Divine Initiative and the Christology of the Damascus Road Encounter

Divine Initiative and the Christology of the Damascus Road Encounter

Timothy W. R. Churchill

◆PICKWICK *Publications* • Eugene, Oregon

DIVINE INITIATIVE AND THE CHRISTOLOGY
OF THE DAMASCUS ROAD ENCOUNTER

Copyright © 2010 Timothy W. R. Churchill. All rights reserved. Except for brief quotations in critical publications or reviews, no part of this book may be reproduced in any manner without prior written permission from the publisher. Write: Permissions, Wipf and Stock Publishers, 199 W. 8th Ave., Suite 3, Eugene, OR 97401.

Pickwick Publications
An Imprint of Wipf and Stock Publishers
199 W. 8th Ave., Suite 3
Eugene, OR 97401

www.wipfandstock.com

ISBN 13: 978-1-60899-325-3

Cataloging-in-Publication data:

Churchill, Timothy W. R.

Divine initiative and the christology of the Damascus Road encounter / Timothy W. R. Churchill.

xxiv + 312 p. ; 23 cm. Includes bibliographical references and indexes.

ISBN 13: 978-1-60899-325-3

1. Paul, the Apostle, Saint — Conversion. 2. Epiphanies. 3. Jesus Christ — History of doctrines. 4. Bible. N.T. Acts — Criticism, interpretation, etc. I. Title.

BS2506 .C55 2010

Manufactured in the U.S.A.

New Revised Standard Version Bible, copyright © 1989, Division of Christian Education of the National Council of the Churches of Christ in the United States of America. Used by permission. All rights reserved.

Scripture quotations taken from the New American Standard Bible®, copyright © 1960, 1962, 1963, 1968, 1971, 1972, 1973, 1975, 1977, 1995 by The Lockman Foundation. Used by permission.

To Kristina—for your unwavering love

Ἀλλὰ ἅτινα ἦν μοι κέρδη,
ταῦτα ἥγημαι διὰ τὸν Φριστὸν ζημίαν

—Apostle Paul

Contents

List of Figures / ix
List of Tables / x
Foreword / xi
Preface / xiii
Acknowledgments / xv
Abbreviations / xvi

1. Introduction / 1
   Survey of Literature • The Christology of the Damascus Road Encounter • Literary-Theoretical Methodology • Conclusion

2. Ancient Jewish Epiphanies / 32
   Introduction • Survey of Literature • Literary Aspects of Ancient Jewish Epiphanies • Conclusion

3. Paul's Epistles / 98
   Introduction • Exegesis • Literary Aspects of the Damascus Road Encounter • Conclusion

4. Acts 9, 22, and 26 / 191
   Introduction • Exegesis • Literary Aspects of the Damascus Road Encounter • Conclusion

5. The Significance of the Damascus Road Encounter / 250
   Ancient Jewish Epiphanies • The Damascus Road Encounter According to Paul • The Damascus Road Encounter According to Acts • Conclusion

Appendix A: Narrative Structure of Selected Epiphanies / 255

Appendix B: Epiphany in Non-Jewish Literature / 258

Bibliography / 261

Author Index / 283

Subject Index / 289

Ancient Document Index / 297

Figures

1. Karel Dujardin, *The Conversion of Saint Paul* / xxiv
2. The Basic Narrative Structure of Epiphany Narratives / 40
3. Type-I Characterization of Epiphanic Beings / 92
4. Type-II Characterization of Epiphanic Beings / 95

Tables

1. Characterization of God as the Angel of Yahweh / 91
2. Narrative Structure of Selected Epiphanies / 255

Foreword

TIM CHURCHILL IS ONE of a new generation of New Testament scholars who look at issues from fresh angles. This clear, lucid, and readable book approaches the Pauline and Lukan accounts of Saul/Paul's Damascus road encounter from the perspective of the one who appeared to Paul. This is a fresh approach, since previous studies have focused on the effects of the encounter on Paul himself, but with little attempt—if any—to consider what we learn about the one who appeared. Dr. Churchill's approach adds to our understanding of the early Christians' beliefs about Jesus, and also contributes to our understanding of how the early believers came to those beliefs.

Dr. Churchill offers particular fresh insight in studying the three Acts accounts of the Damascus road encounter, in recognizing the cumulative and developing force of the three accounts from a christological perspective—again, something which has not really been noticed or studied in any depth in the past.

A further key contribution is Dr. Churchill's consideration of ancient Jewish epiphanies. His analysis of these epiphanies into two major types, which have different implications for the identity of the one encountered in the experience, is fresh and helpful. He develops this theme further by then showing that the accounts of the Damascus road encounter are consistently of one type, where God takes the initiative to reveal himself to humans, rather than of the other type, where a human being seeks an encounter with God. This divine initiative theme is very significant to understanding the Damascus road encounter's Christology, for it places Jesus alongside the God of Israel.

Perhaps most significantly of all, this book will move forward discussion of early Christology, adding to the growing weight of evidence for an early high Christology among followers of Jesus.

I warmly recommend Tim Churchill's work to you—please read it: you'll learn much from it!

Steve Walton
London School of Theology

Preface

I HAVE LONG BEEN fascinated by Jesus' encounter with Paul on the Damascus road. This fascination can be attributed in part to an ongoing curiosity over how heavenly beings are depicted in biblical narratives. When I was much younger I asked a trusted teacher about the identity of Jacob's mysterious wrestling opponent (Gen 32:22–32). Jacob's opponent is initially described as a man (v. 24). Yet following the match, Jacob comments, "I have seen God face to face" (Gen 32:30, NRSV). How could the opponent be described as both a man and God? My old Scottish teacher smiled, and with a twinkle in his eye asked me what I thought. I don't know if he had an answer for me or just wanted me to ponder it a bit more, but I've been thinking about it ever since. Years later, I spent a summer reading E. P. Sanders as part of an independent study course on the New Perspective. I began to question whether Sanders's hypothesis fit the Christology that (I presumed) exists in New Testament accounts of the Damascus road encounter. I will be the first to admit that my Damascus road Christology has changed significantly since then.

The Damascus road encounter also deserves attention on its own merit, since it is significant for many reasons. It is the first purported encounter with the post-ascension Jesus. Accounts of the encounter are contained in some of the earliest Christian documents, particularly the early Pauline epistles and Acts. The Damascus road encounter presents an interesting Christology, as we shall see.

Many others have also been intrigued by the encounter. Seyoon Kim has written perhaps the most well-known monograph on the subject. Yet Kim builds much of his Christology on 2 Cor 4:4–6, which (I argue) likely does not allude to the Damascus road encounter, and is not typical of the Christology of texts that do refer to the encounter.

The Damascus road encounter narratives are located squarely in the tradition of ancient Jewish epiphany texts. In fact, I posit the existence of two distinct patterns for Jewish epiphanies: divine initiative and divine response. The latter is more prevalent in contemporary epiphany narratives. However, the Damascus road encounter is described by Paul and the author of Acts in the pattern of divine initiative, with a more complicated and controversial pattern of divine characterization.

The implications of these findings are significant. I argue against the prevailing view that the Damascus road encounter is a form of *merkabah* vision, which is a subset of the divine response pattern. Furthermore, the characterization of Jesus as divine is highly developed and subtly nuanced. This complicates the question of the origin of divine Christology, or how (on earth) Jesus "became" God, since from the earliest accounts Jesus is already presented as divine.

Therefore, it is my sincere hope that this work makes a contribution to our understanding of christological origins, and rekindles an interest in the identity of the one who appeared to Paul on the Damascus road.

Timothy Churchill
St. John's, Newfoundland
March 2010

Acknowledgments

THIS WORK REPRESENTS THE fruit of my labor in doctoral studies at London School of Theology. A wise man once told me that completing a British doctorate is like being dropped in the middle of a forest without a compass or a map—if you can find your way out, you get the degree. I would like to thank Steve Walton for giving me the freedom to find my own way, yet keeping me focused on the goal, for skillful advice regarding both the big picture and the smallest detail, for encouraging me through many difficulties, and for being a good friend. Thanks to the rest of the faculty at London School of Theology, especially Conrad Gempf and Steve Motyer, and also to the staff, for making the school a home away from home. I would also like to express my appreciation to Tyndale House in Cambridge for new friends, the wonderful library, afternoon tea, and even gardening day. Thanks also to Larry Hurtado for providing an honest critique and challenging me to rethink and strengthen my arguments.

Words cannot express the debt of gratitude I owe my wife, Kristina, for your loving support through the years, and for taking care of our family as I spent long hours away from home in research and writing. Many thanks also to my children, John, Anna, Sarah, and Katie, for the joy you bring to my life, and for forgiving the many hours I was unable to spend with you because of my studies. Special thanks to my parents for your help and inspiration through the years, and especially for proofreading several drafts of my thesis. Thank you as well to my church family at Calvary Baptist Church in St. John's for your constant prayers and support, which sustained me through many difficulties, and for all the love you showed my family while I was away from home. Finally, I would also like to acknowledge Activant Solutions for providing flexibility in my work schedule through three graduate degrees, and Mike Rowe for creating the professional diagrams.

Abbreviations

APOCRYPHA

Tob	Tobit

OLD TESTAMENT PSEUDEPIGRAPHA

Apoc. Ab.	*Apocalypse of Abraham*
Artap.	*Artapanus*
3 Bar.	*3 Baruch (Greek Apocalypse)*
1 En.	*1/2/3 Enoch (Ethiopic Apocalypse)*
2 En.	*2 Enoch (Slavonic Apocalypse)*
3 En.	*3 Enoch (Hebrew Apocalypse)*
Ezek. Trag.	*Ezekiel the Tragedian*
Hist. Rech.	*History of the Rechabites*
Jos. Asen.	*Joseph and Aseneth*
Jub.	*Jubilees*
L.A.B.	*Liber antiquitatum biblicarum (Pseudo-Philo)*
L.A.E.	*Life of Adam and Eve*
Lad. Jac.	*Ladder of Jacob*
Mart. Ascen. Isa.	*Martyrdom and Ascension of Isaiah*
Pss. Sol.	*Psalms of Solomon*
T. 12 Patr.	*Testaments of the Twelve Patriarchs*
T. Ab.	*Testament of Abraham*
T. Isaac	*Testament of Isaac*
T. Jac.	*Testament of Jacob*
T. Job	*Testament of Job*
T. Levi	*Testament of Levi*
T. Reu.	*Testament of Reuben*

DEAD SEA SCROLLS

1Q28b	*Rule of the Blessings* (Appendix b to 1QS; 1QSb)
1QH^a	*Hodayot*^{a} or *Thanksgiving Hymns*^{a}

Abbreviations   xvii

1QM	*Milḥamah* or *War Scroll*
1QS	*Serek Hayaḥad* or *Rule of the Community*
2Q4	*Exod*ᶜ
4Q246	*Apocryphon of Daniel* (4QapocrDan ar)
4Q266	*Damascus Document*ᵃ (4QDᵃ)
4Q400	*Songs of the Sabbath Sacrifice*ᵃ (4QShirShabbᵃ)
4Q403	*Songs of the Sabbath Sacrifice*ᵈ (4QShirShabbᵈ)
4Q404	*Songs of the Sabbath Sacrifice*ᵉ (4QShirShabbᵉ)
4Q405	*Songs of the Sabbath Sacrifice*ᶠ (4QShirShabbᶠ)
4Q554	NJᵃ ar
4Q555	NJᵇ ar
5Q15	NJ ar
11Q18	*New Jerusalem* (11QNJ ar)
11Q19	*Temple Scroll*ᵃ (11QTᵃ)
CD-A	Cairo Genizah copy of the *Damascus Document*ᵃ

PHILO

Fug.	*De fuga et inventione* (On Flight and Finding)
Migr.	*De migratione Abrahami* (On the Migration of Abraham)
Mos.	*De vita Mosis 1/2* (On the Life of Moses)
Prob.	*Quod omnis probus liber sit* (That Every Good Person Is Free)
QG	*Quaestiones et solutiones in Genesin* (Questions and Answers on Genesis)
Somn.	*De somniis* (On Dreams)

JOSEPHUS

Ant.	*Jewish Antiquities*
J.W.	*Jewish War*

RABBINIC WRITINGS

b.	Babylonian Talmudic tractate
Exod. Rab.	Exodus Rabbah
Gen. Rab.	Genesis Rabbah
Ḥag.	Hagigah
Meg.	Megillah
m.	Mishnah

PAPYRI

PDM — *Papyri demoticae magicae*. Demotic texts in PGM corpus as collated in *The Greek Magical Papyri in Translation, Including the Demotic Spells*, ed. H. D. Betz (Chicago: University of Chicago Press, 1992)

PGM — *Papyri graecae magicae: Die griechischen Zauberpapyri*, ed. K. Preisendanz (Stuttgart: Teubner, 1928, 1931)

MISCELLANEOUS

DRE — Damascus road encounter

SECONDARY SOURCES

AB	Anchor Bible
ABD	*Anchor Bible Dictionary*, ed. D. N. Freedman, 6 vols. (New York: Doubleday, 1992)
ABRL	Anchor Bible Reference Library
AFSBSS	American Folklore Society Bibliographical and Special Series
AGJU	Arbeiten zur Geschichte des antiken Judentums und des Urchristentums
AnBib	Analecta biblica
ANRW	*Aufstieg und Niedergang der römischen Welt: Geschichte und Kultur Roms im Spiegel der neueren Forschung*, ed. H. Temporini and W. Haase (Berlin: de Gruyter, 1972–)
ANTC	Abingdon New Testament Commentaries
BDAG	Bauer, W., F. W. Danker, W. F. Arndt, and F. W. Gingrich, *A Greek-English Lexicon of the New Testament and Other Early Christian Literature*, 3rd ed. (Chicago: University of Chicago Press, 2000)
BDF	Blass, F., A. Debrunner, and R. W. Funk, *A Greek Grammar of the New Testament and Other Early Christian Literature* (Chicago: University of Chicago Press, 1961)
BECNT	Baker Exegetical Commentary on the New Testament
Bib	*Biblica*
BKAT	Biblischer Kommentar, Altes Testament, eds. M. Noth and H. W. Wolff
BN	*Biblische Notizen*
BNTC	Black's New Testament Commentaries
BSac	*Bibliotheca sacra*
BT	*The Bible Translator*

BZ	*Biblische Zeitschrift*
BZAW	Beihefte zur Zeitschrift für die alttestamentliche Wissenschaft
CBC	Cambridge Bible Commentary
CBET	Contributions to Biblical Exegesis and Theology
CBQ	*Catholic Biblical Quarterly*
CBQMS	Catholic Biblical Quarterly Monograph Series
CC	Continental Commentaries
CEJL	Commentaries on Early Jewish Literature
CI	*Critical Inquiry*
CSCO	Corpus scriptorum christianorum orientalium, eds. I. B. Chabot et al. (Paris, 1903–)
DPL	*Dictionary of Paul and His Letters*, eds. G. F. Hawthorne and R. P. Martin (Downers Grove, IL: InterVarsity, 1993)
DSD	*Dead Sea Discoveries*
EdF	Erträge der Forschung
EKKNT	Evangelisch-katholischer Kommentar zum Neuen Testament
EvT	*Evangelische Theologie*
ExpTim	*Expository Times*
FF	*Foundations and Facets*
FOTL	The Forms of the Old Testament Literature
FRLANT	Forschungen zur Religion und Literatur des Alten und Neuen Testaments
GBS	Guides to Biblical Scholarship
GGBTB	*Greek Grammar beyond the Basics*, Daniel B. Wallace (Grand Rapids: Zondervan, 1999)
GNS	Good News Studies
HCOT	Historical Commentary on the Old Testament
HNT	Handbuch zum Neuen Testament
HO	Handbuch der Orientalistik
HTA	Historisch Theologische Auslegung
HTKAT	Herders theologischer Kommentar zum Alten Testament
HTKNT	Herders theologischer Kommentar zum Neuen Testament
HTR	Harvard Theological Review
IBC	Interpretation: A Bible Commentary for Teaching and Preaching
ICC	International Critical Commentary
ICT	Issues in Contemporary Theology
IDB	*The Interpreter's Dictionary of the Bible*, ed. G. A. Buttrick, 4 vols. (Nashville: Abingdon, 1962)
Int	*Interpretation*

JBL	*Journal of Biblical Literature*
JBQ	*Jewish Bible Quarterly*
JETS	*Journal of the Evangelical Theological Society*
JJS	*Journal of Jewish Studies*
JLS	*Journal of Literary Semantics*
JPSTC	Jewish Publication Society: The JPS Torah Commentary
JSJ	*Journal for the Study of Judaism in the Persian, Hellenistic, and Roman Periods*
JSJSup	Journal for the Study of Judaism: Supplement Series
JSNT	*Journal for the Study of the New Testament*
JSNTSup	Journal for the Study of the New Testament: Supplement Series
JSOT	*Journal for the Study of the Old Testament*
JSOTSup	Journal for the Study of the Old Testament: Supplement Series
JSP	*Journal for the Study of the Pseudepigrapha*
JSPSup	Journal for the Study of the Pseudepigrapha: Supplement Series
JSS	*Journal of Semitic Studies*
JTS	*Journal of Theological Studies*
KEK	Kritisch-exegetischer Kommentar über das Neue Testament (Meyer-Kommentar)
L&N	*Greek-English Lexicon of the New Testament: Based on Semantic Domains*, eds. J. P. Louw and E. A. Nida, 2nd ed. (New York: United Bible Societies, 1989)
LCL	Loeb Classical Library
LHBOTS	Library of Hebrew Bible/Old Testament Studies
LSJ	Liddell, H. G., R. Scott, and H. S. Jones, *A Greek-English Lexicon*, 9th ed. with rev. suppl. (Oxford: Oxford University Press, 1996)
LSTS	Library of Second Temple Studies
MHT	Moulton, J. H., W. F. Howard, and N. Turner, *A Grammar of New Testament Greek* (Edinburgh: T. & T. Clark, 1906–76)
NA27	*Novum Testamentum Graece*, Nestle-Aland, 27th ed.
NAC	New American Commentary
NDT	New Dictionary of Theology
NEchtB	Neue Echter Bibel
NICNT	New International Commentary on the New Testament
NICOT	New International Commentary on the Old Testament
NIDNTT	*New International Dictionary of New Testament Theology*, ed. C. Brown, 4 vols. (Grand Rapids: Zondervan, 1975–85)

Abbreviations

NIGTC	New International Greek Testament Commentary
NLH	*New Literary History*
NovT	*Novum Testamentum*
NovTSup	Supplements to Novum Testamentum
NRSV	New Revised Standard Version
NSBT	New Studies in Biblical Theology
NSHE	*New Schaff-Herzog Encyclopedia of Religious Knowledge*, Samuel MacAuley Jackson, ed., 12 vols. (London, 1908–12)
NTAbh	Neutestamentliche Abhandlungen
NTBS	New Studies in Biblical Theology
NTD	Das Neue Testament Deutsch
NTL	New Testament Library
NTS	*New Testament Studies*
OBT	Overtures to Biblical Theology
ÖTK	Ökumenischer Taschenbuch-Kommentar
OTL	Old Testament Library
OTP	*Old Testament Pseudepigrapha*, ed. J. H. Charlesworth, 2 vols. (New York: Doubleday, 1983)
PT	*Poetics Today*
RB	*Revue biblique*
RNT	Regensburger Neues Testament
RSR	*Recherches de science religieuse*
S&S	*Science & Spirit*
SBLDS	Society of Biblical Literature Dissertation Series
SBLEJL	Society of Biblical Literature Early Judaism and Its Literature
SBLMS	Society of Biblical Literature Monograph Series
SBLSP	Society of Biblical Literature Seminar Papers
SBLTT	Society of Biblical Literature Texts and Translations
SBS	Stuttgarter Bibelstudien
SBT	Studies in Biblical Theology
SJOT	*Scandinavian Journal of the Old Testament*
SJT	*Scottish Journal of Theology*
SNTSMS	Society for New Testament Studies Monograph Series
S*Philo*	*Studia philonica*
SR	Studies in Religion
SSU	Studia Semitica Upsaliensia
ST	*Studia theologica*
STDJ	Studies on the Texts of the Desert of Judah
TBei	*Theologische Beiträge*
TCGNT	*A Textual Commentary on the Greek New Testament*, B. M. Metzger (London: United Bible Societies, 1994)

TDNT	*Theological Dictionary of the New Testament*, eds. G. Kittel and G. Friedrich, trans. G. W. Bromiley, 10 vols. (Grand Rapids: Eerdmans, 1964–76)
TDOT	*Theological Dictionary of the Old Testament*, eds. G. Johannes Botterweck, Helmer Ringgren, and Heinz-Josef Fabry, trans. J. T. Willis, G. W. Bromiley, and David E. Green, 15 vols. (Grand Rapids: Eerdmans, 1974–2006)
THKNT	Theologischer Handkommentar zum Neuen Testament
TNTC	Tyndale New Testament Commentaries
TS	Texts and Studies
TS	*Theological Studies*
TWOT	*Theological Wordbook of the Old Testament*, eds. R. L. Harris, G. L. Archer Jr., and Bruce K. Waltke (Chicago: Moody, 1980, 1999)
TynBul	*Tyndale Bulletin*
UBS4	*The Greek New Testament*, United Bible Societies, 4th rev. ed.
VT	*Vetus Testamentum*
WBC	Word Biblical Commentary
WC	Westminster Commentaries
WMANT	Wissenschaftliche Monographien zum Alten und Neuen Testament
WUNT	Wissenschaftliche Untersuchungen zum Neuen Testament
ZAW	*Zeitschrift für die alttestamentliche Wissenschaft*
ZBK	Zürcher Bibelkommentare
ZNW	*Zeitschrift für die neutestamentliche Wissenschaft und die Kunde der älteren Kirche*

Divine Initiative and the Christology of the Damascus Road Encounter

FIGURE 1: Karel Dujardin, *The Conversion of Saint Paul*
Photo ©The National Gallery, London

1

Introduction

SURVEY OF LITERATURE

IN COMMENTING ON THE unique significance of the Damascus road encounter (DRE), Jervell remarks:

> Von den anderen Christophanieberichten unterscheidet sich das Damaskusereignis darin, dass Jesus nicht nur als der Auferstandene auftritt, sondern sich als der Erhöhte im Himmel befindet. Eine solche Christophanie kommt nur hier vor, und Paulus ist in der Kirche der einzige, dem eine solche Offenbarung zuteil wird.[1]

Given its remarkable and unique features, the DRE is essential to a proper understanding of NT Christology. Yet Paul's encounter with Jesus on the Damascus road has long been a source of great controversy. Some scholars have minimized or even neglected the DRE,[2] while others have deemed it essential to a correct understanding of Paul's theology.[3] This

---

1. Jervell, *Apostelgeschichte*, 280.

2. Newman notes the general neglect of the DRE: "Since the turn of the century, the Damascus Christophany has suffered through some rather lean years in Pauline scholarship. Though the Christophany is often mentioned, the general tendency has been to downplay its importance for understanding Paul." Newman, *Glory-Christology*, 164.
This neglect of the DRE is particularly evident in the *religionsgeschichtliche Schule*. For example, in Bousset's *Kyrios Christos*, Acts 9:1–9 is only referenced once, in denial of its historicity: "The explanation of Saul's journey to Damascus in Acts 9:1 is unhistorical" (119). Similarly, Beker makes only passing mention of the DRE and no mention of Acts 9:3–9 in particular. In fact, Beker claims that "Paul's conversion experience is not the entrance to his thought." Beker, *Paul*, 10.

3. For example, Kim claims that Paul's theology is understandable "only when" we ascertain that "Paul received his gospel from the Damascus revelation of Jesus Christ." Kim, *Origin*, 335.

study will explore the Christology of the Damascus road encounter between Jesus and Paul from an exegetical and literary-critical perspective. However, before the thesis may be stated in greater detail, it must first be situated within the landscape of contemporary scholarship.

In his epochal *Kyrios Christos*, Bousset proposed a Hellenistic-Gentile hypothesis for the origin of NT Christology which diminished the significance of the DRE.[4] In place of the DRE, Bousset suggested that Paul's theology originated from self-reflection after exposure to various contemporary religious ideas.[5] Bousset's reasoning was highly speculative.[6] Reacting against Bousset, the trend of late has been to emphasize the Jewish origin of NT Christology, particularly among the so-called new *religionsgeschichtliche Schule*.[7]

Several aspects of the DRE dominated scholarly discussion in the years following Bousset.[8] One of the more prominent debates has been

---

4. In Bousset's own words, "we misunderstand the phrase ἐν Χριστῷ εἶναι of Paul if we somehow mean by it the historical Jesus in our sense.... In [the DRE] the Christ is supposed to have appeared to the apostle as a purely supra-terrestrial, divine (II Cor. 4:6) being detached from all earthly connections.... We should remember that [Paul] treated his Damascus vision as an extraordinary and unique fact, not as the first in a series of visions of Christ out of which then his mysticism could have developed, and that therefore in his own testimony he does not afford us a handle for grasping the entire combination.... The fire of his Christ piety was ignited, not at the historical Jesus, nor in the first place at the Christ who appeared to him near Damascus, but rather at the powerful reality of the Kyrios as Paul experienced it in the first Hellenistic communities." Bousset, *Kyrios*, 155–56.

5. "But we may suppose that already in Paul's time there was a body of religious literature which had been completely separated from the connections that had to do immediately with cult and practice and thus was accessible to a wider circle. And the supposition that Paul was acquainted with such semi-literary edifying writings as they were available in the Hermetic tractates, in the edificatory, purely religious parts of the magical literature.... In this way, Paul the Pharisee may have stored up and meditatively thought through many particular speculations and mysterious attitudes in his innermost being.... Then came the strong and stormy impulses which stormed in upon him from the new Christ religion. And as in a thaw the sluggish masses slide into the stream and the ice floes strike against one another and push and pile up, so now the mass of thoughts in Paul has slipped into the stream and has piled up in an amazing heap, and the result was the Pauline theology." Bousset, *Kyrios*, 22.

6. This is confirmed in Bousset's own words: "we may suppose," "and the supposition," "may have," etc.

7. Newman provides a critical summary of the Hellenistic-Gentile approach to the DRE in Newman, *Glory-Christology*, 166–73.

8. Hurtado surveys recent literature related to the DRE in Hurtado, "Convert." Wright also summarizes current scholarship on the DRE, and discusses the implica-

the calling-conversion controversy. Stendahl famously argued against the traditional view[9] in proposing that Paul had not experienced a conversion, but a calling.[10] Stendahl sparked a debate that remains far from settled.[11] Others have examined the DRE from psychological,[12] sociological,[13] physiological,[14] and literary[15] perspectives. The perceived discrepancies between the three DRE accounts of Acts 9, 22, and 26 have also received much attention.[16] However, the most prevalent debates have concerned possible antecedents for the DRE in Jewish religious practice.

---

tions of the DRE with respect to Paul's understanding of resurrection, in Wright, *Resurrection*, 375–98.

In addition to the studies we will consider in the section, see also Lohfink, *Conversion*; Lührmann, "Christologie," 363. According to Lührmann, "die Rechtfertigungsbotschaft des Paulus ist also in der Tat Interpretation und Konsequenz seiner Christologie." Dunn discusses how the DRE affected Paul's relationship to Judaism and the law in Dunn, "Apostate." Gager concludes that Paul maintained two central affirmations: "one, God's unshakable commitment to Israel and to the holiness of the law (=Judaism); and, two, the redemption of the Gentiles through Jesus Christ (=Christianity)." Gager, *Reinventing*, 152.

9. For example, Prokulski boldly asserted that "there can be no doubt today of the conversion of St Paul at Damascus." Prokulski, "Conversion," 453.

10. Stendahl, *Paul*, 10–11.

11. For example, Jasper and Pricket refer to Acts 9:1–9 as "the classic conversion story." Jasper and Prickett, eds., *Bible and Literature*, 300–303. The topic is discussed at length in Gaventa, "Conversion"; *Darkness*.

12. Inglis hypothesized that "[Paul's] personality was stabilized by the redirection of its affective elements to an object in which they found the fullest satisfaction, and this object called forth all his latent capacities for spiritual development." Inglis, "Problem," 231.

13. Fredriksen is quite pessimistic: "What *actually* happened, what the convert actually thought or experienced at the time of his conversion, is thus not accessible to the historian." Fredriksen, "Paul," 34.

14. A molecular biochemist has recently proposed that the DRE was merely an epileptic seizure. Pickover, "Epilepsy." This theory was thoroughly discredited many years earlier by Lilly, "Conversion," 191–96.

15. Baban explores literary aspects of the Acts 9 DRE account as one of three "on the road" Lukan encounters in Baban, *Encounters*, 207–26.

16. Wright's introductory statement is typical of how the DRE in Acts immediately invokes discussion of the perceived discrepancies: "It is notorious both that Luke tells the story of Paul's Damascus road experience no fewer than three times, and that the accounts do not match one another in all respects." Wright, *Resurrection*, 388. So also Munck: "La conversion de Saul est racontée trois fois dans les Actes et les trois récits offrent des divergences considérables." Munck, "La vocation," 133.

The following survey will review some of the more recent major works related to the DRE in approximately chronological order.

Bowker

John Bowker proposes a *merkabah* model for Luke's accounts of the Damascus road encounter in "'Merkabah' Visions and the Visions of Paul."[17] He begins by observing that *merkabah* contemplation was not entirely suppressed in the first century CE, although it was restricted later. This restriction was due in part to the dangers associated with seeing God. Nevertheless, some orthodox rabbis contemporary with Paul, such as Johanan b. Zakkai, did practice *merkabah* contemplation. In fact, *merkabah* contemplation likely required higher training. The main purpose of *merkabah* contemplation was not necessarily to experience a vision, but to gain understanding of the vision of Ezek 1–2.[18] Bowker therefore claims that it is reasonable to suggest that Paul was capable of pursuing *merkabah* contemplation.[19]

Bowker acknowledges that Paul's visions were not likely all of the same kind.[20] In order to demonstrate that one of Paul's visions was a *merkabah* vision, Bowker recognizes that he must establish "points of contact" to other *merkabah* visions.[21] In fact, Bowker does claim that both 2 Cor 12 and the DRE accounts in Acts describe *merkabah* visions.[22] Bowker then presents texts describing the *merkabah* visions of Johanan b. Zakkai and his companions.[23] The main point of contact between Johanan's *merkabah* visions and 2 Cor 12 is the mention of the "third heaven" (2 Cor 12:2).[24]

---

17. Kim acknowledges that "In so far as מרכבה also stands [in the tradition of OT prophetic and apocalyptic theophany visions], it is possible to draw parallels between it and the Damascus vision." Yet he rejects Bowker's claim that Paul's DRE resulted from meditation on Ezek 1 and 2. Kim, *Origin*, 224n3. "I have not found [Bowker's] suggestion convincing." Kim, *Paul*, 180n45.
18. Bowker, "Merkabah Visions," 157–58.
19. Ibid., 158–59.
20. Ibid., 159.
21. Ibid.
22. Ibid.
23. Ibid., 159–66.
24. Ibid., 167.

Finally, Bowker lists seven points of contact between *merkabah* visions and the DRE accounts in Acts: the reference to "on the road" (9:3; 22:6; 26:12); the reference to a time or season (22:6; 26:13); light from heaven (9:3; 22:6; 26:13); falling to the ground (9:4; 22:7; 26:14); a voice speaking (9:4; 22:7; 26:14); apparent uncertainty among the traveling companions over what had occurred (9:7; 22:9); and consequences of the vision (9:9).[25] Bowker acknowledges that "some of the features are likely to occur in the account of *any* vision."[26] He concludes that "if in fact Paul *was*, like the rabbis, reflecting 'on the road' . . . . . . what *may* have happened" is that he experienced a *merkabah* vision of Jesus.[27] Bowker's suggestion that the DRE is a form of *merkabah* vision will be discussed in greater detail following our analysis of the Acts DRE accounts.[28]

Kim

Of all the recent monographs related to the Damascus road encounter, Seyoon Kim's *The Origin of Paul's Gospel* may be the most audacious.[29] In this work, Kim argues against the tendency to overlook the DRE.[30] Instead, he advocates the centrality of the DRE to a proper understanding of Paul. Kim claims that the Damascus road encounter is the basis not only of Paul's apostleship, but also of his theology.[31] In developing his thesis, Kim relies on generally accepted Pauline references to the DRE,[32] as well as other texts from the undisputed[33] and disputed[34] Pauline epistles,[35] while acknowledging the value of the more lengthy accounts

---

25. Ibid., 167–70.

26. Ibid., 170.

27. Others have relied on Bowker's conclusions. For example, see Pate, *Reverse*, 181–86, 319n272.

28. See pp. 234–37 below.

29. Kim also discusses the DRE in Kim, *Paul*, 1–84. Most of the discussion in this later work regards the development of Paul's doctrine of justification.

30. "Ignoring this fundamental testimony of Paul himself, for far too long his modern interpreters have attempted to explain his gospel only by analyzing it in the light of literary and *religionsgeschichtliche* parallels." Kim, *Origin*, 332.

31. Ibid., 31.

32. 1 Cor 9:1; 15:8–10; Gal 1:13–17; Phil 3:4–11.

33. Rom 1:1; 10:2–4; 1 Cor 1:1; 9:16–17; 2 Cor 1:1; 3:4—4:6; 5:16; Gal 1:1.

34. Eph 1:1; 3:1–13; Col 1:1; 23c–29.

35. Kim, *Origin*, 3–31.

of Acts 9, 22, and 26.[36] Kim examines Paul's condition prior to the DRE,[37] rejecting the notion that Paul made any psychological preparations that resulted in the DRE.[38] Kim describes the DRE as an "objective, external" event[39] in which Paul "saw" Christ,[40] resulting in Paul's conversion as well as his apostleship.[41] Kim then develops the theological significance of the DRE in relation to the gospel,[42] Christology, and soteriology.[43]

Kim's discussion of Christology is presented in two parts. The first part examines the christological titles Christ, Lord, and Son of God.[44] Kim considers how these messianic titles came to be applied to Jesus, concluding that Paul did not simply transfer pre-existing notions to Jesus, but rather reinterpreted them according to how Jesus had revealed himself to Paul.[45] Kim concludes the first part with substantial discussions relating to the "pre-existent" Son[46] and Wisdom Christology.[47] The second part examines the identification of Jesus as the εἰκών τοῦ θεοῦ (2 Cor 3:16—4:6; Col 1:15).[48] In this section Kim emphasizes antecedents in ancient Jewish literature as the basis for Paul's description of Jesus as the εἰκών.[49] Also in relation to 2 Cor 3-4, Kim claims that the DRE

36. Ibid., 3.
37. Ibid., 32–50.
38. Ibid., 51–55.
39. Ibid., 56.
40. Ibid., 55.
41. Ibid., 56.
42. Ibid., 67–99. Kim claims that Paul's gospel was "fundamentally different from the apocalyptists' message" in that it "proclaims the salvation that has already been realized in the Messiah Jesus, although it still envisages the *consummation* of that salvation at the *eschaton*" (73). Kim also discusses the "mystery" of the gospel at length, claiming that the "divine plan of salvation" involves a temporal sequence of events: first, the "partial hardening of Israel;" second, the salvation of the Gentiles; third, the salvation of all Israel (85).
43. Ibid., 269–329. Kim's discussion of soteriology focuses on justification (269–311), reconciliation and sonship (311–15), and sonship, transformation, and new creation (315–29).
44. Ibid., 100–136.
45. Ibid., 107.
46. Ibid., 111–21.
47. Ibid., 121–31.
48. Ibid., 137–268.
49. Kim cites OT epiphanies such as Ezekiel, Daniel, *1 En.* 46, *4 Ezra* 13, and Rev 1; OT theophanies such as Gen 18–19, and Philo's commentary on these and similar passages; and other ancient *merkabah* "Throne-Theophanies." Ibid., 205–56.

was a *merkabah* vision.⁵⁰ The relevance of εἰκών-Christology to the DRE and the interpretation of the DRE as a *merkabah* vision both depend on whether 2 Cor 3:16—4:6 alludes to the DRE. We will consider Kim's arguments in favor of a connection between 2 Cor 3:4—4:6 and the DRE as part of our discussion of this passage.[51]

This study is in broad agreement with Kim in areas such as the centrality of the DRE to a proper understanding of Paul's theology and Christology, and especially the reliance upon ancient Jewish epiphany narratives as the proper context for understanding the DRE. However, there are several significant differences. Kim seeks to understand how Paul's theology derived from the DRE; this study will seek to understand the DRE itself.[52] Kim relies on disputed Pauline texts; this study will rely solely on the undisputed Pauline epistles in order to ensure that any christological conclusions are a reflection of Paul's own thought. In addition, Kim relies on Acts to support his arguments related to Paul; this study will examine the accounts of the DRE in Acts separately. Finally, Kim derives his Christology primarily from titles; this study will examine the DRE from a literary perspective, deriving a Christology from numerous other characterizations of Jesus in the DRE texts.

Dunn

Kim's monograph provoked much discussion, including a direct response from James Dunn.[53] Dunn briefly surveys other issues related to the DRE, suggesting that the calling-conversion debate should be secondary since the primary purpose of both Paul[54] and Acts[55] is Paul's mission to the Gentiles, and dismissing the prevailing christological[56] and sote-

---

50. "On the Damascus road Paul must have been convinced that the glorious figure on the divine throne whom he saw in the vision was Jesus Christ whose followers he was persecuting." Ibid., 187. Kim recently reaffirmed that "as a secondary thesis in my *Origin*, I submitted that on the Damascus road Paul saw the exalted Christ on the *merkabah*-throne." Ibid., 194–95.

51. See pp. 130–35 below for a discussion of 2 Cor 4:4–6, and pp. 157–58 below for a discussion of Kim's argument in favor of interpreting the DRE as a *merkabah* vision.

52. This is perhaps analogous to the difference between evolution and the "big bang" theory in science.

53. Dunn, "Light."

54. Ibid., 251–52.

55. Ibid., 253.

56. "The recognition of Jesus' Messiahship is insufficient explanation of Paul's apostolic self-understanding." Ibid., 254.

riological[57] views before proceeding to interact with Kim. Dunn agrees with Kim that 2 Cor 4:4, 6 refers to the DRE, but questions the extent to which it describes "what Paul *saw*."[58] In fact, Dunn seeks to answer that question from other texts (1 Cor 9:1; Gal 1:16).[59] He questions whether the DRE should be considered a "*theophany*" since the evidence appears to reflect traditions of angelic beings or exalted humans.[60] Dunn also disputes Kim's conclusions regarding the Wisdom Christology of the DRE.[61] In arguing these points, Dunn focuses on a few key terms such as "Lord," "Son," and εἰκὼν τοῦ θεοῦ rather than the entirety of christological evidence from the DRE passages. This limitation is unfortunate but natural considering that Dunn is reflecting Kim's emphasis. This study will seek to address Dunn's question concerning the nature of Jesus's appearance by combining a survey of ancient Jewish epiphany texts with a more comprehensive characterization of Jesus in the DRE texts.

Segal

In his essay "Heavenly Ascent in Hellenistic Judaism, Early Christianity and their Environment," Alan Segal proposes that ancient Jewish epiphany texts may be differentiated according to the category of ascent/descent, and provides a detailed analysis of the features of heavenly ascent narratives. Segal claims, in effect, that heavenly ascent is a subgenre of epiphany.[62] However, his assumption that any interaction between God and humans requires a mediator[63] is invalid if it is possible for God to enter the "imperfect [earthly] realm," or for humans to enter the "perfect [heavenly] realm." Segal distinguishes between descent (*katabasis*) and ascent (*anabasis*), depending on the direction of the journey.[64] He next discusses ancient heavenly ascent narratives from both non-Jewish

---

57. Both the "exegetical base and the necessary rationale seem to be inadequate to sustain the case argued." Ibid., 256.

58. Ibid., 259.

59. Ibid., 259–60.

60. Ibid., 260–61.

61. Ibid., 260–62.

62. "Many of the different ascension myths . . . seem to me to show a fundamentally similar structure." Segal, "Heavenly Ascent," 1338.

63. "Communication between [God and humans] ought to be impossible; so when it occurs, it can only be accomplished through the movement of a mediator." Ibid.

64. Ibid., 1340.

and Jewish sources[65] before applying his findings to the New Testament. Segal claims that Jesus may have been associated with earlier depictions of the Angel of Yahweh.[66]

Thus, Segal provides a fascinating account of heavenly ascent in ancient literature. His attempt to classify epiphanies according to the criteria of ascent is useful. However, the distinction between ascent and descent raises certain questions. For example, how should epiphanies such as Jacob's ladder (Gen 28:10–22) and Stephen's martyrdom (Acts 7:55–56) be categorized, since they appear to bridge the divide between the earthly and heavenly realms without a journey? Can dreams or visions properly be described as ascents, since they occur within a person's mind? Furthermore, some epiphanies such as Jacob's ladder identify the one who appears as God and/or Yahweh, thus (apparently) eliminating the prerequisite mediator.

In *Paul the Convert*, Segal interprets the DRE as a precursor of *merkabah* visions.[67] Since Segal argues that both Paul and Acts present the DRE as a *merkabah* vision, his arguments will be discussed in more detail later in the context of both Paul[68] and Acts.[69]

Dietzfelbinger

Another significant, although less discussed monograph on the DRE is Christian Dietzfelbinger's *Die Berufung des Paulus als Ursprung seiner Theologie*. Like Kim, Dietzfelbinger argues that Paul's call was the origin of his theology. Dietzfelbinger presents his argument in three chrono-

---

65. Ibid., 1341–68.

66. "It is probable that Jesus' identity was very early associated with the angel of YHWH who is superior to all angels in that he represents God's name on earth." Ibid., 1371. Most, if not all, of the OT depictions of the Angel of Yahweh involve descent, not ascent, making it noteworthy that Segal should raise this point in a discussion on heavenly ascent.

67. "Paul is an important witness to the kind of experience that apocalyptic Jews were reporting and an important predecessor to merkabah mysticism." Segal, *Paul the Convert*, 40. With three minor exceptions, Kim agrees with Segal: "I find Segal presenting a thesis more or less identical with mine in its main points, with differences only in a few details." Kim, *Paul*, 184. Dunn is ambivalent to Segal's claim. He allows the possibility "that Paul had practiced a form of Jewish mysticism prior to his conversion," yet recognizes that "we should also observe that Paul had made a point of discounting just such experiences ([2 Cor] 12.6–10)." Dunn, *Theology of Paul*, 47.

68. See pp. 158–59 below.

69. See p. 237 below.

logical sections: first, the period in Paul's life prior to the DRE;[70] second, the event itself;[71] third, consequences of the DRE.[72] He prefaces this discussion by identifying the Pauline epistles and the book of Acts as the two earliest and most reliable sources pertaining to the DRE. He gives the Pauline sources primary importance, but values Acts as a significant secondary source since it likely contains not only the Lukan *Paulusbild* but also pre-Lukan material.[73]

In the first section, Dietzfelbinger discusses Paul's persecution of the church prior to the DRE. Paul's comments on this period of his life are "selten und zurückhaltend"; the few relevant passages (Gal 1:13f; 1:22–24; 1 Cor 15:8f; Phil 3:5–6) betray an "eigenartige Sprödigkeit."[74] Dietzfelbinger points to Acts as a more fruitful source of information, but does rely primarily on the autobiographical Pauline testimony. After discussing the nature, extent, authorization, and location of Paul's activities, Dietzfelbinger identifies two primary reasons for the persecution: zeal for the Torah (Gal 1:13),[75] and the cross.[76]

The second section pertains to the Damascus road encounter itself. Dietzfelbinger claims that only four Pauline passages describe the DRE (Gal 1:15–16; 1 Cor 9:1–2; 15:8; 2 Cor 4:6[77]), a "disconcerting shortage."[78] After a brief review of these passages,[79] Dietzfelbinger addresses the nature of Paul's experience. He concludes, regarding 1 Cor 9:1 and 15:8, that Paul claimed to have seen Jesus in an Easter event;[80] regarding Gal 1:15–16, that Paul speaks of his persecution and call using "OT-like

---

70. Dietzfelbinger, *Berufung*, 4–42.
71. Ibid., 43–89.
72. Ibid., 90–147.
73. Ibid., 2–3.
74. Ibid., 4.
75. Ibid., 23–28.
76. Ibid., 29–39. He claims that the Pharisee Paul could not accept the proclamation of one who was crucified as the Messiah. Ibid., 39.
77. Dietzfelbinger acknowledges that connecting 2 Cor 4:6 to the DRE is controversial. Ibid., 49–50. See the discussion of 2 Cor 4:6 on pp. 130–35 below.
78. Dietzfelbinger, *Berufung*, 44. He also notes numerous passages where the DRE stands in the background: Rom 1:1; 5:3; 11:3; 12:3; 15:15, 16, 18; 1 Cor 1:1; 2 Cor 3:7–11; Gal 1:11, 16; 2:2, 7–9; Phil 3:4b–11; 1 Thess 2:16.
79. Ibid., 44–51.
80. Ibid., 56, 60.

narrative elements" of prophetic calls;[81] and regarding 2 Cor 4:6, that Paul had seen in his christophany of Jesus how God's light was on him.[82] Dietzfelbinger concludes his review of the texts by acknowledging uncertainty over what Paul actually saw, and emphasizing the similarities to OT auditory encounters.[83]

Dietzfelbinger then addresses the changes in Paul's theology as a result of the DRE. He examines Paul's newfound Christology under the titles Kyrios, Christ, Son of God, Bearer of Divine Light, and Image of God.[84] Two related questions arise in the course of the discussion: first, whether the titles reflect Paul's immediate understanding of the one who appeared or deductions Paul made later; second, whether Paul appropriated early Christian understandings of these titles, or infused them with his own interpretations.[85] He concludes that the titles reflect Paul's immediate understanding of Jesus in the DRE. For example, he claims that the title Kyrios somehow reflects the change in Paul's perception of Jesus as a result of the DRE;[86] that the application of the title Christ to Jesus, through both the memory of the person and work of Jesus and also a future hope, received a largely new context;[87] that Paul named Jesus as Christ in the immediate context of the DRE due to the "große Umbruch" in Paul;[88] and that the DRE resulted in a radical change that brought Paul to name Jesus as the Son of God.[89]

Next, Dietzfelbinger explores the tradition of Acts 9:1–9.[90] He outlines several apparent conspicuous differences,[91] yet concludes that

---

81. Ibid., 62.
82. Ibid., 63.
83. Ibid., 63–64.
84. Ibid., 64–75.
85. See also ibid., 129f.
86. Ibid., 67.
87. Ibid.
88. Ibid., 71.
89. Ibid., 71–72.
90. Ibid., 75–82. He does not provide a similar discussion of the Acts 22 or 26 accounts.
91. Acts 9 differs from Paul's accounts in that it does not describe an "Easter-Christophany," it does not proclaim Paul's apostleship, that Paul is not sent to the Gentiles, and that it is theologically less significant since it does not raise problems related to the law. Ibid., 81.

the differences are not contradictions since each author reflects his own perspective.[92]

Dietzfelbinger concludes this section by addressing the question of whether Paul made any inner preparations prior to the DRE.[93] He concludes that it is not possible to know whether Paul made any preparations.[94]

The third section considers the consequences of the DRE.[95] Dietzfelbinger proposes the DRE as the starting point for Paul's new understanding of the Torah.[96] He suggests that Paul's encounter with Jesus marked the end of the era of the Torah and the beginning of a new era.[97] He also returns to the Christology of the DRE, concluding that the DRE was necessary for Paul to comprehend the meaning of the cross,[98] thus completing the transformation of Jesus from one cursed under the law[99] to the one whom God used to justify the godless.[100] He also considers whether Paul's apostleship was an immediate result of the DRE or a later development. He suggests that Acts 9 seems to indicate that the call came later.[101] Dietzfelbinger concludes with the existential observation that the "Christ-meeting" became a "self-meeting" for Paul.[102]

Dietzfelbinger raises several interesting issues, particularly related to the questions of whether Paul made any preparations leading up to the DRE,[103] and how the DRE influenced Paul's Christology.[104] However, this study differs in emphasis from Dietzfelbinger's in several areas. First, Dietzfelbinger focuses on Paul and his theology. He develops

---

92. Ibid., 81–82.

93. Ibid., 82–89.

94. "Ob in diesem Rahmen etwas in Paulus vor sich gegangen ist, das ihn für die Erkenntnis von Damaskus reif gemacht hat, wissen wir nicht, und es ist müßig, darüber zu spekulieren." Ibid., 89.

95. Ibid., 90–116.

96. Ibid., 96.

97. Ibid., 125.

98. Ibid., 132.

99. Ibid., 133.

100. Ibid., 137.

101. Ibid., 137–38.

102. Ibid., 147.

103. For a discussion of Paul's preparation for the DRE see pp. 154–57 below.

104. For a discussion of the Christology of the DRE see pp. 166–86 below.

Paul's theology as it relates to the Torah and the cross, both prior to and coming out of the DRE. This study is more interested in the event itself rather than its theological implications. With respect to the event, Dietzfelbinger discusses whether the DRE was an Easter christophany, and also the type of appearance it was (although with little attention to similar events in ancient Jewish literature). This study will seek to analyze the event in greater detail, and within the context of related literature. Dietzfelbinger's discussion of Christology is limited to titles only, with emphasis on how Paul's views changed in the DRE, and whether Paul appropriated earlier Christian meaning of those titles. This study will explore all characterizations of Jesus in the DRE accounts, and not the christological titles alone.[105]

Tabor

In *Things Unutterable: Paul's Ascent to Paradise in Its Greco-Roman, Judaic, and Early Christian Contexts*, James Tabor expands significantly on Segal's earlier work on heavenly ascent.[106] Tabor makes a substantial contribution by demonstrating that a multi-leveled cosmological structure is not uniquely Jewish, but rather "part of the framework of most religions of the period."[107] Tabor further refines the category of heavenly ascent by identifying four subtypes. The first type involves ascent as an "invasion of heaven" in a negative sense, where humans leave the earthly realm to enter heaven temporarily, often to learn that humans ought not to ascend.[108] The second type consists of ascent "to receive revelation."[109] This type of ascent involves positive reports of journeys where the human is privileged to enter heaven for a time in order to receive secret information[110] but must return to earth.[111] The third type involves ascent "to heavenly immortality."[112] In such ascents, the mortal ascends permanently to heaven, achieving immortality.[113] The fourth type consists of

---

105. For a discussion of other means of characterization see pp.173–85 below.
106. Segal, "Heavenly Ascent."
107. Tabor, *Things Unutterable*, 67.
108. Ibid., 69–73.
109. Ibid., 73–77.
110. Ibid., 81.
111. Ibid., 73.
112. Ibid., 77–81.
113. Ibid., 77–78.

ascent "as a foretaste of the heavenly world."[114] Although similar to the first two types, and particularly ascent to receive revelation, this type of ascent anticipates a final, permanent ascent into the heavenly realm.[115]

Having discussed heavenly ascent in detail, Tabor applies his findings to the remarkable and unique accounts from Paul.[116] Tabor concentrates on 2 Cor 12 rather than texts related to the DRE, since it more clearly fits the paradigm of heavenly ascent.[117] Nevertheless, he compares the two events in the following manner: both were "granted to him by the Lord," although for different (but related) purposes.[118] Tabor also briefly discusses several DRE texts in relation to "seeing" (1 Cor 9:1; 15:8).[119] However, Tabor does not claim that the DRE was an ascent. He concludes that "next to his initial calling and conversion . . . [Paul's] ascent to heaven must have been his highest moment."[120]

Tabor's study does provide an extremely helpful analysis of heavenly ascents. However, since it is unclear at this point whether the DRE involved heavenly ascent, and since Tabor makes no such claim himself, the relevance of Tabor's work to this study remains to be determined.[121]

---

114. Ibid., 81–95.

115. "Such a journey anticipates a final ascent or heavenly destiny. It is a highly privileged experience. It often involves the reception of revelation, but is more than that, the journey itself functions as a proleptic 'crossing the bounds,' a move from mortal to heavenly realms. As such, it can be an experience of transformation. It is something granted graciously to the initiate, thus beyond human power and often fraught with potential danger. It often culminates with a face to face encounter with the highest powers of the heavenly world." Ibid., 95.

116. "Ironically, with all this material on ascent, stretching over hundreds of years, Paul's testimony of his own journey to Paradise is perhaps our best evidence that we are dealing with something that was practiced." Ibid., 97.

117. Tabor clearly views the two as distinct and separate events: "[Paul's] extraordinary ascent to heaven [2 Cor 12] . . . is to be compared to his 'Damascus road' vision and calling." In fact, Tabor claims that the vision of 2 Cor 12 "is a higher and more privileged experience." Ibid., 37.

118. The DRE was for Paul's commendation as apostle, 2 Cor 12 for "a highly privileged confirmation of the Lord's commendation." Ibid.

119. Ibid., 20.

120. Ibid., 124.

121. See pp. 166–86 below for a discussion the nature of Paul's DRE text, and pp. 233–34 below for Acts.

Hurtado

Larry Hurtado explores the development of exalted NT Christology within the context of monotheistic Judaism in *One God, One Lord: Early Christian Devotion and Ancient Jewish Monotheism*.[122] He searches for an antecedent to early Christology among Jewish divine agents,[123] including divine attributes and powers such as Wisdom and Logos,[124] exalted humans such as Moses and Enoch,[125] and principal angels such as Michael and Yahoel.[126] Hurtado concludes that while early Christian conceptions of Jesus were likely influenced by the category of divine agency,[127] the worship of Jesus was a unique and significant deviation from the pattern of divine agency.[128] The distinctive features of the early Christian veneration of Jesus include hymns celebrating Jesus's resurrection, prayer to Jesus, the name of Jesus, the Lord's Supper, the confession of Jesus, and prophetic addresses presented as coming from the risen Jesus.[129] Hurtado suggests that early religious experiences such as the DRE may explain how the mutation occurred.[130] With regard to the DRE in particular, Hurtado argues in favor of viewing the DRE as an apocalyptic vision,[131] and cites Kim's interpretation of the DRE as a *merkabah*-like encounter.[132]

---

122. Hurtado, *One God*, 3–26.

123. "God is understood as having given a unique place and role to this or that heavenly figure who becomes something like the grand vizier of the imperial court." Ibid., 39.

124. Ibid., 41–50.

125. Ibid., 51–69.

126. Ibid., 71–92.

127. "At the earliest stages, Christian experience of and reflection upon the risen Jesus were probably influenced by and drew upon the divine agency category." Ibid., 123.

128. "It is likely that the cultic veneration of Jesus was not only a mutation in the divine agency tradition but it was also a mutation of a somewhat singular nature at the time of its origin." Ibid., 69.

129. Ibid., 99–114.

130. "Prominent among the causes of this mutation in Jewish monotheism were powerful religious experiences of the early believers in which Jesus was experienced as exalted to heavenly glory and legitimated by God himself as an object of their devotion." Ibid., 124.

131. Ibid., 118. Segal develops this argument more fully. See pp. 158–59 below.

132. Hurtado, *One God*, 119. See the discussion of 2 Cor 4:4–6 on pp. 130–35 below, and the discussion of Kim's argument in favor of viewing the DRE as a *merkabah* vision on pp. 157–58 below.

Newman

In *Paul's Glory-Christology: Tradition and Rhetoric*, Carey Newman explores Paul's characterization of Jesus as δόξα. He first examines the "tradition-history" of glory in the Old Testament and "Jewish literature of the Second Temple period," and then applies his findings to Paul's use of δόξα, particularly as he applies the term to Jesus.[133] Newman identifies four essentially diachronic uses of glory in the Old Testament: theophanic, involving the arrival of God and the subsequent upheaval; Sinaitic, in connection with the theophany at Sinai in particular; royal, in connection with God, the King, and life in the kingdom of Israel; and prophetic, as it was reinterpreted in the light of the exile.[134] He then considers the use of glory in *merkabah*-related visions, *1 En.*, Ezek 1–2, Dan 7, and various Qumran scrolls, particularly the *Songs of the Sabbath Sacrifice*.[135] Newman observes that "when a seer peers into the heavens, he sees glory—be it associated with God, a throne, or angels,"[136] particularly with respect to the royal and prophetic patterns. He also develops the significance of glory Christology in ancient Jewish literature, finding a significant connection between glory and *merkabah* visions.[137] Newman claims that the LXX translates כבוד as δόξα as a means of distinguishing Yahweh from other gods.[138] He also observes that δόξα is closely associated with divine appearance and light imagery.[139]

Newman then turns his attention to Paul's accounts of the DRE. He concludes that "the Damascus christophany led Paul to weld together the various strands of the glory tradition to arrive at the identification of Christ as δόξα."[140] A significant portion of his argument hinges on the

---

133. Newman, *Glory-Christology*, 12.

134. Ibid., 25–75.

135. Ibid., 83–92.

136. Ibid., 91.

137. "In short, the ramified use of Glory in throne visions and the tradition dependent upon Ezekiel 1 tradition formed the semantic and semiotic building blocks for Paul's identification of Christ as δόξα." Ibid., 104.

138. "So that the manifestation of pagan deities would not be confused with the revelation of Yahweh." Ibid., 152.

139. δόξα "formed part of the lexical field of 'epiphany' and 'light' terminology." Ibid.

140. Ibid., 211–12.

identification of the DRE as a *merkabah* vision[141] of heavenly ascent.[142] We will examine Newman's proposal in greater detail once we have had examined the Pauline DRE texts.[143]

Stuckenbruck

Another substantial angelological study is Loren Stuckenbruck's *Angel Veneration and Christology: A Study in Early Judaism and in the Christology of the Apocalypse of John*. Stuckenbruck examines a specific aspect of the characterization of angels in ancient Jewish literature, the worship of angels, and compares this to the phenomenon of Christ worship as depicted in the book of Revelation.[144] Stuckenbruck examines ancient Jewish literature for evidence relating to angel veneration in two sections. He first considers polemical sources, raising the possibility that of some "attitudes and practices which were suspected as posing a threat to monotheistic belief,"[145] but concludes that the evidence does not permit "any firm or general conclusions" related to angel veneration.[146] He next discusses non-polemical texts from Qumran,[147] the OT Pseudepigrapha,[148] and selected ancient inscriptions.[149] He concludes that there is "little existing evidence" of an "angel cult" in ancient Jewish literature.[150] In apply-

---

141. "If Paul's [Damascus road] Christophany bore any resemblance to a throne vision—akin to the throne visions of early Jewish apocalypses . . ." Ibid., 203.

142. "To Paul the [Damascus road] Christophany and his heavenly ascents could well be similar sorts of experiences." Ibid., 202.

143. See pp. 159–63 below.

144. "The question addressed in the chapters below is whether and to what degree we may speak of a veneration of angels in early Jewish and Christian sources, and then how (if at all) this motif may have been applied to Christology by the author of the Apocalypse." Stuckenbruck, *Veneration*, 42.

145. Ibid., 75.

146. Ibid., 146.

147. Ibid., 150–64.

148. Ibid., 164–80. Here Stuckenbruck discusses three passages at length (Tob 11:14–15 [164–67]; *Jos. Asen.* 14:1–12; 15:11–12x 9 [168–70]; *L.A.B.* 13:6 [170–73]), considers selections from *1 Enoch* (174–76) and *Testaments of the Twelve Patriarchs* (176–78), and briefly mentions several other works (178–79).

149. Ibid., 180–200. Stuckenbruck's discussion of ancient inscriptions is unique and fascinating. Bauckham is less generous, describing the findings as "slender evidence adduced for some kind of veneration of angels by Jews." Bauckham, *God Crucified*, 13 n. 17.

150. Stuckenbruck, *Veneration*, 269.

ing his findings to the Christology of Revelation, he concludes that the "exalted status" of Jesus was not intended as a "breach" of monotheism. While there is a "religio-historical discontinuity" between ancient Jewish angel veneration and the Christology of Revelation, there is a "traditio- and religious-historical continuity" in how the exaltation of both angels and Jesus were accommodated within monotheistic belief systems.[151]

At first glance, Stuckenbruck's study appears to be highly relevant to this study. However, there are crucial differences that unfortunately mitigate the relevance of Stuckenbruck's work to ours. Stuckenbruck's primary concerns are angel veneration and its relation to the Christology of Revelation. Obviously, the Christology of Revelation is of limited relevance to the DRE. However, the relevance of Stuckenbruck's survey of angel veneration is also limited. Stuckenbruck considers few epiphanies in his analysis of ancient Jewish sources. Therefore, his analysis of ancient Jewish sources is also of limited value for our purposes. Furthermore, he considers only one aspect of the characterization of one type of heavenly being; our study will consider the characterization of heavenly beings in general.

Fletcher-Louis

Crispin Fletcher-Louis also discusses the subject of angelomorphic Christology in *Luke-Acts: Angels, Christology, and Soteriology*. Fletcher-Louis argues that Jesus's appearance to Paul on the Damascus road may be an "angelophanic mode of the risen and ascended Christ."[152] He does not argue for the identification of Jesus as an angel, but rather for a combination of "angelomorphic characteristics with a higher-than-angelic Christology."[153] The characterization of angels, and especially the Angel of Yahweh, will merit careful consideration in our discussion of christological antecedents.

Gieschen

While the preceding studies are related to the nature of the seer's experience, others emphasize the characterization of heavenly beings. Angels have received much attention as intermediary beings that may

---

151. Ibid., 272.
152. Fletcher-Louis, *Luke Acts*, 50–57.
153. Ibid., 56–57.

have provided an antecedent for the development of early Christology. In *Angelomorphic Christology: Antecedents and Early Evidence*, Charles Gieschen explores the possibility that the New Testament describes Jesus in language previously reserved for angels.[154] While Gieschen does not address the DRE at length, he does mention it several times. Gieschen claims that Paul's transformation after the DRE may be related to Enoch's transformation after his *merkabah* vision (*2 En.* 22:8–10), which seems to imply that the DRE should be understood as a kind of *merkabah* vision.[155] He also argues that the DRE was partly responsible for Paul's concept of mystical union with Christ ("in Christ").[156]

Donaldson

In *Paul and the Gentiles*, Terence Donaldson seeks to address "the nature and the origin of Paul's convictions about the Gentiles and their place in salvation."[157] Donaldson dismisses the notion that the DRE was the source of Paul's call to the Gentiles as begging the question[158] or tautologous.[159] He cites four points that require explanation: that Paul's earlier life in Judaism was a "stable framework of meaning" corresponding to Sanders's "covenantal nomism"; that Paul viewed Jesus's followers as a threat; that Paul's "conversion experience" resulted in a new opinion of

---

154. "Angelomorphic traditions, especially those growing from the Angel of the Lord traditions, had a significant impact on the early expressions of Christology to the extent that evidence of an Angelomorphic Christology is discernible in several documents dated between 50 and 150 CE." Gieschen, *Angelomorphic Christology*, 6. Gieschen's criteria for divinity are listed on p. 29 below.

155. Gieschen, *Angelomorphic Christology*, 322. He also notes that the mystical experience described in 2 Cor 12 is likely not the DRE. Ibid., 321n25.

156. While this is a rather unremarkable interpretation of Jesus's query, "Why are you persecuting me?" (Acts 9:4), Gieschen's reasoning is new: the mystical union with Christ "can be best understood if one accepts that Paul believed Christ to be the manifestation of God with a mystical body of gigantic proportions." Ibid., 340.

157. Donaldson, *Paul*, 13. Similarly, "Paul's apostolic interest in the Gentiles, formerly seen as axiomatic, now emerges as a problem in need of a solution." Ibid., 22.

158. Sanders's view that "the call to reveal God's Son to the Gentiles is the point of departure for everything else" can, according to Donaldson, "be disposed of rather quickly.... [since] it either begs the question or renders Paul's convictional shift arbitrary and inexplicable—or both." Ibid., 250.

159. "To account for Paul's Gentile mission simply by saying that his Damascus experience was really a call to be an apostle to the Gentiles is ultimately tautologous. The problem remains." Ibid., 18.

Jesus; and that Paul started his "Torah-free" ministry to Gentiles at a later point.[160] He argues that the change in Paul's views regarding Jesus and the mission to the Gentiles is best understood as a paradigm shift"[161] which involved a "reconfiguration rather than a repudiation of his essential Jewishness."[162]

After discussing Paul's basic theological views concerning God, humanity, Jesus, the Torah, and Israel,[163] Donaldson reaches three conclusions: first, that Paul began as a covenantal nomist; second, that Paul opposed the Christian movement since it promoted Jesus rather than the Torah as the defining boundary of God's covenant people; third, that Paul's experience of the risen Jesus resulted in the conviction that Jesus is Christ and Lord, shifted his understand of God's purposes with respect to Israel and the Gentiles, and "galvanized his own personal involvement with the Gentile world."[164] In other words, the DRE changed Paul's view of Jesus, which led him to reconsider the place of Gentiles within the people of God.[165] Thus, the DRE primarily affected Paul's view of Jesus, which later resulted in his conviction that he was called to a Gentile ministry.[166]

Donaldson's argument explains how Paul could account for a Gentile mission, but does not explain why Paul was personally convicted to undertake such a mission.[167] His solution is based on the "assumption that prior to Damascus [Paul] believed that only proselytes would share in Israel's salvation," which is then combined with the "assumption that in addition he had already been personally involved in the process by

---

160. Ibid., 26–27.

161. Ibid., 45.

162. Ibid., 49.

163. Ibid., 81–248.

164. Ibid., 259; see 295–99 for a more detailed summary.

165. Donaldson relates this to Paul's pre-DRE views concerning Gentiles, which he argues that the Pharisee Paul had held: "only those Gentiles who in this age became proselytes—full members of the community of the elect—would have a share in the age to come." Ibid., 251.

166. "But the experience in its initial impact and import, I maintain, concerns Jesus and the belief that God had raised him, not Paul and the belief that God had called him." Ibid.

167. Donaldson acknowledges this difficulty: "Why did [Paul] feel that he himself was called to take the lead in this enterprise?" Ibid., 260.

which Gentiles became proselytes."¹⁶⁸ In other words, the combination of a new understanding of Jesus and his former proselytizing activity led Paul to understand himself to be called by Christ to a mission among the Gentiles.¹⁶⁹

To summarize, Donaldson raises a valid and difficult question: given Paul's past in covenantal nomism, how did his convictions regarding Gentiles arise? His solution is also substantial and noteworthy: Paul's new assessment of Jesus caused a reconfiguration of his views concerning the boundaries of the people of God. Yet Donaldson does not appear to account fully for Paul's own testimony regarding the origin of his Gentile mission. His dismissal of the notion that the call to Gentile mission was contained in the DRE as begging the question or tautologous is too facile. Surely it is possible that Jesus could have called Paul as apostle to the Gentiles during the DRE, a claim that Paul himself appears to make (Gal 1:15–16).¹⁷⁰ Conversely, Donaldson's alternative account of the origin of Paul's Gentile mission is based on three assumptions: first, that Paul held a particular belief concerning proselytes, of which we have little evidence; second, that Paul had been involved in proselytizing Gentiles prior to the DRE, an assumption which is curiously absent from Paul's account of his prior life (cf. Phil 3:4b–6); and third, that Paul somehow came to view himself as the apostle to the Gentiles on his own, which Paul repeatedly denies (cf. Rom 1:1, 5; 15:15, 18; 1 Cor 1:1, 17; 2 Cor 1:1; Gal 1:1, 15–16). In other words, Donaldson's explanation for the origin of Paul's Gentile mission either directly contradicts Paul's testimony or relies on unsubstantiated assumptions. Furthermore, Donaldson fails to explain the purpose of the DRE if it were not to call Paul to the Gentile ministry.¹⁷¹ While it appears that Donaldson's argument has merit as an explanation for how Paul's views changed following the DRE, it does not adequately explain the relationship between the DRE and Paul's missional call to the Gentiles.

---

168. Ibid. Yet he does acknowledge that Paul's DRE-motivated paradigm shift led directly to his Gentile mission: "In all likelihood, then, Paul's convictions about the Gentile mission were the direct result of the Damascus experience." Ibid., 271.

169. Ibid., 299.

170. The initiative and the purpose of the DRE are discussed on pp. 154–57 above.

171. For a discussion of the purpose of the DRE see pp. 165–66 below.

Eskola

In *Messiah and the Throne: Jewish Merkabah Mysticism and Early Christian Exaltation Discourse*, Timo Eskola considers the influence of *merkabah* mysticism on the development of early Christology.[172] He defines "throne mysticism" as a heavenly ascent in which the adept is escorted before God's throne, often featuring worship in the heavenly temple and possible angelic intermediaries.[173] Eskola's literary-critical methodology[174] is similar to ours. However, Eskola relies on some different areas of literary theory since his purpose is somewhat different.[175]

Following a survey of ancient Jewish literature,[176] Eskola concludes that *merkabah* mysticism involves a heavenly ascent and a vision of God's throne, using "traditional terminology" from the OT to describe the heavenly realm, which may include a heavenly temple.[177] Eskola identifies several "starting point[s]" for relating *merkabah* mysticism to early Christology, including *merkabah* as a model for enthronement, the exaltation of angels, priestly figures, and the Davidic Messiah.[178] He then examines NT Christology in the light of these points of contact with *merkabah* mysticism,[179] concluding that "the earliest exaltation Christology is not comprehensible without the background of Jewish merkabah mysticism."[180] Of particular interest to this study, of course, is

---

172. Eskola's purpose is stated more clearly on Eskola, *Messiah and Throne*, 17: "*to investigate the relationship between Jewish merkabah mysticism and New Testament exaltation Christology by focusing on the central metaphor of the throne.*"

173. Ibid., 6.

174. Ibid., 17–42.

175. See the discussion of literary theory on pp. 24–31 below.

176. Eskola, *Messiah and Throne*, 67–108. Eskola considers Ezek 1–3 (67–68), *Testament of Levi* (77–69) *1 Enoch* (72–74; 91–96), Philo (96–98), *4 Ezra* (98–100), *Testament of Job* (100–103), *2 Enoch* (103–5), *Apocalypse of Abraham* (105–7), and *Ladder of Jacob* (107–8). Most of Eskola's observations related to these texts are summarized on p. 123. However, he does note a significant exception in the case of *2 Enoch*: "the enthronement itself does not display standard features" (105).

177. "The symbolic universe of traditional Old Testament religion maintained its relevance in the literature of Jewish mysticism." Ibid., 123.

178. Ibid., 156–67.

179. Ibid., 159–390.

180. Ibid., 390.

Eskola's discussion of the DRE between Paul and Jesus.[181] Eskola claims that Paul interpreted the DRE as a *merkabah* vision.[182]

Summary

The preceding survey reveals the diversity of approaches and opinions related to the Damascus road encounter between Jesus and Paul. The question of how the DRE relates to contemporary ancient Jewish religious beliefs and practices is central to recent interpretations of the DRE. In particular, scholars such as Bowker, Kim, Segal, Hurtado, and Eskola have argued that the DRE was a *merkabah*-like vision. It is within the context of this current scholarly discussion that we seek to consider the Christology of the DRE.

THE CHRISTOLOGY OF THE DAMASCUS ROAD ENCOUNTER

This study will examine the Christology of the DRE as depicted by the undisputed Pauline epistles and the book of Acts within the genre of ancient Jewish epiphanies[183] up to the first century CE using an exegetical and literary-critical[184] methodology. The central hypothesis that we will assess is that both Paul and Acts characterize Jesus as not only in unique relationship to God the Father, but also as divine.[185]

---

181. Ibid., 199–202.

182. Ibid., 201. Eskola's argument in relation to the DRE is discussed at length on pp. 163–64 below.

183. Epiphany may be defined as an encounter between God, angels, or other heavenly beings, and humans.

184. For a brief introduction to literary theory, see Chatman, *Story and Discourse*; Culler, *Literary Theory*, 82–93; Genette, *Narrative Discourse*, 25–32; Waugh, ed., *Literary Theory*. For an earlier approach to literary theory, see Richards, *Literary Criticism*.

For a review of the literary critical approaches to biblical hermeneutics, see Longman, "Bible as Literature"; Merenlahti and Hakola, "Characterization"; Petersen, *Literary Criticism*; Powell, *Narrative Criticism*; Prickett, "Hermeneutics"; idem, "Biblical and Literary Criticism"; Resseguie, *Narrative Criticism*.

185. "Divine" will normally be used as a direct reference to God, rather than a vague term that might equally apply to angels and other creatures. Bauckham notes that this important question, namely "what, in the Jewish understanding of God, really counts as 'divine'—is rarely faced with clarity." Bauckham, *God Crucified*, 4–5. This concern cannot be overemphasized. Much of the confusion regarding the identity of God, Jesus, and various intermediary figures may be related to a rather slippery definition of "divine," which often appears to be a moving target meaning anything from "God" to "heavenly."

This study will focus on Jewish sources rather than non-Jewish sources. This approach has become common recently, especially within the new *religionsgeschichtliche Schule*. Furthermore, both Paul (Gal 1:13–14; Phil 3:4b–6) and Luke (Acts 22:3–5; 26:4–11) place the DRE in a Jewish context. Paul also casts the encounter as a prophetic call using the language of Isaiah and Jeremiah (Gal 1:15–16).[186]

This study will focus on the characterization of Jesus in the undisputed Pauline epistles and the book of Acts, and not in the disputed Pauline epistles. The undisputed Pauline epistles capture the thoughts of a single (implied) author, as does the book of Acts; the authorship of the disputed Pauline epistles is not certain. As well, there is little material pertaining to the DRE in the disputed Pauline epistles (cf. Eph 3:1–12; Col 1:25–29; 1 Tim 1:12–17; 2:7).[187] On the other hand, Acts contains three accounts of the DRE by a single author, which may be used to construct a comprehensive portrait. Since Acts purports to describe the same even on the Damascus road as the undisputed Pauline epistles, it should prove interesting to compare and contrast these two portraits, just as many OT epiphanies may be compared to corresponding rewritten accounts in the OT Pseudepigrapha and Josephus.

LITERARY-THEORETICAL METHODOLOGY

This study will examine how Jesus is characterized in the DRE accounts of Paul and Acts. It seems natural to apply literary theory in the study of the DRE, since it is a story, having its own setting, plot, and characters. Our only evidence is literary, from the accounts of Paul[188] and Acts. Therefore, it is reasonable that the tools and methods developed in the study of literature should be applied to the DRE.[189]

---

186. A brief survey of non-Jewish epiphany narratives is provided in appendix B.

187. The disputed Pauline epistles are discussed on pp. 148–49 below.

188. The relevance of narrative criticism to the Pauline epistles is discussed on p. 98 below.

189. While the literary-critical methodology employed in this study pertaining to genre and character was developed for fictional literature, it is not necessary to assume that the biblical narratives are also fictional. White discusses the connection between history and narrative, but seems to raise more questions than he answers. White, "Value of Narrative," 267–68.

Recent studies of NT Christology have also used a literary methodology.[190] For example, Eskola relies on literary theory related to semiotics and semantics in order to provide a theoretical foundation for his assertion that the symbolic universe of ancient Judaism, and *merkabah* mysticism in particular, is essential to an understanding of early NT Christology.[191] Literary theory also provides a solid theoretical foundation for the comparison of texts by different authors (such as the DRE narratives of Paul and Acts, and the many works included within the genre of ancient Jewish epiphany). As Eskola observes, "in the study of Christology intertextual criticism may help us define the relation between early christological statements and earlier Jewish descriptions of heavenly figures and heaven residences."[192] The relationship between the NT and earlier Jewish texts has long been recognized.[193] While Eskola's study focuses on symbology, since he is concerned with the distinctive metaphors of *merkabah* mysticism, our emphasis will be on the literary theory related to genre.

At the level of individual narratives, it is possible to employ the more familiar tools of narrative criticism.[194] This study will rely on a narrative critical methodology to examine individual texts. A general familiarity with narrative criticism is assumed throughout the study, although key concepts will be defined where necessary. Concepts such as metalepses,[195] repetition,[196] time,[197] focalization,[198] evaluative point of view,[199] and irony[200] will be used to interpret the DRE texts. However,

---

190. For example, see the collection of essays in Longenecker, ed., *Narrative Dynamics*.

191. Eskola, *Messiah and Throne*, 17–28.

192. Ibid., 187.

193. "In this area the study of the New Testament has been ahead of its time." Ibid., 38.

194. For more information on narrative criticism see Powell, *Narrative Criticism*; Resseguie, *Narrative Criticism*.

195. See p. 40 n. 32 below.

196. See p. 225 n. 203 below.

197. See p. 36 n. 22 below.

198. See p. 37 n. 23 below.

199. See p. 203 n. 76 below.

200. See p. 241 n. 273 below.

this study will rely most heavily on the literary theory related to genre and characterization.²⁰¹

Genre

Since this study will interpret the DRE accounts within the genre of ancient Jewish epiphany, it is necessary to discuss the literary theory related to genre.²⁰² Genre has been described as "the most powerful explanatory tool available to the literary critic."²⁰³ Abbott defines genre as

---

201. A review of the literature reveals that character has received poor treatment in recent decades. For a discussion of character, see Abbott, *Narrative*, 123–37; Keen, *Narrative Form*, 55–72; Rimmon-Kenan, *Narrative Fiction*, 29–42. Barthes even went so far as to proclaim the death of character: "What is obsolescent in today's novel is not the novelistic, it is the character; what can no longer be written is the Proper Name." Barthes, *S/Z*, 95. Hochman attributes the decline of character in literature to the decline of character in the larger world: "literature reflects life with regard to character as in other respects." Hochman, *Character*, 13. Rimmon-Kenan observes that "structuralists can hardly accommodate character within their theories, because of their commitment to an ideology which 'decentres' man and runs counter to the notions of individuality and psychological depth." Rimmon-Kenan, *Narrative Fiction*, 30. Culler also admits as much: "Character is the major aspect of the novel to which structuralism has paid least attention and has been least successful in treating." Culler, *Structuralist Poetics*, 230.

Yet this neglect did not deter some from continuing the study of character. In fact, Knapp observes a renewal in the study of character: "Until quite recently, the construct in various hermeneutic theories and literary criticism known as character has been neglected in literary studies." Knapp, "Self-Preservation," 1.

202. Generic criticism has a wide variety of proponents, including Frye, Derrida, and Keen. Frye notes that "the critical theory of genres is stuck precisely where Aristotle left it." Frye, *Anatomy*, 13. "There is a place for classification in criticism.... The strong emotional repugnance felt by many critics toward any form of schematization in poetics is again the result of a failure to distinguish criticism as a body of knowledge from the direct experience of literature, where every act is unique, and classification has no place" (29). Frye's model for genology involves four generic categories: romantic, tragic, comic, and ironic/satiric (162). The various "phases" between the categories are neatly summarized in two diagrams by Hernadi. *Beyond Genre*, 133–34. Derrida states, "the genre has always in all genres been able to play the role of order's principle: resemblance, analogy, identity and difference, taxonomic classification, organization and genealogical tree, order of reason, order of reasons, sense of sense, truth of truth, natural light and sense of history." Derrida, "Genre," 81. The study of genre was a feature of Chicago criticism. Shereen, "Literary Theory," 238–39. See also Keen, *Narrative Form*, 141–53.

203. "[Genre] is our most valued way of talking about and valuing the literary text. When both genre and its definitional nature are made explicit rather than denied, our explanations acquire the defensive strengths of self-awareness and internal consistency. They thereby reduce their vulnerability to ironic discounting or extramural deconstruction." Rosmarin, *Genre*, 39.

a "recurrent literary form" that applies to "large categories like the novel" as well as "subsets of these large categories, like the picaresque novel (the episodic adventures of a rascal, told in the first person)."[204] The task of determining genre is left to the literary critic.[205] Genres may span a variety of authors and time periods. This is most apparent in broad genres such as the novel, but is also applicable to narrower genres such as the picaresque novel or folktales.[206]

More specifically, this study claims that epiphany in ancient Jewish literature constitutes a genre. If epiphany is defined as a human encounter with God, angels, or other heavenly beings, then epiphany narratives may be identified throughout the OT, Apocrypha, OT Pseudepigrapha, and other ancient Jewish writings, including those of Josephus. Therefore, since epiphany is a recurrent literary form, it may be considered a genre.[207] The genre of epiphany will be developed using an approach similar to those of Rodway[208] and Todorov:[209] a working hypothesis will be presented, and then refined through the study of specific epiphanies.[210]

---

204. Abbott, *Narrative*, 45. For an extensive discussion on the theory of genre, see Rosmarin, *Genre*, 3–51.

205. "Generic studies are by nature definitive. The task of the student of the novel or of any other genre is to uncover and examine those attributes which are specific to the genre, which define the class." Firmat, "Genres," 271. "When a critic asserts that a particular genre is like a particular literary text, he makes a conceptual promise to his reader. He fulfills this promise by displaying both the *extensiveness* of his metaphor's power, showing how it subsumes surprisingly many poems, and its *intensiveness*, showing how it unfolds a given poem in surprising detail." Rosmarin, *Genre*, 47.

206. See Propp, *Folktale*.

207. Keesey, *Contexts*, 312.

208. Rodway explains that the hermeneutical dilemma may be escaped "by edging out, tacking from evidence to hypothesis to further evidence to renewed hypothesis." Rodway "Generic Criticism," 94. "Few subjects outside mathematics can avoid [this spiral]; literature least of all." Ibid., 97.

209. "We actually deal with a relatively limited number of cases, from them we deduce a general hypothesis, and we verify this hypothesis by other cases, correcting (or rejecting) it as need be." Todorov, *Fantastic*, 4.

210. The genre of ancient Jewish epiphany is explored in more detail on pp. 32–41 below.

Characterization

The close connection between action and character in the DRE is quite obvious:[211] the Christology of the DRE involves the characterization of Jesus within a specific event. Our initial focus will be on the genre of epiphany, thus placing the focus on action. Then action will be subordinated to character as we focus on the characterization of heavenly beings within epiphanies. The characterization of these heavenly figures presents some unique challenges. For example, the restriction of our field of research to epiphany texts removes most personifications, hypostases, and other such literary devices from consideration, since they do not normally appear as characters within epiphany narratives. This means that some of the literature used by other scholars will not be examined in our discussion of ancient Jewish literature.[212] Furthermore, the heavenly characters who appear in epiphanies are generally not human, which creates some unusual difficulties.[213] As Forster observes, "since the novelist is himself a human being, there is an affinity between him and his subject-matter which is absent in many other forms of art."[214] In an epiphany, there is much less affinity to the one who appears. Indeed, the lack of affinity to the resurrected Jesus may help to explain why the characterization of Paul tends to receive the majority of the attention in theological and artistic presentations of the DRE, rather than the characterization of Jesus.[215]

---

211. Rimmon-Kenan recognizes the competing interests of action and character: "it is legitimate to subordinate character to action when we study action but equally legitimate to subordinate action to character when the latter is the focus of our study." Rimmon-Kenan, *Narrative Fiction*, 36. She identifies two problems related to the "mode of existence" of character: "people or words" and "being or doing." Ibid., 31–36.

212. For example, the personification of wisdom has long been proposed as a Christological antecedent. E.g., Witherington gives wisdom the first mention in the section on "Christ's Divinity" in Witherington, "Christology," 105. Bauckham sees great value in the use of personifications and "hypostatizations of aspects of God" as paradigms for New Testament Christology. Bauckham, *God Crucified*, 20–22. However, the relevance of literary devices as a legitimate precursor for the characterization of a person is debatable. See Hurtado, *One God*, 47.

213. For example, Forster's chapter on characterization is entitled "People," since "the actors in a story are usually human." The only exceptions he sees are animals. Forster, *Novel*, 30.

214. Ibid.

215. Artistic depictions of Jesus in the DRE are quite fascinating, and seem to illustrate this lack of affinity. For example, Karel Dujardin's *The Conversion of Saint Paul* (oil on canvas, 1662, National Gallery, London) substitutes two cherubs in the place of Jesus

The Characterization of God and Other Heavenly Beings

Many scholars have attempted to characterize God and other heavenly beings. For example, Gieschen lists five criteria for divinity.[216] The first criterion, divine position, may attribute divinity to a being on or near God's throne, or on a throne near God's throne, or even standing near God. The second criterion, divine appearance, involves the physical characteristics of the angelomorphic being in comparison to God's visible features from various theophanies. It may also consider the physical size of the being. The third criterion, divine functions, attributes divinity to beings that carry out actions typically ascribed to God. The fourth criterion, divine name, involves the use of Yahweh in reference to a being. The fifth criterion, divine veneration, may accord divinity to those beings who receive worship.[217]

Bauckham proposes three ways in which God is uniquely categorized. The first involves how God is identified in covenant relationship to Israel, both by his activities and by his character.[218] The second involves God's "unique relationship to the whole of reality," particularly as Creator and Ruler.[219] The third is monolatry, "the exclusive worship of the one God."[220]

The debate over criteria for divinity is closely related to the debate over the definition of monotheism. For example, Hurtado associates monotheism ("the universal sovereignty and uniqueness of the one God

---

(see p. xxiv above). Caravaggio's *The Conversion on the Way to Damascus* (Michelangelo Merisi da Caravaggio, oil on canvas, 1600, Cerasi Chapel, Santa Maria del Popolo, Rome) depicts Paul, but not Jesus. Of five paintings of the DRE in the Louvre, only one contains a depiction of Jesus (Nicolò dell' Abate, *La Conversion de Saint Paul*, ink on paper, sixteenth century); the others do not (anonymous, *Saint Paul sur le Chemin de Damas*, ink on paper, c. 1600; Christoph Zimmermann, *Saint Paul sur le Chemin de Damas*, ink on paper, c. 1614; Eugène Delacroix, *Saint Paul Renversé sur le Chemin de Damas*, lead on paper, nineteenth century; Eugène Delacroix, *Saint Paul sur le Chemin de Damas*, watercolor and lead on paper, nineteenth century).

216. Gieschen, *Angelomorphic Christology*, 31–33.

217. Gieschen's criteria do not appear to be equally useful for making clear distinctions between God and other beings. For example, the book of Revelation makes reference to 24 beings seated on thrones encircling God's throne (Rev 4:4), who are not God yet meet Gieschen's criterion of divine position. Eskola provides a thorough critique of Gieschen's criteria in Eskola, *Messiah and Throne*, 137–46.

218. Bauckham, *God Crucified*, 9.

219. Ibid., 10.

220. Ibid., 13.

of Israel") with monolatry (the "reservation of cultic worship ... for this one God").[221] Bauckham also argues that there is a clear line between God, who is worshipped, and other heavenly beings "who, being only servants of God, may not be worshipped."[222] Stuckenbruck builds on Hurtado's proposal,[223] but reaches a slightly modified conclusion that several ancient Jewish texts do depict the worship of angels "as beings aligned with and subordinate to God."[224]

Rather than relying on predefined categories such as Bauckham's and Gieschen's, this study will take a more inductive approach to the characterization of heavenly beings in ancient Jewish epiphany texts, and Jesus in the DRE. We will explore the Pauline DRE texts to see how Jesus is characterized, and then compare this to how other ancient Jewish epiphanic figures are characterized.

Direct and Indirect Characterization

In order to bring structure to the data related to the characterization of Jesus, the term "direct characterization" will refer to christological names[225] and titles, and "indirect characterization" to other means of characterization.[226] Indirect characterization involves narration and

---

221. Hurtado, "Monotheism," 25.

222. Bauckham, *God Crucified*, 19.

223. Stuckenbruck, *Veneration*, 15–21.

224. Ibid., 269.

225. Docherty devotes a chapter to the important role of names in Docherty, *Character*, 43–86.

226. Several literary critics use similar categories. Garvey uses the term "identification of character" for "the attribution of a name or a definite description," and "characterization" when a character is invested with "an attribute or set of attributes ... which add descriptive material of a particular sort to the argument node." Garvey, "Characterization," 63. Garvey later uses the terminology "directly" and "indirectly" to refer to characterization by "explicit statements" and "dramatically," respectively. Ibid., 67.

For Rimmon-Kenan, "direct definition" involves naming a character trait by an adjective, abstract noun, or some other noun or part of speech. "Indirect presentation" involves the mentioning of a trait through action, speech, external appearance, or the environment. She argues that these traits may be reinforced through the use of analogy. Rimmon-Kenan, *Narrative Fiction*, 59–71.

Bar-Efrat distinguishes between the direct and indirect "shaping" of characters. Methods of direct shaping include outward appearance and inner personality, including statements concerning character traits and mental states. Methods of indirect shaping include speech, actions, and minor characters. Bar-Efrat, *Narrative Art*, 47–92.

dialog,[227] as well as grammatical and lexical aspects of the text.[228] In the words of Garvey, "even the most trivial detail may provide relevant material for characterization."[229] This is especially true of the DRE since the data is sparse.

CONCLUSION

Now that we have surveyed the scholarly landscape and presented a proposal for examining the Christology of the DRE, we may proceed. We begin with a study of the genre of epiphany in ancient Jewish literature up to the first century CE, followed by an examination of the NT DRE texts. Paul's accounts will be considered first, since they not only predate Acts but also presume to be eyewitness testimony.[230] Finally, we will consider the implications of our findings as we seek to understand the Christology of the Damascus road encounter between Jesus and Paul.

---

227. Booth discusses the distinction between telling (narration), where the author "'intrudes" to "tell us something about his story," and showing (dialog), where the author "thinks of his story as a matter . . . to be so exhibited that it will tell itself. Booth, *Fiction*, 8. Darr also uses the categories of telling, or "direct narrative descriptions and evaluations of characters," and showing. Darr, *Character Building*, 44.

Berlin also comments on indirect characterization: "The reader reconstructs a character from the information provided to him in the discourse: he is told by the statements and evaluations of the narrator and other characters, and he infers from the speech and action of the character himself." Berlin, *Poetics*, 34.

228. Alter observes that both syntax and related texts may be of particular use for understanding character: "One must be constantly aware of two features: the repeated use of narrative analogy, through which one part of the text provides oblique commentary on another; and the richly expressive function of syntax, which often bears the kind of weight of meaning that, say, imagery does in a novel by Virginia Woolf or analysis in a novel by George Eliot. Attention to such features leads not to a more 'imaginative' reading of biblical narrative but to a more precise one." Alter, *Biblical Narrative*, 21.

229. Garvey, "Characterization," 68.

230. As Gaventa suggests, beginning with Paul is "a far better approach" than beginning with Acts. Gaventa, *Darkness*, 18.

2

Ancient Jewish Epiphanies

INTRODUCTION

A<small>NCIENT JEWISH LITERATURE ABOUNDS</small> with depictions of humans encountering heavenly beings.[1] Some narratives describe fresh encounters, others retell these familiar accounts, while many weave new tales involving legendary figures of old. Taken together, these ancient Jewish epiphany narratives offer an opportunity to understand Jewish conceptions of epiphany up to the time of the Apostle Paul.[2]

We will begin by examining recent approaches to the classification of epiphanies, and the inherent difficulties of these approaches. A new literary approach will then be proposed and applied to a representative sample of epiphany narratives. We will then examine the genre of epiphany from a literary perspective, with particular attention to the presentation of event and character.

Recent Approaches to the Classification of Epiphanies

Epiphanies have typically been classified according to various categories. Perhaps the most obvious classification is based on the type of epiphanic

---

1. Horbury surveys current understandings of Second Temple period theology in Horbury, "Herodian," 16n1. He lists the four most common approaches as strict monotheism, supreme deity and exalted angel, Trinitarian anticipated, and monotheism with some acknowledgement of other divine beings. Sanders exemplifies the latter view; see Sanders, *Judaism*, 247. Horbury argues for an inclusive type of monotheism.

2. It has recently become common practice, particularly in the new *religionsgeschichtliche Schule*, to view the literature of the Second Temple period as antecedent to NT Christology. Consider the following quotation from Nickelsburg: "The first Christians interpreted the person and activity of Jesus in light of this whole range of figures, or conversely, Christian beliefs about any or several of these figures were almost uniformly tied to Jesus of Nazareth." Nickelsburg, *Origins*, 117.

figure. Thus, theophanies are frequently separated from angelophanies. For example, the *Anchor Bible Dictionary* has separate entries for appearances of God[3] and angels,[4] yet no article for epiphany in general. Epiphanies are also grouped according to purpose. The call narrative is a classic example of this approach,[5] although even this category is often subdivided.[6] Epiphanies are even classified according to kinds of appearances such as visions, dreams, or external encounters, or even more specific groupings such as "auditory message dreams" or "visual-symbolic dreams."[7] Segal notes the similarly unhelpful distinction between apocalypticism and mysticism.[8]

There are numerous difficulties with these classifications. For example, there are obvious difficulties with classification according to the type of epiphanic being. First, the precise identity of the epiphanic figure is often in dispute. For example, the Angel of Yahweh has been subjected to a seemingly neverending series of speculations.[9] Appearances of the Angel of Yahweh are distinguished from theophanies by those who do

---

3. Hiebert, "Theophany in the OT." Interestingly, there is no corresponding entry in *ABD* for "Theophany in the NT."

4. See Newsom, "Angels."

5. Hubbard identifies the structure of the call narrative as: introduction, confrontation, reaction, commission, protest, reassurance, and conclusion. Hubbard, "Commissioning Accounts," 187, 191–92. See also Hubbard, "Commissioning Stories," 103–26. Mullins, "Commission Forms," discusses some of the themes that appear frequently in call narratives. Kutsch's proposed form for call narratives consisted of: communication of the call by Yahweh, objection by the appointee, dismissal of the objection with the promise of Yahweh, and signs as confirmation that Yahweh has given the mission. As cited in Schmitt, "Berufungsschema," 202. There is a great danger of circular reasoning inherent in this approach, since the form is used to determine the type of call, but the type of call determines the form. Consider the circular reasoning of the following quotation: "Recognizing the form of the commissioning story allows the interpreter to understand the primary intent of such stories: 'to commission someone to carry out a divinely-instigated task.'" Bailey and Vander Broek, *Literary Forms*, 146.

6. See Childs, *Exodus*, 54.

7. Gnuse, "Dreams," 32.

8. He suggests that "scholars have carried a distinction in literary genre into the realm of experience without sufficient warrant." Segal, *Paul the Convert*, 38.

9. Newsom presents a selection of such theories ("a sort of hypostasis of the deity; . . . a functional identity exists between messenger and sender; . . . the phrase mal'ak yhwh is a late, pious interpolation; . . . the alternation between Yahweh and mal'ak yhwh has to do with point of view; etc."), and concludes by proposing yet another theory: that the מלאך יהוה is a paradox. Newsom, "Angels," 252.

not view the Angel Yahweh as God,[10] even though many texts seem to characterize him as such.[11] Second, the epiphanic figure is often characterized by multiple terms in a single passage, or multiple types of beings appear in a single event. For example, Gen 18–19 refers to an appearance of Yahweh (18:1), three men (18:2), and two angels (19:1). In such cases, it is not possible to classify the epiphany according to a single type of being. Third, the characterization of certain epiphanic figures is disputed even where the identity of the epiphanic figure seems beyond doubt. For example, Westermann argues vehemently against the view that Gen 18 is a theophany: "There is no way in which one can consider the present event an appearance of God."[12]

Other difficulties are introduced because the various methods of classification are not mutually exclusive. It is entirely possible to classify a single epiphany according to the type of epiphanic being, the purpose of the appearance, and the kind of appearance.[13] This dilemma is clearly illustrated in Gnuse's struggle to classify the initial encounter between Yahweh and Samuel (1 Sam 3). This epiphany was originally classified as a call narrative.[14] Gnuse first proposed that the epiphany is instead an "auditory message dream."[15] He later retracted this opinion, concluding that "the account in its final form appears to be a mixed genre, combining elements of a prophetic call narrative with the dream report."[16] However, the distinction between the call narrative and the auditory message dream is unnecessary, since there is no reason why a particular epiphany could not be both a call narrative according to purpose, and an auditory message dream according to the kind of appearance. In fact, it is rather absurd that 1 Sam 3 has ever been considered a call narrative since the narrative does not contain a call,[17] and equally absurd that

---

10. For example, Hiebert, "Theophany."
11. See the discussion of the Angel of Yahweh on pp. 89–91 below.
12. Westermann, *Genesis 12–36*, 275.
13. Such as a dream (1 Kgs 3:5) or an external encounter (Judg 6:11).
14. Gnuse, *Dream Theophany*, 168n133. Gnuse cites scholars such as Gressmann, Jepsen, von Rad, Caird, Murray Newman, Ackroyd, Stoebe, Jenks, Hubbard, Ehrlich, Fichtner, Galling, and Bardtke who held that 1 Sam 3 is a call narrative.
15. Ibid., 157. Moberly disagrees with Gnuse's assessment that this narrative is a dream theophany. Moberly, "Call of Samuel," 447–49.
16. Gnuse, "Dreams," 44.
17. Moberly notes the absence of a call: "Although YHWH addresses Samuel, He does not call him to a specifically prophetic vocation. Samuel is not in fact told to say

it was originally classified as a dream narrative since Samuel is awake throughout!

Furthermore, many of the categories and subcategories are unnecessarily specific. For example, Coats appears to create the subgenre of annunciation from a single account (2 Kgs 4:8–17).[18] He then speculates that Gen 18:1–15 is an annunciation, and proceeds to draw several remarkable conclusions from the differences.[19] Coats's entire argument hinges on two precarious assumptions: that 2 Kgs 4:8–17 provides the definitive prototype for annunciations, and that Gen 18:1–15 is an annunciation.

In addition, reliance on such overly specific categories may lead to unnecessary conclusions. For example, Westermann begins with the genres "promise of a child to a childless couple" and "visit of a divine messenger . . . who rewards the reception and hospitality with a gift." Since Gen 18 fits neither of these subgenres, Westermann concludes that the text must have originally been two narratives that "overlapped and fused into one."[20] Westermann provides a hypothetical explanation for the origin of the text, but does not properly account for the genre of the text in its final form.

Thus, a plethora of difficulties are associated with the current classification of epiphanies. Propp notes a similar tendency in the classification of folktales:

> The most common division is a division into tales with fantastic content, tales of everyday life, and animal tales. At first glance everything appears to be correct. But involuntarily the question arises, "Don't tales about animals sometimes contain elements of the fantastic to a very high degree?" And conversely, "Don't ani-

---

anything at all." Moberly, "Call of Samuel," 445. Hertzberg notes the apparent omission, observing that the narrative "depicts as it were the call of Samuel." Hertzberg, *I & II Samuel*, 41. Klein rightly observes that "the call genre can really only be maintained by claiming that vv 11–14 have replaced an original commission." Klein, *1 Samuel*, 31.

18. "The expected pattern would be (1) recognition of the problem, (2) annunciation (birth, name, destiny, although the series may not be stated in full), (3) expression of doubt, and (4) fulfillment of the annunciation." Coats, *Genesis*, 138.

19. "[Gen 18:1–15] does not develop the pattern in full. . . . This narrative is thus not a distinct unit, but part of a larger narration in J (→ 16:1–21:1). It may, of course, properly be analyzed form-critically since it is an element of a larger whole. Indeed, it may hide evidence of an annunciation tale, originally quite distinct and independent. But in its current position as an element, it has no independent structural role." Ibid.

20. Westermann, *Genesis 12–36*, 274.

mals actually play a large role in fantastic tales?"... If a division into categories is unsuccessful, the division according to theme leads to total chaos."[21]

The division of epiphanies according to themes and categories has resulted in the same situation for epiphanies that Propp found with folktales: "total chaos."

The Basic Narrative Structure of Epiphany

Rather than seeking to classify epiphanies according to various themes and categories, we will apply a more literary approach to epiphany narratives similar to that of Barthes. Barthes proposes that the main obstacle to the analysis of a given text is its complex "atemporal matrix structure." The solution, he suggests, involves "dechronologizing" and "relogicizing" the narrative in order to give a "structural description of the chronological illusion."[22] We will now examine the chronological structure of epiphany using an approach similar to Barthes's.

The basic chronological structure of the genre of epiphany consists of five elements. First, there is an initial period during which the human experiencing the epiphany has no contact with the heavenly being or beings who will appear. Second, there is a transition period during which the two parties come into contact with and become aware of each other. This generally involves the human party becoming aware of the heavenly presence, or ascending into the presence of the heavenly being(s). Third, there is a period of contact between the heavenly party and the human party. This typically involves the communication of a message by the heavenly party, an action by the heavenly party, or the experience of the presence of the heavenly party. Fourth, there is a transition period as

---

21. Propp, *Folktale*, 5, 7.

22. "Structurally narrative institutes a confusion between consecution and consequence, temporality and logic. This ambiguity forms the central problem of narrative syntax. Is there an atemporal logic lying behind the temporality of narrative?... [A]ll contemporary researchers (Lévi-Strauss, Greimas, Bremond, Todorov)... could subscribe to Lévi-Strauss's proposition that 'the order of chronological succession is absorbed in an atemporal matrix structure.'... Analysis today tends to 'dechronologize' the narrative continuum and to 'relogicize' it, to make it dependent on what Mallarmé called... 'the primitive thunderbolts of logic'; or rather, more exactly (such at least is our wish), the task is to succeed in giving a structural description of the chronological illusion—it is for narrative logic to account for narrative time." Barthes, *Narratives*, 98–99.

the heavenly party separates from the human party, after which the two parties are no longer in contact. Fifth, there is a period immediately after the parties have separated during which the human party may experience some aftereffects of the encounter. Every epiphany must go through these five stages chronologically. However, every stage may not be narrated in a given epiphany text.

These five stages correspond roughly with the five stages of any narrative event: introduction, focalizer, action, defocalizer, and conclusion.[23] Since we are concerned with these stages as they relate to epiphany narratives in particular, we will use these more specific terms: introduction, appearance, message, departure, and conclusion. Each of the five elements is composed of subelements that may be reordered, repeated, and/or omitted. We will now discuss the five basic structural elements of epiphany in detail.

The introduction element provides a transition from the larger narrative context. The introduction is preliminary to the appearance of the heavenly party. The introduction may consist of a title, background information, setting, and/or a continuation of the preceding narrative. The title provides a convenient summary of the epiphany by declaring who appeared to whom. Therefore, the title may assist in identifying the one who appears. Setting often includes references to time, including the age of a person (Gen 17:1; *T. Levi* 2:2), the time of year (Ezek 8:1; *Jub.* 15:1), the time of day (2 Chr 7:12), or even the time since a previous event (Ezek 3:16). Setting may also include the location (*3 Bar.* 1:2; cf. Dan 10:4), and a list of those present at the epiphany (Judg 13:9).[24] The introduction often merges seamlessly into the larger narrative.

The appearance element is present in most epiphany narratives. It generally consists of descriptive details, actions, and responses as the two parties make initial contact. A description is present in most epiphanies. It announces the presence of the epiphanic figure, and may also specify the

---

23. Focalization "identifies the governing perspective" of a text. Wadenpfuhl, "Glossary," 326. Focalization involves the temporal distance between the event and the narration. "Narration may focalize events from the time at which they occurred, from shortly afterwards, or from long afterwards." Culler, *Literary Theory*, 88. Events that are narrated long after they occur may be focalized as they were perceived at the time, or with the later benefit of hindsight. For a discussion of the five stages of narrative texts see Funk, *Poetics*, 17.

24. For a detailed description of setting, see Resseguie, *Narrative Criticism*, 94–114. Resseguie provides a useful bibliography for setting in ibid., 262–65.

kind of appearance, such as a dream (1 Kgs 3:5) or an external encounter (Judg 6:11). It may be brief ("God appeared to . . ."; 2 Chr 7:12), or lengthy (*2 En.* 3–21). Actions by the heavenly party are frequently narrated in the appearance. The heavenly party may identify itself, identify or greet the human party by name, and/or command the human party (Exod 3:5). The heavenly party may also perform an action (e.g., Num 22:22–23). A human reaction may be present. Physical reactions appear to be more common than verbal reactions. Common physical reactions include fear (Dan 8:17; 10:7–8; Tob 12:16a), falling (Gen 17:3; Num 22:31; Josh 5:14; Ezek 1:28; Tob 12:16b), and bowing (Gen 18:2; 19:1). The heavenly party may respond to the human reactions (Judg 13:11b).

The message element is central to most epiphanies. The majority of epiphanies contain a message of some sort.[25] Most messages are verbal, although some epiphanies involve an action or actions rather than a message, and others use images rather than words to convey their message. A given epiphany may contain multiple message elements. Most messages consist of a combination of statements, commands, questions, and actions. Frequently, due to the unexpected content of the heavenly message, the epiphany will record the recipient's immediate reaction, either physical or verbal. Questions concerning the content of the message, or the recipient's ability to perform the requested task, are often raised. There is normally an immediate response to any questions raised by the recipient. The question and answer cycle may be repeated several times. Nearly all of these aspects of the message are illustrated in Exod 3:7—4:17.[26]

The departure element describes the separation of the two parties (Gen 35:13), with possible human reactions if the departure is unusual (Judg 13:20; 2 Kgs 2:12). The departure element is frequently omitted.[27]

The conclusion element resolves the epiphany by describing the immediate effects of the appearance on the recipient. It is similar to the departure element in that it may contain narrative descriptions and human responses (*Jub.* 12:27).

---

25. Gen 32:1–2 is a noteworthy exception, having an introduction, appearance, and conclusion, but no message.

26. See p. 51 below.

27. See Appendix A: Narrative Structure of Selected Epiphanies.

Epiphany narratives are generally written from a human perspective.[28] For example, the introduction normally describes the human setting, and rarely mentions the heavenly setting (see Job 1:6–12). The conclusion describes the effects of the epiphany on the human party, not the heavenly party. This human perspective naturally limits the revelation, in terms of both what may be known, and when.[29] For example, most epiphanies do not reveal anything about the one who appears, other than what might be observed from a human perspective during the epiphany. However, there are some notable exceptions. In some third-person narrative accounts, the narrator may provide unexpected and tantalizing details. For example, Yahweh's soliloquy in Gen 18:17–19 would appear to be beyond human knowledge, since it does not appear that God spoke those words to Abraham.[30] However, it is useful to note that the events are generally described from a human point of view, with the attendant limits of perspective.

This structure is summarized in figure 2. The X-axis represents the progression of story time. The Y-axis indicates the proximity of the heavenly and human parties within the implied reality of the implied author's narrative world. The solid line traces the path of the heavenly party; the dotted line, the human party. At first, the two parties are not in contact (introduction). The two parties meet (appearance), interact (message), and separate (departure) as story time progresses. Finally, the heavenly party is no longer in contact with the human party (conclusion).

A particular epiphany narrative may vary from this basic structure in a number of ways. First, one or more elements may be omitted. For example, the departure is frequently omitted (e.g., Gen 16:12–13), presumably because it is not as interesting, relevant, or necessary as the other elements. Second, multiple overlapping epiphanies may complicate the basic structure (e.g., Gen 18–19). Third, the elements may be presented out of sequence. In other words, there may be discrepancies between story time and discourse time.[31] This is frequently due to narrative com-

---

28. *Jubilees* is a notable exception.

29. For a discussion on focalization and the limitations of knowledge, see Culler, *Literary Theory*, 89–90.

30. I.e., the narrator appears to be omniscient.

31. There are two basic types of time related to narrative texts. First is narrative or discourse time, "the time it takes to peruse the discourse." Second is story time, "the duration of the purported events in the narrative." Chatman, *Story and Discourse*, 62. Genette describes this as "connections between the temporal *order* of succession

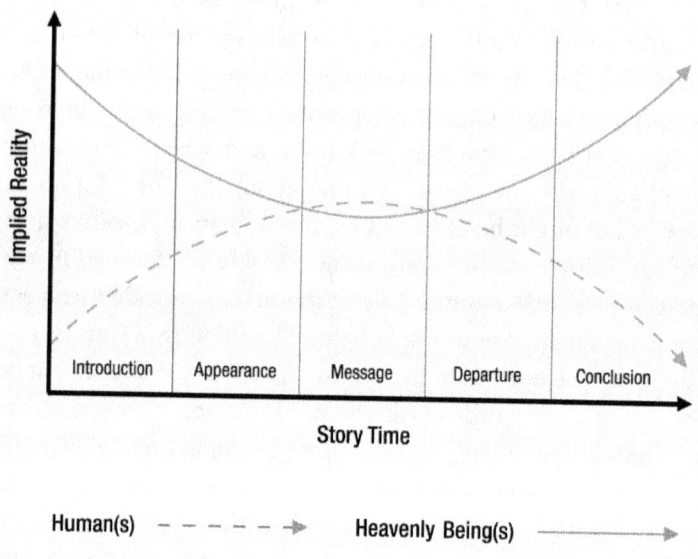

FIGURE 2: The Basic Narrative Structure of Epiphany Narratives

plexity or stylistic concerns, particularly in the introduction and appearance elements. For example, in Judg 6:11 the appearance is announced before the setting is given. Fourth, the epiphany may not be the primary focus of the narrative, so that its form is greatly abbreviated. This is seen, for example, in Num 22:9–12, 20, where God appears to Balaam twice, but within the larger context of Balaam's encounter with Balak's men. Fifth, there may be complications arising from metalepses.[32] In such cas-

---

of the events in the story and the pseudo-temporal order of their arrangement in the narrative." Genette, *Narrative Discourse*, 35. Anachrony is defined as any discrepancy between story time and narrative time (35–36). Anachronies that occur entirely outside of narrative time are external, those that occur within the narrative are internal, and those that overlap the story time are mixed (49). Analepses are events narrated belatedly; prolepses, prematurely. Powell, *Narrative Criticism*, 37. See also Genette, *Narrative Discourse*, 48–49, 67. The use of time is critical to many narrative texts. For example, the television program *24* is based on the interesting premise that episodes occur in "real time"; that is, discourse and story time are said to be identical.

32. Multiple levels within a narrative text. Genette designates the universe of the first narrative as the diegesis; the world of the second narrative, or metanarrative, as the metadiegesis. Genette, *Narrative Discourse*, 228. For example, in Acts 22 Paul's speech is diegetic, and the account of the DRE within the speech is metadiegetic. Genette describes three types of relationships between the levels of a narrative. First, the explanatory relationship involves "direct causality between the events of the metadiegesis and

es, the epiphany is often presented at the metadiegetic level (e.g., in Acts 22, the DRE is presented within a speech). Sixth, other information may be present within the structure of the epiphany. This typically involves parenthetical background information (e.g., Gen 18:10b–11). Despite these narratological variations, the basic structure of most epiphanies may be identified without difficulty.

The basic structure of epiphany is useful for identifying anachronies and other chronological features of the narrative, recognizing patterns and common features within each section, comparing two or more narratives, and isolating developments in the genre of epiphany over time.

Divine Initiative and Divine Response

One of the distinctions we will consider within the genre of epiphany that has not received much attention is initiative. There appear to be two basic classes of epiphanies: those involving the appearance of heavenly beings without the prior knowledge or expectation of their human counterparts, in order to deliver a message or perform an action that is entirely unanticipated; and those involving the appearance of heavenly beings in response to a human request for a vision or appearance, or in answer to a human question or desire for knowledge. The former shall be designated as Divine Initiative epiphanies; the latter, Divine Response.[33]

It is usually possible to identify either the human party or the heavenly party as providing the initiative for an epiphany. For example, the initiative may be attributed to the heavenly party in cases where the human party is not expecting the heavenly party. Conversely, the initiative may be attributed to the human party in cases where the human party initiates the encounter by petitioning a heavenly party to appear, or by performing rituals in preparation for an ascent.

---

those of the diegesis." Second, the thematic relationship involves contrast or analogy, in which there is "no spatio-temporal continuity between the metadiegesis and diegesis." The third relationship involves no explicit connection between the two levels, in cases of distraction or obstruction. Ibid., 232–33. For further discussion on narrative levels, see Rimmon-Kenan, *Narrative Fiction*, 92–95. Malina sees the effects of metalepses in a continuum, from "startling diversion through destabilization and disorientation to outright violation." Malina, *Breaking the Frame*, 3.

33. I would like to offer special thanks to Larry Hurtado for suggesting these terms.

SURVEY OF LITERATURE

Ancient Jewish epiphany narratives are as diverse as they are numerous. It is not possible to provide a detailed analysis of every epiphany narrative from this period. Instead, key passages will be highlighted from as many texts as possible.[34] Particular attention will be paid to the narrative structure and initiative of these epiphanies, as well as the character of the heavenly beings that are encountered.

In order to emphasize any developments that might be encountered, documents from the period will be presented in approximately chronological order. The OT will be considered first. The Apocrypha and OT Pseudepigrapha, containing some of the next oldest works, will then be examined, followed by the Dead Sea Scrolls, Philo, Josephus, and rabbinic works.

Old Testament

Given the large number of epiphany narratives in the OT, it is not possible to discuss each in detail. Instead, we will analyze four narratives: Gen 18:1—19:29; Exod 3:1—4:17; 1 Sam 3:1—21; Ezek 1:1—3:15. These four narratives have been selected as a representative sample according to a wide range of factors, including chronology (from the early Pentateuch through to the later prophets), narrative complexity (from a fairly simple structure such as Exod 3–4 to the more complex structure of Gen 18–19), kinds of appearances (i.e., external appearances, dreams, and visions), types of messages, and types of epiphanic figures (i.e., Yahweh, the Angel of Yahweh, other angels, and "men"). These epiphanies are also significant theologically, and are therefore often controversial. It is hoped that the following analysis will illustrate not only how the structure may be applied to specific epiphany texts, but also that it is a valid approach to OT epiphany in general. We will begin with Abraham and Sarah's unexpected encounter in Gen 18–19.

GENESIS 18:1—19:29

The appearance of Yahweh to Abraham (Gen 18) and the two angels to Lot (Gen 19), is "one of the most graphically and finely written narratives in the OT."[35] The two chapters form a complex narrative structure

---

34. The results of this analysis are summarized in appendix A.
35. Driver, *Genesis*, 191.

that encompasses two intertwined appearances with a third, intervening message somewhat independent of the others. As Westermann notes, "Gen. 18:1–16a, in its present context, is part of a larger narrative complex which covers chs. 18–19."[36] Gen 18 consists of two sections.[37] In 18:1–16, three men, presumably Yahweh and two angels,[38] deliver a message to Abraham and Sarah. In 18:17–33, Yahweh interacts with Abraham alone.[39] In Gen 19, the two angels rescue Lot and his family from the destruction of Sodom.[40]

The complex structure has led to the conjecture that Gen 18–19 was formed by combining several independent narratives. However, there is evidence to the contrary. Hamilton provides a sampling of the similarities between chapters 18 and 19: similar vocabulary, similar actions, the two angels in 19 come from 18, similar lingering (Yahweh in 18; Lot in 19), and destruction of Sodom in 19 completes the promise of 18.[41]

An unusual feature of this epiphany is the prolonged interaction of Yahweh and the angels with humans, both of Yahweh and the angels eating with Abraham and Sarah (18:2–8), and of the angels with Lot and the townspeople (19:1b–11, 15–23).

Narrative Structure

The structure of this narrative text will be discussed in two sections: first 18:1–33, then 19:1–29.

---

36. Westermann, *Genesis 12–36*, 274.

37. "The chapter divides into two distinct parts. Verses 1–15 tell of the appearance of the angelic visitors to Abraham, while verses 17–33 deal with the intended divine visitation upon Sodom and Gomorrah. Verse 16 effects the transition between the sections." Sarna, *Genesis*, 128.

38. Waltke notes that the two men (Gen 18:22) are "presumably the two angels/messengers" (18:1; 19:1). Waltke, *Genesis*, 269.

39. For an excellent reading of Gen 18:16–33 with emphasis on Yahweh rather than Abraham, see MacDonald, "Abraham and Yhwh," 25–43. For a discussion of the traditional Jewish interpretations of the text, see Blenkinsopp, "Judge." For a historical-critical perspective, see Ben Zvi, "Abraham and YHWH."

40. For a narrative critical analysis of Gen 19, see Gunn, "Narrative Criticism," 179–90.

41. Hamilton, *Genesis 18–50*, 30.

Genesis 18:1–33

Introduction (1)

I₁ *Title* (1a). Yahweh appears to Abraham (literally, "And Yahweh appeared to him"). This is clearly titular.⁴² Abraham is not mentioned by name, since the passage continues the narrative from the previous chapter.⁴³

I₂ *Setting* (1b). Both the spatial and the temporal setting are given.⁴⁴ The spatial setting consists of topographical ("by the trees of Mamre")⁴⁵ and architectural ("while he sat at the tent door")⁴⁶ elements.⁴⁷ The temporal setting is described as "in the heat of midday."

Appearance (2–9)

A₁ *Description* (2–9). The title introduced Yahweh, but the appearance begins by identifying three men. Thus, it appears that Yahweh may be described as a man. Similarly, the angels (19:1) are also referred to as men, both here and elsewhere.

Message 1 (10–15)

M1₁ *Statement* (10a). Yahweh announces that Sarah will have a son.

M1₂ *Background* (10b–11). Sarah and Abraham were beyond childbearing years.

M1₃ *Verbal Reaction* (12). Sarah laughs.

M1₄ *Response* (13–14). Yahweh responds to Abraham.

M1₅ *Verbal Reaction* (15a). Sarah denies laughing.

M1₆ *Response* (15b). Yahweh corrects Sarah.

---

42. Or, as Sarna describes it, "A general statement followed by a detailed description." He observes that that this is "the only example of this formula being used without some verbal declaration immediately following." Sarna, *Genesis*, 128.

43. "The lack of an explicit naming of Abraham here ... shows it is part of a sequence of narratives." Wenham, *Genesis*, 2:45.

44. For an overview of a narrative understanding of setting, see Powell, *Narrative Criticism*, 70–75.

45. For a discussion of topographical setting, see Resseguie, *Narrative Criticism*, 95–100.

46. For a discussion of architectural setting, see ibid., 100–105.

47. Ska discusses the tree and the tent. He notes that the setting seems to disappear during the scene: "Il n'est plus question ni de l'arbre, ni de la tente. En fait, tout est devenu transparent: il n'y a pas d'obstacles à la connaissance de YHWH." Ska, "L'arbre," 388.

Departure 1 (16, 22)

D1₁ *Description* (16). The men get up to leave.

D1₂ *Description* (22). The angels depart; Yahweh does not.

Message 2 (20–21; 23–32)

M2₁ *Background* (17–19). Yahweh's soliloquy.[48]

M2₂ *Statement* (20–21).

M2₃₋₁₄ *Repeated Verbal Reaction and Response* (23–32). Abraham presses Yahweh not to destroy Sodom if fifty, forty-five, forty, thirty, twenty, and finally, ten righteous men are found there.[49]

Departure 2 (33)

D2₁ *Description* (33). Both Yahweh and Abraham depart. This is an excellent example of a departure element containing the departure of both parties.

[Conclusion]

The conclusion element is omitted.

The departure has been split into two parts (16, 22), illustrating the tension between story time and discourse time. This illustrates that a narrative may not be presented in chronological order even though the events certainly fit a chronological structure. In this case, discourse time varies from story time because the single appearance of Yahweh and two angels must now diverge into two separate events as Yahweh continues with Abraham, while the angels depart for Sodom.

There are also stylistic considerations. In the transition from the first message (10–15) to the second (20–21, 23–32), the narrator must describe both the departure of the angels, and Yahweh's decision to stay with Abraham. He does this by beginning the departure element, providing a soliloquy to justify Yahweh's change of heart, followed by a new message from Yahweh to Abraham. Only then does he indicate the departure of the angels. This propels the narrative by maintaining a tension ("what happened to the other two men from verse 16?") that is not resolved until the more important action (Yahweh discloses the fate

---

48. For a discussion of the "ethical complexity" of Gen 18:17–32, see Kahn, "Abraham," 155–57.

49. Wenham notes that this doubling of the common threefold repetition is used for emphasis. Wenham, *Genesis*, 2:51.

of Sodom to Abraham) has been narrated. As Hamilton observes, "It is possible to read the end of v. 16, skip vv. 17–19, and continue smoothly with v. 20."[50]

Genesis 19:1–29

Introduction

I_1 Setting (1a). The angels arrive in Sodom. Lot is at the city gate.

Appearance (1b–10)

A_1 Reaction (1b–3). Lot reacts to the men/angels.

A_2 Reaction (4–10). The townspeople react to the angels as if they were men, calling them men, and even pursuing sexual relations with them.

A_3 Response (11). The angels' response reveals that they are not ordinary men.

Message (12–22)

M_1 Command/Statement (12–13). The angels deliver their message of impending destruction to Lot.

M_2 Reaction (14). Lot reacts by telling his family, to no avail.

M_3 Command (15). The angels again warn Lot to flee.

M_4 Reaction (16a). Lot again delays his departure.

M_5 Response (16b). The angels force Lot to flee.

M_6 Command (17). The angels warn Lot not to look back as they escape.

M_7 Reaction (18–20). Lot expresses his desire to flee to a different city.

M_8 Response (21–22). The angels accept Lot's proposal.

[Departure]

The departure element is omitted.

Conclusion (23–29)

C_1 Description (23–29). Lot arrives in Zoar, Yahweh destroys Sodom and Gomorrah (24–25), Lot's wife turns into a pillar of salt (26), and Abraham observes the destruction from a distance (27–28). The narrative ends with the summarizing

---

50. Hamilton, *Genesis 18–50*, 17.

statement that Yahweh destroyed Sodom (29). In a sense, 19:27–29 serves as a conclusion to the larger narrative (Gen 18–19), and provide closure for 18:1–33, which ended without a conclusion.

Event

Gen 18–19 is a Divine Initiative epiphany, since Yahweh and the two angels appear unexpectedly to accomplish divine purposes. The title announces that Yahweh appeared to Abraham (18:1). As Speiser indicates, "this is the author's aside to the reader who is thus prepared at the outset for the surprise that is in store for Abraham."[51] Following the delivery of each message, human reactions reveal ignorance or disbelief. Thus, Sarah laughs when she hears that she will have a child, Abraham engages in an extended argument with Yahweh concerning the fate of Sodom, and Lot warns his disbelieving family (19:14), then hesitates himself (16a) until he is forcibly removed from the city (16b), at which point he presses the angels to permit him not to flee so far (18–22).

The purpose of the epiphany in Gen 18–19 is threefold, each aspect involving the accomplishment of a divine goal. First, Yahweh appeared to deliver a divine promise to Abraham and Sarah regarding the birth of their son (18:1–16).[52] Second, Yahweh appeared in order to warn Abraham of the imminent destruction of Sodom (18:20–33). Third, the angels appeared to Lot in order to warn him of the coming devastation (19:1–29). Thus, in each case the purpose for the appearance is the delivery of a divine message. In fact, the delivery of a divine message appears to be the primary purpose of many epiphanies.

Characterization of the Epiphanic Figures

The characterization of the heavenly visitors in Gen 18–19 has long been the subject of debate. Many scholars have hesitated to affirm the opening words of the narrative: that Yahweh appeared to Abraham. For example, Calvin denied that Yahweh appeared, preferring instead to view all the figures as angels.[53] Sarna also makes the assertion that this theophany is

---

51. Speiser, *Genesis*, 129.

52. "The purpose of the men's visit is the promise that Sarah will have a son." Westermann, *Genesis 12–36*, 279.

53. "God's majesty had been manifested in the angels.... The word of the Lord is so precious to the Lord himself that he should be acknowledged as present whenever he speaks through his ministers." Having identified the men as angels, Calvin makes

"mediated ... through angelic messengers." He later notes that the "three men" (18:2) are "repeatedly designated 'men,' although they are also called 'angels,'"[54] while he fails to note that one of the three is also repeatedly designated Yahweh (cf. 18:1, 13, 14, 17, 19, 20, 22, 26, 33). Sarna later argues that "God and His angels often speak interchangeably,"[55] pointing to evidence related to the "angel of the Lord."[56] Even this claim is debatable, since Yahweh is not only said to speak, but also to appear (18:1) and depart (18:33). Furthermore, there is no mention of the Angel of the Lord in this account.

Gaster identifies the three men as angels.[57] Gunkel[58] and Westermann[59] also emphasize the anthropomorphic aspects of the encounter. Westermann further claims that "the narrative 18:1–16b does not belong to any of the types of divine appearance in the Old Testament."[60] Skinner is willing to grant the encounter the "value of a theophany,"[61] yet claims that Yahweh was not visibly present in it.[62] Alston moves in the opposite direction. He rejects the notion that "God is one of the three men and the others two divine deputies," and argues instead that "God is, or is represented by, all three."[63]

However, as we have seen, the narrative describes the epiphanic figures as Yahweh (18:1, 13, 14, 17, 19, 20, 22, 26, 33), three men (18:2; cf. 18:16), and two angels (19:1). Brueggemann argues:

---

the seemingly contradictory claim that "whenever the Lord manifested himself to the fathers, Christ was the Mediator between him and them." Calvin, *Genesis*, 175.

54. Sarna, *Genesis*, 128–29. Sarna is not alone in making such unsupported assertions or blatant omissions. Such interpretations appear to reveal more about the presuppositions of the interpreter, rather than the meaning of the narrative.

55. Ibid., 130.

56. Ibid., 383–84.

57. "Angels appear to men in human form. Abraham entertained them as guests without being aware of their true identity (Gen 18)." Gaster, "Angel," 129.

58. Gunkel entitles this "legend," "The Three Men Visit Abraham in Hebron." Gunkel, *Genesis*, 192.

59. Westermann entitles his discussion, "Die drei Männer bei Abraham." Westermann, *Genesis 12-36* (BKAT), 329.

60. "Die drei Männer bei Abraham." Ibid.

61. Skinner, *Genesis*, 298.

62. Ibid., 299.

63. Alston, "Genesis 18," 398–99. Dancy also claims that the three men "in some mysterious way represent the LORD." Dancy, *Divine Drama*, 65.

There is no need either to harmonize the two versions or to divide into sources . . . The story is an unreflective account of a revelatory disclosure. That is enough. The vacillation of identity heightens the hidden source from which the disclosure comes. The interpreter will do well to present the story as it is and allow for playfulness in this regard.[64]

Brueggemann plainly declares, "It is especially in Genesis 18 that Abraham has direct interaction with Yahweh."[65] Alter also confirms that the three men were "God Himself" and "two human-seeming angels of destruction" (Gen 18:10, 13–15),[66] as does Waltke, who equates the "three men" with "'the LORD' and two angels."[67]

If we accept that those who appeared to Abraham and Lot were Yahweh and two angels, we are still left with an incredible narrative feature. Yahweh and the angels are characterized interchangeably as both human and heavenly. In fact, the angels are not characterized as such until after their encounter with Abraham and Sarah (Gen 19:1).[68]

Finally, the contrast between the characterization of Yahweh and the angels is also apparent in how they communicate their messages to their respective human audiences. Yahweh speaks in the first person, as the one who has the authority to act (e.g., "if I find," אִם־אֶמְצָא, 18:26). In contrast, the angels are not God, but identify themselves as messengers from Yahweh ("And Yahweh has sent us," וַיְשַׁלְּחֵנוּ יְהוָה, 19:13).

Thus, the text characterizes the three men who appeared to Abraham as Yahweh and two angels.

Exodus 3:1—4:17

In this epiphany God reveals his name to Moses at the burning bush.[69] Habel describes Exod 3:1-12 as a call narrative with the following structure:

---

64. Brueggemann, *Genesis*, 157–58.
65. Brueggemann, *Theology*, 570.
66. Alter, *Genesis*, 77.
67. Waltke, *Genesis*, 265.
68. Takahashi notes this fluidity of characterization, mentioning several similar occurrences (Gen 21:17–18; Judg 6:7–24; 13). Takahashi, "Angelology," 346–48. Hamilton also mentions the notion of fluidity in his commentary on the passage. Hamilton, *Genesis 18–50*, 6–7.
69. This passage has been a favorite among source critics, since it mentions both God and Yahweh. For example, see Noth, *Exodus*, 30–35. More recently, Renaud, "Moïse"; Wyatt, "Exodus 3." Den Hertog does not agree that the two names indicate different

(i) the divine confrontation vv. 1–3, 4a

(ii) the introductory word, vv. 4b–9

(iii) the commission, v. 10

(iv) the objection, v. 11

(v) the reassurance, v. 12a

(vi) the sign, v. 12[70]

Habel's structure may be viewed as a subset of the basic narrative structure of epiphany. The divine confrontation and introductory word are part of the appearance element, while the commission, objection, reassurance, and sign are part of the message. The introduction is also present (3:1–2a),[71] but the departure and conclusion are not.

Narrative Structure

Introduction (3:1–2a)

I_1 Setting (3:1). How Moses came to Horeb.

Appearance (3:2–6)

A_1 Description (3:2–4a). The Angel of Yahweh appeared to Moses "in a flame of fire from the midst of the bush."[72]

A_2 Calling (3:4b). Double vocatives are most frequently used by Yahweh to initiate contact with an individual during a theophany (Gen 46:2; Exod 34:6; 1 Sam 3:10), but Gen 22:11 records the Angel of Yahweh calling Abraham.

---

sources: "This is not self-evident. It is quite possible to read the narrative in a literary and holistic way." Den Hertog, "Prophetic Dimension," 216.

More recently, Moberly has restated a twelfth-century proposal of Ibn Ezra that undercuts the source critical theories, namely, that "all the occurrences of YHWH in Genesis were additions to the stories made by Moses himself." Moberly, *Old Testament*, 37. Seitz follows a similar approach in critiquing traditional source criticism. Seitz, "Call of Moses."

The meaning of the name Yahweh is discussed in Gianotti, "YHWH." For an interesting note concerning the translation of Exod 3:14–15, see Osborn, "My Name."

70. Habel, "Call Narratives," 298. Habel's theory is also cited by Childs, *Exodus*. Sarna divides the narrative into three sections: theophany at the burning bush (3:1–6), divine call (3:7–10), and Moses's dialog with God (3:11–4:17). Sarna, *Exodus*, 13.

71. Although 3:2a may be viewed as the opening of the appearance, it also presents a summary of the encounter. Childs notes that it "serves as a type of superscription to the narrative," parallel to Gen 18:1. Childs, *Exodus*, 53.

72. Janzen's reading of the burning bush as "a veiled promise of divine-human intimacy" is intriguing. Janzen, "Bush," 220. For further discussion of the burning bush, see Wyatt, "Burning Bush."

A_3 *Verbal Reaction* (3:4c).

A_4 *Statement* (3:5).

A_5 *Identification* (3:6a).

A_6 *Physical Reaction* (3:6b). Hiding and fear are common human reactions to the divine presence.

Message (3:7—4:17)

M_1 *Statement* (3:7–10). God will use Moses to deliver the Israelites from Egypt.

M_2 *Verbal Reaction* (3:11). Moses questions his ability to go before Pharaoh.

M_3 *Response* (3:12). God answers Moses.

M_4 *Verbal Reaction* (3:13). Moses questions his ability to go the Israelites.

M_5 *Response* (3:14–22). God answers Moses.[73]

M_6 *Verbal Reaction* (4:1). Moses doubts that the people will believe him.

M_7 *Response* (4:2–9). God provides Moses with signs to convince the people.

M_8 *Verbal Reaction* (4:10). Moses doubts his speaking abilities.

M_9 *Response* (4:11–12). God responds to Moses.

M_{10} *Verbal Reaction* (4:13). Moses asks God to send someone else.

M_{11} *Response* (4:14–17). God promises Moses that Aaron will assist him.

[Departure]

[Conclusion]

Event

Exod 3–4 is a Divine Initiative epiphany, since God appears to Moses unexpectedly to call Moses to his new vocation. When confronted by the message, Moses voices so many objections that "God's anger burned against Moses" (4:14). Von Rad remarks that "neither previous faith nor personal endowment had the slightest part to play in preparing a man who was called to stand before Jahweh for his vocation."[74] The purpose,

---

73. Addinall, "Exodus III," discusses the interpretation of v. 19.
74. Von Rad, *OT Theology* 2:57.

revealed in the message element (3:7–10), is divine: Yahweh appears to Moses in order to call him to be the deliverer of the Israelites from Egyptian slavery.

Characterization of the Epiphanic Figure

The epiphanic figure is directly characterized in several different ways. In the title element (3:2a), the narrator introduces the "Angel of Yahweh" in the midst of a bush. This is the only mention of the Angel of Yahweh. In verse 4, Yahweh sees Moses, and God calls to Moses from the midst of the bush.

Ibn Ezra poses the question that has vexed scholars for centuries: "What reason is there to mention this angel?"[75] Numerous explanations have been proposed. Robinson suggests that for early readers,[76] the presence of the Angel of Yahweh would emphasize "the transcendence of the deity," while the dialog between God and Moses would "portray Moses as the spiritual progenitor of Hebrew prophets down the centuries."[77] Carroll concludes that the mention of the Angel of Yahweh suggests that Yahweh was absent from the burning bush.[78] Propp takes the opposite view.[79] Jacobsen discusses the ancient Near Eastern ability to view the cult statue simultaneously as both god and not god.[80] Sarna posits that "most likely, the angel is mentioned only to avoid what would be the gross anthropomorphism of localizing God in a bush."[81] Noth differentiates between the angel and God.[82] Durham claims that the "fluid interchange between symbol, representative, and God himself . . . the

---

75. Ibn Ezra, *Exodus*, 53.

76. Robinson takes a literary critical approach that "seeks to discover what [the text] will have meant to its original readers." Robinson, "Moses," 107.

77. Ibid., 112.

78. "Not YHWH but one of the other beings from the pantheon encountered Moses that day on Horeb." Carroll, "Strange Fire," 41–42.

79. "One might initially identify the angel with the flame that burns in the bush. Having captured Moses' attention, Yahweh himself then calls down from heaven. That is probably incorrect, however. God himself is within the bush." Propp, *Exodus 1–18*, 198. Propp discusses the ambiguous nature of the angel in great detail.

80. Jacobsen, "Graven Image," 18–19. The explanation, he claims, is in their monotheistic (as opposed to the modern dualistic) worldview.

81. Sarna, *Exodus*, 14.

82. "First of all he has the 'angel of the Lord.' . . . Later, however, when we have a personal address to Moses and are dealing no longer with the 'appearance' of God but with his 'speech', it is Yahweh himself who acts." Noth, *Exodus*, 40.

addition of Elohim (v 4) to the messenger, the fire and Yahweh of v 2 simply provided four designations of the same and single reality."[83] The diversity of scholarly opinion concerning the identity of the epiphanic figure(s) is astounding.

Despite the variety of scholarly opinion, the characterization of the epiphanic figure within the narrative is straightforward from a literary perspective. The narrative directly characterizes the epiphanic figure in three ways: the Angel of Yahweh (3:2), Yahweh (3:4), and God (3:4).[84]

1 SAMUEL 3:1–21

In this passage, Yahweh appears to the boy Samuel. As previously discussed,[85] this passage has been variously treated as a call narrative, an auditory message dream, or both.[86]

Narrative Structure

Samuel's encounter with God corresponds with the basic narrative structure of epiphany.[87]

> *Introduction (1–3)*
>
> I_1 *Narration* (1). This verse provides a bridge to Samuel's theophany, and might possibly be considered a background element.[88]
>
> I_2 *Setting* (2–3). Time and location are presented.

---

83. Durham, *Exodus*, 31.

84. Thompson reaches a similar conclusion: "Whatever our understanding, and whatever solutions we might suggest to the variance and fluidity of the divine protagonists in these early pentateuchal stories, the regularity and consistency in the patterns of usage discourage us from seeing these variations as either insignificant or as accidental. Nor is the problem easily solved by assigning different divine characters to different story sources, for what is striking about both Genesis and the exodus analogies to the theophany stories of Exodus 3 and 6 is that the story episodes in which the divine names are found are much more coherent in their plots than a jumbled complex of distinct sources would allow." Thompson, "Yahweh," 68.

85. See pp. 34–35 above.

86. And neither: Campbell claims, somewhat unhelpfully, that the "nocturnal revelation to Samuel" fits the genre of "story." Campbell, *1 Samuel*, 56.

87. For a more detailed analysis of the structure of the entire chapter, see Watson, "Structure." Also see the response by Wicke, "1 Samuel 3."

88. Eli's fading eyes are discussed in Sasson, "Eyes of Eli."

Appearance (4–10)

A_1 *Calling* (4a, 6a, 8a, 10b). Alter notes the "intensifying pattern," a "folk-tale structure of three repetitions with a final reversal."[89]

A_2 *Verbal response* (4b, 10c).

A_3 *Interaction with others* (5, 6b, 8b–9).

A_4 *Background* (7). Samuel is called four times, apparently due to his prior lack of intimacy with Yahweh.

Message (11–14)

M_1 *Statement* (11–14). Yahweh reveals to Samuel the fate of Eli and his family.

[Departure]

Conclusion (15–21)

C_1 *Description* (15–21). Samuel's immediate reaction to the theophany (staying in bed, 15a), his reluctance to share the message with Eli (15b), and final acquiescence (16–18) are followed by a summary of the status of Samuel and Eli in Israel (19–21).[90]

Event

This epiphany corresponds to the pattern of Divine Initiative. God must call Samuel four times before the boy realizes who is talking to him. The purpose of this epiphany is also divine. Yahweh appears to Samuel in order to reveal the future destruction of Eli and his household.

Characterization of the Epiphanic Figure

The narrator repeatedly and consistently characterizes the one who appears to Samuel as Yahweh (1, 3, 4, 6, 7, 8, 9, 10, 11, 15, 18, 19, 20, 21).

EZEKIEL 1:1—3:15

In Ezek 1–3, the prophet Ezekiel experiences a vision of God in human form. The textual boundaries of the narrative have been debated. It is possible to understand Ezek 1:1–3 as an introduction to the entire book,

---

89. Alter, *David*, 17.

90. It is possible to limit the conclusion to 15a, 15–18, or 15–21, or to consider 15–21 as separate from the theophany in 1–14. Again, this uncertainty is due to the fact that the theophany, while of primary importance in 2–14, is functioning within a larger narrative (1–21), which itself is part of the larger text of 1 Sam.

rather than to this epiphany in particular.[91] The epiphany's terminus is also debated.[92] We will consider Ezek 1:1—3:15 to be the narrative text, although the precise boundaries are not significant for our purposes.

The genre of this epiphany is much debated. Long classifies it as a "dramatic word-vision."[93] Allen remarks that Ezekiel's encounter shares the pattern of "vision and instruction" of "the visionary call narrative," "the report of a theophany," and "a commissioning message."[94] Block notes the distinction between the "protested call" and "overwhelming call" forms, and states that "the tendency to draw the distinctions between the two types of call narratives too sharply has blinded interpreters to the reality that both types merge in this account."[95] Odell makes the fascinating proposal that Ezek 1 is within the Israelite theophanic tradition, but influenced by Assyrian royal ideology and iconography.[96] Such an approach rightly emphasizes the theophanic aspect of the vision, while seeking to explain its unique features. Yet the narrative is clearly an epiphany, and certainly fits the proposed structure of epiphany.

Block defines the basic structure of the narrative as:

A. Superscription (1:1–3)
B. Inaugural Vision (1:4–28a)
C. Commissioning of Ezekiel (3:12–15)
D. Preparation of Ezekiel (3:12–15)
E. Yahweh's Induction Speech (3:16–21)
F. Initiation of Ezekiel (3:22–27)[97]

---

91. Zimmerli is unwavering in claiming that "1:1—3:15 must undoubtedly be understood in its present form as a complete unit." Zimmerli, *Ezekiel*, 1:95. Hals proposes a combination of the two, stating that 1:1–3 "constitutes a fusion of both the introduction to the vision of 1:1–3:15 (vv. 1–2; 3b) and the SUPERSCRIPTION to the book as a whole (v. 3a)." Hals, *Ezekiel*, 11. Zimmerli seems correct in placing 1:1–3 with the rest of the epiphany, but Hals is perhaps more perceptive in recognizing its function for the entire book. See also Berry's conclusion that Ezek 1:1–3 is not typical of book titles. Berry, "Title," 54.

92. Block makes a case for 3:27 as the end of the narrative. Block, *Ezekiel 1–24*, 77. The more natural ending is 3:15, which Block concedes is generally accepted.

93. Long, "Visions," 362–63.

94. Allen, *Ezekiel 1–19*, 14. Previously, Allen had suggested that Ezek 1 features alternating sections of "storm theophany" and "throne theophany." Allen, "Ezekiel 1:1," 160.

95. Block, *Ezekiel 1–24*, 78.

96. Odell, "Ezekiel Saw," 175–76.

97. Block, *Ezekiel 1–24*, 78. Habel gives the structure as: divine confrontation (1:1–

Disregarding sections E and F, since they extend beyond the end of the epiphany, Block's structure is analogous with the proposed epiphany structure. The superscription corresponds to the introduction; the inaugural vision, to the appearance; the commissioning and preparation, to the message.

Narrative Structure

    Introduction (1:1–3)

    I_1 Setting (1–3). Ezekiel provides chronological,[98] social, and geographic[99] setting.

    I_2 Title (1b). "I saw visions of God."

    Appearance (1:4—2:2)

    A_1 Description (1:4–14). Ezekiel describes the four living creatures.[100]

    A_2 Description (1:15–21). Heavenly wheels.[101]

    A_3 Description (1:22–25). A voice speaks from the heavenly dome.

    A_4 Description (1:26–28a). A human figure appears on the throne.[102]

    A_5 Physical Reaction (1:28b). Ezekiel falls.

    A_6 Command (2:1). God commands Ezekiel to stand.

    A_7 Physical Reaction (2:2). Ezekiel stands.

---

28), introductory word (1:29—2:2), commission (2:3–5), objection (implied in 2:6, 8), reassurance (2:6–7), and sign (2:8—3:11). Habel, "Call Narratives," 313. Allen provides an extended discussion of the structure in Allen, "Ezekiel 1:1"; see also Allen, *Ezekiel 1–19*, 14–17.

98. The "Thirtieth Year" has been the subject of much dispute. See Taylor, "Thirtieth Year"; Whitley, "Thirtieth Year"; and more recently, Miller, "Thirtieth Year."

99. Block, *Ezekiel 1–24*, 83–84.

100. The LXX differs considerable at certain points of Ezek 1–2 (1:3, 8–9, 14, 24, 27; 2:2). These differences are discussed in Lind, "Ezekiel 1," 137–39.

101. The interpretation of the "rims" of the wheels is discussed by Waldman, "Ezekiel 1:18."

102. Driver suggests that the fire and brightness might be understood as imagery from a Babylonian brass foundry. Driver, "Ezekiel," 62. Wacholder draws a comparison between the *merkabah* language of Ezekiel with the language of creation in Gen 1. Wacholder, "Ezekiel's Merkabah."

Message (2:3—3:11)

M_1 *Statement* (2:3-8). God commissions Ezekiel as his messenger.

M_2 *Action* (2:9-10). Ezekiel receives a scroll.

M_3 *Command* (3:1). God commands Ezekiel to eat the scroll.

M_4 *Physical Reaction* (3:2). Ezekiel opens his mouth.

M_5 *Command* (3:3a). God commands Ezekiel to eat the scroll.

M_6 *Physical Reaction* (3:3b). Ezekiel eats the scroll.

M_7 *Statement* (3:4-11). God again commissions Ezekiel as his messenger.

Departure (3:12-14)

D_1 *Description* (12-14). The spirit lifts Ezekiel. The Lord departs. Ezekiel returns.

Conclusion (3:15)

C_1 *Description* (15). Ezekiel sits overwhelmed for seven days.

Event

This epiphany may be classified as Divine Initiative,[103] since Ezekiel does not initiate the appearance ("the heavens were opened," 1:1).[104] The purpose of the epiphany is also divine, as the message reveals (2:3; 3:4). God appears to call Ezekiel as his messenger to the Israelites in exile.

Characterization of the Epiphanic Figure

In the introduction, the one who appears to Ezekiel is identified as God. The characterization of the epiphanic figure at the outset of the narra-

---

103. "The prophet is the one who has been summoned. The summons is described as an unsolicited and unanticipated event, a personal transformation accompanied by extraordinary experiences and profoundly disturbing spiritual and psychological upheaval." Blenkinsopp, *Ezekiel*, 17-18. So also Eichrodt: "Ezekiel therefore possesses an unshakable certitude, that the indescribable vision which he has been found worthy to see does not proceed from his own spiritual power, but that God in person is introducing him into a new dimension of reality, the strangeness and terrifying sublimity of which far transcend all that is imaginable to man." Eichrodt, *Ezekiel*, 54.

104. Greenberg proposes that Ezekiel sought divine solace at the Chebar canal, and "by way of response,... the heavens opened and the Majesty of God appeared, vindicating the nonconformist and proving that right and divine favor were with him, not with the many." Greenberg, *Ezekiel 1-20*, 80. Even if Greenberg is correct, God was not under any obligation to appear, nor is it apparent that Ezekiel was expecting, or even requesting, to see the things that were revealed to him.

tive is a pattern repeated in many OT epiphanies (cf. Gen 18:1; 19:1; Exod 3:2a). The being who appears is also described as "a likeness as an appearance of a human (דְּמוּת כְּמַרְאֵה אָדָם, 1:26b), and "the likeness of the appearance of the glory of Yahweh" (מַרְאֵה דְּמוּת כְּבוֹד־יְהוָה, 1:28b).[105] Thus, the epiphanic figure is characterized as both God and human.[106]

Apocrypha and Old Testament Pseudepigrapha

The Apocrypha and Old Testament Pseudepigrapha *(OTP)* are two collections that cover the entire Second Temple period. Two works from the Apocrypha will be considered: Tobit and 2 Esdras. The former is an OT expansion not unlike many Pseudepigraphical works; the latter also appears in the *OTP* as *4 Ezra*. Given these similarities, it is appropriate that the Apocryphal works should be considered together with those from the *OTP*.

The *OTP* is a collection of documents written during or after the Second Temple period. Charlesworth rightly claims that the *OTP* is essential to an understanding of early Judaism,[107] further noting that "many specialists on Paul now emphasize that he was profoundly shaped by Jewish apocalypticism."[108] Most of the works are presumably Jewish, although many show signs of Christian editing in their current form. Indeed, it is often difficult to determine if a document is the Christian redaction of a Jewish work, or a Christian work influenced by Jewish thought. We will consider only those documents exhibiting Jewish authorship.

The *OTP* contains works from a variety of genres. Charlesworth identifies six categories: apocalyptic; testaments; expansions of the OT and legends; fragments of Judeo-Hellenistic works; wisdom and philo-

---

105. Greenberg questions whether the nouns can be understood in any literal sense: "It looked like torches, sapphire, a human being, but that is not to say that torches, sapphire, and a human being were actually there. The use of these buffer terms indicates that the prophet wished to have his audience supposing he had any reservations respecting the visual likeness in these comparisons." Ibid., 53.

106. See Allen, *Ezekiel 1–19*, 35: "When Yahweh appears in a recognizable form in the OT, the human form is regarded as the natural and characteristic one for him to assume." Kutsko emphasizes the literary connection between the glory of Yahweh (1:28a) and the human likeness (26b): "The opening theophany concludes in v. 28a with a description chiastically related to v. 26b." Kutsko, *Between Heaven and Earth*, 88–89.

107. Charlesworth, "Pseudepigrapha, OT," 537.

108. Ibid., 539.

sophical; prayers, psalms, and odes.[109] Of these, the first four provide the bulk of relevant material, particularly: the *Apocalypses of Adam* and *Abraham*, *1 Enoch*, *2 Enoch*, *4 Ezra*, and *3 Baruch*; the *Testaments of Abraham*, *Levi*, and *Job*; the OT expansions of *Jubilees*, *Ladder of Jacob*, *Joseph and Asenath*, and the *History of the Rechabites*; and the Judeo-Hellenistic fragment Artapanus.

These works will be examined chronologically rather than according to Charlesworth's categories, in the hope that any chronological developments might be more clearly revealed. A primary difficulty in detecting chronological developments is that regrettably few works can be dated with any precision. Upper limits may occasionally be established using external evidence, such as the presence of a manuscript in the Dead Sea Scrolls, or a quotation in another ancient source that has been reliably dated. Unfortunately, many documents are dated by correlating their content to historical events such as the destruction of the temple in 70 CE. Obviously, this sort of necessary speculation does not always provide a desirable degree of certainty.

Finally, it must be noted that some *OTP* works containing relevant material have been excluded because they are dated outside the period of interest. For example, *3 Enoch* includes a detailed *merkabah* vision of Enoch, but has been excluded due to its late date (fifth–sixth century CE), particularly the "patently additional" *3 En.* 48BCD.[110]

We will consider seven works that are generally accepted as having pre-Christian origins, and eight works that are roughly contemporary with Paul. The pre-Christian works include Tobit, *1 Enoch*, Artapanus, *Jubilees*, *Testaments of the Twelve Patriarchs*, *Testament of Job*, and *Joseph and Asenath*. The contemporary works include *2 Enoch*, *Ladder of Jacob*, *3 Baruch*, *4 Ezra*, *Apocalypse of Abraham*, *Testaments of the Three Patriarchs*, and the *History of the Rechabites*.

While epiphanies in Tobit and *Jubilees* are presented in detail, the narrative structures of many other epiphanies have been summarized in Appendix A: Narrative Structure of Selected Epiphanies.

Let us proceed, then, to a chronological examination of the Apocryphal and Pseudepigraphical works of the Second Temple period.

---

109. Ibid., 538.
110. Alexander, "3 Enoch," 234.

Tobit (250–175 BCE)[111]

Tobit's encounter with the angel Raphael (5:4—12:22) is an excellent example of an extended epiphany. The introduction (5:4a) and appearance (5:4b) elements are brief. After much narrative detail (5:5—12:5), the message element concludes with an exhortation from Raphael (12:6-10), followed by the disclosure of his true identity (12:11-15), a typical fear reaction from Tobit and Sarah (12:16), and response from Tobit (12:17-20a). The departure element is present (12:20-21), as is a conclusion (12:22).

Narrative Structure

Introduction (5:4a)

I_1 Background (5:4a). Tobit goes in search of Gabael.

Appearance (5:4b)

A_1 Description (5:4b). Tobit encounters Raphael, but does not realize that he is an angel.

Message (5:5—12:20a)

M_1 Description (5:5—12:5). Extended narration of Tobit's encounter with Raphael.

M_2 Statement (12:6-15). Raphael exhorts Tobit and Sarah, and reveals his angelic identity.

M_3 Physical Reaction (12:16). Tobit and Sarah fall in fear.

M_4 Response (12:17-20a). Raphael reassures Tobit and Sarah.

Departure (12:20b-21)

D_1 Statement (12:20b). Raphael announces his departure.

D_2 Description (12:20c). Raphael ascends.

D_3 Reaction (12:21). Tobit and Sarah notice Raphael's departure.

---

111. The book of Tobit has not been dated precisely. "There is little evidence on which to date the book of Tobit." Otzen, *Tobit and Judith*, 57. Fragments of Tobit found at Qumran have been dated no later than 100 BCE. This solitary fact, unsupported by any internal evidence that could be used to narrow the range, has led Dancy to date Tobit to 250–200 BCE. Dancy, *Shorter Books*, 10. DeSilva is slightly more generous, suggesting the period 250–175 BCE. DeSilva, *Apocrypha*, 69. Moore concludes that a date "no earlier than ca. 300 BCE [is] quite plausible." Moore, *Tobit*, 42. Fitzmyer suggests a date near the end of 225–175 BCE. Fitzmyer, *Tobit*, 52. Knibb has recently suggested that Tobit dates from around 200 BCE. Knibb, "Temple," 408.

Conclusion (12:22)

C_1 *Description* (12:22). Tobit and Sarah praise God for the encounter.

Event

Tobit's encounter with Raphael is an example of a Divine Initiative epiphany, since Tobit and Sarah remain unaware that Raphael is an angel until the end of the epiphany. Raphael reveals the divine purpose of the epiphany: "I was sent to you to test you. And at the same time God sent me to heal you and Sarah your daughter-in-law" (12:14, NRSV).

Characterization of the Epiphanic Figure

The characterization of the angel Raphael is noteworthy. Through much of the narrative, he is seen by everyone to be a normal human being (5:5—12:10), even though the narrator has revealed to the reader that he is an angel (3:17; 5:4b). As in numerous OT epiphanies (e.g., Gen 18–19), the heavenly figure is indistinguishable from a person for much of the appearance. Raphael is clearly and consistently identified as being distinct from God,[112] both by the narrator (3:16–17a) and Raphael himself (12:14–15).[113]

ARTAPANUS (250–100 BCE)[114]

The third fragment of Artapanus describes Moses's actions in Egypt. While the text does not describe an epiphany, it does mention a divine voice several times (3.27:21, 36). The first encounter with the divine voice is in response to Moses's prayer (21); initiative of the second encounter

---

112. Fitzmyer remarks that Raphael is "different from 'the angel of the Lord' (Gen 16:7–11; Exod 3:2; Num 22:22) or 'the angel of God' (Gen 21:17; Exod 14:19; Judg 6:20), i.e. the theophanic angel." Fitzmyer, *Tobit*, 160. Schüngel-Straumann compares Raphael's self-revelation to those by God in Exod 20:2 and Deut 5:6, although the basis of the comparison seems to be limited to an introductory "I am" before the name. Schüngel-Straumann, *Tobit*, 157.

113. Raphael is identified more precisely as "seven angels who stand ready and enter before the glory of the Lord" (Tob 12:15, NRSV). Skemp notes other texts that mention angels standing in the presence of God (*T. Levi* 3:4–8; Luke 1:19; Rev 4:5; 8:2), as well as others where the actual phrase "angels of the presence" is used (*Jub* 2:2, 18; 1QH^a XIV, 13; 1Q28b IV, 25–26). Skemp, "Avenues," 51.

114. *Artapanus* is dated towards the end of the third century BCE. Collins, "Artapanus," 891. Attridge notes that Artapanus "certainly wrote before Alexander Polyhistor and thus not later than 100 B.C.E." Attridge, "Historiography," 168. Barclay dates Artapanus between 250–100 BCE. Barclay, "Manipulating Moses," 31.

is uncertain. The description of the encounters is too brief to permit a more detailed analysis of the events or the nature of the divine voice.

JUBILEES (160–150 BCE)[115]

In its opening line, *Jubilees* claims to be an account of the revelation that Moses received from the Lord on Mount Sinai. The "angel of the presence," clearly distinguished from the Lord (*Jub.* 1:27, 29), reveals the creation story to Moses "by the word of the Lord" (2:1).[116] We will consider three epiphanies that are typical of many in *Jubilees*.

Jubilees 12:16–27

Abraham's initial call from God (12:16–24) differs from the antecedent Genesis account (Gen 12:1–3) in that it presents God's command as a response to Abraham's prayer for guidance. Furthermore, the account in *Jubilees* is mediated by the angel of the presence. For example, the angel states: "The word of the Lord was sent to him by my hand" (22; cf. 25, "And the Lord God said to me, 'Open his mouth...'").[117]

Narrative Structure

> *Introduction* (16–21)
>
> I_1 *Setting* (16). The setting is described as the night of the new moon of the seventh month, in the sixth week of the fifth year of Abram's stay in Haran.
>
> I_2 *Description* (17–21). Abram asks God if he should remain in Haran or return to Ur.
>
> *Appearance* (22a)
>
> A_1 *Description* (22a). God sends the angel of the presence to Abram with the answer to his question.
>
> *Message* (22b–26)
>
> M_1 *Statement* (22–24). The angel delivers God's answer to Abram's question.

---

115. *Jubilees* has been dated to 160–150 BCE. VanderKam, *Jubilees Guide*, 21; Wintermute, "Jubilees," 44. Knibb raises the possibility that *Jubilees* should be dated earlier than 168 BCE. Knibb, "Temple," 409.

116. VanderKam notes that some passages identify the angel as the author (1:27; 30:12, 21; 50:6, 13), while others name Moses (1:5, 7, 26; 2:1; 23:32; 33:18). VanderKam, *Jubilees* (CSCO), 6 n. 27.

117. Crawford suggests that the angelic narration is due to a desire for the book to be accepted as divinely inspired. Crawford, "Rewritten Bible," 184.

M_2 *Parenthesis* (25). God tells the angel to teach the Hebrew language to Abram.

M_3 *Description* (26). The angel teaches Abram Hebrew.

[*Departure*]

Conclusion (27)

C_1 *Description* (27). Abram studies for six months.

Event

The initiative for this appearance appears to be human, since the angel appears in response to Abraham's question (21). The purpose of this appearance is also human, since the angel appears to answer Abraham's question, "Shall I return unto Ur of the Chaldees. . . . Or shall I dwell here in this place" (21). Thus, *Jub.* 12:16–27 follows the Divine Response pattern of epiphany.

Characterization of the Epiphanic Figure

The angel of the presence is distinguished from God (22, 25–26).

Jubilees 15:1–24

The epiphany in *Jub.* 15 parallels Gen 17:1–16. This time, God's appearance is not mediated ("And the Lord appeared to Abram," 15:3; "And the Lord spoke to him, saying," 15:5:).

Narrative Structure

Introduction (1–2)

I_1 *Setting* (1a). The date is identified precisely within the jubilee.

I_2 *Description* (1b–2). Abraham sacrifices several animals on the altar.

Appearance (3–5a)

A_1 *Description* (3a). The Lord appears to Abraham.

A_2 *Statement* (3b–4). The Lord identifies himself to Abraham.

A_3 *Physical Reaction* (5a). Abraham falls.

Message (5b–21)

M_1 *Statement* (5b–10). God confirms his covenant with Abraham.

M_2 *Statement (11–14)*. God commands Abraham to circumcise the males in his house.

M_3 *Statement (15–16)*. God promises a son for Abraham and his wife Sarah.

M_4 *Physical reaction (17a)*. Abraham falls on his face.

M_5 *Verbal reaction (17a–18)*. Abraham doubts that Sarah can have a son, and requests that God accept Ishmael instead.

M_6 *Response (19–21)*. God denies Abram's request, affirming that Sarah will have a son.

Departure (22)

D_1 *Description (22)*. God ends the conversation and ascends.

Conclusion (23–24)

C_1 *Description (23–24)*. Abram obeys God's command of circumcision.

Event

The initiative for this appearance is unclear. In Gen 17:1, there is no indication that God appeared in response to actions by Abraham. In *Jub.* 15:1–2, however, Abraham offers sacrifices that seem to evoke God's presence. The purpose for this appearance remains divine, since God reaffirms his covenant with Abraham (4–16) and promises a son (17–21).

Characterization of the Epiphanic Figure

Unlike Gen 17:1–16, God's appearance is not mediated ("And the Lord appeared to Abram,"15:3; "And the Lord spoke to him, saying," 15:5).

Jubilees 16:1–4

In this epiphany, the author of *Jubilees* retells the story of Gen 18–19.

Narrative Structure

Introduction (1a)

I_1 *Setting (1a)*. Both temporal and spatial settings are specified.

Appearance (1b)

A_1 *Description (1b)*. The angels appear to Abraham.

Message (1c–4)

M_1 *Statement (1c)*. The angels inform Abraham that Sarah will have a son.

M_2 *Physical Reaction* (2a). Sarah laughs.

M_3 *Response* (2b). The angels admonish Sarah.

M_4 *Verbal Reaction* (2c). Out of fear, Sarah denies that she laughed.

M_5 *Statement* (3-4). The angels tell Sarah that her son will be named Isaac, and that he will be born at a set time.

[*Departure*]

[*Conclusion*]

Event

This narrative maintains the pattern of Divine Initiative (1b) of the original Genesis account. The purpose (1c, 3-4) is also divine.

Characterization of the Epiphanic Figure

The Gen 18-19 appearance of Yahweh and two angels to Abraham is paralleled in *Jub.* 16:1-4. The author of *Jubilees* replaces Yahweh with angels ("we," 1b; cf. 1:27f). VanderKam speculates that this may have been done to maintain Yahweh's transcendence, or to remove any apparent confusion from the passage.[118]

Summary

We have seen that in several cases, the author of *Jubilees* maintains the identity of the one who appears (15:3; 16:1); in another, he introduces a mediator (12:22). Similarly, in one case divine initiative and purpose are maintained (16:1-4); in another, they are replaced by human initiative and purpose (12:16-24).

Testaments of the Twelve Patriarchs (137-107 BCE)[119]

The *Testament of Levi* contains an angelophany in which Levi is led through a vision of the three heavens (*T. Levi* 2-5). The "angel of the

---

118. As VanderKam observes, "The wording of Gen. 18:1-3 can leave a reader puzzled because it is difficult to determine exactly who visits the patriarch as he sits at the entrance to his tent.... Did Abraham have one visitor or three, one of whom was the Lord? *Jubilees* simplifies matters by saying simply that 'we appeared to Abraham' (16.1), that is, some angels of the presence were the ones who visited him." VanderKam, *Jubilees Guide*, 51.

119. Despite the obvious Christianization of the *Testaments of Abraham* and *Jacob*, their Jewish origin is recognized. Sanders argues that *T. Ab.* is "unmistakably Jewish."

Lord" who appears to Levi (2:7) is differentiated from God: "I am the angel who makes intercession for the nation Israel" (5:6). The angel opens the gates of heaven for Levi, who can then see "the Holy Most High sitting on the throne" (5:1). This vision is clearly a dream ("Then sleep fell upon me," 2:5; "And after this I awoke," 5:7). The vision appears to exhibit human initiative, since it is presented as a consequence of Levi's prayer for deliverance ("I prayed to the Lord that I might be delivered," 2:4). While the encounter is described as a Divine Response epiphany, the nature of the purpose is less certain. God responds to Levi's pleas by making him a priest ("The Most High has given heed to your prayer that you be delivered from wrongdoing, and that you should become a son to him, as minister and priest in his presence," 4:2). Since Levi did not request that God make him a priest, the purpose may be divine; however, it is also possible that Levi's priesthood is a result of his initial request.

TESTAMENT OF JOB (100 BCE–100 CE)[120]

The *Testament of Job* begins with an epiphany. God's messenger appears to Job in response to Job's questions (*T. Job* 2:1-4). This is a Divine Response epiphany, since both the initiative and the purpose are human. The messenger, presumably an angel, is introduced as "a loud voice ... in a very bright light" (3:1), and later metonymically as "the light" (4:1).[121] After the message is imparted to Job, the angel departs (5:2).

JOSEPH AND ASENATH (100 BCE – 115 CE)[122]

Chapters 14–17 of this book describe Asenath's encounter with a heavenly man who was the "chief of the house of the Most High" (*Jos.*

Sanders, "Testament of Abraham," 875. Stinespring identifies *T. Jac.* as the "product of Egyptian Judaism." Stinespring, "Testament of Isaac," 904. The *Testaments of the Twelve Patriarchs*, and the *Testament of Levi* in particular, have been dated to the second century BCE, possibly during the reign of John Hyrcanus (137–107 BCE). Kee, "Twelve Patriarchs," 1:778.

120. Spittler claims that the *Testament of Job* is an essentially Jewish work with some possible Christian editing, "probably [written] during the first century B.C. or A.D." Spittler, "Testament of Job," 833. Collins places it from 100 BCE to 150 CE. Collins, "Testaments," 353.

121. ἐμοὶ εἶπες τὸ φῶς ... Schaller, "Testaments Hoibs," 59. καὶ ἀωοκριθεὶς μοι τὸ φῶς εἶπεν ... Kraft et al., eds., *Testament of Job*, 24.

122. The date of *Joseph and Asenath* has been the focus of recent rebate. Until recently, it had been recognized as a pre-Christian work. Philonenko dates the work to the beginning of the second century: "... placer la compostion [sic] de *Joseph et Asénath* au

Asen. 15:12x). The epiphany follows the normal pattern of introduction (14:1a), appearance (14:1b-15), message (15:1—17:6), departure (17:7-8), and conclusion (17:9-10). Asenath's concluding comment, "I did not know that [a] god came to me" (17:9),[123] has several variations for "a god," including a fifteenth-century manuscript which reads "God," and an ambiguous sixth-century Syriac version which reads "God from heaven."[124] This is a Divine Response epiphany, since both the initiative and the purpose are human according to both Asenath ("So the Lord God listened to my prayer, because this star rose as a messenger and herald of the light of the great day," 14:2) and the heavenly man ("Behold, I have heard all the words of your confession and your prayer," 15:2).

2 *Enoch* (1–100 CE)[125]

The structure of the epiphany is apparent from the outset of *2 Enoch*. The introduction (*2 En.* 1:1-3) is followed by the appearance of two "huge men" (1:4-5), and Enoch's reaction (1:6-7). The content of the vision is described in the following chapters, as Enoch ascends in *merkabah*-like fashion through seven levels of heaven to the throne of God (21:1-6). Enoch sees God (22:1), and receives revelations from God (24:2, etc.).

---

début du second siècle serait assez naturel." Philonenko, *Joseph et Asénath*, 109. Burchard claims that "every competent scholar has ... affirmed that *Joseph and Asenath* is Jewish, with perhaps some Christian interpolations; none has put the book much after A.D. 200, and some have placed it as early as the second century B.C." He argues for a date between 100 BCE and the Jewish revolt under Trajan (115-17 CE). Burchard, "Joseph and Asenath," 187. Similar reasoning has led others to the same conclusion. For example, see Chesnutt, *Death to Life*, 80-85; also Bohak, *Heliopolis*, 84-87; Evans, "Stories," 61-62. More recently, Kraemer has argued at length for a date "no earlier than the third century C.E." Kraemer, *Asenath*, 239. Collins seems to argue for an early date with "late antique elements." Collins, "Jewish or Christian?" 111. It is not clear whether Kraemer's evidence will gain acceptance. Docherty notes that Kraemer's arguments "have won little support." Docherty, "Rewritten Bible?" 31. Burchard, however, calls Kraemer's work "ingenious and stimulating," without necessarily agreeing with her dating. Burchard, "Reconsidered," 91. Brooke observes that "in light of recent understandings of angelomorphism in the Dead Sea scrolls we are back where we started before Kraemer made her contribution." Brooke, "Men and Women," 177.

123. Burchard gives the Greek text as καὶ οὐκ ᾔδειν ὅτι θεὸς ἦλθε πρός με. Burchard, *Joseph und Asenath*, 228.

124. Burchard, "Joseph and Asenath," 231.

125. Andersen dates *2 Enoch* in the first century CE, although this is not certain due to its unknown origin. Andersen, "2 Enoch," 91.

The initiative of this epiphany is somewhat uncertain, but it appears to be likely human. While Enoch does not specifically request ascent, the appearance of the two men may be viewed as a response to Enoch's "great distress" (1:3).

LADDER OF JACOB (1–100 CE)[126]

The *Ladder of Jacob*[127] opens with a retelling of God's appearance to Jacob in Genesis 28:11–13f (*Lad. Jac.* 1:1–12). The second chapter is a song of Jacob in response to the vision. In the third chapter, the angel Sariel appears to explain the vision of the ladder. The appearance element is similar to *Hist. Rech.* 1:3. As Jacob prays, a voice comes "before face"[128] and commands the angel Sariel to explain the first vision to him (*Lad. Jac.* 3:1–2). Immediately Sariel appears and interprets the vision. Thus, the two visions are closely connected. Both are Divine Initiative epiphanies. The initiative and the purpose of the first vision are both divine, as in Genesis 28:11–13f. The initiative and the purpose of the second vision are also both divine, since Sariel is sent to explain the first vision ("Sariel . . . go and make Jacob understand the meaning of the dream he has just had," 3:2).

3 BARUCH (70–300 CE)[129]

3 Baruch presents an apocalyptic vision of five heavens mediated by an angel (Phanuel, according to the introduction of the Slavonic version).[130] The vision (1:3f) occurs in response to Baruch's repeated questioning of the destruction of Jerusalem by Nebuchadnezzar, "Lord, why have you

---

126. Lunt dates *Ladder of Jacob* in the first century CE. Lunt, "Ladder of Jacob," 401. The evidence for this date is uncertain. Ibid., 404–5.

127. Kugel summarizes the content of "one of the strangest texts" in Kugel, "Ladder of Jacob."

128. For more on the meaning of the face, see Orlov, "Face."

129. The date of *3 Baruch* has been widely disputed. As with many pseudepigraphical texts, there are two opposing views for its origin: it is either a Christian work that incorporated Jewish traditions, or a Jewish work with later Christian revisions. Harlow provides a helpful summary of the debate in Harlow, "Christianization," 416–20. Gaylord does not choose between the two in suggesting that *3 Baruch* be dated in the first to third centuries CE. Gaylord, "3 Baruch," 656. Harlow seems to suggest a date shortly after 70 CE, stating that "3 Baruch provides a response to the circumstances attending Jerusalem's destruction." Harlow, *3 Baruch*, 15.

130. Orlov provides a summary of the content of *3 Baruch* in Orlov, "Flooded Arboretums."

done this?" (1:2). Therefore, it may be classified as a Divine Response epiphany. Furthermore, Baruch is barred from entering the fifth heaven (11:1-2), and thus prevented from seeing God.

4 EZRA 14:1-26 (80-100 CE)[131]

4 Ezra is comprised of a Christian introduction (*4 Ezra* 1-2), seven visions of a Jewish nature (3-14), and an appendix (15-16).[132] The first vision begins with Ezra questioning God (3:1-36). The angel Uriel appears (4:1) and answers Ezra at length (4:2—5:13), followed by the conclusion of the vision (5:14-20). The next three visions follow a similar pattern, in which an angel appears to give God's answer to Ezra's questions. The fifth vision recounts Ezra's eagle dream, followed by Ezra's request for, and reception of, its interpretations. The sixth vision mirrors the pattern of the fifth, in which Ezra dreams of a man from the sea, who is also described as the Son of the Most High (13:37).[133] The seventh vision, in which the Lord appears to Ezra, invokes Moses's burning bush encounter implicitly (14:1-2) and explicitly (14:3), followed by a message from God (14:4-26).

Although *4 Ezra* 14 presents Ezra primarily as the second Moses "in accordance with his role as the restorer of the scriptures,"[134] it also alludes to other OT epiphany narratives. For example, the introduction places the appearance "under an oak" (14:1a). This is clearly reminiscent of God's appearance to Abraham at the oaks of Mamre (Gen 18:1). The appearance, described as a voice from the bush (*4 Ezra* 14:1b), recalls Exod 3:2-4. The voice then identifies itself as the one who "revealed myself in a bush and spoke to Moses when my people were in bondage in Egypt" (*4 Ezra* 14:3, NRSV). The message element (5b-26) consists of a command (5b-18), Ezra's questioning response (19-22), and God's answer (23-26). There are no departure or conclusion elements.

---

131. *4 Ezra* is generally dated near the end of the first century CE. "Most scholars would place the date of the composition of 4 Ezra somewhere around 100 CE." Willett, *Eschatology*, 53. Internal evidence, particularly the identification of Domitian in the symbolism of the eagle vision (4 Ezra 11-12), suggests a date during or immediately after his reign (81-96 CE). Coggins and Knibb, *1 & 2 Esdras*, 105; deSilva, *Apocrypha*, 323; Longenecker, *2 Esdras*, 13; Myers, *I & II Esdras*, 129; Stone, *4 Ezra*, 10.

132. Metzger, "4 Ezra," 517.

133. For a discussion of the vision of 4 Ezra 13, see Hayman, "Man from the Sea."

134. Coggins and Knibb, *1 & 2 Esdras*, 273.

It is "most significant," as Stone rightly observes, that Ezra talks directly to God without the "*angelus interpres*" of the previous chapters.[135] Yet *4 Ezra* 14 also removes reference to the Angel of Yahweh from Exod 3–4. In the latter the narrator of Exodus uses the terms Angel of Yahweh (3:2), Yahweh (3:4), and Elohim (3:4) interchangeably; the one who appears also uses the terms Elohim (3:6) and Yahweh (3:15).[136] In *4 Ezra*, however, the only narrative descriptor for the message-bringer is "a voice." The one who speaks does not use any divine names. Ezra refers to the speaker as "Lord" twice (2, 19). Thus, much of the fluidity of identification found in Exod 3 has been removed in *4 Ezra* 14, particularly in the characterization of God as the Angel of Yahweh.

The visions appear to fit the Divine Response pattern. The sequence occurs in response to Ezra's lengthy plea to the Lord (3:1–36; cf. 5:21–30; 6:36–59; 9:27–37). The interpretation of the later visions is the result of Ezra's requests (12:3b–9; 13:14b–20).

APOCALYPSE OF ABRAHAM (70–150 CE)[137]

In the initial seven chapters of the apocalypse, Abraham searches for a revelation from God. Abraham's desire to see God culminates in his plea: "If [only] God will reveal himself by himself to us!" (7:12). God does then appear to Abraham, in the form of a personified or hypostatic voice (8:2).[138] God calls Abraham using a double vocative, and delivers a message echoing Genesis 12:1 (*Apoc. Ab.* 8:4). The voice then speaks a second time (9:1), using messages reminiscent of two biblical Abrahamic theophanies (cf. Gen 15:9 with *Apoc. Ab.* 9:5; Gen 22:2 with *Apoc. Ab.* 9:8) in calling Abraham to offer sacrifices. A third epiphany immediately follows (10:3f), in which the angel Iaoel is sent to bring Abraham to heaven to receive various revelations from God. The remainder of the apocalypse recounts Abraham's obedience to the command to sacrifice (12:1–15:1), and the heavenly visions that follow (15:4f.). As in the earlier theophany accounts, Abraham hears the voice of God, but does not

---

135. Stone, *4 Ezra*, 411.

136. See pp. 52–53 above.

137. *Apocalypse of Abraham* is typically dated after 70 CE due to its description of the destruction of Jerusalem (*Apoc. Ab.* 27). Rubinkiewicz claims a late first century CE date is "commonly held." Rubinkiewicz, "Abraham," 683. Charlesworth is less certain. Rubinkiewicz, "Abraham," 683 n. 15,16.

138. Charlesworth discusses the hypostatic voice in Charlesworth, "Hypostatic Voice," 33–37.

see God (19:1), a restriction the angel explicitly states to Abraham before they approach God: "You will not look at him himself" (16:3).

These epiphanies correspond with the pattern of Divine Response, since they occur as a direct result of Abraham's request (7:12). They appear to have a human purpose, since they reveal the answers to Abraham's questions ("For who is it, or which one is it who made the heavens crimson and the sun golden ... and who has sought me out in the perplexity of my thoughts," 7:11).

Testaments of the Three Patriarchs (75–125 CE)[139]

The *Testament of Abraham* recasts the story of Abraham so that the Master God communicates with Abraham through the archangel Michael (*T. Ab.* 1:4, 2:1, 5:1, etc.). The same pattern is seen in the *Testament of Isaac* (*T. Isaac* 2:1, 5:4; cf. *T. Jac.* 1:6, 2:5).

The *Testament of Abraham* is a Divine Initiative epiphany. The Master God commands Michael to "go down to Abraham and tell him about his death" (1:4). The same is true for the *Testament of Isaac*.

1 Enoch (70–260 CE)[140]

1 En. 14 recounts Enoch's vision of God which came to him in a dream (*1 En.* 14:2). As Enoch enters into heaven, he sees the temple filled with cherubim (14:8–17), the throne of God (14:17–19), and presumably God himself (14:20–25). The next chapters contain God's message to Enoch (15–16), followed by various visions in the presence of angels (17–36). Stone remarks that *1 En.* 14 is "the oldest Jewish ascent vision."[141]

---

139. The *Testament of Abraham* has been dated between the third century BCE and the third century CE, with Munoa favoring a date "no later than the early second century C.E." Munoa, *Four Powers*, 17–18. E. P. Sanders is more confident, suggesting a date of 100 CE, "plus or minus twenty-five years." Sanders, "Testament of Abraham," 875. Allison has an extensive discussion on the dating of the Testament of Abraham in Allison, *Testament of Abraham*, 35–40. The *Testaments of Isaac* and *Jacob* are later. Stinespring, "Testament of Isaac," 904; Stinespring, "Testament of Jacob," 1:913.

140. The dating of *1 Enoch* is more complicated due to its composite nature. The opening section (*1 En.* 1–36) is dated to the third century BCE. Stone, "Enoch," 192. The Book of Parables (*1 En.* 37–71) is not present in the Qumran versions of *1 Enoch*; therefore, the date of the Parables is disputed. Milik proposes that it dates to the middle of the third century CE. Milik, *Enoch*, 95–96. Black concludes that it dates to "the early Roman period, probably pre-70 A.D." Black, *1 Enoch*, 188. Isaac argues that *1 Enoch* included the Parables by 100 CE. Isaac, "1 Enoch," 7. Stone views this dating as "not implausible." Stone, "Enochic Pentateuch," 210.

141. Stone, "Enoch," 193.

1 *Enoch* is filled with visions and epiphanies, but the vision of the Son of Man (45–57) in the Book of the Parables (37–71) stands out among them.¹⁴² In the vision, Enoch sees two beings (46:1). The first is identified as the Lord of the Spirits. This second is commonly known as the Son of Man (46:3), but throughout the vision is also called the Elect One (45:3f), the Chosen One (48:6), the Anointed One (48:10), and the Righteous One (53:6).¹⁴³ VanderKam rightly notes that "the writer is careful to provide enough information in the text to demonstrate that he is referring through these designations to only one, not four individuals."¹⁴⁴ Although carefully distinguished from the Lord of the Spirits, the Son of Man is closely identified with him, having been chosen by the Lord of the Spirits (46:3; 48:6) to judge not only kings (46:4–8), but also the risen dead in the final judgment (51:2), and even Azaz'el (55:4). These judgments shall be from the very throne of the Lord of the Spirits (51:3; 55:4). While the Son of Man does appear to be a highly exalted being, he is consistently distinguished from the Lord of the Spirits. Bauckham, who cites the Son of Man as the "one exception which proves the rule" that only God may be worshipped, concludes that the Son of Man's "inclusion in the divine identity" is "partial" and "equivocal."¹⁴⁵ Hays concurs with Bauckham's assessment.¹⁴⁶

The Book of Parables concludes with the statement that Enoch himself is the Son of Man (71:14).¹⁴⁷ This revelation is obscured by

142. The pre-Christian origin of the Parables is not certain. Its absence from the Qumran scrolls is particularly noteworthy. "No MS corresponding to any part of *1 En.* 37–71 has been recovered from Qumran." Davidson, *Angels*, 25.

143. These names are also used elsewhere in the Parables: the Elect One (39:6; 40:5; 45:3, 4; 49:2, 4; 51:3 (B and C; A omits), 5; 52:6, 9; 53:6; 55:4; 61:5, 8, 10; 62:1); the Anointed One, or Messiah (48:10; 52:4); the Righteous One (38:2; 53:6); the Son of Man (46:2, 3, 4; 48:2; 62:5, 7, 9, 14; 63:11; 69:26, 27, 29; 70:1).

144. VanderKam, "Biblical Interpretation," 116.

145. Bauckham, *God Crucified*, 19–20. Bauckham also cites *1 En.* 61:8; 62:2, 5; 69:27, 29 as pertinent references to the Son of Man.

146. "Taken alone, this text [*1 En.* 38] could be understood simply as a portrayal of God's activity in the final judgment, and 'the Righteous One' could be God himself. However, as the visionary description unfolds, 'the Righteous One' is clearly identified with a figure distinct from God, 'the Elect One of righteousness and of faith.'" Hays, "Righteous One," 193–94.

147. The Greek text reads σὺ ἔι ὁ υἱὸς τοῦ ανθρώπου (walda be'si). Black, *1 Enoch*, 363. Nickelsburg and VanderKam translate this as "You are that son of man." Nickelsburg and VanderKam, *1 Enoch Translation*, 95. Knibb notes the possibility that chs. 70–71 are a later addition to the Parables. Knibb, "1 Enoch 70.1," 340–41.

Isaac's translation, "You, son of man, ..."[148] In commenting on the relation of the Parables to Christianity, Black notes that "the Son of Man who is to come as the Judge of all mankind is identified, not with Jesus of Nazareth, *but with Enoch himself.*"[149] Several of the names applied to the transcendent figure are also used for humans. The name "son of man" is used for Enoch (60:10), and "righteous ones" for other humans (45:6). The *OTP* has emended *1 En.* 45:5 to read "Elect One" where the text has "elect ones."[150]

Thus, the Son of Man in *1 Enoch* is as a semi-divine, exalted human[151] who shares attributes of angels,[152] and who possibly even receives worship, yet who is never characterized as God.

The initiative and purpose of the vision in the Book of the Parables are uncertain, since the vision is presented without an introduction, appearance, departure, or conclusion. Thus, it is difficult to classify the vision as either Divine Initiative or Divine Response.

HISTORY OF THE RECHABITES (1–500 CE)[153]

This text opens with an angelophany. An angel is sent by God to Zosimus in response to his prayers. The text mentions both a voice and an angel: "A voice came to him and an angel came toward him and said to him ..." (1:3). God's presence is presented in a hypostatic voice (1:2–3), but is immediately replaced by the presence of the angel. Thus, the angel and the voice are distinct, but the initial presence of the voice gives the angel divine authority.

---

148. Isaac, "1 Enoch," 50.

149. Black, *1 Enoch*, 188.

150. Isaac, "1 Enoch," 34 n. 45m.

151. "The assumption of Enoch to heaven, and his greeting as 'Son of Man,' raises the question whether a human being can be exalted to a divine, or semidivine, state, in a Jewish context." Collins, "Powers," 15.

152. "The son of man/Chosen One/Righteous One of the parables is a heavenly figure who assumes salvific and judicial functions that other sections of *1 Enoch* ascribe to angelic figures and to Enoch himself." Nickelsburg, "Response," 102.

153. *History of the Rechabites* may be dated from the first to fourth centuries CE. Charlesworth, "Rechabites," 443. Knights hesitates to give any date, claiming that "the dating of *The History of the Rechabites* is most problematic." Knights, "Rechabites," 330–33.

This is a Divine Response epiphany, since both the initiative and the purpose of the epiphany are human ("I praised and exalted God, who had answered me and heard my petition and fulfilled my desire," 18:1).

Dead Sea Scrolls

The Dead Sea Scrolls provide invaluable insights into the eschatology of the Qumran community. The scrolls date from about 150 BCE, when the community was established, to 68 CE, when it was destroyed.[154] This range should be sufficient, since this general period establishes that the scrolls are relevant for the purposes of this study and since most documents from sources other than Qumran are dated with less precision than the general period of the Dead Sea Scrolls.

Apocalyptic language is found throughout the scrolls. The following survey explores some of the more noteworthy features of the scrolls as they relate to epiphany.

The scrolls reveal the hope of God's future appearance. For example, *Damascus Document* speaks of a future day "when God will make a visitation" (CD-A VIII, 2–3;[155] cf. 4Q266 3 iii, 25);[156] *Temple Scroll*, of a future day when God's glory will "settle" on the temple (11Q19 XXIX, 8–9).[157] Furthermore, the community is living in anticipation of God's coming. For example, *War Scroll* refers to Israel as being "those who hear the glorious voice and see the holy angels" (1QM X, 10–11).[158] The community also expressed a desire to ascend to heaven. For example, *Rule of the Blessings* requests the visitation of the Lord, and the glorification of the blessed:

> May He lift up His countenance toward your entire congregation! May He place [a crown] upon your head [ ] [ ] with [perpetual] glo[ry. May He] sanctify your descendants with glory without end. (1Q28b III, 2–4)[159]

---

154. Vermes, *Introduction*, 27–28.

155. Martínez and Tigchelaar, *Dead Sea Scrolls* 1:561.

156. Parry and Tov, eds., *DSS Reader* 1:91.

157. Ibid., 3:165.

158. Ibid., 1:227. Stuckenbruck argues against a proposed connection to Col 2:18 (θρησκείᾳ τῶν ἀγγέλων). Stuckenbruck, *Veneration*, 151–52.

159. Parry and Tov, eds., *DSS Reader* 5:429.

In these texts, the appearance of God is a future event to be sought, rather than the experience of a member of the community. These passages reflect the hope of a future appearance of God, or the hope of a future ascension to heaven. There is no narrative account of God appearing to a member of the Qumran community.

Apocalyptic language of the *merkabah* vision is also present in *Songs of the Sabbath Sacrifice*.[160] The repetition of "seven" throughout the opening of *Songs of the Sabbath Sacrifice*[d] is reminiscent of the heavenly levels in *merkabah* visions (4Q403 I, 1–27). Not surprisingly, this is followed by heavenly throne room imagery (4Q403 II, 1–17), culminating with: "And the chariots of his *debir* praise together . . ." (4Q403 II, 15).[161] The following song also has "seven" as a central theme (II, 18f), as does *Songs of the Sabbath Sacrifice*[e] (4Q404 2, 4–9; 11, 1–2; 16, 3–4).[162] *Songs of the Sabbath Sacrifice*[f] follows a similar pattern, culminating in fragments 4Q405 20–23.[163] Phrases such as "the seat of the throne of his kingship," "the chariots of his glory," "the glorious seats of the chariots," "the chariots of his glory when they move" (4Q405 20, 2–5), etc., reflect the *merkabah* tradition.[164] Yet there is no account of an individual experiencing a *merkabah* vision. Frennesson concludes that "descriptions of ascensions, or even references to ascensions . . . are simply not [present in Qumran texts]."[165]

The Qumran scrolls also exhibit an interest in angels and other heavenly beings. In *Rule of the Community*, the "Angel of Truth" and the "Angel of Darkness" are contrasted, as are their followers (1QS III, 13—IV, 1).[166] *Thanksgiving Hymns*[a] speaks of "powerful spirits" who changed into angels, stars, luminaries, stormy winds, thunder, and lightning (1QH[a] IX, 10–12).[167] As well, *Songs of the Sabbath Sacrifice* contains

---

160. Stuckenbruck discusses the *Songs* in Stuckenbruck, *Veneration*, 156–61, 163–64. Stuckenbruck concludes that apparent angel veneration "is not understood as contradictory to the worship of God; indeed, recognition of the angelic superiority derives at least partly from their exemplary worship of God." Stuckenbruck, *Veneration*, 163.

161. Parry and Tov, eds., *DSS Reader* 5:375–81.

162. Ibid., 5:385–89.

163. Ibid., 5:401–5.

164. Vermes, *Introduction*, 54.

165. Frennesson, *Common Rejoicing*, 102. Frennesson mentions "one single exception," (4Q491 11 I), but notes that it lacks features typical of later *Hekhalot* texts.

166. Parry and Tov, eds., *DSS Reader* 4:152–53.

167. Ibid., 5:15–17.

much angelic language. It identifies an entire class of heavenly beings as: "the gods" (4Q400 1 i, 1); "the eternal holy ones," "priests," "the servants of the Presence," "deities" (i, 4); "holy ones" (i, 17); and "divine beings" or "gods" (אלים; ii, 17). Such beings are consistently distinguished from God, as they are from humans; for example, humans and angels are clearly distinguished: "What is the offering of our tongue of dust (compared) with the knowledge of the divinities?" (4Q400 2, 7).[168]

It has recently been suggested that the community understood itself in angelomorphic terms, either at that time or in the future. Fletcher-Louis asserts that "much of the language within the Songs, though not all, refers to the Qumran community members who now have a heavenly, angelic and divine identity."[169] One key text used to support this view is the following simile from *Rule of the Blessings*:

> May you (abide forever) as an Angel of the Presence in the holy habitation, to the glory of the God of hosts[s. May you serve the Lord forever and b]e all around. May you / the kingdom of God, ordering destiny with the Angels of the Presence, a Council of the Yaḥad [with the Holy Ones] forever, for all the ages of eternity. (1Q28b IV, 24–26)[170]

Yet the passage does not assert that members of the community will become angels. Rather, a simile is employed to indicate a fervent wish for a blessed hope. Regardless of whether the community understood itself in angelomorphic terms, it is clear that there is no fluidity of characterization between God and either humans or angels.

Several other theories have been proposed regarding the relationship between humans and angels. Martínez suggests that angels were already present in the Qumran community.[171] Schuller is perhaps more realistic in claiming that humans may one day join angels in praising God.[172]

The "son of God" figure in 4Q246 has also drawn attention. It is difficult to draw many conclusions from this Aramaic fragment. It is brief, consisting of only nine lines. It is also rather vague and ambiguous. Yet it does describe a pre-Christian figure who is in a unique relationship

---

168. Ibid., 5:357–59.
169. Fletcher-Louis, "Heavenly Ascent," 369.
170. Parry and Tov, eds., *DSS Reader* 5:431.
171. Martínez, "Apocalypticism," 184.
172. Schuller, "Theory," 137.

to God.[173] Collins notes that the title "does not necessarily imply metaphysical divine status. It can be understood as an adoptive formula, as in Psalm 2, or simply as an honorific title."[174]

Thus, the Dead Sea Scrolls contain the anticipation of God's appearance, often couched in *merkabah*-like language, with a highly developed angelology. Yet the scrolls do not contain examples of epiphany.[175] In its characterization of heavenly figures, God remains distinct from angels, as well as from humans. Even the hoped-for ascension to the presence of God does not involve the deification of the blessed. There is no ambiguity in the distinction between God and other beings in the language of the Qumran community.

Philo of Alexandria

Philo was a leading member of the Jewish community in Alexandria during the first half of the first century CE. The exact dates of Philo's birth and death are unknown, but he is known to have led the Jewish delegation from Alexandria to Rome in 39–40 CE. Borgen estimates that he lived from about 20 BCE to 50 CE.[176] Philo was also a prolific writer who interpreted the Hebrew Scriptures allegorically. Unfortunately, Philo does not provide any narrative accounts of epiphanies. However, two aspects of Philo's writing are applicable to this study: his depiction of heavenly beings such as two gods and the Logos, and his depiction of exalted human beings.

---

173. The text is discussed in detail in Martínez, *Apocalyptic*, 162–79. Collins seeks to make a connection between the "son of God" in 4Q246 and the "son of Man" in Dan 7. Collins, *Scepter*, 167. Dunn rightly rejects this assertion. Dunn, "Son of God." Fitzmyer also discusses the text in Fitzmyer, *Origins*, 41–72.

174. Collins, "Powers," 21.

175. "There is no clear evidence that the Qumranites themselves authored pseudepigraphic apocalypses." Nickelsburg, "Nature," 91. Similarly, Davidson notes that "in apocalypses . . . the role of the angel as communicators to the seers is quite explicit. Yet this kind of idea is not found in the Qumran literature, with the possible exception of the *Description of the New Jerusalem* [5Q15]." Davidson, *Angels*, 205; see also 241–42. The *New Jerusalem* fragments (2Q4, 4Q554, 4Q555, 5Q15, and 11Q18) are reminiscent of Ezek 40–48, but without any indication of who is leading the narrator to do the measurements.

176. Borgen, "Philo," 333.

Two Gods and the Logos

In *De Somniis* I, Philo urges his readers to "examine precisely" if Gen 31:13 (LXX) mentions "two gods" (*Somn.* 1.228).[177] The ensuing discussion reveals that Philo does not interpret the passage, or other similar texts, as referring to two gods ("There is one true God," 1.229). He interprets the anthropomorphic language of OT epiphanies as catering to the "dullness" (ἀμβλύς) of humans (1.234–36).

In *Quaestiones et solutiones in Genesin*, Philo discusses an enigmatic figure he terms the Logos:

> For nothing mortal can be made in the likeness of the most high One and Father of the universe but (only) in that of the second God [τὸν δεύτερον θεόν], who is His Logos [ἐκείνου λόγος]. ...But He who is above the Logos (and) exists in the best and in a special form...God most justly avenges...men...because they have a certain kinship with His Logos, of which the human mind is a likeness and image. (*QG* 2.62)

The relationship of the Logos to both God and humanity is revealed in this passage. The Logos has such an affinity to God, and is sufficiently exalted above humanity, that it merits the title "second God." Yet Philo also understands the "most high One and Father" to be "above the Logos."[178]

These two characteristics of the Logos (namely, being simultaneously exalted above humanity yet distinct from God) are also seen in *De fuga et inventione*. The Logos is high above all the symbols of Moses's tabernacle, being the image of God (εἰκὼν θεοῦ, *Fug.* 101). Yet the Logos is not characterized as God: "while the Logos is the charioteer of the Powers, He Who talks is seated in the chariot, giving directions to the charioteer for the right wielding of the reins of the Universe" (*Fug.* 101). Thus, Philo presents the Logos in close proximity to the One God, even deeming him a "second God," but does not equate him with the One God.

---

177. Segal claims that "it is clear that Philo uses and approves of the term 'second God' which the rabbis later would find repugnant." Segal, *Two Powers*, 165–66.

178. Segal claims that Philo uses the Logos to explain "human representations of God," and that the Logos is one of "God's powers," an "intermediary who is divine," or even "God's human form." Segal, "Heavenly Ascent," 1355. Yet *QG* 2.62 appears to distinguish "the most high One and Father" from the Logos in that God is above the Logos.

Exalted Humans

Moses

Philo presents several OT figures in highly exalted terms. For example, Philo writes that Moses "was named god and king (θεὸς καὶ βασιλεύς) of the whole nation" (*Mos.* 1.158). Despite this apparent deification, Philo maintains a distinction between the ascended human and the "God of gods":

> The legislator of the Jews in a bolder spirit went to a further extreme and in the practice of his "naked" philosophy, as they called it, ventured to speak of him who was possessed by love of the divine and worshipped the Self-existent only, as having passed from a man into a god, though, indeed, a god to men, not to the different parts of nature, thus leaving to the Father of all the place of King and God of gods. (*Prob.* 43)

As Niehoff observes, although Moses had become a "god," he was still "to be sure, subordinate to the creator God and did not apparently enjoy any direct worship."[179] Scott reaches the same conclusion:

> Of course, there is an ontological change in Moses which distances him from the rest of humanity. We may even say that Moses is no longer simply human, but occupies a middle point between humanity and God.... He still remains entirely dependent on the one God, claiming nothing in and of himself.[180]

Thus, Philo's Moses is an exalted human, and even a "god," but is not given the exalted status of the "God of gods."

High Priest

Another OT figure that Philo describes in highly exalted form is the High Priest.[181] Philo reasons that the High Priest was "not a man, but a divine word" (*Fug.* 108), a conclusion he reaches after allegorizing the High Priest's death (*Fug.* 106). Interestingly, the High Priest is also identified with the Logos. Philo names him "the High Priest the Logos" (*Migr.* 102), but does not equate this figure with God.[182]

---

179. Niehoff, *Philo*, 84.

180. Scott, "Moses," 109. So also Runia, who states that Moses is "neither God nor man but rather occup[ies] a midway position." Runia, "Philo," 63.

181. Philo's High Priest is discussed in LaPorte, "High Priest."

182. Borgen, "Philo," 339.

Summary

Philo introduces both the Logos and ascended human figures as intermediary beings between God and humanity. This is a well-known observation, which Borgen affirms: "Some scholars have pointed to the tendency to bridge the gap between the transcendent God and man by intermediaries, such as Logos, the powers, etc."[183] Yet in developing these intermediaries, Philo maintains a clear distinction between them and God.

Flavius Josephus

Josephus, born Joseph ben Mattathias in about 37 CE, was a Jewish historian who wrote during the second half of the first century CE.[184] In the *Jewish Antiquities*, Josephus retells many OT epiphany narratives. Other epiphanies do not have an OT antecedent. Both types are valuable to this study.

Rewritten Old Testament Epiphanies

Many OT epiphanies are retold by Josephus in the *Jewish Antiquities*. These parallel accounts are invaluable for revealing how Josephus's understanding of epiphany varied from the OT authors. The following brief survey will illustrate the range of variation.

Perhaps the most noteworthy modifications occur in the characterization of epiphanic figures. In some cases Josephus does characterize some figures using OT-like terminology. For example, in the case of Hagar's second expulsion, both characterize Hagar's rescuer as an angel of God (מַלְאַךְ אֱלֹהִים, Gen 21:17; θεῖος ἄγγελος, *Ant.* 1:219).[185] The accounts of Hagar's first expulsion vary slightly. The OT uses the title Angel of Yahweh (מַלְאַךְ יְהוָה, Gen 16:9), while Josephus uses angel of God (ἄγγελος θεῖος, *Ant.* 1:189). Josephus also introduces some variations. While the OT is fairly consistent in the use of the term מלאך for messenger or angel, Josephus introduces the term φάντασμα ("phantom"

---

183. Ibid.

184. Feldman, "Josephus," 981–82.

185. Although, as Feldman remarks, the miracle "is lessened and to a great degree rationalized here." Feldman, *Antiquities 1–4*, 3:82–83.

or "apparition"[186]) and uses it interchangeably with ἄγγελος (*Ant.* 1:325, 1:331–33).[187]

Yet Josephus also alters the identity of some figures. In Gen 18–19 Abraham receives three visitors, men whom the narrator identifies as יהוה (18:1, 10, 13–14, 17, 19–20, 22, 26, 33) and שְׁנֵי הַמַּלְאָכִים ("two angels," 19:1). Josephus introduces the three as angels (τρεῖς ἀγγέλους, *Ant.* 1:196), and later describes them revealing their own identities to Abraham as angels, or messengers, of God (ἀγγέλους τοῦ θεοῦ, 1:198).[188] God is presented as receiving Abraham's plea to spare the city of Sodom (1:199–201), but not as one of those who appeared. The narrative structure of these two epiphanies mirrors that of Gen 18–19. Josephus presents the encounter with Abraham with an introduction (196a), appearance (196b–97a), and message (197b–200a). The encounter with Lot is narrated with an introduction (200b), appearance (200c–202a), message (202b), and conclusion (202c).

Another example is found in the retelling of Num 22–24. Levison attributes the modifications to Josephus's audience:

> Nor was recounting the biblical story at face value an option, with its assertions that God without mediation opened the ass's mouth and put a word in Balaam's mouth, given Josephus's desire to present an acceptable, respectable history to his readers.[189]

Levison rightly observes that Josephus frequently introduces mediators between God and humans. However, his conclusion does not account for the fact that Josephus is not consistent in the introduction of intermediaries.

Thus, Josephus maintains the identity of some divine figures, but also removes multiple characterizations in other instances. Josephus is not averse to showing interactions between God and humans (1:199–201), but does have a tendency to eliminate direct appearances of God when retelling Old Testament accounts. This removes any multiple characterizations from the affected passages.

---

186. Crane, *Perseus*, online: http://www.perseus.tufts.edu/hopper/morph?l=fanta%2Fsmata&la=greek&d=Perseus:text:1999.01.0145:book=1:section=325&i=1.

187. Feldman mentions several other places where Josephus replaces "angel of God" with "apparition" (*Ant.* 5.213, 277). Feldman, *Antiquities 1–4*, 1:120.

188. Feldman notes the differences in ordering between Gen 18:1–6 and *Ant.* 1.194–95 without observing the change in identity. Feldman, "Rearrangement," 257.

189. Levison, "Divine Spirit," 137–38.

Other Epiphany Narratives

Alexander's dream theophany is an example of an epiphany narrative without an OT parallel: "While he slept after the sacrifice, God warned (ἐξρημάτισεν . . . ὁ θεός) him in the dream to take courage . . ." (*Ant.* 11:327).[190] The narrative lacks sufficient detail for an analysis of its narrative structure. Fletcher-Louis uses this account as an example of "precedent in mainstream Jewish cultic practice for the worship of a human being,"[191] although he concedes that "the degree of recognition of Alexander's divinity" is "not entirely clear."[192]

Summary

Josephus is not compelled to modify the identity of figures from OT epiphanies. Yet he does demonstrate a tendency to eliminate ambiguity by introducing intermediaries that are clearly distinct from God.

Rabbinic Writings

Most of the rabbinic material available today is dated centuries later than Paul.[193] The Talmud consists of the Mishnah and Gemara. The Mishnah was compiled early in the third century CE;[194] while the Gemara, a commentary on the Mishnah, was first collected late in the fifth century, but did not reach its current form until centuries later.[195] The midrashim were not assembled until at least 400 CE.[196] Despite these late dates, the sources are still of some value not only because they confirm developments already seen in other sources, but also because they draw upon source material which extends as far back as 50 BCE.[197]

---

190. This account is discussed by Koet; unfortunately, he does not mention *Ant.* 11.327. Koet, "Dreams," 94–100.

191. Fletcher-Louis, "Alexander," 71.

192. Ibid., 102.

193. "It is nearly impossible to be sure of the wording of rabbinic traditions before 200 C.E. much less before 70 C.E." Segal, *Two Powers*, 43.

194. Brooks, "Mishnah," 871.

195. Porton, "Talmud," 313.

196. Neusner, *Genesis* 1:xi.

197. Brooks, "Mishnah," 871.

Mishnah and Talmud (post-200 CE)

The Mishnah is largely silent on matters relating to epiphany. It does, however, contain at least two intriguing prohibitions regarding *merkabah* visions. The first disallows the reading of Ezekiel's throne vision: "They do not use as the prophetic lection the selection of the chariot," although this opinion is not unanimous: "R. Judah permits" (*m. Meg.* 4:10 F, G).[198] Another section warns against even discussing *merkabah* visions:

> They do not expound upon the laws of prohibited relationships before three persons, the works of creation before two, or the Chariot before one, unless he was a sage and understands of his own knowledge. (*m. Ḥag.* 2:1 A-B)[199]

The Babylonian Talmud's commentary on this passage has an interesting comment concerning the number of firmaments: "R. Judah said: There are two firmaments . . . Resh Lakish said: seven . . ." (*b. Ḥag.* 12b).[200] It is perhaps more than a coincidence that seven is also the number of heavens most commonly found in *merkabah* visions, despite the rabbinic prohibition on discussing such visions.

Midrash (400–500 CE)

The Midrash on Genesis exhibits a tendency to introduce intermediaries. For example, in the commentary to Gen 18:1 Rabbi Hiyya introduces the angel Michael in the place of the Lord: "R. Hiyya taught on Tannaite authority, 'It was to the most important of them, Michael, that he spoke'" (*Gen. Rab.* 48:10 1B).[201] A similar modification is found in commentary on the appearance of the Angel of the Lord to Moses in the burning bush (Exod 3:2). Three rabbis are mentioned; each modifies the OT text by naming the angel:

> R. Johanan said: This is Michael; R. Hanina said it was Gabriel. Whenever they saw R. Jose the tall, they used to say, *there goes our holy Rabbi*, so also whenever Michael appeared, it was realized that there was the Glory of the *Shechinah*. (*Exod. Rab.* 2:5)[202]

---

198. Neusner, *Mishnah*, 324.
199. Ibid., 330.
200. *Babylonian Talmud*, 69.
201. Neusner, *Genesis* 2:184.
202. Lehrmah, *Exodus* 3:53.

It was demonstrated in the earlier discussion that in Exod 3–4 the Angel of the Lord is also characterized as God and Yahweh. In contrast, the rabbis characterize the angel as Michael, not God.

Summary

The rabbinic material considered in this section was compiled too late to be given primary significance. Yet it does confirm two trends already observed in earlier writings. First, there is evidence of an increasingly complex ouranology. Second, there is a tendency to introduce intermediaries when discussing OT texts, seemingly to remove ambiguity and eliminate confusion surrounding the identification of God with various angels.

LITERARY ASPECTS OF ANCIENT JEWISH EPIPHANIES

The literary aspects of ancient Jewish epiphany narratives will now be considered. We will first discuss aspects pertaining to event, or how the action of epiphanies is depicted. We will then consider the characterization of heavenly figures within epiphany narratives.[203]

Event

A number of observations may now be made with respect to the genre of epiphany in ancient Jewish literature. Many descriptive details such as bright lights and heavenly voices are common throughout the body of literature, as are specific human reactions such as fear and falling. In addition to these shared features, it is also possible to identify ways in which epiphany narratives differ. For example, setting seems to exhibit development over time. In later epiphanies it becomes more common for the adept to ascend into heaven, rather than for God to descend to earth. The heavenly realms to which the adept ascends become increasingly complex, from three levels (*T. Levi* 2:7) to five (*3 Bar.* 11:1–2), seven (as seen in accounts such as *2 Enoch*, the *Martyrdom and Ascension of Isaiah*, *3 Baruch*, and the *Apocalypse of Abraham*),[204] and possibly even ten.[205] An angelic escort may also appear to guide the adept through the

---

203. Literary criticism is discussed on pp. 24–31 above.

204. Poirier argues for the authenticity of an eighth level of heaven in the Apocalypse of Abraham. Poirier, "Ouranology," 393–408.

205. Cf. *2 En.* 22:1[J].

heavens to God's throne. For example, the angel Iaoel is sent to guide Abraham through heavenly visions (*Apoc. Ab.* 10:4); Phanuel guides Baruch (*3 Bar.* 1:1); two "huge men" accompany Enoch (*2 En.* 1:4–5); an angel takes Isaiah through seven heavens into God's presence (*Mart. Ascen. Isa.* 7:2); an angel of the Lord escorts Levi through three heavens to God's throne (*T. Levi* 2–5); and elsewhere (cf. *Apoc. Zeph.* A:(1), B:8, 2:1). In *4 Ezra*, the angelic escort remains even after the vision ends (*4 Ezra* 5:14–20). The increasingly complex ouranology practically requires the presence of such escorts.

In addition to these diachronic developments, it appears that epiphanies may be grouped into two distinct categories. The first category of Divine Initiative includes epiphanies where heavenly beings appear without the prior knowledge or expectation of their human counterparts in order to deliver a message or perform an action that is entirely unanticipated. In these epiphanies, heavenly beings do not appear at the behest of humans, but intrude unexpectedly into the lives of those to whom they appear. In such cases, the epiphany is not an end in itself. God and other heavenly beings do not appear merely in order to be seen, but in order to deliver a divine message or to accomplish a divinely appointed task. Some prominent examples include epiphanies we have already considered: Gen 18–19; Exod 3–4; 1 Sam 3; Tob 5–12; *Jub.* 16:1-4; *2 Enoch*; *Ladder of Jacob*; and *Testament of Abraham*.

The second category of Divine Response includes epiphanies where heavenly beings appear in response to a human request for a vision or appearance, or in answer to a human question or desire for knowledge. The most obvious cases of the Divine Response pattern involve an expression of the adept's desire to ascend, followed immediately by an epiphany in response to that desire.[206] *3 En.* 1:1-3 clearly illustrates this pattern:

> When I ascended to the height to behold the vision of the chariot, I entered six palaces, one inside the other, and when I reached the door of the seventh palace I paused in prayer before the Holy One, blessed be he; I looked up and said: "Lord of the Universe, grant, I beseech you, that the merit of Aaron . . . may avail for me now . . ." At once the Holy One, blessed be he, summoned

---

206. Rowland notes the pattern of ascent followed by *merkabah* vision: "Particularly worthy of note is the fact that in the apocalyptic texts the vision of the *merkabah* is preceded by an ascent to heaven." Rowland, "Apocalyptic," 173.

to my aid his servant, the angel Metatron, Prince of the Divine Presence.

Many earlier epiphany texts follow the same pattern. For example: Abraham's initial encounter with the angel comes in response to Abraham's prayer for guidance ("Shall I return to Ur . . . [o]r shall I dwell here in this place," *Jub.* 12:21); Baruch's *merkabah*-like vision is in response to his earlier questioning of God (*3 Bar.* 1:1–2); and God's appearance to Abraham follows a plea for revelation (*Apoc. Ab.* 7:12—8:2). Many such epiphany texts reveal a desire on the part of the human participant to have a vision of God, or to make an ascent to the throne. Of this pattern, Rowland comments that "such a need to travel to the world above to see visions of God contrasts with the biblical visions in which the heavenly journey plays no part."[207] Alexander also recognizes the desire for ascent, admitting uncertainty as to why the shift occurred: "It is not at all clear why the adepts wanted to make the ascent to the Merkabah."[208]

A significant number of other accounts also exhibit the Divine Response pattern, including: Job 38–42, in response to Job's petition (31:35); Hab 2:2–20, in response to Habakkuk's demand (2:1); Dan 9:21–27, in response to Daniel's prayer; *Testament of Levi*; *Testament of Job*; *Joseph and Asenath*; *3 Baruch*; *4 Ezra*; *Apocalypse of Abraham*; and *History of the Rechabites*. Not all of these accounts involve ascent, but they all involve epiphany in response to human initiative.

A significant difference between Divine Initiative and Divine Response epiphanies involves the certainty of outcome. The successful completion of Divine Initiative epiphanies is seldom in doubt, perhaps since initiative and purpose are associated with God through the epiphanic figure.[209] In contrast, Divine Response epiphanies may not reach a successful conclusion. While many ascents apparently[210] reach a

---

207. Rowland, *Open Heaven*, 80.

208. Alexander, "3 Enoch," 234.

209. One possible example of an unsuccessful outcome in a Divine Initiative epiphany is be found in Exod 33:7—34:28. While communing with God, Moses asks to see God's glory (33:18). God denies this request (33:20), but does grant that Moses may see his back (33:23; 34:5–7). Yet the divine purpose is achieved in the appearance (34:1–3), and Moses's request is partially granted (34:5–7).

210. Charlesworth takes the view that no adept ever sees the face of God. Charlesworth, *Pseudepigrapha*, 66.

successful conclusion (e.g., *1 En.* 14; *2 En.* 22; *T. Levi* 5:1), some do not. For example, Abraham hears God's voice and has visions of heaven but is not permitted to see God (*Apoc. Ab.* 16:3; 19:1), while Baruch is not permitted past the fifth heaven (*3 Bar.* 11:1–2). Rowland observes this phenomenon, noting the increasing tendency to avoid descriptions of God's appearance.[211]

The recognition of these categories of Divine Initiative and Divine Response epiphanies leads to several interesting questions. What is the relationship between the categories? Why do these categories exist? What are some of the implications of their existence? The relationship between Divine Initiative and Divine Response is well defined in most cases. The categories appear to be fairly static. Rewritten OT epiphanies tend to maintain their initial classification, although *Jub.* 12 is a notable exception. However, it is difficult to determine the appropriate classification of some specific epiphany narratives. For example, the appearance of the Angel of Yahweh to Manoah and his wife occurs in two stages. The angel first appears to Manoah's wife (Judg 13:2–7). When Manoah is told by his wife that a "man of God" had appeared to her (6), Manoah asks God to send the man again so that he can talk to him (8). In response, the man again appears (9–20). The initial appearance follows the Divine Initiative pattern, the second, clearly Divine Response. Yet the entire sequence, if taken as a whole, may be classified as Divine Initiative since the man of God does not initially appear in response to Manoah's wife.

The existential question may be addressed from a literary perspective. The categories may reflect a difference in perspective or emphasis for the various implied authors. In Divine Initiative epiphanies, the implied author uses an unexpected external event to propel the plot in an unanticipated direction (from the point of view of the human characters). The subsequent plot is often dependent on the unexpected message revealed in the epiphany, such as the birth of a child (e.g., Gen 18–19; *Jub.* 16) or the call of a prophet (Exod 3–4; 1 Sam 3). Conversely, in Divine Response epiphanies the implied author presents the human characters as participating in the development of the plot. In some cases the epiphany is an end in itself (e.g., *3 Baruch*). The implications for the two categories are primarily related to the role of God and other heavenly beings within the narrative. Divine Initiative places the onus for plot development on God, who acts independently from humans. In

---

211. Rowland, *Open Heaven*, 86.

Divine Response epiphanies, the relationship between God and humans is more cooperative.

There also appears to be a relationship between initiative and purpose. The purpose of Divine Initiative epiphanies appears to be typically divine. God usually initiates encounters so that a message might be communicated or an action performed. On the other hand, Divine Response epiphanies may have a human purpose that is related to the initial human request, such as seeing God or having a question answered (*Jub.* 12:16–17; *T. Job* 2–5; *Jos. Asen.* 14–17). Alternatively, Divine Response epiphanies may have a divine purpose that is unrelated to the initial human request (cf. *T. Levi* 2–5).

Character

The characterization[212] of epiphanic figures in ancient Jewish literature is daedal.[213] An overwhelming variety of heavenly beings appear, including: God (e.g., 2 Chr 1:7); the Angel of Yahweh (e.g., Gen 31:10); other angels (e.g., Gen 32:1; *Jub.* 1:27); cherubim (e.g., Gen 3:24; Ezek 10:1–22; *1 En.* 14:11); seraphim (e.g., Isa 6:2, 6; *1 En.* 61:10); men who seem to be more than human (e.g., Gen 18–19; Judg 13:6); a "divine hand" (e.g., Dan 5:24); the Son of Man (*1 En.* 46:3); a "mystically transformed"[214] human closely identified with God; "the chief of the house of the Most High" (*Jos. Asen.* 15:12x); and "the man from the sea," also described as the "Son of the Most High" (*4 Ezra* 13:37).

From this range of epiphanic figures, two distinct patterns of characterization for heavenly beings emerge. Type-I characterization involves depictions of God in angelomorphic or anthropomorphic form. Type-II characterization involves depictions of God in neither human nor angelic form.

In Type-I epiphanies, God is characterized in angelic or human form. This is particularly evident in early epiphanies. We have discussed several epiphanies that exhibit Type-I characterization, including Gen 18–19 (Yahweh, 18:1; three men, 18:2; two angels, 19:2), Exod 3–4 (Angel of Yahweh, 3:2; God, 3:5; Yahweh, 3:7), and Ezek 1–3 (God, 1:1; a man, 1:26; Yahweh, 2:4).

---

212. Literary theory related to characterization is discussed on pp. 28–31 above.
213. "Skillful, artistic; intricate." *Merriam-Webster's Collegiate Dictionary*, 11th ed.
214. Segal, "Risen Christ," 305.

Type-I characterization is also present in early Angel of Yahweh epiphanies. Scholars have characterized the Angel of Yahweh as a being distinct from Yahweh,[215] a transitional figure,[216] a primitive attempt to bridge the gap between God's immanence and transcendence,[217] a hypostasis,[218] a paradox,[219] a redactional artifact,[220] and a euphemism,[221] among other things.[222] A literary analysis of the OT Angel of Yahweh texts is revealing. In some cases, the epiphanic figure is directly characterized only as the Angel of Yahweh (Exod 14:19; 1 Kgs 19:5–7; 2 Kgs 1:3–4, 15; 19:35; Isa 37:36). In other cases, an angel similar to the Angel

---

215. "The Angel of the Lord is certainly distinguished from Jehovah." Liddon, *Divinity*, 53.

216. Westermann claims that the Angel of Yahweh is a convenient "transitional mode" between the "directness of God's revelation" to the Patriarchs and his later "withdrawal into the distance" during the time of the Judges. Westermann, *Prophetic Speech*, 100.

217. Dunn suggests that the Angel of Yahweh is most obviously explained as "an early, still unsophisticated attempt to speak of God's presence and activity on earth without resorting to even less sophisticated anthropomorphism or abandoning belief in God's holy otherness." Dunn, "Monotheistic," 323–24.

218. Gieschen is one of the more recent scholars to propose that the Angel of Yahweh is a divine hypostasis. He defines hypostases as "aspects of God that have degrees of distinct personhood." Gieschen, *Angelomorphic Christology*, 122.

219. The alternation between God and the Angel of Yahweh, according to Newsom, is "the expression of a tension or paradox: Yahweh's authority and presence in these encounters is to be affirmed, but yet it is not possible for human beings to have an unmediated encounter with God.... The unresolved ambiguity in the narrative allows the reader to experience the paradox." Newsom, "Angels," 252.

220. Newsom rightly observes that "the apparent interchangeability of the *mal'ak yhwh* and Yahweh cannot be resolved by assuming a clumsy merging of two traditional stories." Ibid.

221. White suggests that the Angel of Yahweh "is a euphemism for God used both to create tension in the narrative and to emphasize the transcendence of Yahweh." White, "Angel," 299.

222. Durham claims that the terms Yahweh, God, and Angel of Yahweh are used in Exod 3–4 to refer to "the same and single reality." Durham, *Exodus*, 31. Moberly qualifies his opinion with "apparently" and "virtually": "For the most part YHWH is a presence who speaks and who can be spoken to, but who does not usually appear in a form accessible to sight and touch. However, he does sometimes appear in the form (apparently) of a normal human being, most famously to Abraham at Mamre (Gen 18:1–33) and to Jacob at the ford of Jabbok (Gen 32:22–32), and is sometimes represented by an 'angel' (*mal'ak*, literally messenger) who is virtually indistinguishable from YHWH himself (Gen 22:11)." Moberly, *Genesis 12–50*, 20. Sarna notes that "the demarcation between God and His angels is often blurred." Sarna, *Genesis*, 383.

TABLE 1: Characterization of God as the Angel of Yahweh

Epiphany Text	Direct, by Narrator	Direct, by Angel	Direct, by Others	Indirect (by Angel)	Related Passages
Gen 16:7–14	Yes (13)		Yes (13)	Yes (10)	
Gen 21:17–21	Yes (17, 19)			Yes (18)	
Gen 22:11–19				Yes (12)	
Gen 31:10–13		Yes (13)		Yes (13)	Yes (Gen 28:13)
Exod 3:1–4:17	Yes (3:4)	Yes (6)		Yes (3:7f)	
Num 22:2–35	Yes? (22)			Yes (35)	Yes (Num 23:4–5, 16)
Judg 2:1–5				Yes (3)	
Judg 6:11–24	Yes (14)			Yes (14)	
Judg 13:1–23			Yes (22)		
2 Sam 24:15–25	No? (16)				
1 Chr 21:14–30	No? (15)				
2 Chr 32:21	No (21)				
Zech 1–3	No (1:12)				

of Yahweh is mentioned, but the title "Angel of Yahweh" is not used (Exod 23:20–33; 32–33). In these cases, the angel is distinguished from God.[223]

The remaining Angel of Yahweh texts may be divided into two sets according to the relationship between the Angel of Yahweh and God. In one set of epiphanies, the Angel of Yahweh appears to be characterized as God (Gen 16:7–14; 21:17–21; 22:11–19; 31:10–13; Exod 3:1–4:17; Num 22:2–35; Judg 2:1–5; 6:11–24; 13:1–23); in the other, the Angel of Yahweh is distinguished from God (2 Sam 24:15–25; 1 Chr 21:14–30; 2 Chr 32:21; Zech 1–3). The analysis of these texts is summarized in table 1 below. The table reveals that each epiphany is internally consistent in its own presentation of the Angel of Yahweh, especially where the Angel

---

223. In Exod 23, Yahweh refers to "an angel" (20), "my angel" (23). In Exod 32–33, the phrase "my angel" is repeated in 32:34; 33:2. This angel is not characterized as Yahweh, because the angel will go with the people (33:2) but Yahweh will not (33:3). The Angel of Yahweh is also mentioned throughout Zechariah.

of Yahweh is also characterized as God. The indirect evidence from these Angel of Yahweh narratives is also startling. In nearly every case where the angel is directly characterized as Yahweh, the angel speaks as though he were Yahweh (Gen 16:10; 21:18; 22:12; 31:13; Exod 3:7f; Num 22:35; Jug 2:3; 6:14).[224]

Thus, God is characterized as the Angel of Yahweh in numerous early epiphanies (Gen 16:7-14; 21:17-21; 22:11-19; 31:10-13; Exod 3:1-4:17; Num 22:2-35; Judg 2:1-5; 6:11-24; 13:1-23). God is also characterized as human or angelic in three previously considered epiphanies (Gen 18-19; Exod 3-4; Ezek 1-3). Similar Type-I characterization also occurs in other early epiphanies. For example, the figure who wrestles with Jacob (Gen 32:24-30) is characterized as both a man (24) and God (30). Similarly, the figure who appears to Joshua (Josh 5:13-6:5) is characterized as a man (5:13), the commander of Yahweh's army (5:15), and Yahweh (6:2). In each of these cases, humans are not characterized as anything other than human, while angels may appear in human form (Gen 19).

The relationships of Type-I characterization are illustrated in figure 3 below. The arrows from God to angels and humans indicate that God may also be characterized as angelic or human. The arrow from angels to humans indicates that angels may be characterized as humans. The arrows are directional, indicating that humans are not characterized as divine or angelic, and angels are not characterized as God.

Type-II characterization differs from Type-I in that God is portrayed distinctly from other beings, rather than in angelomorphic or anthropomorphic terms. First, God is not described in angelomorphic terms. This distinction between God and angels is seen in numerous epiphanies that mention an angel of Yahweh or God (e.g., Exod 23:20-33; 32-33; 2 Sam 24:15-25; 1 Chr 21:14-30; 2 Chr 32:21; Zech 1-3; *T. Levi* 2:7; *3 Bar.* 3:1). Named angels are also distinguished from God, including Gabriel (Dan 8:15-16; 9:21), Michael (*T. 12 Patr.*), Uriel (*4 Ezra* 4:1-2), and Iaoel (*Apoc. Ab.* 10:1). Even narratives that place angels and God in close proximity maintain this distinction. For example, the angel who appears to Zosimus is differentiated from the voice of God (*Hist. Rech.* 1:3).

---

224. This is typically not true of angels who are characterized as distinct from God (e.g., Gen 19:13).

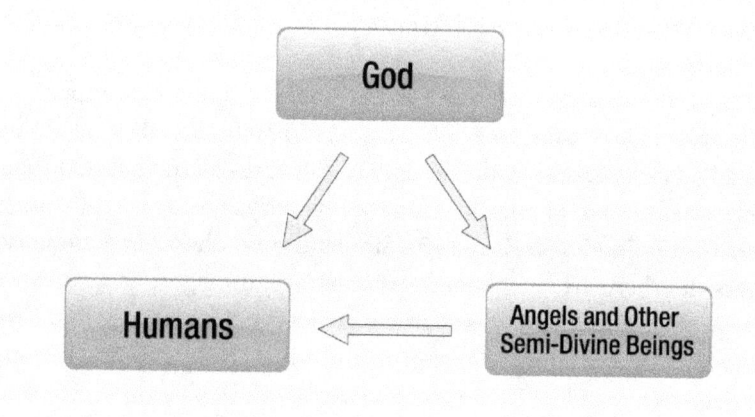

FIGURE 3: Type-I Characterization of Epiphanic Beings

Second, God is not described in anthropomorphic terms. This assertion has been disputed by some, including Fletcher-Louis, who argues that individuals "could at the same time be human, angelomorphic, and divine to the extent that they received worship."[225] Fletcher-Louis cites four examples in support of his claim: the High Priest (Diodorus Siculus), Moses (Ezekiel the Tragedian), Adam (*Life of Adam and Eve*), and the Son of Man (*1 Enoch*). An examination of these texts reveals that humans are indeed characterized as exalted heavenly beings, but are never characterized as God. We have already seen that Enoch's Son of Man is not characterized as God.[226] The same is true in each of the other three cases. Hecataeus describes the High Priest as a messenger (ἄγγελον) of God's commandments. The people worship (προσκυνεῖν) the High Priest when he expounds God's commandments to them.[227] Yet the High Priest is not characterized as God. Moses is not characterized as God in Ezekiel the Tragedian. Lines 68–82 describe a vision similar to Ezek 1–3, with a man on a heavenly throne (68–73). The

---

225. Fletcher-Louis, *Luke Acts*, 213–14.
226. See pp. 71–73 above.
227. Diodorus Siculus, *Library of History* 40.3.3–5.

man withdraws from the throne, gives Moses the scepter and crown, and asks him to mount the throne (74–6). Moses sees visions from the throne, but then wakes from his dream (77–82). The dream is then interpreted by Moses's father-in-law: "God gave you this as a sign for good.... For you shall cause a mighty throne to rise, and you yourself shall rule and govern men" (83–86). Yet Moses is not characterized as God. In *Life of Adam and Eve*, the devil tells of how he was cast out of heaven after the creation of Adam because he would not worship Adam as the image of God with Michael and the other angels (13:1—16:3). Yet, once again, Adam is not characterized as God. Each of these humans is distinguished from God,[228] even though the High Priest and Adam are described in angelomorphic terms.

Thus, the characterization of Type-II epiphanic figures may be summarized by the following three points. First, the boundary between God and all other beings, including other heavenly beings and humans, is impermeable. God is not characterized as either angelic or human, but remains utterly transcendent. He appears only as himself, or perhaps not at all (e.g., *Apoc. Ab.* 16:3; *3 Bar.* 11:1–2). In fact, Rowland notes the increasing tendency to avoid descriptions of God's appearance,[229] while Charlesworth claims that no adept ever sees the face of God.[230] Second, other heavenly beings are described in more exalted, God-like terms.[231] However, these exalted heavenly beings are simultaneously distinct from God.[232] Third, the boundary between angels and humans is completely

---

228. Hurtado agrees: "Conscientious Jews also maintained a distinction between the God of Israel and any of the exalted figures who could be seen as prominent in God's entourage, such as principal angels or revered human figures like Moses or Enoch ... This distinction was most clearly maintained in discouraging the worship of these figures." Hurtado, *Lord Jesus Christ*, 91.

229. Rowland, *Open Heaven*, 86.

230. Charlesworth, *Pseudepigrapha*, 66.

231. "God's activity, role and position in heaven are all more and more assumed by other entities (either an angelic figure, the Messiah himself, or some other hypostatization!)." Kreitzer, *Eschatology*, 89. Kreitzer recognizes the increasing category of "other entities," yet implicitly recognizes that they are still distinguishable from God in characterizing them as "other entities."

232. Hurtado makes a similar observation: "The exalted descriptions of the principal angel figure go hand in hand with a distinction between him and God.... The principal angel, however majestic his status in comparison to all other servants of God, and however closely he is associated with the exercise of God's will, remains essentially distinct from God." Hurtado, *One God*, 85–86. Likewise, Bauckham claims that most Jews "drew the line of distinction between the one God and all other reality clearly,

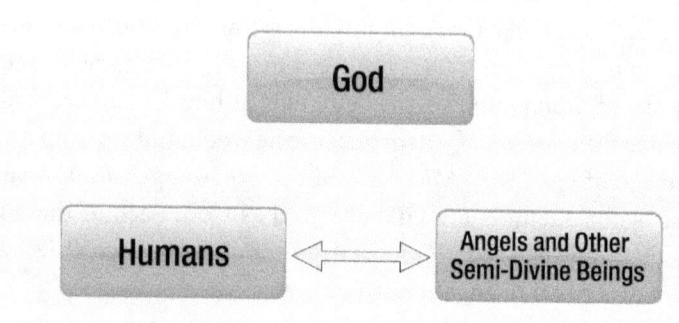

Figure 4: Type-II Characterization of Epiphanic Beings

permeable. As in epiphanies with Type-I characterization, angels may be described anthropomorphically. However, unlike Type-I epiphanies, humans may be characterized as exalted or angelomorphic beings.[233] While this phenomenon reaches perhaps its fullest expression centuries later in the exaltation of Enoch/Metatron (*3 En.* 4:1—16:5), we have already seen evidence of it in the Son of Man (*1 En.* 37–71) and Adam (*L.A.E.* 13:1—16:3). These relationships are illustrated in figure 4.

The relationship between the Type-I and Type-II patterns of characterization may best be observed in rewritten OT epiphanies.[234] Some of these rewritten narratives simply restate the original story, thus

---

and were in the habit of distinguishing the one God and all other reality by means of certain clearly articulated criteria. So-called intermediary figures were not ambiguous semi-divinities straddling the boundary between God and creation." Bauckham, *God Crucified*, 3. Stuckenbruck also notes the distinction between angels and God with respect to worship: "In none of the passages discussed is there any hint that in Judaism a *cultus* was being organized around angelic beings.... At the same time, the Jewish sources containing language in which angels are venerated cannot be pressed so neatly into a *non-cultic* category." Stuckenbruck, "Herodian," 68.

233. As we have seen, "Texts where humans are *angelomorphic*—angelic in status or nature, though without necessarily having their identity reduced to that of an angel—have been the subject of a flurry of studies in recent years." Fletcher-Louis, "Reflections," 292.

234. Alexander proposes the "principal characteristics" of the "rewritten Bible" in Alexander, "Retelling," 116–18.

maintaining the earlier type of characterization. However, a wide range of sources replace Type-I characterization with Type-II. For example, we have already seen that *Jubilees* introduces intermediaries in several cases (*Jub.* 12:24, 16:1-4). The *Ladder of Jacob* introduces the archangel Sariel as the one who changes Jacob's name (*Lad. Jac.* 4:1-3). Ezra's commission, echoing Exod 3-4, introduces a voice to replace the Angel of Yahweh/Yahweh/Elohim (*4 Ezra* 14:1b). Similarly, the epiphanies of Abraham, Isaac, and Jacob are retold with the archangel Michael acting as the intermediary between the Master God and the patriarchs (*T. Ab.* 1:4; 2:1; 5:1; *T. Isaac* 2:1, 5:4; *T. Jac.* 1:6, 2:5). Josephus also introduces intermediaries in retelling OT epiphanies.[235] For example, the three men of Gen 18-19 are also characterized as God and two angels; Josephus characterizes them as three angels (*Ant.* 1.196-98). A similar shift is also found in rabbinic writings. For example, in the Midrash on Gen 18, the angel Michael is introduced in the place of God (*Gen. Rab.* 48:10 1B). Similarly, in the Midrash on Exod 3-4, Michael replaces the Angel of Yahweh (*Exod. Rab.* 2:5). The Septuagint also replaces Type-I characterization with Type-II in some cases.[236] For example, "and they saw the God of Israel" is changed to "and they saw the place there where the God of Israel stood" (Exod 24:10); "and they saw God" to "and they were seen in the place of God" (Exod 24:11); "I said, 'I will not see Yah'" to "I said, 'I will no longer see the salvation of God'" (Isa 38:11); "I will see God" to "for from the Lord these things will be accomplished for me" (Job 19:26). In these cases, direct contact with God is replaced by indirect contact, or removed entirely.

The reasons for this dynamic relationship between Type-I and Type-II characterizations are unclear. It may be that the implied authors of Type-II epiphanies viewed the original Type-I characterization as unrealistic, unintelligible, unacceptable theologically, or unhelpful for their implied readers. For example, Josephus's changes have been attributed to his Gentile Roman audience.[237] Or, it may be that the later implied authors are reflecting a different understanding of God, or of the rela-

---

235. Levison, "Divine Spirit," 137-38.

236. "The LXX altered the texts that speak of a vision of God apart from theophanies and visions (Ex. 24:10-11; Isa. 38:11; Ps. 63:3[2]; Job 19:26-27; 33:26; cf. Ps. 11:7; 17:15), substituting another object for 'God'... translating a different text... or using a passive construction." Fuhs, "רָאָה," 13:242.

237. Levison, "Divine Spirit," 137-38.

tionship between God and humans. Or, the changes may reflect cultural changes or foreign influence.[238] Whatever the reasons may be, it does appear that Type-I characterization is less common and less familiar than Type-II.

It is difficult to propose why the two types of characterization exist, particularly in light of the tendency for Type-I characterization to be replaced by Type-II. It is possible that different implied authors are wrestling with the characterization of such an unfamiliar character as God. Epiphanies that describe God in Type-I terms use human language to depict him. In other words, the other is described in familiar ways. Conversely, in Type-II epiphanies God remains distinctly other, even though humans and angels are described in increasingly fantastic or exaggerated anthropomorphic terms.

The relationship between the patterns of initiative and character appears to be complex. Type-I characterization appears frequently in early Divine Initiative epiphanies such as the Gen 18–19 and the early Angel of Yahweh epiphanies; it also occurs in later Divine Initiative epiphanies such as Ezek 1–3. Yet Divine Initiative epiphanies may also exhibit Type-II characterization, such as in some rewritten OT epiphanies. Divine Response epiphanies seem to prefer Type-II characterization; yet Job may be an example of a Divine Response epiphany with Type-I characterization. Therefore, it is not possible to determine the pattern of characterization based solely on the type of initiative, or vice versa.

CONCLUSION

Several key observations have emerged from this discussion of ancient Jewish epiphany narratives. First, there appear to be two distinct patterns pertaining to event. In Divine Initiative epiphanies, heavenly beings appear without the prior knowledge or expectation of their human counterparts in order to deliver a message or perform an action that is entirely unanticipated. In Divine Response epiphanies, heavenly beings appear in response to a human request for a vision or appearance, or in answer to a human question or desire for knowledge. Second, there appear to be two distinct patterns of characterization. Epiphanies with Type-I characterization depict God in angelomorphic or anthropo-

---

238. Rowland asserts that "the conditions existed within Jewish religion for the ready acceptance" of a more developed cosmology. Rowland, *Open Heaven*, 83. It seems reasonable that a similar argument might be made for the changes in characterization.

morphic form. Epiphanies with Type-II characterization do not depict God in either human or angelic form. These fundamental categories of event and character will inform our discussion of Paul's Damascus road encounter.

3

Paul's Epistles

INTRODUCTION

According to the New Testament, Paul's life as a follower of Jesus began when Jesus appeared to him on the Damascus road. Paul's epistles are written from a first-person perspective.[1] Therefore, in his epistles Paul is both narrator of and participant in the DRE. For the most part, the epistles are not presented in narrative form.[2] Fortunately, the narrative substructure of the DRE is most clearly seen in Gal 1–2, which contains Paul's most extensive discussion of the DRE.[3] While Gal 1 is the primary account, Paul also references the DRE elsewhere in his epistles. All the relevant evidence will be considered in order to reconstruct a composite portrait.[4]

We will now examine Paul's own testimony concerning this pivotal event in two sections. In the first section, an exegetical analysis of the relevant DRE texts will be performed. In the second section, the literary aspects of the DRE texts will be discussed, particularly in relation to the event itself, and the characterization of Jesus within the DRE.

---

1. For a discussion of first-person narration, see Romberg, *First-Person*.

2. Hays proposes a narrative approach to Paul, but his approach involves a search for the narrative of the gospel, not of Paul's life. Hays, *Faith*, 29. Hays is credited with "(re)introducing" this approach to Paul; so Dunn, "Narrative Approach," 218. Hays observes that other scholars have identified the narrative aspects of Gal 1–2. Hays, *Faith*, 29–30. See also the various discussions in Longenecker, ed., *Narrative Dynamics*.

3. "It is significant that, with the exception of Gal 1–2, Paul in his extant writings never actually tells a story." Watson, "Story," 239.

4. Barclay discusses the narrative aspects of Gal 1:10—2:14 in Barclay, "Paul's Story." Dunn discusses the dangers of a narrative approach to Paul in Dunn, "Narrative Approach."

EXEGESIS

In order to avoid any doubts concerning the authenticity of the conclusions that result from this study, only the undisputed Pauline epistles will be examined. We will examine the letters chronologically, with one possible exception. Galatians will be examined first, primarily because it contains the most explicit discussion of the DRE. However, it may also be first chronologically if the South Galatian theory is accurate.[5] The other epistles containing allusions to the DRE will be examined according to the generally accepted chronological order: 1 and 2 Corinthians, Romans, and Philippians.[6]

Paul makes reference to his DRE on at least several occasions. According to Murphy-O'Connor, the allusions "on which all agree" include Gal 1:12, 16; 1 Cor 9:1; 15:8.[7] Other texts have been suggested by various scholars.[8] For instance, Kim includes Rom 1:1; 12:3; 15:15; 1 Cor 1:1; 3:10; 9:16–17; 2 Cor 1:1; 3:4–4:6; 5:16; Gal 1:1–2:9; Phil 3:4–11.[9] Wright considers Gal 1:11–17; 1 Cor 9:1; 15:8–11; 2 Cor 4:6; 12:1–4.[10] Schnelle identifies 1 Cor 9:1; 15:3–8; Gal 1:12–16; 2 Cor 4:6; Phil 3:4b–11.[11] Newman lists even more.[12] Rather than relying solely on the analysis of others, we will begin with a broad range of texts, and eliminate those whose relevance cannot be established.

---

5. For example, Longenecker dates Galatians no later than 49 CE. Longenecker, *Galatians*, lxxiii, lxxxviii.

6. For example, see Betz, "Paul," 191–92; Fitzgerald, "Philippians," 322; Schnelle, *Apostle Paul*, 192–386.

7. Murphy-O'Connor, *Critical Life*, 71.

8. Dietzfelbinger lists four primary texts (Gal 1:15; 1 Cor 9:1; 15:8; 2 Cor 4:6) and numerous others where the DRE stands in the background (Rom 1:1; 5:3; 11:3; 12:3; 15:15, 16, 18; 1 Cor 1:1; 2 Cor 3:7–11; Gal 1:11, 16; 2:2, 7–9; Phil 3:4b–11; 1 Thess 2:16). Dietzfelbinger, *Berufung*, 44.

9. Kim, *Origin*, 3–29. Kim also includes the deutero-Pauline texts of Eph 3:13 and Col 1:23c–29 (20–25).

10. Wright, *Resurrection*, 378–88.

11. Schnelle, *Apostle Paul*, 87–90.

12. 1 Cor 9:1; 15:3–11; Gal 1:11–17; Phil 3:2–15; 2 Cor 3:4—4:6; Rom 10:2–4; 1 Cor 9:16–17; 2 Cor 5:16; Eph 3:1–13; Rom 1:5; 15:15; 1 Cor 3:10; 15:10; Gal 1:9; Eph 3:2, 7, 8; Col 1:25. Newman, *Glory-Christology*, 165–66.

Galatians

Rather than beginning with the more limited pericope of Gal 1:11–17, we will investigate the passage from the salutation (1:1–17).

In addition to Kim, many scholars consider Gal 1:1–10 to be related to the DRE. For example, Dunn remarks that Paul "clearly . . . had his experience on the Damascus road already in mind."[13] Similarly, Burton comments that Paul "affirms in the very salutation of the letter his *direct commission as an apostle from Jesus Christ and God the Father*."[14] The connection of 1:1–10 to the DRE will become more apparent as we examine the text in detail. Some of the more obvious connections include both Paul's claim to be a messenger from Jesus and God the Father (1–5; cf. 15–16b) and the origin of his message (6–10; cf. 11, 16b).

Since this text is so crucial to our understanding of the DRE, it is translated in its entirety below. This translation reflects the NA[27] text. Textual variants that may affect this discussion are noted in the footnotes. Uncertainties that affect the meaning of the text will also be raised in the exegetical notes.

> **1:1** Paul, an apostle neither from people nor by a person, but by Jesus Christ and God the Father who raised him from the dead,
>
> **2** and all the brothers with me,
>
> To the churches of Galatia,
>
> **3** Grace and peace to you from God our[15] Father and the Lord Jesus Christ, **4** who gave himself for[16] our sins, that he might res-

---

13. Dunn, *Galatians*, 27.

14. Burton, *Galatians*, 1. Goulder states that the opening verse of Galatians is "the opening broadside of a battle running from 1:11 to 2:14." Goulder, "Pauline Epistles," 489. Hübner concurs. "Ansatzweise ist aber schon das Präskript in die theologische Argumentation des Briefes einbezogen." Hübner, *Paulus*, 2:58. Fung notes that the salutation "occasionally [anticipates] the contents of the letter in summary fashion." Fung, *Galatians*, 35.

15. The position of ἡμῶν relative to θεοῦ πατρὸς and κυρίου Ἰησοῦ Χριστοῦ is in doubt. The NA[27] text, based primarily on the evidence of ℵ A and "Paul's usage elsewhere." (*TCGNT*, 520), places ἡμῶν with the former; 𝔓[46, 51vid] B D et al., with the latter; less reliable witnesses omit ἡμῶν or include a ἡμῶν with both. Fortunately, the placement of ἡμῶν is not critical to this discussion.

16. The text, supported by 𝔓[51] ℵ[1] B et al., reads ὑπέρ. Other variants, such as 𝔓[46] ℵ* A et al., read περί. Ὑπέρ and περί are frequently interchanged (BDAG, 1030) due to their overlapping semantic domains. Ὑπέρ is preferred, but περί is its semantic equivalent in this case.

cue us from the present evil age,[17] according to the will of God our Father, 5 to whom be the glory for evermore, amen.

6 I marvel at how quickly you are turning away from the one who called you by the grace of Christ,[18] to a different gospel 7 (which is not another gospel)—but some are confusing you and wish to distort the gospel of Christ. 8 But even if we or an angel from heaven should proclaim[19] to you[20] contrary to what we proclaimed to you, let him be cursed. 9 As we have already said, even now I say again: if anyone preaches to you contrary to what you received, let him be cursed.

10 Am I now striving to persuade people or God? Or am I now seeking to please people? If I am still pleasing people, I am not being a slave of Christ.

11 For[21] I make known to you, brothers, that the gospel preached by me is not according to a person—12 for I neither received it from a person, nor[22] was I taught it—but by a revelation of Jesus Christ.

13 For you have heard[23] of my way of life while in Judaism, that to an extraordinary degree I persecuted the church of God and

---

17. The text, supported by 𝔓[46, 51vid] ℵ* A B et al., places the adjective ἐνεστῶτος in the second attributive position. Other manuscripts, including ℵ² D F G, place it in the first attributive position. Both readings have the same meaning, and NA²⁷ uses the better supported variant.

18. Χριστοῦ is present in 𝔓[51vid] ℵ A B Ψ 33 81 614 1739, Ἰησοῦ Χριστοῦ in D. On the other hand, ἐν χάριτι has no qualifying genitive in 𝔓[46vid] G H[vid] and numerous church fathers. NA²⁷ encloses Χριστοῦ in square brackets to indicate the uncertainty as to whether it is a later addition.

19. The verb has three primary variants. Only one weakly supported reading, εὐαγγελίζεται, is not subjunctive. The other two main variants, εὐαγγελίζηται and εὐαγγελίσηται, are subjunctive; the former has stronger support (𝔓[51vid] B D(*) F G et al.).

20. The text reads εὐαγγελίζηται ὑμῖν. The pronoun is in doubt, but has strong support from many important witnesses (including 𝔓[51vid] ℵ² A B D(*) H K L P 6 33 81), and is implied by the middle form of εὐαγγελίζω ("w. mention of the thing proclaimed, as well as of the pers. who receives the message," BDAG, 402) in any event.

21. Some witnesses contain the subordinating conjunction γάρ, which is favored by NA²⁷. Others contain the coordinating conjunction δέ. Metzger notes that that the evidence is "almost evenly balanced" between the two. *TCGNT*, 521.

22. The NA²⁷ reading οὔτε is supported only by 𝔓⁴⁶ B D¹ 𝔐. Οὐδέ is support by ℵ A D*·ᶜ F G al. The difference between the two "and not's" is insignificant.

23. Ἠκούσατε is functioning as a consummative aorist (*GGBTB*, 559–60; cf. NRSV, NASB: "you have heard").

sought to destroy it, **14** and that I advanced in Judaism beyond many contemporaries among my people, being a far greater zealot for the traditions of my forefathers. **15** But when [God,][24] the one who separated me from my mother's womb and called me by his grace, was pleased **16** to reveal his son to me so that I might preach him among the nations, I did not immediately consult with flesh and blood **17** nor did I go up[25] to Jerusalem to those who were apostles before me, but I went to Arabia and again returned to Damascus.

Galatians 1:1–5

It may be unexpected that the salutation merits our attention. Yet Paul seizes every opportunity from the very outset to confront the Galatians with his divine authority as a messenger from God. Therefore, it is not surprising that the salutation is pertinent to the DRE.

Galatians 1:1

In many respects, the salutation of the epistle to the Galatians is quite typical. It contains the three elements common to the salutation of most Greek letters: author (1–2a), recipients (2b), and greeting (3–5).[26] However, Paul also uses the salutation in a unique way: not only to introduce himself, but also to establish from the outset his authority as a messenger from God.

The author identifies himself by name, Παῦλος, and title, ἀπόστολος. The title ἀπόστολος has the general meaning of messenger,[27] yet in the

---

24. ὁ θεὸς is present in some reliable witnesses (א A D Ψ et al.), but absent from others ($\mathfrak{P}^{46}$ B F G et al.). The editorial committee for NA[27] included ὁ θεός based on the "preponderance of external testimony." *TCGNT*, 521. Indeed, the best argument in favor of ὁ θεός may be the diversity of versions that include the reading "God." Early versions listed by UBS[4] in support of this reading include it[d] (V), cop[sa] (IV), eth (VI), and geo (V). Metzger dissents, claiming that ὁ θεός is more likely a scribal gloss, which would not likely be omitted from the text if it were original. *TCGNT*, 521–22. Metzger's view is also compatible with many early versions, including it[b] (V), it[f] (VI), it[o] (VII), vg (IV/V), and syr[p] (V). Since the evidence appears to be evenly divided, it is impossible to declare with certainty whether ὁ θεός should be included in the text given the nearly equal division of evidence.

25. The text reads ἀνῆλθον, per א A Ψ et al. Other witnesses, including $\mathfrak{P}^{51}$ B D F G, read ἀπῆλθον. $\mathfrak{P}^{46}$ reads ἦλθον. The directionality of ἀνῆλθον and ἀπῆλθον is not significant to the meaning of the text.

26. Longenecker, *Galatians*, 1.

27. L&N, §33.194.

NT it may refer to a special messenger of Jesus Christ.[28] Paul invokes this second, more specific meaning in claiming divine authority from the outset of the letter. As Burton succinctly notes, "the title is certainly not . . . a mere title of dignity, but involves an assertion, the maintenance of which is essential to the purpose of the letter."[29]

Paul begins with a twofold denial of any human involvement in his commissioning. First, Paul denies that the ultimate agent[30] is human: οὐκ ἀπ' ἀνθρώπων. The preposition ἀπό is used to indicate the ultimate agent,[31] or "more remote cause."[32] The construction ἀπό + genitive normally occurs with a passive verb when expressing agency.[33] In this case, however, it modifies the verbal noun ἀπόστολος. The agent ἀνθρώπων indicates that Paul denies any ultimate human responsibility for his apostolic authority. Paul next denies that the intermediate agent of his apostleship is human: οὐδὲ δι' ἀνθρώπου. The preposition διά is used to indicate agency,[34] or more precisely, the intermediate agent.[35] By denying both ultimate and intermediate human agency, Paul forges a thorough, considered, and exhaustive denial of human responsibility for his apostleship.

Having thus denied human origin, Paul now affirms the divine origin of his calling: ἀλλὰ διὰ Ἰησοῦ Χριστοῦ καὶ θεοῦ πατρὸς τοῦ ἐγείραντος αὐτὸν ἐκ νεκρῶν. Ἀλλά introduces the contrast from the preceding denials[36] as Paul moves from a negative to a positive identification of his sender.

---

28. L&N, §53.74.

29. Burton, *Galatians*, 1–2.

30. Wallace delineates three types of agency. *GGBTB*, 431–35. First, the ultimate agent, also known as the principal or sole cause, the originator, or the source, refers to the one who is finally responsible for an action. Second, the intermediate agent, also known as the efficient cause, or simply the agent, refers to one who may be used by an ultimate agent to complete an action. The third type of agency, impersonal means, refers to what an agent may use to complete an action; however, "means does not indicate agency, except in a broad sense" (431).

31. *GGBTB*, 432.

32. BDAG, 106.

33. *GGBTB*, 433.

34. BDAG, 225.

35. *GGBTB*, 432.

36. BDAG, 44.

The relationship between the negative and positive assertions is not entirely clear. The former section contains both ἀπό and διά; the latter, only διά. The function of this second διά has been a matter of some controversy. Bruce notes the difficulty of this section, calling it "strange" to find διά repeated before Ἰησοῦ Χριστοῦ.[37] One possible resolution involves interpreting the second διά differently from the first; another approach views the section as a chiasm[38] with an implied ἀπό before θεοῦ πατρός. Bruce is typical of the former position. He interprets the second διά "in the more general sense of agency" rather than with reference to intermediate agency in particular.[39] Fung agrees,[40] which appears to contradict his earlier statement that Paul "asserts that his apostolic commission, with regard to both its source and its mediation, was from God and Christ."[41] Indeed, this statement seems to acknowledge the symmetry of the section. Betz notes that "'through Jesus Christ' stands juxtaposed with 'through [a] man' as 'God the Father' is contrasted with 'through men.'"[42] Longenecker,[43] following Bligh,[44] understands the section to be chiastic in nature, although Betz makes it clear that it is not necessary to complete the chiasm by assuming ἀπό before θεοῦ πατρός.[45] Betz's interpretation seems most likely. The two-fold affirmation of Jesus and God the Father complements the two-fold denial in the opening statement.[46]

---

37. Bruce, *Galatians*, 72.

38. Scholer and Snodgrass define chiasm by its two fundamental elements: "inversion and balance," which are often accompanied by a third, "climactic centrality, when the inversion has a middle element." Scholer and Snodgrass, "1992 Preface," vii. Resseguie omits the element of balance, preferring to emphasize inversion, which he terms "the crossover pattern of words, phrases, clauses or ideas." See Resseguie, *Narrative Criticism*, 58–60. For a discussion on the use of chiasm, see Lund, *Chiasmus*, 30–47. See also Welch, "Introduction." Welch lists fifteen criteria for identifying chiasms in Welch, "Identifying Chiasmus."

39. Bruce, *Galatians*, 73.

40. Fung, *Galatians*, 37.

41. Ibid., 36.

42. Betz, *Galatians*, 39.

43. Longenecker, *Galatians*, 5.

44. Bligh, *Galatians*, 61.

45. Betz also makes the apparently contradictory assertion that διά should be interpreted "more in terms of ultimate source than agency." Betz, *Galatians*, 39n23.

46. See pp. 176–77 above.

Paul identifies the one who commissioned him as Ἰησοῦ Χριστοῦ καὶ θεοῦ πατρός. Jesus is presented first, before God the Father. This is surprising for several reasons. First, it gives Jesus the prominence of first mention, rather than God the Father. Paul obviously did not have any difficulty in mentioning Jesus before the Father (cf. Rom 1:1), yet several commentators have noted this ordering as a potential problem. Longenecker calls the ordering strange, without providing an explanation.[47] Betz views this as a function of the text, with Paul returning to the "proper hierarchical order" in verse 3.[48] Apparently, Paul views the first mention of Jesus as neither strange nor improper.

Equally unexpected is the fact that Paul mentions a person, Jesus Christ, immediately after his vehement denials of any human agency. This should not be viewed as a denial of Jesus's humanity. Indeed, Paul explicitly affirms Jesus's humanity in Rom 5:15 with phrase τοῦ ἑνὸς ἀνθρώπου Ἰησοῦ Χριστοῦ.[49] Thus, it is unlikely that Paul is denying Jesus's humanity. Why, then, would he choose to exclude Jesus from humanity? Fung proposes that he may be ascribing a glorified status to Jesus.[50] This appears to echo Bruce, who refers to Jesus as "risen and exalted."[51] Yet Jesus's exalted status does not appear to be a sufficient explanation for his exclusion from humanity, since Paul could surely afford Jesus such a status without denying his humanity. Rather, it appears that Paul views Jesus as much more than a mere human. He presents Jesus as inseparable from the Father.

This close association between Jesus Christ and God the Father is also affirmed grammatically by their union under the single preposition διά.[52] Jesus and God the Father are presented as the single source of Paul's apostleship.[53] Jesus's close connection with God the Father may be

---

47. Longenecker, *Galatians*, 4.

48. Betz, *Galatians*, 41.

49. A similar statement is found in a disputed Pauline epistle: ἄνθρωπος Χριστὸς Ἰησοῦς (1 Tim 2:5).

50. "The juxtaposition of 'Jesus Christ' and 'God the Father' under one preposition reflects the exalted status which Christ holds in Paul's understanding." Fung, *Galatians*, 37.

51. Bruce, *Galatians*, 73.

52. Blass notes that "the originator is probably also denoted by διά instead of the agent." BDF, §223(2).

53. Burton observes that "Jesus Christ and God the Father are not separated in his mind as sustaining different relations to his apostleship, but are conceived of jointly and as sustaining one relation." Burton, *Galatians*, 5.

just as shocking as his exclusion from humanity. Indeed, the remainder of the διά clause strengthens the close connection that Paul is making between Jesus Christ and God the Father. The clause is structured as follows:

    A – διὰ Ἰησοῦ Χριστοῦ καὶ
    B – θεοῦ πατρὸς
    B' – τοῦ ἐγείραντος
    A' – αὐτὸν [ἐκ νεκρῶν,]

This presentation of Jesus Christ and God the Father forms a chiasm.[54] Just as Paul has united Jesus with God semantically, as distinct from humanity, and grammatically, under one preposition, he now does so literally, within a tightly woven chiasm. It is therefore not unreasonable to conclude that the source of Paul's apostleship is a single strand which leads inseparably to both Jesus Christ and God the Father.

Galatians 1:3-5

Paul, having introduced himself and addressed the recipients of his letter, now closes the salutation with a greeting. The invocation, χάρις ὑμῖν καὶ εἰρήνη, is typically Pauline (cf. Rom 1:7; 1 Cor 1:3; 2 Cor 1:2; Phil 1:2; 1 Thess 1:1; 2 Thess 1:2; Phlm 3), but the subsequent qualifying prepositional clause is much more interesting. Having already presented himself as a messenger from God (1), Paul now gives a précis of his message (3–4). Once again, God the Father and Jesus Christ are united under one preposition. Here, they are united under ἀπό as the joint single source of grace and peace. Yet again, they are found in chiasm:

    B – ἀπὸ θεοῦ πατρὸς ἡμῶν
      A – καὶ κυρίου Ἰησοῦ Χριστοῦ
      A' – τοῦ δόντος ἑαυτὸν ὑπὲρ τῶν ἁμαρτιῶν ἡμῶν,
      A" – ὅπως ἐξέληται ἡμᾶς ἐκ τοῦ αἰῶνος τοῦ ἐνεστῶτος πονηροῦ[55]
    B' – κατὰ τὸ θέλημα τοῦ θεοῦ καὶ πατρὸς ἡμῶν

Paul presents Jesus Christ and God the Father in a chiasm similar to that of Gal 1:1. Here, however, Paul reverses the order in which the Father and Jesus are presented. Thus, the two chiasms in the salutation of

---

54. This structure is not noted by commentators such as Betz, Bruce, Burton, Dunn, Fung, and Longenecker.

55. This chiasm has a tripartite center. In his first law of chiastic structure, Lund confirms that a chiasm may take such a form: "*(1) The centre is always the turning point.* The centre . . . may consist of one, two, three, or even four lines." Lund, *Chiasmus*, 40.

Galatians have the form ABBA and BAAAB. In other words, Paul interchanges Jesus with the Father twice, and even interchanges the order of presentation. These reversed chiasms reveal how closely Paul associates Jesus Christ with God the Father, and vice versa. Furthermore, it shows that, for Paul, the order in which the two occur is irrelevant. He does not consistently give priority of first mention to either.

Thus, Paul's salutational presentation of Jesus Christ and God the Father is fascinating. They maintain distinct identities, as witnessed by their different names. They also maintain distinct roles, with Jesus as "the one who gave himself for our sins" (3), and the Father as the one "who raised [Jesus] from the dead" (1). Yet, for Paul, they share a bond that supersedes Jesus's very humanity.

GALATIANS 1:6–10

In this section, Paul marvels at how quickly the Galatians turned away from the gospel of Christ (τὸ εὐαγγέλιον τοῦ Χριστοῦ, v. 7). Verses 8 and 10 in particular merit our consideration.

Galatians 1:8

In verse 8, Paul emphasizes the primacy of his message by contrasting it with any other non-divine message. The earlier distinction between humans and God (1) reappears with further refinement.

The verse takes the form of a third-class conditional sentence, having ἐάν with a subjunctive verb in the protasis.[56] The entire protasis may be translated, "But even if we or an angel from heaven should preach to you contrary to what we preached to you." While the situation being described is theoretically possible, it is also "somewhat doubtful," as the subjunctive mood suggests.[57] The subject is compound: ἡμεῖς ἢ ἄγγελος ἐξ οὐρανοῦ. The first half of the subject, "we," may refer to Paul and the ἀδελφοί with him (2),[58] or more likely Paul alone[59] if taken as an epistolary plural.[60] The second half, "an angel from heaven," is rather more interesting. The primary meaning for ἄγγελος is messenger,[61] which may

---

56. *GGBTB*, 689.
57. Longenecker, *Galatians*, 16.
58. Fung, *Galatians*, 47.
59. Martyn, *Galatians*, 113.
60. *GGBTB*, 396.
61. BDAG, 8.

or may not be human. Paul clearly implies that the messengers are angels by including the phrase ἐξ οὐρανοῦ, "from heaven." Thus, Paul begins the protasis by grouping humans together with angels.

The apodosis, "let him be cursed," reveals the fate of one who would deliver a different message. Although God is not mentioned explicitly by the text, he is clearly understood as the one who curses.[62]

Thus, Paul has constructed another contrast regarding his message, the gospel of Christ, to which he has been called as an apostle. Earlier, he distinguished humans from Jesus Christ and God the Father (1). Here, he distinguishes both human and heavenly messengers from God. The two contrasts may be taken together, since both relate to the veracity of Paul's message. The combination provides a startling conclusion. Paul views humans and angels in contrast to God the Father, yet understands Jesus to be united with God the Father as the sole source of his message. In other words, Paul places Jesus on the same plane as God the Father, even in contrast with angels from heaven.[63]

Galatians 1:10

In this verse Paul draws several related contrasts. The verse begins with a question (Ἄρτι γὰρ ἀνθρώπους πείθω ἢ τὸν θεόν;) and ends with a second-class (contrary to fact) conditional statement (εἰ ἔτι ἀνθρώποις ἤρεσκον, Χριστοῦ δοῦλος οὐκ ἂν ἤμην).[64] In the former, Paul contrasts humanity and God; in the latter, he contrasts humanity and Jesus. Based on the parallelism between the question and the statement, Paul has once again united God and Jesus in contrast to humanity.

---

62. Louw and Nida suggest that this may be translated as "I would wish that God himself had cursed me" (§33.474). Behm notes that the curse involves "the delivering up to the judicial wrath of God." Behm, "ἀνάθεμα, ἀνάθημα, κατάθεμα," 1:354. For Martyn, God is clearly implied: "Paul does not need literally to identify it as *God's* curse." Martyn, *Galatians*, 114.

63. Longenecker proposes that Paul "seems to equate the 'angel of God' with 'Christ Jesus'" (Gal 4:14). Longenecker, "Motifs," 532. He repeats this claim in Longenecker, *Christology*, 31. In the light of Gal 1:8, I find Longenecker's proposal that Paul "seems to equate the 'angel of God' with 'Christ Jesus'" (Gal 4:14) to be rather dubious. Here, Paul uses a pattern of intensification from "we" to "an angel of heaven." The angel is clearly the greatest level of being to which he could conceivably appeal, since it would be inconceivable for Paul that Jesus could preach a different gospel. In the later verse, Paul uses a similar pattern of intensification, from an "angel of God" to "Christ Jesus" (Gal 4:14). Paul seems to mark Jesus as being greater than an angel of God, rather than merely identifying him in angelic terms.

64. Such conditional sentences are rare in Paul. See BDF, §360(4); *GGBTB*, 695–96.

Galatians 1:11–17

In the preceding verses (7–10), Paul expresses his displeasure with the Galatians concerning their departure from his gospel message. He now moves to establish the authority of his message by revealing the nature and source of his calling. Therefore, this pericope forms the basis of Paul's argument in the epistle. It is also the most explicit autobiographical account of Paul's calling in the undisputed Pauline corpus. Hence, it deserves detailed attention.

Here is the basic narrative structure[65] of Paul's account, which will provide a useful framework for the exegesis of the passage:

Introduction (11–14)
I_1 *Title* (11–12)
I_2 *Background* (13–14)

Appearance (15–16a)

Message (16b)

Conclusion (16c–17)

Introduction (1:11–14)

The introduction to Paul's encounter with the risen Jesus consists of a title summarizing his experience and background information concerning his life prior to the encounter.

Title (1:11–12)

Paul begins his account with a rather lengthy summary of his encounter with Jesus. He launches into an extended parenthetical denial that his gospel has any human origin before finally asserting that it came through Jesus:

> Γνωρίζω γὰρ ὑμῖν, ἀδελφοί,
> τὸ εὐαγγέλιον τὸ εὐαγγελισθὲν ὑπ' ἐμοῦ
> ὅτι οὐκ ἔστιν κατὰ ἄνθρωπον·
>   οὐδὲ γὰρ ἐγὼ παρὰ ἀνθρώπου παρέλαβον αὐτὸ
>   οὔτε ἐδιδάχθην,
> ἀλλὰ δι' ἀποκαλύψεως Ἰησοῦ Χριστοῦ.

---

65. See pp. 36–41 above.

The transition into Paul's account of his calling begins with the verb γνωρίζω, indicating that Paul is about to reveal something that the Galatians had perhaps forgotten,[66] or more likely would prefer to forget![67]

The direct object, εὐαγγέλιον, is the focus of 11–12. This "good news" refers to a specific message (τό) that God is communicating to humans.[68] Τὸ εὐαγγέλιον is modified by the adjectival phrase τὸ εὐαγγελισθὲν ὑπ᾽ ἐμοῦ. The participle εὐαγγελισθέν is cognate with the preceding noun in an obvious Hebraism. The entire phrase is rather awkward, and appears to be structured so that Paul can avoid claiming ownership of the message (cf. τὸ εὐαγγέλιόν μου, Rom 2:16; 16:25), while still identifying it as the one he proclaimed. It seems logical that Paul should not claim ownership of the message here, since he is about to deny that its origin is human, claiming rather that it came from Jesus Christ.

Paul first denies that his message has a human origin. This complements the earlier denial that his apostleship had a human origin (1).[69] In this instance, this denial consists of a main clause (οὐκ ἔστιν κατὰ ἄνθρωπον) modified by a compound subordinate explanatory clause (οὐδὲ γὰρ ἐγὼ παρὰ ἀνθρώπου παρέλαβον αὐτὸ οὔτε ἐδιδάχθην). The essence of the denial rests in the prepositional phrase "not according to a human." The preposition κατά, "according to,"[70] includes aspects of both ultimate and intermediate agency,[71] thereby mirroring the earlier functions of ἀπό and διά (1). The object of the preposition, ἄνθρωπος, refers to humanity in general.[72] Thus, the message is "not according to

---

66. Fung, *Galatians*, 51.

67. Betz, *Galatians*, 56.

68. BDAG, 402.

69. Paul's claim "is complementary to the one made in verse 1, since, in Paul's eyes at least, apostleship and preaching of the gospel were inextricably bound together." Dunn, *Galatians*, 53.

70. BDAG, 512. Harris describes κατά as a "marker of norm of similarity or homogeneity." Harris, "Prepositions and Theology," 3:1200.

71. "The complete phrase κατὰ ἄνθρωπον suggests both source and agency." Longenecker, *Galatians*, 23.

72. Human "in status" (BDAG, 81). Danker further defines ἄνθρωπος in this context as "*in a human way, from a human standpoint* [which] emphasizes the inferiority of human beings in comparison w. God." BDAG, 81. Of the six Pauline instances of κατὰ ἄνθρωπον cited (Rom 3:5; 1 Cor 3:3; 9:8; 15:32; Gal 1:11; 3:15; Rom 7:22, κατὰ τὸν ἔσω ἄνθρωπον, is not mentioned), five do appear to emphasize human inferiority with respect to God. However, as with ἀπ᾽ ἀνθρώπων and δι᾽ ἀνθρώπου (Gal 1:1), it is not

a human" in the sense that it does not come from a human source or agent.

The phrase κατὰ ἄνθρωπον is clarified by the subsequent γάρ clause. The conjunction γάρ indicates that the clause is both subordinate and explanatory.[73] The coordinating conjunctions οὐδὲ ... οὔτε ... indicate that two distinct negative qualifications are being made.[74] The first qualification indicates that Paul did not receive his message from a human source: οὐδὲ γὰρ ἐγὼ παρὰ ἀνθρώπου παρέλαβον αὐτό. Paul first emphasizes that he, ἐγώ, is the subject. The verb, παρέλαβον, translated "receive,"[75] has the sense of gaining control of, or receiving jurisdiction over.[76] Louw and Nida suggest the gloss "learn from someone," which implies a tradition that has been taught.[77] The antecedent for αὐτό is clearly Paul's message, τὸ εὐαγγέλιον. The final portion of this clause is the prepositional phrase παρὰ ἀνθρώπου. Παραλαμβάνω is commonly used in constructions with παρά,[78] but here the preposition is emphasized by its position before the verb. Παρά indicates from whom the message was (or, in this case, was not) received; in other words, the ultimate agent.[79] Thus, παρά is analogous to ἀπό in verse 1, but is used instead to complement the verb παραλαμβάνω. Longenecker notes that παρά also has reference to the ultimate agent, "with ἀπό and παρά appearing indistinguishably in parallel accounts."[80] Once again, the object of the preposition is ἄνθρωπος. Thus, Paul has again denied that his message was received from a human source.

---

certain that the phrase κατὰ ἄνθρωπον in Gal 1:11 is emphasizing inferiority as much as it is making a simple distinction between humans and God. Longenecker is perhaps closer to the mark when he remarks that "the noun ἄνθρωπον conveys simply the thought of 'human' without any more exact discrimination." Longenecker, *Galatians*, 23.

73. *GGBTB*, 761.

74. The combination of οὐδέ and οὔτε is rare in the NT, occurring only twice elsewhere (Rev 5:3; 9:20).

75. LSJ, 1315.

76. BDAG, 768.

77. L&N, §27.13.

78. BDAG, 768.

79. Ibid., 756.

80. Longenecker, *Galatians*, 23.

The second qualification is that Paul's message was not received from any human teaching: οὔτε ἐδιδάχθην. The verb is a simple passive.[81] Thus, Paul flatly denies that his message was received from a human intermediate agent by means of teaching. Once again, this complements the earlier denial of human intermediate agency with regard to Paul's apostleship (1).[82]

Having exhaustively rejected that the source of his message was human, Paul now reveals the true source: ἀλλὰ δι' ἀποκαλύψεως Ἰησοῦ Χριστοῦ. As in verse 1, ἀλλά marks the transition from negative to positive identification. The phrase δι' ἀποκαλύψεως Ἰησοῦ Χριστοῦ is a pithy synopsis of Paul's message. Διά here has a causal sense,[83] indicating the instrument or means by which the message was given to Paul.[84] Paul indicates that instrument was a revelation, ἀποκάλυψεως,[85] but gives no further hint as to the type of revelation.

In fact, the only detail Paul provides concerning the revelation at this point is that it pertains to Ἰησοῦ Χριστοῦ. The function of the genitive has been much debated. Since ἀποκάλυψις is a verbal noun, the genitive Ἰησοῦ Χριστοῦ is likely functioning either subjectively or objectively.[86] The objective genitive view has the most support,[87] although the subjective genitive view is also widely held.[88] Given the evidence in support of both positions, this may be a case where the plenary genitive

---

81. The simple passive indicates that the subject received (or in this case, did not receive) the action. See *GGBTB*, 439–40.

82. Longenecker also makes a connection to the phrase οὐδὲ δι' ἀνθρώπου from v. 1, and concludes that οὔτε ἐδιδάχθην thus refers to the intermediate agent. Longenecker, *Galatians*, 23.

83. LSJ, 338.

84. BDAG, 224.

85. L&N, §28.38; LSJ, 201; BDAG, 112. Danker further suggests "revelations of a particular kind, through visions, etc...." Since there is nothing in this verse to indicate the type of revelation, the suggestions "of a particular kind" and "through visions, etc." are unhelpful.

86. Betz notes that "the answer must be given from the context, because grammatically it can be either." Betz, *Galatians*, 63.

87. See Bruce, *Galatians*, 89; Burton, *Galatians*, 41–43; Fung, *Galatians*, 54. Dunn comments that "'Jesus Christ' is not thought of as the source of the revelation, but as its content ... the gospel is not simply 'from Christ' but is Christ." Dunn, *Galatians*, 53–54.

88. Ἀποκάλυψις "with genitive of the author." BDAG, 112. Wallace cites this very phrase as his primary example of the subjective genitive. *GGBTB*, 113. See also Longenecker, *Galatians*, 23–24.

might be preferred. In other words, the revelation is both by and about Jesus Christ.

Thus, Gal 1:11–12 summarizes Paul's autobiographical epiphany account. Paul is careful not to claim the gospel as his own. Indeed, he denies that it originated from any human source. Instead, he insists that his message came through the revelation of Jesus Christ.

Background (1:13–14)

Having provided a summary of his experience, Paul describes his background prior to the revelation of Jesus:

Ἠκούσατε γὰρ τὴν ἐμὴν ἀναστροφήν ποτε ἐν τῷ Ἰουδαϊσμῷ,
ὅτι
    καθ' ὑπερβολὴν
    ἐδίωκον τὴν ἐκκλησίαν τοῦ θεοῦ
    καὶ
    ἐπόρθουν αὐτήν, καὶ
    προέκοπτον ἐν τῷ Ἰουδαϊσμῷ ὑπὲρ πολλοὺς συνηλικιώτας...,
        περισσοτέρως ζηλωτὴς ὑπάρχων τῶν πατρικῶν μου
        παραδόσεων.

Paul summarizes his life prior to the DRE in a single statement with two explanatory clauses. The opening verb, ἠκούσατε, functions in several significant ways. First, it is an important rhetorical device. By appealing directly to his readers using the second person, Paul draws them in to what follows. Second, it is helpful in establishing the truthfulness of the whole message. By appealing to his readers' own knowledge of past events, he presents himself as a reliable source, thereby increasing the likelihood that they will trust the information he is about to reveal (cf. γνωρίζω, v. 11).

Paul now recounts his life prior to Jesus's revelation: τὴν ἐμὴν ἀναστροφήν ποτε ἐν τῷ Ἰουδαϊσμῷ (13). The word ἀναστροφήν, translated "conduct,"[89] involves a way of life, or behavior according to certain principles.[90] The enclitic particle ποτε involves a generalization of time, "once, formerly,"[91] or "when."[92] Finally, Ἰουδαϊσμῷ refers to the practice

---

89. L&N, §41.3.
90. BDAG, 73.
91. Ibid., 856.
92. L&N, §67.30.

of Judaism,⁹³ or the Judean way of life.⁹⁴ Thus, Paul refers to the time that preceded the DRE as "his former way of life in Judaism."

The conjunction ὅτι connects the preceding statement with what follows. It indicates that the next two statements will further refine what Paul means by his life in Judaism.⁹⁵ The first statement following the ὅτι describes Paul's activities against the church; the second, his progress within Judaism.

Regarding Paul's relationship to the church, Paul writes: καθ' ὑπερβολὴν ἐδίωκον τὴν ἐκκλησίαν τοῦ θεοῦ καὶ ἐπόρθουν αὐτήν (13). This "quite classical" prepositional phrase καθ' ὑπερβολήν, meaning "excessively" or "beyond all measure," is used only by Paul in the NT.⁹⁶ It appears to modify both coordinate clauses, ἐδίωκον τὴν ἐκκλησίαν τοῦ θεοῦ and ἐπόρθουν αὐτήν (13). The first coordinate clause reveals that Paul persecuted the church. The verb ἐδίωκον uses the imperfect tense in a customary or habitual sense,⁹⁷ indicating that Paul persecuted the church on a regular basis. The noun ἐκκλησία has reference to a body of Christians, whether specific (cf. Gal 1:2) or in general, as it appears to be used here.⁹⁸ The second coordinate clause reveals that Paul sought not only to persecute the church, but also to destroy it. The verb ἐπόρθουν is evidently a conative imperfect,⁹⁹ since Paul's attempts were unsuccessful. Both verbs are intensified by the prepositional phrase καθ' ὑπερβολήν, "to an extraordinary degree, beyond measure, utterly."¹⁰⁰ Thus, Paul sought to persecute and annihilate the church to an extraordinary degree prior to the DRE.

Regarding his status within Judaism, Paul writes: προέκοπτον ἐν τῷ Ἰουδαϊσμῷ ὑπὲρ πολλοὺς συνηλικιώτας ἐν τῷ γένει μου, περισσοτέρως ζηλωτὴς ὑπάρχων τῶν πατρικῶν μου παραδόσεων. The customary im-

---

93. Ibid., §41.33.

94. BDAG, 479. Dunn remarks that the term "only came into currency with 2 Maccabees... [and] clearly received its distinctive emphasis as the antithesis to 'Hellenism.'" Dunn, *Galatians*, 56.

95. BDAG, 731.

96. Bruce, *Galatians*, 90.

97. *GGBTB*, 548.

98. BDAG, 304. It is interesting to note that Paul identifies the church as belonging to God, a distinction significantly omitted from his description of Judaism.

99. *GGBTB*, 550.

100. BDAG, 1032.

Paul's Epistles

perfect verb προέκοπτον[101] indicates Paul's continual progress within Judaism.[102] Paul's progress in Judaism is qualified by the prepositional phrase ὑπὲρ πολλοὺς συνηλικιώτας ἐν τῷ γένει μου, indicating it was beyond that of his peers. The adverbial clause περισσοτέρως ζηλωτὴς ὑπάρχων τῶν πατρικῶν μου παραδόσεων provides the reason for this: Paul was a greater enthusiast for the traditions of his fathers.[103] In other words, since Paul had greater zeal for the traditions of Judaism he made continual progress beyond that of his peers. It is interesting to note that Paul presents himself as being extreme both against the church (καθ' ὑπερβολήν) and within Judaism (περισσοτέρως). The term ζηλωτής does not suggest that Paul is claiming to be a member of the "Zealot" faction, since that did not exist prior to 66 CE.[104] However, ζηλωτής may be an allusion to Phinehas, an OT figure who was described as being "zealous for [Yahweh's] zeal" (ἐν τῷ ζηλῶσαί μου τὸν ζῆλον, Num 25:11 LXX) because he killed an apostate Israelite.[105] This allusion to Phinehas affirms Paul's earlier depictions of both the church and himself. Paul had viewed the "church of God" (Gal 1:13) as apostate, just as Phinehas judged those who had "yoked themselves to the Baal of Peor" (Num 25:5, NRSV) as apostate. Therefore, Paul felt justified in persecuting the church, just as Phinehas had obeyed Moses's call to kill those who had worshipped Baal (Num 25:5-8).[106]

The phrase τῶν πατρικῶν μου παραδόσεων (14b) is used synonymously for Judaism. This is noteworthy, since it emphasizes the human aspect of Judaism after such strenuous and repeated denials of a human origin for Paul's own message and mission (1, 8-9, 10, 11-12). Not only that, it contrasts with his description of the church as τὴν ἐκκλησίαν τοῦ

---

101. *GGBTB*, 548.

102. Burton notes that "the nature of this advance in Judaism is not defined." Burton, *Galatians*, 46.

103. BDF notes that Paul appears to use περισσοτέρως in "a still stronger force" (§60[1]).

104. Barnett, "Revolutionary Movements," 818.

105. Dietzfelbinger observes that Phinehas was the model for Jewish zeal for the Law. Dietzfelbinger, *Berufung*, 9, 11.

106. Donaldson summarizes the contemporary Jewish understanding of zeal in Donaldson, *Paul*, 285–86. "The basic pattern of zeal was derived from the popular Old Testament prototypes—Phinehas (Num 25), Elijah (1 Kgs 18–19), and Simeon and Levi (Gen 34). Zeal was more than just a fervent commitment to the Torah; it denoted a willingness to use violence against any—Jews, Gentiles, or the wicked in general—who were contravening, opposing, or subverting the Torah."

θεοῦ (13). By associating Judaism with human traditions, Paul discredits its authority as being merely human, while simultaneously denying it the divine status granted to the church (and, by implication, to his message also).[107]

Prior to the DRE, then, Paul gives no indication that he was anything but successful in his zealous pursuit of Judaism.[108]

Appearance (1:15–16a)

Here Paul describes the nature of his encounter with the risen Jesus. He does so concisely, using OT allusions that give added depth to the account. Interestingly, the appearance and message are found in a subordinate clause. Paul's description of Jesus's appearance begins as follows:

Ὅτε δὲ
 εὐδόκησεν
 [ὁ θεὸς]
 ὁ ἀφορίσας με ἐκ κοιλίας μητρός μου
 καὶ καλέσας διὰ τῆς χάριτος αὐτοῦ ἀποκαλύψαι τὸν υἱὸν αὐτοῦ ἐν ἐμοί

Paul suddenly changes the time, topic, and subject of the discourse at the start of verse 15. Until now, the focus has been on Paul's former life in Judaism (13–14). But in this verse, the first three words mark an abrupt change. The temporal particle[109] ὅτε indicates a change in time, ending the discussion of Paul's life in Judaism. The conjunction δέ functions transitionally,[110] indicating a change in topic.[111] The verb εὐδόκησεν reveals the shift from first person (13–14) to third, indicating a change in subject. Thus, in the space of only three words, Paul has changed the time, topic, and subject. Therefore, the beginning of verse 15 signals a dramatic shift in the discourse.

The structure of the subordinate clause containing the appearance and message is complex. In order to maintain clarity, we will discuss the subject in its entirety before proceeding to the predicate. To make

---

107. Martyn is one of the few to note this contrast: "the undifferentiated Law ... turns out here to be tradition as distinguished from apocalyptic revelation, thus lying on the human side of the divine/human antinomy." Martyn, *Galatians*, 155.

108. "As a Jew he had no reason to leave Judaism." Betz, *Galatians*, 68.

109. BDAG, 731.

110. *GGBTB*, 674.

111. Fung notes that this "'but then' ... signals that a complete break occurred in Paul's life when God called him to be an apostle." Fung, *Galatians*, 63.

matters worse, the presence of ὁ θεός at the beginning of the clause is in doubt. Indeed, ὁ θεός appears to be a later addition "for the sake of explicitness."[112] Fortunately, it is not essential to the meaning of the text, since the subject can only be God.[113]

Excluding ὁ θεός, the subject consists of two singular, personal substantive participles joined by καί and preceded by an article. This is a classic instance of the Granville Sharp construction,[114] which means that the subject is a single person, namely, God the Father. The first participle, ἀφορίσας, is from the verb ἀφορίζω, meaning to set apart or appoint,[115] especially for a particular office.[116] The object με obviously refers to Paul. The prepositional phrase ἐκ κοιλίας μητρός μου is a Septuagintalism[117] meaning "from my mother's womb." A less literal translation would be "from my birth" or even "from before my birth."[118] Thus, Paul is asserting that he had been set apart by God not only prior to the appearance of Jesus, but even before his birth, despite Paul's actions to the contrary (13).[119]

The second participle, καλέσας, is from καλέω, meaning to call or name. In this case, it suggests a specific task.[120] The prepositional phrase διὰ τῆς χάριτος αὐτοῦ indicates that grace was the means God used to call Paul to a task he had actively opposed.

---

112. Bruce, *Galatians*, 92.

113. Longenecker, *Galatians*, 30.

114. *GGBTB*, 271–72.

115. BDAG, 158; L&N, §37.97.

116. LSJ, 292. Ἀφορίζω is used by Paul with the same sense in Rom 1:1, and also by Luke of Paul and Barnabas in Acts 13:2.

117. Cf. Judg 16:17; Job 1:21; Ps 22:10 (21:11 LXX); 71:6 (70:6 LXX); Isa 49:1.

118. Longenecker, *Galatians*, 30.

119. Donaldson suggests that Paul's concern for the Gentiles should therefore be viewed as "somehow part of God's dealings with [Paul] from the beginning" rather than as a "radical *novum*." He further argues that this is "at least consistent" with his view that "the roots of [Paul's] Gentile concern are to be found in a pre-Damascus orientation toward the Gentiles." Donaldson, *Paul*, 255. Yet Paul here appears to be contrasting his former life with God's intentions prior to the DRE, rather than suggesting that he was somehow involved with a Gentile mission prior to the DRE (which is absent from the list of Paul's former activities in verses 13–14).

120. To "choose for receipt of a special benefit or experience" (BDAG, 502); "to urgently invite someone to accept responsibilities for a particular task, implying a new relationship to the one who does the calling" (L&N, §33.312).

The combination of καλέω and χάρις is unusual. In fact, it only occurs four times in the NT (cf. Gal 1:6, 15; 2 Tim. 1:9; 1 Pet 5:10), and is entirely absent from the LXX. Both instances in the undisputed Pauline epistles are found in Gal 1; the former attributes grace to Jesus (6),[121] the latter to God the Father (15). Longenecker rightly asserts this "interchange . . . in phraseology highlights the fact that Paul thought of God and Christ as completely at one in mankind's salvation."[122]

Paul describes the initiative for the revelation in the predicate. The main verb, εὐδόκησεν, precedes the subject. It means "to determine or resolve," or more precisely here, "to consider something as good and therefore worthy of choice."[123] In other words, God the Father chose to act at a point he determined. The precise nature of the action is revealed in the complementary aorist infinitive ἀποκαλύψαι.[124] The infinitive may be interpreted "to reveal or disclose," or more specifically, to reveal "divine revelation of certain transcendent secrets."[125] There are several noteworthy parallels with the title (11–12). Ἀποκαλύπτω is cognate with ἀποκάλυψις (12). The object of the revelation, τὸν υἱὸν αὐτοῦ, is parallel with Ἰησοῦ Χριστοῦ (12). The final element, ἐν ἐμοί, which does not have a corresponding title element, identifies Paul as the one who received the revelation.

An examination of the predicate raises several significant issues regarding the nature of the appearance and the identity of the one who appeared. First, there is some debate concerning the kind of appearance that Paul is describing. Danker,[126] Louw and Nida,[127] and Blass[128] suggest that ἐν is used only to identify Paul as the one to whom Jesus appeared.[129] Dunn takes the more nuanced position that ἐν ἐμοί (16a) likely refers

---

121. Χριστοῦ is included in the text of NA[27]. Its enclosure within square brackets is apparently due to its absence from 𝔓[46].

122. Longenecker, *Galatians*, 30.

123. BDAG, 404. See also LSJ, 710.

124. *GGBTB*, 598.

125. BDAG, 112.

126. A "marker denoting the object to which something happens." BDAG, 329.

127. A "marker of an experiencer of an event." L&N, §90.56.

128. Ἐν "appears also to stand for the customary [dative] proper . . . 'to me.'" BDF, §220(1).

129. Hays interprets ἐν instrumentally, indicating that "God has chosen Paul as his eschatological messenger to the Gentiles." Hays, "Christology," 281.

to the "personal transformation" within Paul,[130] yet he also claims that the DRE was "auditory" and "visual."[131] On the other hand, Betz claims that the DRE occurred in Paul's mind.[132] Wikenhauser even claims that verses 15 and 16 refer not to the DRE, but instead to another "special interior revelation from Christ."[133] It may even be true that Jesus's appearance to Paul had aspects of both external appearance and vision.[134] However, based on the lexical evidence, the only reasonable conclusion that can be drawn from this verse is that Paul received the appearance; the phrase ἐν ἐμοί cannot be used to draw conclusions regarding the kind of appearance that he experienced.[135]

The other relevant feature of the predicate is its characterization of Jesus as τὸν υἱὸν αὐτοῦ. Since Paul has already mentioned God "the Father" several times (1, 3, 4), his description of Jesus as the Son is not unexpected. Dunn claims that the term reflects the uniqueness of the relationship between God the Father and Jesus.[136] The use of the title "son" will be significant in the later discussion of Paul's characterization of Jesus.[137]

A final aspect of the appearance is its striking similarities to several prophetic passages from the OT.[138] First, Paul alludes to the Servant passage of Isa 49:1 (LXX):

> Ἀκούσατέ μου, νῆσοι, καὶ προσέχετε, ἔθνη, διὰ χρόνου πολλοῦ στήσεται, λέγει κύριος. ἐκ κοιλίας μητρός μου ἐκάλεσεν τὸ ὄνομά μου.

---

130. Dunn, *Galatians*, 64.
131. Ibid., 64.
132. Betz, "Paul," 187.
133. Wikenhauser, *Pauline Mysticism*, 135.
134. Bruce speaks of "outward vision and inward illumination." Bruce, *Galatians*, 93.
135. "It would seem, therefore, that *en emoi* refers to the revelation to Paul (simple dative) that enabled him to preach to the Gentiles." Gaventa, *Darkness*, 27. Wright gives two alternatives: "as emphasizing either god's [sic] revelation of his son *to* Paul, or his revelation of his son *through* Paul." Wright, *Resurrection*, 380.
136. "The first reference to Jesus' sonship presupposes that his relation to God had a unique character which marked it off from other relationships." Dunn, *Galatians*, 64.
137. See pp. 171–73 above.
138. Sandnes suggests that "Gal 1:15–16a ... forms a structure which corresponds to OT call-narratives." Sandnes, *Paul*, 68. Munck discusses the connection to Isa 49:1–6 and Jer 1:4–5 in Munck, "La vocation," 137–38. See also Wright, *Resurrection*, 379–80.

The parallels are obvious. The phrase ἐκ κοιλίας μητρός μου (Gal 1:15) is repeated exactly. Καλέω appears in both, as an aorist active participle (Gal 1:15) and an indicative verb (Isa 49:1). The reference to "nations," ἔθνη, is found in both (Gal 1:16; Isa 49:1, 6).

Paul also appears to invoke Jer 1:5 (LXX):

> Πρὸ τοῦ με πλάσαι σε ἐν κοιλίᾳ ἐπίσταμαί σε καὶ πρὸ τοῦ σε ἐξελθεῖν ἐκ μήτρας ἡγίακά σε, προφήτην εἰς ἔθνη τέθεικά σε.

Jeremiah's references to being set apart from the womb (κοιλία), and his call to the nations (εἰς ἔθνη), are both echoed by Paul.

There are at least two possible motives for these OT allusions.[139] First, Paul may have a personal motivation. He may have viewed himself in the tradition of the OT prophets, and intentionally reflected this self-assessment in the description of his call. Second, Paul may have been motivated by his audience. Regardless of how he viewed himself, he may have alluded to OT prophetic passages in order to establish his authority in the minds of his audience. Given Paul's careful argumentation to this point, the latter seems likely. Paul is attempting to persuade his readers of his authority. An implicit claim to prophetic authority would, no doubt, catch the attention of many of his readers.[140] Yet the former is also possible, since Paul has presented himself as a messenger on a divine mission.

Message (1:16b)

The message is found at the end of the extended subordinate clause (15–16). Paul concludes the clause with a statement of purpose: ἵνα εὐαγγελίζωμαι αὐτὸν ἐν τοῖς ἔθνεσιν. Ἵνα is a purpose conjunction,[141] indicating that Paul is about to unveil the purpose for Jesus's appearance. The appearance was not, in Paul's opinion, an end in itself—it served a purpose beyond simply being an epiphany. As Dunn rightly states, "the revelation of Christ had no other purpose than [preaching Christ among the nations]."[142]

---

139. Longenecker explains these allusions with the suggestion that Paul "thought of his apostleship not just along the lines of . . . a representative messenger or envoy . . . but also in terms of Israelite prophetology." Longenecker, *Galatians*, 30.

140. Hübner also draws the connection to Isa 49, but discusses at greater length a less obvious connection between Gal 1:4 and Isa 53. Hübner, *Paulus*, 2:58–61, 325.

141. *GGBTB*, 676.

142. Dunn, *Galatians*, 65. Bruce concurs: "The purpose of the revelation, that Paul

The verb εὐαγγελίζωμαι is significant. It is in the subjunctive mood, which is to be expected following ἵνα. Its lexical form is εὐαγγελίζω,[143] meaning to bring good news or announce.[144] In the NT, εὐαγγελίζω refers specifically to the good news about Jesus Christ.[145] The verb εὐαγγελίζωμαι is first person singular, to which Paul now returns after the temporary switch in verse 15. The verb demonstrates that Jesus was revealed for the purpose of calling Paul to preach the good news. The theme of good news is prominent in this chapter. The verb εὐαγγελίζω previously appeared in verses 8, 9, and 11; its cognate noun, εὐαγγέλιον, in verses 6, 7, and 11.

Paul was terse in his description of Jesus's appearance; he is equally short in his description of the message. The εὐαγγέλιον is described simply as αὐτόν, a third-person singular pronoun referring to τὸν υἱὸν αὐτοῦ.[146] In the undisputed Pauline epistles, the verb εὐαγγελίζω occurs nine times in DRE-related texts (Rom 1:15; 15:20; 1 Cor 1:17; 15:1, 2; Gal 1:8, 9, 11, 16, 23), and only eight times elsewhere (Rom 10:15; 1 Cor 9:16, 18; 2 Cor 10:16; 11:7; Gal 1:23; 4:13; 1 Thess 3:6). Thus, Paul closely associated preaching with the DRE.

The recipients of Paul's preaching are identified by the phrase ἐν τοῖς ἔθνεσιν. The term ἔθνος refers generally to a people or nation. For a Jew of Paul's time (cf. Gal 1:13–14), τὰ ἔθνη (plural) would refer to those who believe "in other gods or in false gods,"[147] "the entire world population apart from the Jews."[148] Given that the message pertains to Jesus, Paul's call extended to those in all nations who did not know the good news about Jesus.

Finally, the ἵνα clause establishes the close connection between the appearance, the message, and the messenger. Jesus appeared for the purpose of calling Paul to be his messenger to the nations. Paul is a messenger (ἀπόστολος) called to preach (εὐαγγελίζω) a message (εὐαγγέλιον).

---

should proclaim the gospel of Christ among the Gentiles, was part of the revelation itself." Bruce, *Galatians*, 93.

143. So BDAG, 402; L&N, §33.215. LSJ uses εὐαγγελίζομαι as the lexical form (704).

144. BDAG, 402; LSJ, 704.

145. L&N, §33.215.

146. Burton, *Galatians*, 53.

147. L&N, §11.37.

148. Betz, *Galatians*, 72.

These three are inseparably connected, and they all originate from the ἀποκάλυψις of Jesus.

Thus, the appearance and the message, as presented in Gal 1:15–16b, reveal the essence of Paul's encounter with Jesus. The verse opens with a sudden shift in perspective from Paul to God the Father. God chose Paul from birth for the task he was about to be given in the appearance of Jesus. The nature of the event is barely discussed, apart from two details. First, it was a revelation of Jesus by God to Paul. Second, it had the specific purpose of commissioning Paul to preach Jesus to the nations. Paul's call as apostle, his message, and his task of preaching to the nations are thus inseparable, and inseparably linked to Jesus's appearance. Paul accomplished this using language that reflects OT language from the prophetic call of Jeremiah and the Servant of Isaiah.

Conclusion (1:16c–17)

The events following Jesus's appearance and presumed departure are discussed in Gal 1:16c–17. The main clause begins with the temporal adverb εὐθέως (16c), indicating that the events in this section followed immediately after Jesus's departure.[149] Paul returned to Damascus after traveling to Arabia (17), which implies that Jesus's appearance occurred at Damascus.[150]

GALATIANS 1:18—2:20

Paul continues his narrative with the events that followed Jesus's appearance. A few details of these later events are relevant to the DRE. First, Paul declares to the leaders of the church in Jerusalem his vocation to preach to the nations (2:2). This declaration affirms Paul's calling (1:15–16). Unfortunately, no additional information is provided here.

Galatians 2:7–9 delves more deeply into the connection between Jesus's appearance and Paul's calling as apostle to the nations. There are several parallels between this section and the earlier account (1:11–17), including: the connection of grace to the call (2:9; cf. 1:15), the claim to be a passive recipient of the message (πεπίστευμαι, 2:7; τὴν χάριν τὴν δοθεῖσάν μοι, 2:9; cf. 1:15–16), and the identification of the message's

---

149. Burton, *Galatians*, 53–54.

150. Gal 1:17b is "an indirect confirmation of Acts that Paul's conversion and commission took place at Damascus." Longenecker, *Galatians*, 34.

audience as the nations (τὰ ἔθνη, 2:8; cf. 1:16; the synonym ἀκροβυστίας is also used in 2:7).

Thus, Gal 1:1—2:20, and 1:1–17 in particular, is a rich source of information concerning both the nature of the DRE, as well as the characterization of Jesus within that event.

1 Corinthians

Paul also makes reference to the DRE in 1 Corinthians. Such references are found in the salutation (1 Cor 1:1), as well as throughout the remainder of the letter (1:17; 9:1; 15:1–11).

1 Corinthians 1:1

The salutation of 1 Corinthians is similar to, although much shorter than, those of Galatians and Romans. Here, Paul identifies himself as Παῦλος κλητὸς[151] ἀπόστολος Χριστοῦ Ἰησοῦ[152] διὰ θελήματος θεοῦ. The term κλητός refers to being called or summoned to an office.[153] The cognate verb καλέω appears in the context of Jesus's appearance in Gal 1:15. Both the noun and the verb involve action on the part of another. In other words, Paul did not take apostleship for himself; rather, it was given to him by another. The genitive phrase Χριστοῦ Ἰησοῦ appears to be used subjectively, indicating that Paul is a messenger sent from Christ Jesus. There are two main grounds for this view. First, the subjective genitive, identifying Jesus as the one who sent Paul, works best in conjunction with the following prepositional phrase διὰ θελήματος θεοῦ, which identifies the means Jesus used in sending Paul. Second, the subjective genitive fits the context of verse 17, where Paul directly states that Jesus sent him to proclaim the gospel.[154] Schrage comments that Paul's call did not come from "Menschen, Gemeinden oder bestimmte Gruppen in ihnen," but from "Jesus Christus selbst."[155]

---

151. Absent from 𝔓⁶¹ᵛⁱᵈ A D 81.

152. Metathesis of Χριστοῦ Ἰησοῦ in ℵ A Ψ 1739 1881 et al. is outweighed by 𝔓⁴⁶ B D F G 33 et al., but for our purposes the difference is insignificant.

153. L&N, §33.314. See also BDAG, 549.

154. Fee concurs, stating that the phrase "emphasize[s] the origin of Paul's apostleship." Fee, *1 Corinthians*, 30.

155. Schrage, *1 Korinther*, 1:100.

In the following phrase, διά is used with the genitive θελήματος as a marker of means[156] or efficient cause.[157] In other words, Paul is an apostle from Jesus by means of the will of God. This is noteworthy in that it appears to reverse the roles of Jesus and God the Father in relation to Paul's call as presented in Gal 1:1, where God the Father (the ultimate agent) uses Jesus (the intermediate agent) to call Paul; in other words, God the Father called Paul by means of Jesus. In 1 Cor 1:1, Jesus called Paul by means of the will of God. Yet it is not a true reversal, since 1 Cor 1:1 refers to "the will of God," and not God himself.

Finally, the phrase διὰ θελήματος θεοῦ emphasizes that the catalyst for Paul's call was a cause outside of himself.

1 Corinthians 1:17

This verse is similar in content to the salutation (1), but it does provide additional light on the task for which Paul was sent. The relevant portion of the verse reads: οὐ γὰρ ἀπέστειλέν με[158] Χριστὸς βαπτίζειν ἀλλὰ εὐαγγελίζεσθαι.[159] Paul is clearly discussing his apostolic call to evangelize the nations using verbal cognates of the more frequently used nouns ἀπόστολος and εὐαγγέλιον. The first cognate, ἀπέστειλεν, refers to the action of sending;[160] the second, εὐαγγελίζεσθαι, refers to the act of proclaiming the message.[161]

In this statement Paul explicitly claims that Jesus is the one who sent him: ἀπέστειλέν με Χριστός. The purpose of the call[162] is clarified by the infinitives βαπτίζειν and εὐαγγελίζεσθαι. The inclusion of these infinitives demonstrates that Paul was sent for a specific purpose. Paul first denies that he was sent to baptize.[163] He then affirms that he was

---

156. *GGBTB*, 368–69.

157. Fee, *1 Corinthians*, 29n8. Also BDAG, 224.

158. Several important witnesses include the article ὁ before Χριστός, including 𝔓[46] B F G 343. The weight of evidence supports the NA[27] reading. In any event, the presence or absence of the article is not relevant to this discussion.

159. Only B 365 read εὐαγγελίσασθαι.

160. L&N, §15.66.

161. Ibid., §33.215.

162. *GGBTB*, 89.

163. Conzelmann makes the memorable comment that for Paul "to wander about as a baptizer would be a nonhistoric mode of existence." Conzelmann, *1 Corinthians*, 36–37.

sent to proclaim the good news. The purpose for Paul's call by Jesus was, specifically, that he would proclaim the gospel message.

While this verse is not commonly listed as a DRE text, its content certainly reflects Paul's DRE experience.[164]

1 Corinthians 9:1

Here Paul transitions from a discussion of Christian freedom (ἐξουσία, 1 Cor 8:9) to a defense of his authority (cf. esp. 1 Cor 9:3, "This is my defense to those who question me").[165] Schrage calls the connection to the preceding verse "sinnvoll und sachlich."[166] Paul poses four rhetorical questions, each of which expects a positive response:[167]

> Οὐκ εἰμὶ ἐλεύθερος;
> Οὐκ εἰμὶ ἀπόστολος;[168]
> Οὐχὶ Ἰησοῦν τὸν κύριον ἡμῶν ἑόρακα;
> Οὐ τὸ ἔργον μου ὑμεῖς ἐστε ἐν κυρίῳ;

Paul poses these questions in respect of himself, as demonstrated by the first-person singular verbs in the first three questions and the uniquely personal nature of the last question.[169]

The relationship between the four questions has been debated.[170] For example, Schrage comments, "Ihr Verhältnis zueinander ist nicht einheitlich,"[171] which may be related to his view that the quartet

---

164. Kim does not include this verse in his list of DRE texts, but does refer to it frequently in the context of the DRE. Kim, *Origin*, 26, 58, 93n2, 94.

165. See Wright's discussion in Wright, *Resurrection*, 381–82.

166. Schrage, *1 Korinther*, 2:278.

167. Schnabel comments, "Paulus erinnert zu Beginn dieses Abschnitts die korinthischen Christen mit vier rhetorischen Fragen an sein Wirken als Apostel." Schnabel, *1 Korinther*, 476.

168. D F G Ψ 𝔐 reverse the order of ἐλεύθερος and ἀπόστολος, but the weight of evidence (including 𝔓⁴⁶ ℵ A B P 33 104 365 629 630 1175 1739 1881) supports the NA²⁷ reading.

169. Conzelmann affirms the personal aspect of Paul's claims: "He does not speak about the freedom of Christians in general, but about his own particular freedom; nor yet about apostleship in general, but about his own particular apostleship." Conzelmann, *1 Corinthians*, 152.

170. For example, see Gaventa, "Conversion," 126–37.

171. Schrage, *1 Korinther*, 2:286.

is a digression.¹⁷² However, the questions do appear to follow a logical sequence.

The first question establishes Paul's own freedom. The second question asserts Paul's apostleship, presumably as the basis for his freedom. The connection between these two questions has not been widely discussed. Barrett indirectly asserts that the basis for Paul's freedom is his apostleship: "If any Christian can claim to be free I can do so, for am I not an apostle?"¹⁷³ Conzelmann suggests that no explanation is required:

> How does he come to this apologia? In itself it does not require any particular reason. The freedom of the missionary was a standard theme of the wandering Cynic preachers. But in the present instance there later emerges a concrete controversy. Because of this, Paul brings the apostle title into play.¹⁷⁴

In other words, Paul raises the topic of freedom, as any wandering Cynic preacher might, which led to an assertion of apostolic authority in response to the controversy at hand. This explanation seems wholly inadequate. There are at least two closely related explanations for the apparent connection Paul makes between his freedom and apostleship. First, Paul connects his freedom in Jesus to being a slave of Jesus. In fact, Paul has already drawn this connection: ὁ ἐλεύθερος κληθεὶς δοῦλός ἐστιν Χριστοῦ (1 Cor 7:22). In addition, Paul also associates being a slave of Jesus to the apostolic call he received in the DRE (cf. Rom 1:1; 11:13; 15:16). For Paul, freedom means slavery to Jesus, and slavery to Jesus is a direct result of his apostolic call. A second, closely related explanation lies in the hendiadys "grace and apostleship," which Paul associates with Jesus's appearance (cf. Rom 1:5). The grace God showed to Paul may have led to his freedom, yet it also entailed service to Jesus as an apostle. Thus, Paul is likely connecting freedom to slavery in relation to Jesus's appearance.

The third question expands on Paul's encounter with the resurrected Jesus: οὐχὶ Ἰησοῦν τὸν κύριον ἡμῶν ἑόρακα; The verb ἑόρακα is first person singular perfect¹⁷⁵ from ὁράω. Danker defines this as "to perceive by the eye," and in this instance, "of the perception of personal

---

172. Ibid., 2:279. So also Lindemann, *Korintherbrief*.
173. Barrett, *1 Corinthians*, 200.
174. Conzelmann, *1 Corinthians*, 152.
175. BDF notes that the perfect emphasizes the continuing effect of Jesus's appearance on Paul (§342[2]).

beings that become visible in a transcendent manner."[176] Louw and Nida appear to make no such distinction, preferring the simpler "see."[177] This naturally leads to speculation whether Paul is speaking of seeing Jesus in physical form,[178] or whether it was a more "spiritual" experience. It is difficult to draw either conclusion based on this text alone, but the possibility that the encounter was external is certainly not excluded.

The fourth question concerns the fulfillment of Paul's call. He refers to his Corinthian audience as "my work in the Lord." This is entirely consistent with the audience Paul cites elsewhere in connection with his call, τὰ ἔθνη (Gal 1:16; cf. Rom 1:5; 11:13; 15:16).

Thus, Paul begins the verse in the context of freedom. Paul connects his freedom with his service to Jesus, which in turn he associates with the appearance of Jesus. He concludes by recalling his response to the call of Jesus. This sequence of four rhetorical questions neatly encapsulates the entirety of Paul's encounter with the risen Jesus.

1 Corinthians 15:1–11

First Corinthians 15 begins with these words: Γνωρίζω δὲ ὑμῖν, ἀδελφοί, τὸ εὐαγγέλιον ὃ εὐηγγελισάμην ὑμῖν. The cognates εὐαγγέλιον and εὐαγγελίζω indicate that Paul is about to discuss the message he preaches. As might be expected, some of his comments are pertinent to his call experience.[179]

The section opens with the verb γνωρίζω in first person singular, present active indicative form. This form is found four times in the undisputed Paulines (1 Cor 12:3; 15:1; Phil 1:22; Gal 1:11), and only twice at the beginning of a sentence (1 Cor 15:1; Gal 1:11). Remarkably, both of these introduce a discussion of Jesus's appearance.

---

176. BDAG, 719.

177. L&N, §24.1.

178. "Paul believed that his experience was more than a mere vision. For him it was a resurrection appearance of a kind with all the others." Fee, *1 Corinthians*, 395.

179. Wright discusses this passage at length in Wright, *Resurrection*, 317–29.

Verses 3–8 begin:

παρέδωκα γὰρ ὑμῖν ἐν πρώτοις,
ὃ καὶ παρέλαβον,[180]
ὅτι
    Χριστὸς ἀπέθανεν ὑπὲρ τῶν ἁμαρτιῶν ἡμῶν κατὰ τὰς γραφὰς
    καὶ ὅτι ἐτάφη
    καὶ ὅτι ἐγήγερται τῇ ἡμέρᾳ τῇ τρίτῃ κατὰ τὰς γραφὰς
    καὶ ὅτι ὤφθη Κηφᾷ . . .

Three terms are used to elucidate τὸ εὐαγγέλιον from verse 1: what I first entrusted to you (3), what I received (3), and the extended ὅτι clause (3–8). The first and second clauses reflect similar thoughts from Galatians 1. In Gal 1:8, Paul warns the Galatians concerning any gospel that differs from what he preached (ὃ εὐηγγελισάμεθα ὑμῖν). He repeats the warning in the next verse, replacing ὃ εὐηγγελισάμεθα ὑμῖν with ὃ παρελάβετε (Gal 1:9). He then begins an account of the εὐαγγέλιον (Gal 1:11), claiming that he did not receive (παρέλαβον) it from a human source, but through the appearance of Jesus. Paul makes the same argument in 1 Cor 15. He equates what the Corinthians had received to what he had received. He does not state how he received the message or from whom (1 Cor 15:3), as he did in Galatians (Gal 1:11). However, Paul is about to reveal that he received his gospel from Jesus.

The ὅτι clause consists of a series of chronological statements regarding Jesus: that he died (3), was buried (4), was raised (4),[181] and appeared to a number of people (5–8).[182] Scholars have conjectured that verses 3–7 reflect a pre-Pauline tradition.[183]

Verse 8 begins the section concerning Paul in particular: ἔσχατον[184] δὲ πάντων ὡσπερεὶ τῷ ἐκτρώματι ὤφθη κἀμοί. The verse forms a "fein

---

180. Three versions omit this phrase.

181. For an extensive bibliography related to resurrection, see Thiselton, *1 Corinthians*, 1178–83.

182. Schrage suggests that this sequence forms a chiasm: "a) er starb, b) er wurde begraben, b) er wurde auferweckt, a) er erschien." Schrage, *1 Korinther*, 4:48.

183. Kloppenborg claims that 3b–7 is pre-Pauline. Kloppenborg, "Formula," 351. Webber affirms this claim in Webber, "Note," 265. Schrage is less certain about the origin of verse 6. Schrage, *1 Korinther*, 4:20. Murphy-O'Connor argues that 3–5 are pre-Pauline, 6 is Pauline, and 7 is an appended pre-Pauline transition to 8. Murphy-O'Connor, "Tradition," 589. Lindemann concludes that, regardless of the origin assigned to 6a and 7, 8 is certainly not part of a pre-Pauline tradition. Lindemann, *Korintherbrief*, 326.

184. Jones, "Paul," discusses the meaning of "last."

Paul's Epistles

Scharnier"[185] that connects the prior list of witnesses to Paul's statements concerning the DRE. Jesus's appearance to Paul was post-resurrection, since it comes at the end of a series of chronological statements (3–8). Each of these appearances, including Paul's, involves the verb ὤφθη, from ὁράω (cf. 1 Cor 9:1). Since Paul places the DRE at the end of a series of encounters, and since he uses precisely the same verb to describe his experience, it is likely that the DRE should be understood as occurring in the same manner as the previous encounters.[186] However, whether the vision was external or internal has been greatly disputed.[187] Wright in particular makes a strong case that the DRE was an external event: "The resurrection of Jesus was a real event as far as Paul was concerned, and it underlay the future real event of the resurrection of all God's people."[188]

Verses 9–10 expand on the appearance. First, Paul presents his background prior to Jesus's appearance: "I persecuted the church of God" (ἐδίωξα τὴν ἐκκλησίαν τοῦ θεοῦ). This is reminiscent of the Galatians account (Gal 1:13),[189] which contains the identical phrase except for the tense of the verb διώκω (aorist in 1 Cor 15:9, imperfect in Gal 1:13). Because of his background, Paul considers himself to be "the least of the apostles" (ὁ ἐλάχιστος τῶν ἀποστόλων), and "not worthy to be called an apostle" (οὐκ εἰμὶ ἱκανὸς καλεῖσθαι ἀπόστολος).

Since Paul considers himself unworthy to be an apostle, he attributes his calling to God's grace: χάριτι δὲ θεοῦ εἰμι ὅ εἰμι. Paul has used the noun χάρις frequently in relation to his call (Gal 1:3, 6, 15; 2:9; cf. Rom 1:5; 15:15). Here it is in the dative case, indicating instrumentality. Grace is the means God used to make Paul an apostle.

---

185. Schrage, *1 Korinther*, 4:60.

186. Wright makes a strong case for an external appearance. Wright, *Resurrection*, 382–84.

187. Thiselton discusses the matter at length in Thiselton, *1 Corinthians*, 1197–203. The type of vision is not of great concern to this study. However, the appearance to more than 500 simultaneously (6) suggests that the visions were external. "Paul is here referring to his having seen the risen Lord on the Damascus road, which he did not consider a visionary experience but an actual resurrection appearance of a kind with the others in the series." Fee, *1 Corinthians*, 732.

188. Wright, *Resurrection*, 317–18.

189. Schrage, *1 Korinther*, 4:68.

2 Corinthians

In his Second Epistle to the Corinthians, Paul makes several allusions to Jesus's appearance. Unfortunately, the connection to the DRE is not certain in several cases.

2 Corinthians 1:1

In the salutation to his second Corinthian epistle, Paul identifies himself as Παῦλος ἀπόστολος Χριστοῦ Ἰησοῦ διὰ θελήματος θεοῦ. This is identical to the description in 1 Cor 1:1,[190] save for the omission of κλητός. Therefore, this verse merely confirms the conclusions that have already been reached.

2 Corinthians 4:4–6

In 2 Cor 4, Paul uses a combination of vivid imagery (τὸν φωτισμὸν τοῦ εὐαγγελίου τῆς δόξης τοῦ Χριστοῦ, 4) and christological claims (ὅς ἐστιν εἰκὼν τοῦ θεοῦ, 6) that may allude to the DRE. While some scholars have denied that these verses are connected to the DRE,[191] others have argued in favor of such a connection.[192] For example, Dietzfelbinger claims that since Paul relies on the DRE in defense of his apostleship (Gal 1:15–16;

---

190. Furnish notes that this is a "briefer form of the phrase... in 1 Cor 1:1." Furnish, *II Corinthians*, 99.

191. Wright states that "2 Corinthians 4 is not describing [the DRE], and we cannot take elements of what it says (e.g. that the light shines 'in our hearts', which is certainly not a description of the Damascus Road event), and read them back into, let alone make them determinative for, Paul's original 'seeing' of Jesus." Wright, *Resurrection*, 398. Gaventa also denied the connection: "Several scholars regard 2 Cor 4:6 as an allusion to the conversion.... However, recent work regarding these early chapters of 2 Corinthians makes such a conclusion unlikely.... Thus, when Paul speaks of God 'shining in our hearts,' it is likely that he has in mind a much broader event than merely his own change of mind." Gaventa, "Conversion," 190–92. However, Gaventa's later position is less certain: "Paul may have had conversion in mind when he writes [2 Cor 2:4]." Gaventa, *Darkness*, 2. Donaldson does not list 2 Cor 4:4–6 as a DRE text, claiming that Paul speaks of the DRE "infrequently and tangentially (Gal 1:15–16; 1 Cor 15:8–10; and probably 1 Cor 9:1)." Donaldson, *Paul*, 293. Although Schnelle does view the passage as an allusion to the DRE, he does acknowledge that "whether there is a reference to the Damascus event in 2 Cor. 4:6 is a disputed point." Schnelle, *Apostle Paul*, 90.

192. Hawthorne and Martin suggest that "Paul may well have his own conversion-call in mind." Martin, *2 Corinthians*, 80. Bruce says of these verses, "[Paul's] choice of language is most probably based on his Damascus-road vision." Bruce, *Galatians*, 93. Segal suggests that the "glory of the Lord" is a reference to the "angel of the Lord, or the angel of his presence." Segal, "Presuppositions," 170. See also Kim, *Origin*, 229–32.

1 Cor 9:1; 15:8), one might expect that he would do so here as well.[193] Yet he also admits that Paul does not rely exclusively on the DRE in such situations (cf. 2 Cor 10:13). Dietzfelbinger also argues that there is an "inner agreement" with the other DRE texts in relation to creation.[194] However, since Dietzfelbinger relies on a non-DRE text (2 Cor 5:17) in order to make the connection, his argument that 2 Cor 4:4–6 alludes to the DRE is not convincing.

Perhaps the most comprehensive argument in favor of the connection between 2 Cor 4:4–6 and the DRE is presented by Kim, who claims that 2 Cor 3:4—4:6 is "an obvious allusion to the Damascus revelation."[195] Kim defends this assertion at length in the first chapter.[196] He begins by listing scholars who share this view,[197] then carefully considers three "points of caution" raised by Windisch: first, that Paul may be describing a typical experience rather than a specific vision; second, that Paul is speaking of "pure internal seeing" rather than a vision; third, that the passage may be understood without reference to the DRE of Acts 9.[198] Kim addresses each of Windisch's cautions in turn.

First, Kim considers the subject of 2 Cor 4:1–6. He argues that the subject is not ἡμεῖς πάντες (3:18), but that it has shifted to Paul and his coworkers,[199] and more specifically to Paul himself.[200] Yet in either case, Kim assumes that verse 6 refers to a conversion experience. He claims that even if Paul is not speaking of himself alone, "it must be understood

---

193. Dietzfelbinger also acknowledges that the DRE connection is controversial: "Daß 2Kor 4,6 vom Damaskusereignis handelt, ist umstritten." Dietzfelbinger, *Berufung*, 49.

194. Dietzfelbinger suggests that since 2 Cor 4:6 alludes to creation (Gen 1:3), and that since Paul speaks of being a new creation (2 Cor 5:17) and connects the DRE to new life (cf. 1 Cor 15:8), then 2 Cor 4:6 is an allusion to the DRE. Dietzfelbinger, *Berufung*, 50.

195. Kim, *Paul*, 45n2. Segal makes a similar claim (2 Cor 4:6 describes Paul's "own conversion and ministry, as he described it in Galatians 1") without any supporting arguments. Segal, *Paul the Convert*, 61.

196. Kim, *Origin*, 5–13.

197. Ibid., 5n4.

198. Ibid., 5.

199. Ibid., 5.

200. "Paul frequently involves his co-workers when he makes assertions primarily about himself." Ibid., 5–6 n. 7.

that in v. 6 Paul is describing a typical conversion experience by means of his own."[201]

Second, Kim discusses Paul's description of the event as being as ἐν ταῖς καρδίαις ἡμῶν (4:6). Kim claims that this is reminiscent of ἐν ἐμοί from Gal 1:16. Based on this perceived parallel, he concludes that "Paul is not here [2 Cor 4:6] describing 'a purely internal setting' (whatever it may be) but God's objective disclosure of the risen Christ which 'touched' the heart (in its Biblical sense!) of Paul."[202]

Third, Kim suggests that 2 Cor 4:6 "can be better understood if it is supposed that [it] refer[s] to the Damascus event."[203] Kim discusses Paul's contextual allusions to creation (4:6)[204] and Moses (3:7, 13, 15, 18),[205] as well as allusions to OT prophetic calls in Gal 1:15–16,[206] but claims that ἔλαμψεν (4:6) refers to a "definite point of time in the past, the moment of the Damascus event."[207] In order to sustain an association between 2 Cor 4:4–6 and the DRE, Kim also appeals to the Acts DRE accounts. Kim claims that Jesus "must have" appeared to Paul "accompanied by the radiance of light which was perceived by him as the divine glory."[208] Yet Luke never states that Paul actually saw Jesus, but rather encountered a light (9:3; 22:6, 9, 11; 26:13). In fact, he twice states that Paul was blinded (9:8; 22:11). Kim's detailed conclusion regarding what Paul "must have" seen is speculative since Luke never describes Paul as seeing Jesus's face, only encountering Jesus in a blinding light. Kim also claims that 2 Cor 4:1–5 contains other allusions to the DRE, particularly the references to proclaiming the gospel (4:3–5),[209] mercy, and ministry (4:1).[210]

Kim's suggestion of allusions to the DRE in Paul's comments regarding the proclamation of the gospel and ministry (4:1–5) may be valid, since Paul often makes such allusions when discussing the DRE. However, his claims regarding the details of 2 Cor 4:6 in particular re-

---

201. Ibid., 6.
202. Ibid., 7.
203. Ibid.
204. Ibid., 7–9.
205. Ibid., 8, 12–13.
206. Ibid., 10–11.
207. Ibid., 7.
208. Ibid., 8.
209. Ibid., 10–11.
210. Ibid., 11.

quire close attention. In Kim's first response to Windisch, he argues that the verse describes either Paul's conversion or a typical conversion in terms of Paul's own conversion. Kim makes an underlying assumption in both cases: that the verse describes a conversion experience. Kim never seeks to establish this assertion, but rather assumes that it is obviously true. However, numerous other possible explanations for this verse will be discussed below.

Kim's second response relies on interpreting the phrase ἐν ταῖς καρδίαις ἡμῶν as a specific event: "God's objective disclosure of the risen Christ" in the DRE.[211] Yet Paul uses variations of the phrase ἐν ταῖς καρδίαις ἡμῶν on numerous occasions without reference to a particular vision or encounter such as the DRE.[212] Therefore, it is unlikely that he uses the phrase in 2 Cor 4:6 in the technical sense of denoting a specific "objective" vision of Jesus.

Since Kim's responses to the first two objections are not convincing, his response to the third objection is critical to the argument that 2 Cor 4:6 refers to the DRE. Kim claims that 4:1-6 is best understood in reference to the DRE. However, Paul explicitly refers to both creation (4:6)[213] and the theophany to Moses at Sinai (3:7, 13, 15, 18)[214] in the passage. Kim seeks to associate 4:6 with the DRE because of associations with light and glory. Yet he acknowledges that "nowhere else in his letters does Paul mention explicitly light or glory in connection with the Christophany on the Damascus road."[215] There appears to be strong evidence that the imagery of 4:4-6 is an allusion to an early Christian connection between creation and the incarnation and ministry of Jesus, and not the DRE. John 1:1-14 parallels 2 Cor 4:6 in its application of δόξα (14) in reference to Jesus, and φῶς (4, 5, 7, 8, 9) and σκότος/σκοτία (5) in connection to creation (1-5).[216] Thus, John 1:1-14 describes Jesus with

---

211. Ibid., 7.

212. Rom 2:15; 5:5; 10:6, 8, 9; 1 Cor 7:37; 2 Cor 1:22; 3:2, 3; 5:12; 7:3; 8:16; Phil 1:7. Cf. Eph 3:17; Col 3:15, 16.

213. Dietzfelbinger also makes this connection in Dietzfelbinger, *Berufung*, 50.

214. "The reference to 'glory . . . in the face of Christ' reverts to the preceding discussion in chap. 3, especially at 3:7 . . . and 3:18 . . . as Fitzmyer shows . . . and William H. Smith's dissertation has developed." Martin, *2 Corinthians*, 80-81.

215. Kim, *Origin*, 7.

216. Kim mentions John 1:1-18 in relation to the εἰκὼν τοῦ θεοῦ, even though "John never uses the word εἰκών." Kim, *Origin*, 140. Kim notes that 2 Cor 4:4 and John 1:1-18 share similar themes related to creation and the incarnation, but does not mention the stronger verbal connection between John 1:1-14 and 2 Cor 4:6.

specific reference to both glory and light, the two aspects cited by Kim as significant in 2 Cor 4:6. Furthermore, the other key argument arising from Kim's analysis of 2 Cor 4:4–6 involves the εἰκὼν τοῦ θεοῦ (4). The only other use of this phrase in the NT occurs in Col 1:15,[217] which speaks of Jesus as the εἰκὼν τοῦ θεοῦ in relation to creation (πρωτότοκος πάσης κτίσεως, Col 1:15; ἐν αὐτῷ ἐκτίσθη τὰ πάντα, Col 1:16) and the resurrection (πρωτότοκος ἐκ τῶν νεκρῶν, Col 1:18).[218] Therefore, in 2 Cor 4:4–6 Paul may be alluding to an early Christian association between creation and the incarnation using the imagery of δόξα, φῶς, and εἰκών, rather than to the DRE.

Another possible connection to 2 Cor 4:6 that has received little attention is the vision of 2 Cor 12:1–4. Kim claims that the verb λάμπω (4:6) "refers back to a definite point of time in the past, the moment of the Damascus event."[219] Yet if 4:6 does refer to a specific event, it does not necessarily follow that the specific event must be the DRE. In the context of 2 Corinthians, the most explicit reference to a vision is found in 12:1–4, where Paul claims to have entered the third heaven, paradise. He claims that this experience was a vision (ὀπτασία, 12:1), an appearance (ἀποκάλυψις, 12:1). Therefore, the seeing to which Paul refers (4:6) may have come from the vision that he mentions later in the same epistle (12:1–4),[220] rather than the DRE.[221] Indeed, Paul's allusion to Moses's vision (2 Cor 3:7–18) refers to Moses's encounter with Yahweh at Sinai (cf. Exod 34:29–35), and not his initial encounter with God at the burning bush (Exod 3:1—4:17).[222]

---

217. Col 1:15–20, while part of a disputed Pauline epistle, has (ironically) been identified as pre-Pauline: "It is generally agreed that at this point the writer(s) have included an already formed hymn." Dunn, *Colossians*, 83.

218. Thrall cites Col 1:15–20 as evidence that "the idea of Christ as God's εἰκών existed already [i.e., prior to 2 Cor 4:4] in the liturgical tradition of the early church." Thrall, *2 Corinthians*, 1:309.

219. Kim, *Origin*, 7.

220. The integrity of 2 Cor has been questioned. See Harris, *2 Corinthians*, 8–51.

221. Segal, having already identified 2 Cor 4:6 as a DRE text, also associates it with the vision of 2 Cor 12: "When reading [2 Cor 4:6] in terms of Paul's later description of the ascension of the man to the third heaven . . ." Segal, *Paul the Convert*, 61. Segal does not claim that the two events are identical, but that they are similar.

222. The major commentators all discuss the possibility that 2 Cor 4:4–6 alludes to the DRE, but do not appear to raise the possibility that it may allude to the vision of 2 Cor 12.

Finally, Kim's argument that 2 Cor 4:6 has primary reference to Paul alone does not explain why he would make such a similar statement in 3:18. Paul clearly associates seeing and glory not just with himself but also with "we all," including the Corinthians, in the immediate context of 4:6.

Thus, it appears that 2 Cor 3:4—4:6 is functioning on many levels simultaneously. At different points Paul is speaking as an individual, together with coworkers, and collectively with the letter's recipients, concerning a reality that he compares to their conversion and/or current experiences (3:18), the theophany at Sinai (3:7, 13, 15, 18), creation (4:6), and the incarnation (4:4, 6), in an epistle that refers to a vision other than the DRE (12:1–4). Therefore, it is not possible to identify specific themes such as glory, image, and light as allusions to the DRE with any degree of certainty,[223] particularly since Paul himself never mentions these details in relation to the DRE elsewhere.

Therefore, 2 Cor 4:4–6 cannot be considered a primary DRE text since its connection to the DRE is so uncertain. As a result, Kim's assertions regarding εἰκών-Christology and *merkabah* cannot be accepted as pertaining to the DRE directly.

2 Corinthians 10:8

This verse contains the phrase τῆς ἐξουσίας ἡμῶν ἧς ἔδωκεν ὁ κύριος, which may be an allusion to the authority Paul has as the Lord's messenger. Indeed, Thrall claims that "Paul does have his initial calling in view ... [as] indicated by the aorist tense of ἔδωκεν."[224] However, the connection to the DRE is not certain, and in any case the verse adds nothing new to the discussion.

2 Corinthians 10:13

In verse 13, Paul speaks of "the field that God has assigned to us, to reach out even as far as you" (NRSV). This may be an allusion to his appointment as apostle to the nations. Barnett does make the connection to

---

223. Furnish comments that "even MacRae, who believes ... that there is an allusion to Paul's own conversion [in 2 Cor 4:4–6] must acknowledge that the language is 'so imprecise that he seems to have wished to generalise to the level of the Christian experience of conversion.'" Furnish, *II Corinthians*, 251.

224. Thrall, *2 Corinthians*, 2:624.

Jesus's "commission to Paul on the Damascus Road."[225] However, since the verse introduces no new elements to the discussion, and since its connection to the DRE itself is rather weak at best, it will be excluded from consideration.

2 Corinthians 12:1–4

In this section Paul continues the defense of his apostolic authority over the Corinthians. Many fascinating questions are raised in the interpretation of this passage. Is Paul writing in the third person about another person's experiences, or his own? What is the location of the third heaven? Is paradise to be equated with the third heaven, or is the vision of paradise a separate event? Was the event a spiritual vision or an external experience? While these are all intriguing questions, the chronology in verse 2 disqualifies the section from consideration as a DRE text. The vision of the third heaven is dated fourteen years prior, πρὸ ἐτῶν δεκατεσσάρων, to the writing of this letter. This section of the epistle is normally dated about 56 CE, which would place the vision near 43 CE, well after Paul's initial encounter with Jesus on the Damascus road.[226] Therefore, 2 Cor 12:1–4 is likely not a reference to the DRE.[227]

Although 2 Cor 12 does not refer to the DRE, it does describe an event that differs fundamentally from the DRE. Paul speaks of someone being "caught up" (ἡρπάγη, 2) to the third heaven, a clear reference to heavenly ascent,[228] which is absent from his depictions of the DRE. He cannot describe whether the encounter was "in the body" or without (2, 3). Unlike the DRE, the message of this vision could not be told to others (4). The reference to the "third heaven" may allude to a

---

225. Barnett, *2 Corinthians*, 485.

226. Harris, *2 Corinthians*, 835.

227. Bowker also views 2 Cor and the DRE as distinct ("... the visions of II Cor. xii. i ff., and on the road to Damascus,..."). Bowker, "Merkabah Visions," 159. Tabor also distinguishes between the DRE and the vision of 2 Cor 12: "[Paul's] extraordinary ascent to heaven [2 Cor 12] ... is to be compared to his 'Damascus road' vision and calling. ... [2 Cor 12] is a higher and more privileged experience." Tabor, *Things Unutterable*, 37. Segal is more hesitant to reach the same conclusion, but does recognize that "it would be unwise to proclaim that 2 Cor 12 was definitely Paul's conversion." Segal, *Paul the Convert*, 37.

228. For an analysis of Paul's heavenly ascent, see Tabor, *Things Unutterable*, 113–25. Tabor suggests that the conclusions one may reach concerning this vision are sparse. Beyond the message of the vision, the expectation of Jesus's return, and Paul's mission, "there is little one can say" regarding the significance of the event (124).

merkabah-like multitiered cosmology (*T. Levi* 2:7–9; cf. *3 Bar.* 11:1–2; *2 Enoch*; *Martyrdom and Ascension of Isaiah*; *Apocalypse of Abraham*) that is entirely absent from the depictions of the DRE. Finally, Paul gives no indication regarding how the event was initiated; it cannot be classified as either Divine Initiative or Divine Response. Despite the lack of critical data, it is clear that the vision of 2 Cor 12 differs significantly from the DRE. Thus, Paul describes various types of epiphanies. It is therefore not possible to generalize about Paul's experiences based on a single event.

Furthermore, the variety of encounters that Paul describes should emphasize the unique aspects of the DRE. For example, Paul repeatedly emphasizes the message he received in the DRE,[229] but declines to reveal the message that was received in 2 Cor 12. This suggests that message is critical to the DRE, and that Paul's revelation of the message to his readers is not perfunctory but intentional. Indeed, it is noteworthy that Paul does not attribute the unique features of 2 Cor 12 to the DRE, even though he was certainly aware of encounters involving both heavenly ascent and multitiered heavenly realms.

Romans

In the Epistle to the Romans, Paul makes several references to his encounter with the risen Jesus. As in Galatians and 1 Corinthians, Paul's close connection with Jesus is obvious in the salutation (1:1–6), as well as at several other points (11:13; 15:15–20).[230]

ROMANS 1:1–6

The opening verses appear to be related to the DRE. Few have recognized this connection.[231] Yet, as we shall see, Paul introduces himself in language reminiscent of his call in Gal 1.

---

229. See pp. 153–54 below.

230. Du Toit notes the striking similarities between Rom 1:1–17 and 15:14 in du Toit, "Persuasion," 198–200.

231. Kim views the opening verses of Romans, 1 and 2 Corinthians, and Galatians, as well as Ephesians and Colossians as alluding to the DRE. Kim, *Origin*, 27. Segal mentions the connection with Rom 1:1 in Segal, *Paul the Convert*, 70. Wright mentions Rom 1:3–4 in the context of the DRE in Wright, *Resurrection*, 380–81. Hurtado discusses Rom 1:1–4, albeit not in the context of the DRE. Hurtado, *One God*, 95.

Paul begins the salutation with an extended self-identification consisting of three descriptive phrases in apposition to his name (Παῦλος).[232]

The first phrase, δοῦλος Χριστοῦ Ἰησοῦ, defines Paul in relation to Jesus. The term "slave" indicates Paul's devotion and service. Other terms used by Paul in Rom 1:1, particularly "called" and "set apart," closely parallel not only Gal 1:15, but also the Servant passage of Isa 49:1–6. Thus, it is not surprising to find that δοῦλος is also used in Isa 49:1–6 with reference to Isaiah's Servant (cf. Isa 49:3a LXX, καὶ εἶπέν μοι Δοῦλός μου εἶ σύ).[233] Thus, Paul's claim to be a slave may be not only a statement of his current devotion to Jesus, but also a reference to his call. Furthermore, Paul also uses the phrase δοῦλος Χριστοῦ in the context of his call in Gal 1:10. Therefore, the term may be best understood as yet another allusion to the DRE.

Paul refers more directly to his call in the second appositional phrase, κλητὸς ἀπόστολος. The phrase κλητὸς ἀπόστολος is reminiscent of 1 Cor 1:1, although here Paul does not identify the source of his apostleship. From the context, it is apparent that either Χριστός Ἰησοῦς (1a; cf. 1 Cor 1:1), θεός (1b), or both are in view. Since both are presented as the source of Paul's apostleship in Gal 1:1–2, it is likely that the calling is to be associated with both. The term ἀπόστολος identifies Paul by position, as a messenger from God. He appears to make the claim of apostleship in order to establish his authority from the outset of the letter, as he did in Galatians (cf. Gal 1:1). Thus, Paul presents himself as a messenger from God by divine appointment.[234]

Paul's self-identification continues in the third phrase, ἀφωρισμένος εἰς εὐαγγέλιον θεοῦ. Previously, he claimed to be a messenger; now, he discusses his message. The participle ἀφωρισμένος is reminiscent of ἀφορίσας from Gal 1:15. The passive form indicates that Paul viewed the source of his vocation as external, rather than something he sought to attain, just as the active form (Gal 1:15) attributed the act of setting apart to God. The repetition of ἀφορίζω in the context of Paul's call is

---

232. Cranfield, *Romans*, 1:51.

233. For more on the connection to Isa 49, see Dunn, *Romans*, 1:8. Cranfield cites various other texts connected to the "servant of Yahweh" (Josh 14:7; 24:29; Judg 2:8; 2 Kgs 17:23; Ps 89:3) without reference to Isa 49. Cranfield, *Romans*, 1:50.

234. "The word κλητός here expresses the thought of divine calling in opposition to human self-appointment." Cranfield, *Romans*, 1:51.

striking when one considers that this verb appears only twice elsewhere in the undisputed Pauline canon (2 Cor 6:17; Gal 2:12). The preposition εἰς indicates that Paul was set apart for a purpose: the proclamation of the gospel of God. This closely mirrors the sequence of Gal 1:15–16, where God the Father (the one who set Paul apart) chose to reveal Jesus (his Son), in order that Paul might preach the gospel to the nations. Interestingly, the noun εὐαγγέλιον indicates the purpose in Rom 1:1; the cognate verb εὐαγγελίζω is used in the purpose clause of Gal 1:16. The term εὐαγγέλιον is also connected with Jesus's appearance in Galatians (1:11; cf. 1:6, 7; 2:2, 7), and refers simply to Paul's message concerning the "good news of Jesus Christ."[235] The function of the genitive θεοῦ is debated. It has been variously identified as a subjective[236] and plenary genitive,[237] as well as a genitive of origin[238] and source.[239] Given the context, it appears that genitive of source is most likely. Since Paul has just identified himself as a messenger called by God, it is logical that he should describe his message as coming from God. In the words of Dunn, "'of God' is the source and authority behind the message."[240]

It should also be noted that Paul alternates between describing the gospel as being from God (cf. Rom 1:1; 15:16, 2 Cor 11:7; 1 Thess 2:2, 8, 9) and from Jesus (Rom 15:19; 1 Cor 9:12; 2 Cor 2:12; 9:13; Gal 1:7; Phil 1:27; 1 Thess 3:2). Several of these alternations appear in close proximity (Rom 15; 1 Thess 2–3). There does not appear to be a pattern to this alternation: Paul appears to choose freely between God the Father and Jesus as the source of his gospel.

The next three verses (2–4) elaborate on the εὐαγγέλιον (1).[241] The content of the gospel is Jesus (περὶ τοῦ υἱοῦ αὐτοῦ, 3). Paul summarizes the gospel chronologically, from the OT prophets (2), to Jesus's birth (3), death, and resurrection (4),[242] to Paul's own relationship with Jesus (5).

---

235. Dunn, *Romans*, 1:10.
236. Moo, *Romans*, 43n18.
237. *GGBTB*, 121.
238. BDF, §163; Cranfield, *Romans*, 1:55n1.
239. Dunn, *Romans*, 1:10.
240. Ibid.
241. These verses are also significant for understanding the relationship between Jesus and the Spirit. "In Pauline literature, I Cor xv. 45 apart, there is no more important passage on this subject than Rom. i. 3–4." Dunn, "Flesh," 40.
242. Dunn argues that Jesus's relation to the Spirit (Rom 1:4) explains both the continuity and the difference between the historical Jesus and the exalted Jesus. Dunn, "Romans 1:3–4," 151.

Since the progression is chronological, Paul presents his encounter with Jesus as a post-resurrection event.

The reference to Jesus Christ as God's son (τοῦ υἱοῦ αὐτοῦ, 3; υἱοῦ θεοῦ, 4) is especially significant in his characterization by Paul (cf. Gal 1:16). Hurtado notes that the definite article marks Jesus as "singled out for special honor and status."[243]

Romans 1:5 summarizes Paul's call by the resurrected Jesus:

δι' οὗ ἐλάβομεν
χάριν καὶ
ἀποστολὴν
   εἰς ὑπακοὴν πίστεως
     ἐν πᾶσιν τοῖς ἔθνεσιν
     ὑπὲρ τοῦ ὀνόματος αὐτοῦ

The preposition διά identifies Jesus as the intermediate agent (antecedent of οὗ, 4), which is reminiscent of Gal 1:1.[244] The aorist verb ἐλάβομεν is an epistolary plural,[245] since Paul is the sole author of the letter[246] (*pace* Dunn[247]). While the verb is active, its action is passive ("we received"). This indicates that Paul was a recipient, a passive participant, which corresponds with the intent of κλητός and ἀφορισμένος (1).

Jesus's gift to Paul is described by the nouns χάρις and ἀποστολή, grace and apostleship. It may be surprising to observe how closely χάρις is linked to Paul's encounter with Jesus. Paul mentions χάρις in connection to his calling at least four times in Galatians alone (1:3, 6, 15; 2:9). Paul's apostleship is also intimately tied to Jesus's appearance (Gal 1:1). In fact, Paul may be using the phrase χαρίς και ἀπόστολη as a hendiadys[248] to summarize that experience.[249]

The preposition εἰς introduces the purpose for which the "grace and apostleship" were given. The precise interpretation of the genitive phrase

---

243. Hurtado, "Sonship," 225.

244. Dunn comments that δι' οὗ refers to Jesus as "an active agent and participant in the process of salvation." Dunn, *Romans*, 1:16.

245. *GGBTB*, 395.

246. "So most commentators." Moo, *Romans*, 51n61.

247. Dunn, *Romans*, 1:16.

248. Cranfield, *Romans*, 1:65.

249. Fitzmyer agrees with no hesitation: "... 'grace and apostleship,' a hendiadys ..." Fitzmyer, *Romans*, 237.

ὑπακοὴν πίστεως has been much debated.²⁵⁰ For our purposes, it is sufficient to observe that Paul was sent in order to elicit a response from "all the nations," ἐν πᾶσιν τοῖς ἔθνεσιν (cf. Gal 1:16; 2:2, 8, 9). Here "nations" must refer to the Gentiles in particular.²⁵¹ The message is preached for the sake of Jesus's name, ὑπὲρ τοῦ ὀνόματος αὐτοῦ.

Thus, in Rom 1:1–6 Paul affirms his call to be Jesus's apostle to the nations, using language reminiscent of Gal 1. Since Paul received that call in the DRE, we may conclude that Rom 1:1–6 pertains to the DRE.

ROMANS 11:13

In the midst of an argument concerning the relationship of Israel and the Gentile nations to God, Paul has a brief aside in which he discusses his call as apostle to the nations:

Ὑμῖν δὲ λέγω τοῖς ἔθνεσιν· ἐφ᾽ ὅσον μὲν οὖν εἰμι ἐγὼ ἐθνῶν ἀπόστολος, τὴν διακονίαν μου δοξάζω²⁵²

This dependent clause contains the pithy phrase ἐθνῶν ἀπόστολος, which neatly summarizes both Paul's office (messenger from God) and his calling (to bring the gospel to the nations). This identification is entirely consistent with the previous descriptions of Galatians, 1 Corinthians, and Romans. Paul has already claimed to be an apostle (cf. Gal 1:1; 1 Cor 1:1; 2 Cor 1:1; Rom 1:1), and that he has been sent to the nations (cf. Gal 1:16).²⁵³

In the following independent clause, Paul identifies his apostleship to the nations as his ministry, τὴν διακονίαν μου. In other words, Paul's call as apostle to the nations involves service, presumably to Jesus as well as to the nations. The term διακονία does not refer to a particular church

---

250. Cranfield interprets it to be a genitive of apposition, "obedience which consists in faith." Cranfield, *Romans*, 1:66. Others favor some combination of the genitives of apposition and source. See Dunn, *Romans*, 1:24; Fitzmyer, *Romans*, 237. Moo suggests that the genitives of apposition and source ought to be understood as "mutually interpreting." Moo, *Romans*, 52.

251. Moo, *Romans*, 53.

252. Several witnesses, including 𝔓⁴⁶ F G Ψ 33 1175, read δοξάσω.

253. Fitzmyer observes, "Here [Paul] plays on the 'grace and apostolate' mentioned in 1:5 and is fully aware of his commission to preach the gospel to the Gentiles." Fitzmyer, *Romans*, 612.

office.[254] Since service is often rendered by a servant,[255] this appears to echo Paul's self-identification as δοῦλος Χριστοῦ Ἰησοῦ (Rom 1:1). Thus, in fulfilling his call as apostle to the nations, Paul's service made him a servant of Jesus.

Therefore, this verse appears to be related to the DRE since it discusses Paul's call as apostle to the Gentiles. However, the verse will only be used as supporting evidence since the connection to the DRE is indirect.

ROMANS 15:15–20

Once again, this passage is rarely cited as pertaining to the DRE.[256] However, we shall see that the content of these verses does reveal a connection to the DRE.

In this section Paul begins to summarize what he has written to this point. He says that he has written boldly (15a), and then explains why he assumed such authority (15b–16). His explanation features many of the elements we have already seen in the context of his call:

> διὰ τὴν χάριν τὴν δοθεῖσάν μοι ὑπὸ[257] τοῦ θεοῦ εἰς[258] τὸ εἶναί με λειτουργὸν Χριστοῦ Ἰησοῦ εἰς[259] τὰ ἔθνη, ἱερουργοῦντα τὸ εὐαγγέλιον τοῦ θεοῦ, ἵνα γένηται[260] ἡ προσφορὰ τῶν ἐθνῶν εὐπρόσδεκτος,[261] ἡγιασμένη ἐν πνεύματι ἁγίῳ.

The justification for Paul's boldness is captured in the phrase τὴν χάριν τὴν δοθεῖσάν μοι ὑπὸ τοῦ θεοῦ: "the grace given to me by God." As previously noted, Paul frequently speaks of grace in the context of his call (cf. Gal 1:3, 6, 15; 2:9; Rom 1:5). Paul next explains how the grace was given. The verb δίδωμι reverses the perspective of Rom 1:5, where the exchange was viewed from the perspective of the receiver rather than the giver. The close relationship between the verbs δίδωμι and λαμβάνω is con-

---

254. Dunn concurs that "it should not be rendered 'office.'" Dunn, *Romans*, 2:656.

255. Cf. Luke 12:37 for an example of δοῦλος used in conjunction with διακονέω (cognate with διακονία).

256. Kim does cite Rom 15:15 as a DRE text. Kim, *Origin*, 25.

257. A few witnesses (ℵ* B F) read ἀπό, but the clear majority ($\mathfrak{P}^{46}$ ℵ² A C D G Ψ 33 1739 1881 𝔐) read ὑπό.

258. $\mathfrak{P}^{46}$ alone reads διά.

259. B omits εἰς.

260. B and 1881* read γένηθῃ.

261. F and G omit εὐπρόσδεκτος.

firmed by Louw and Nida, who include both in the "Possess, Transfer, Exchange" domain.²⁶² Both the verb δίδωμι, and the noun χαρίς in particular, suggest that Paul viewed his apostleship as something given rather than taken. In the prepositional phrase ὑπὸ τοῦ θεοῦ, Paul names God as the giver. The construction involving ὑπο indicates that God is the ultimate agent.²⁶³

The remainder of verse 16 confirms many previous observations. The clause begins with εἰς τὸ εἶναι, once again indicating that Paul was called for a particular purpose.²⁶⁴ The predicate accusative λειτουργόν refers to a servant.²⁶⁵ Not surprisingly, this is semantically close to the term διακονία²⁶⁶ used in Rom 11:13, and δοῦλος in Rom 1:1 (cf. 1 Cor 9:1).²⁶⁷ Once again, he renders his service to Jesus (cf. Rom 1:1). He also reaffirms that his call to the nations involves the proclamation of the gospel (τὸ εὐαγγέλιον). The gospel is associated with God in this case (cf. Rom 1:1; although cf. Gal 1:6; Rom 15:20). Paul also reiterates that his call is to the nations, τὰ ἔθνη.

In addition to being a generic reference to service,²⁶⁸ the term λειτουργός is also used with a more specific application to the OT priesthood.²⁶⁹ The remainder of verse 16 confirms that Paul does indeed view his ministry in the light of the OT priesthood. Thus Schreiner correctly claims that λειτουργός "denotes priestly ministry here."²⁷⁰ The verb ἱερουργέω, which appears here as the present active participle ἱερουργοῦντα, is a *hapax legomenon* in the NT, and is absent from the LXX. It pertains to performing sacred rites.²⁷¹ Paul continues the priestly

---

262. L&N, §57.

263. *GGBTB*, 433.

264. Moo, *Romans*, 889n28. "We take εἰς τὸ εἶναί to indicate purpose (cf., e.g., Cranfield; Schlier)."

265. L&N, §35.23.

266. Ibid., §35.19, 21.

267. Oddly, Louw and Nida place δοῦλος in a different semantic domain, but its cognate verb δουλεύω is placed in the same domain as λειτουργός and διακονία. Ibid., §35.27.

268. Cf. 2 Sam 13:18; 1 Kgs 10:5; 2 Kgs 4:43; 6:15; 2 Chr 9:4; Ps 103:21 (LXX 102:21); 104:4 (LXX 103:4).

269. Cf. Ezra 7:24; Neh 10:39 (LXX 40); Isa 61:6.

270. Schreiner, *Romans*, 766. Wilckens comments that Paul represents his apostolic service "im Bilde eines priesterlichen Opferdienstes." Wilckens, *Römer*, 3:118.

271. *LSJ*, 823.

analogy in the next phrase, saying that he desires the nations to be an offering to God.

Barth is a notable exception to the view that Paul is presenting himself in a priestly role. He interprets Paul's words as a reference to a Levitical role. As such, Paul is "witness to Christ as the priest who is about to offer the lost world of the Gentiles to God as an acceptable sacrifice."[272] Barth's distinction between priests and Levites appears unnecessary. Paul's language is not particular to Levites only, nor does it exclude priests. To quote Dunn, the distinction between priest and Levite is "too strained,"[273] since it discounts Paul's role as the one performing sacred rites (ἱερουργέω). Thus, despite Barth's objection, it is not unreasonable to conclude that Paul viewed himself in the tradition of the OT priesthood. This connection between Paul's service and the priestly office appears to complement the similar connection between Paul's call and the OT prophets (Gal 1:15).

Verses 17–19 contain a summary of the practical outworking of Paul's call in the period after his call, culminating in the observation that he has always considered it an honor to proclaim the gospel where Jesus was not named (20).

Thus, in this epistle Paul restates his DRE calling using familiar terms. He identifies the entire experience as one of grace. He reaffirms that the task was given to him, and not something he sought. He claims that God is the one who is ultimately responsible for his call. He views himself as a servant of Jesus in obedience to the call, and that he has been called to preach to the nations. In addition to these familiar elements, Paul also introduces the connection between his call and the priestly office.[274]

Philippians

In Philippians 3, Paul provides a unique glimpse into the personal aspects of his encounter with Jesus.

---

272. Barth, *Romans*, 177.

273. Dunn, *Romans*, 2:859.

274. Donaldson also discusses Paul's use of cultic language to describe his call. Donaldson, *Paul*, 255–57. He concludes that "the cultic elements in Paul's language of mission, then, join with the prophetic and Isaianic Servant elements to reinforce the Israel-centered nature of his understanding of his apostolic role." Donaldson, *Paul*, 257.

Philippians 3:4–14

In Phil 3:1–3, Paul warns his readers of those who require circumcision (2), who place their confidence ἐν σαρκί (3). Paul then contrasts this lifestyle with the superiority of life in Jesus (4–11).

This passage's connection to the DRE has been generally accepted.[275]

To begin, Paul gives five reasons[276] supporting his claim to have more confidence in the flesh than his opponents (4–6):

περιτομῇ ὀκταήμερος,
ἐκ γένους Ἰσραήλ, φυλῆς Βενιαμίν, Ἑβραῖος ἐξ Ἑβραίων,
κατὰ νόμον Φαρισαῖος,
κατὰ ζῆλος διώκων τὴν ἐκκλησίαν,[277]
κατὰ δικαιοσύνην τὴν ἐν νόμῳ γενόμενος ἄμεμπτος.

The five claims are as follows: first, his circumcision according to the Jewish law;[278] second, his Jewish lineage; third, his being a Pharisee; fourth, his persecution of the church; fifth, his claim of being blameless according to the righteousness which is found in the law.

The content of these claims is quite similar to that of Gal 1:13–14, particularly in his ardent pursuit of the law and persecution of the church. The language is similar as well. For example, the term ἐκκλησία is used in both epistles to describe the followers of Jesus, although apparently[279] without the qualifier τοῦ θεοῦ in Phil 3:6. The verb διώκω is used in both to summarize his actions against the church. In Phil 3:6, the noun ζῆλος is used to describe Paul's persecution of the church; in Gal 1:14 the cognate ζηλωτής is used to describe his pursuit of Judaism.[280] Thus, both the content and language of this section are reminiscent of

---

275. So Kim, *Origin*, 3. See also Schnelle, *Apostle Paul*, 91–92. Marshall views verses 4–7 in reference to Paul's "conversion and calling." Marshall, *Acts*, 167.

276. Most commentators count seven claims, taking "of the people of Israel," "of the tribe of Benjamin," and "a Hebrew of Hebrews" separately, rather than as a single expression of Paul's Jewish lineage. Bockmuehl, *Philippians*, 195; Fee, *Philippians*, 307; O'Brien, *Philippians*, 368.

277. F G (0282 629) and a few others insert θεοῦ, which is present in other passages relating to Paul's persecution of the church (cf. 1 Cor 15:9; Gal 1:13) but lacks sufficient support to be included here.

278. Περιτομῇ is a dative of respect. BDF, §197.

279. θεοῦ is present in F and G.

280. Hawthorne and Martin take this as an allusion to Num 25:1–18, describing Paul as a "new Phinehas." Hawthorne and Martin, *2 Corinthians*, 187.

the Gal 1 account, and confirm the details of Paul's life prior to his encounter with Jesus.[281]

In verses 7–11, Paul contrasts this old life with his new life in Jesus. He now considers his achievements as "loss." This claim is repeated four times (7–8):

ταῦτα ἥγημαι ... ζημίαν
ἡγοῦμαι πάντα ζημίαν
τὰ πάντα ἐζημιώθην
ἡγοῦμαι σκύβαλα

The term ζημία, and its cognate verb ζημιόω, both refer to suffering loss.[282] Apparently not satisfied with simply dismissing his past accomplishment, he denigrates them further as σκύβαλα.[283]

Jesus is quite clearly the reason for this change. Paul cites Jesus four times as the reason for his change in perspective (7–8):

διὰ τὸν Χριστόν ...
διὰ τὸ ὑπερέχον τῆς γνώσεως Χριστοῦ Ἰησοῦ τοῦ κυρίου μου ...
δι' ὅν ...
ἵνα Χριστὸν κερδήσω ...

Paul discounts his past life for these reasons: because of Christ; because of the surpassing greatness of knowing Christ Jesus his Lord; because of him (Jesus); and that he might gain Christ. Paul now has a single-minded focus on Jesus, which diminishes everything about his former life. In fact, the gains (κέρδη) of his past are replaced by a desire to gain (κερδήσω, cognate with κέρδη) Jesus. This incredible shift echoes Paul's description of the DRE in Gal 1:13–16a.[284]

Verses 9–11 describe how this transformation affected Paul's life. Therefore, they do not pertain to the DRE itself. Verse 9 equates the rather vague concepts of gaining Christ (Χριστὸν κερδήσω, v. 8), and being found in him (εὑρεθῶ ἐν αὐτῷ, v. 9), with having a certain form of righteousness. Paul contrasts two types of δικαιοσύνη; namely, his

---

281. For example, Silva observes that "the matters he brings up [in Phil 3:4–6] parallel clearly his claims in Gal. 1:13–14." Silva, *Philippians*, 150.

282. L&N, §57.69.

283. "Rubbish" (L&N, §6.225); or more pointedly, "excrement" (LSJ, 1616).

284. "Although not explicitly mentioned, his conversion on the Damascus road is the presupposition of this re-evaluation of 'fleshly' values." O'Brien, *Philippians*, 384. See also Kim, *Origin*, 298.

former righteousness (cf. v. 6) and his present righteousness.²⁸⁵ Verses 10–11 indicate the purpose of Paul's transformation:

τοῦ γνῶναι
αὐτὸν
καὶ τὴν δύναμιν τῆς ἀναστάσεως αὐτοῦ
καὶ [τὴν] κοινωνίαν [τῶν]²⁸⁶ παθημάτων αὐτοῦ,
συμμορφιζόμενος τῷ θανάτῳ αὐτοῦ,
εἴ πως καταντήσω εἰς τὴν ἐξανάστασιν τὴν ἐκ²⁸⁷ νεκρῶν

The articular infinitive γνῶναι indicates purpose;²⁸⁸ namely, Paul desires to gain Christ and be found in him (8b–9a) so that he might know Christ.²⁸⁹ The first καί appear to be epexegetical.²⁹⁰ For Paul, knowing Jesus involves knowing the power of his resurrection and the fellowship of his suffering.

Verse 12 reveals Paul's progress in this endeavor: "not that I have already received [it] or have already been made perfect. But I pursue [it], that I may also attain [it]." What is Paul seeking to attain? ἐφ' ᾧ καὶ κατελήμφθην ὑπὸ Χριστοῦ [Ἰησοῦ].²⁹¹

The verbs κατελήμφθην, and καταλάβω from earlier in the verse, are both from καταλαμβάνω, meaning to attain²⁹² or to acquire with significant effort.²⁹³ Κατελήμφθην is passive, indicating that Paul received the action. In other words, Jesus took hold of Paul. This appears to be a

---

285. Schenk views this verse as a chiasm. His analysis has been accepted by Silva and O'Brien. Bockmuehl's interpretation is similar. See Bockmuehl, *Philippians*, 209; O'Brien, *Philippians*, 394; Schenk, *Philipperbriefe*, 250–51; Silva, *Philippians*, 159–60. Fee suggests a two-part structure with three parallel phrases describing the two types of righteousness. Fee, *Philippians*, 321–22.

286. The articles are absent from various witnesses, but supported by more. The meaning of the text is little affected by either reading.

287. The words τὴν ἐκ are supported by 𝔓⁴⁶ ℵ A B D P Ψ 33 81 104 365 1175 1505 1739ᶜ et al. The reading τῶν is found in 075 1739* 1881 𝔐, and τῶν ἐκ in F G. The NA²⁷ reading has overwhelming support.

288. BDF, §400.

289. Bockmuehl, *Philippians*, 213.

290. O'Brien, *Philippians*, 402.

291. The NA²⁷ reading is supported by 𝔓⁴⁶, ⁶¹ᵛⁱᵈ ℵ A Ψ 075 1739 1881 𝔐 et al. These witnesses do appear to outweigh slightly those in which Χριστῷ is not present, including B D⁽²⁾ F G 33 et al. See *TCGNT*, 548.

292. BDAG, 519.

293. L&N, §57.56.

direct reference to the DRE.²⁹⁴ Furthermore, it affirms that the initiative and purpose of the DRE are divine rather than human.

Verses 13 and 14 reiterate the claims of verse 12. Paul is continuing to pursue εἰς²⁹⁵ τὸ βραβεῖον τῆς ἄνω κλήσεως²⁹⁶ τοῦ θεοῦ ἐν Χριστῷ Ἰησοῦ.²⁹⁷

It is not certain if the "upward call" pertains to the earlier event in which Jesus "attained" Paul (12), or whether it anticipates the future event in which Paul is made perfect (12).²⁹⁸

Thus, in Phil 3:4–14 Paul evokes the DRE both in the recollection of his life prior to the DRE (4–6), and also in the attribution of the initiative and purpose of the DRE to Jesus rather than to himself (12). This section also provides a fascinating glimpse into the mind of one who has experienced an epiphany. Such reports are rare, particularly in biblical narrative where a salient feature of human characterization is reticence,²⁹⁹ and most narrative accounts do not delve beneath the surface of the experiencer's psyche. Many of the first-person accounts in ancient Jewish literature are pseudepigraphical, and therefore present fictional accounts of epiphany experiences. On the other hand, Paul provides a firsthand account not only of his experience, but also of its affects on his life and thinking.

Disputed Pauline Epistles

The few references to the DRE in the disputed Pauline epistles differ little from what is found in the undisputed Paulines. For example, Eph

---

294. "Paul's eager pursuit has as its goal to apprehend the very prize (cf. 14) for the sake of which Christ Jesus took hold of him on the Damascus road." Bockmuehl, *Philippians*, 221; emphasis original.

295. D F G 075 𝔐 read ἐπί, but εἰς has far stronger support (𝔓¹⁶,⁴⁶ ℵ A B I Ψ 33 81 365 1175 1241 1505 1739 1881 2464 etc.).

296. 1739ᵛ·ˡ· reads ἀνεγκλησίας, meaning "a deed of indemnity" (LSJ, 129)—an unsupported reading if there ever was one!

297. There is little doubt concerning the certainty of the phrase τοῦ θεοῦ ἐν Χριστῷ Ἰησοῦ. It is present in 𝔓⁶¹ ℵ A B D¹ I Ψ 075 33 1739 1881 𝔐 et al. 𝔓¹⁶ reverses the order of the final two words. Competing readings have weak support: θεοῦ alone is found in 𝔓⁴⁶ ; ἐν κυρίου Ἰησοῦ Χριστοῦ is found in F G; τοῦ θεοῦ ἐν κυρίου Ἰησοῦ Χριστοῦ in D*.

298. "Perhaps the interpretation of Paul's words should not be defined too precisely. It is God who calls in Christ Jesus, and he calls the believer into eternal fellowship with him. This is the prize for which Paul is still contending." Bockmuehl, *Philippians*, 223.

299. Alter, *Biblical Narrative*, 114–30.

3 mentions the "revelation made known" to Paul (3; cf. Gal 1:12, 16), God's grace (2, 7, 8; cf. Rom 1:5; 15:15; 1 Cor 15:10; Gal 1:15), becoming a servant of the gospel (7; cf. Rom 1:1; 15:16; Gal 1:10), and preaching to the Gentiles (8; cf. Rom 1:5; 11:13; 15:16, 18; Gal 1:16). Col 1 also speaks of becoming a servant by God's commission (25) to declare the gospel to the Gentiles (27). 1 Tim 1–2 again describes Paul's appointment by Jesus to his service (1:12) and receiving grace (1:13), and also mentions Paul's past as a "blasphemer and persecutor and violent (man)" (1:13; cf. Gal 1:13–14; Phil 3:6). Since the disputed Pauline epistles make little reference to the DRE, and in those few references add little that is not contained in the undisputed Pauline epistles, and since their authorship is not certain, they will not receive prominent attention.

Summary

The Damascus road encounter was transformative in the life of the apostle Paul. From his own testimony in the undisputed Pauline epistles, we can trace the contours of the DRE from Paul's background prior to the encounter to the circumstances of the event itself, including the characterization of the one who appeared to Paul. Literary features of the Pauline DRE accounts will be explored in the following section.

LITERARY ASPECTS OF THE DAMASCUS ROAD ENCOUNTER

Now that the relevant texts from the undisputed Pauline epistles have been considered, the literary aspects of the DRE accounts may be explored. The event itself, including its narrative structure, will be examined first. Then Paul's characterization of Jesus in the DRE will be investigated.

Event

Paul's account of the DRE presents a challenge to the literary critic. Paul's epistles are not presented in narrative form. In fact, the details of the DRE are scattered throughout various epistles. As a result, some of the more common aspects of epiphany are omitted. For example, there is no description of the location, no recounting of the events that immediately preceded the encounter, and no hint as to Paul's initial response when confronted with the risen Jesus. Despite these deficiencies, there remains an abundance of evidence that may be used to reconstruct a detailed picture of the event as Paul describes it.

Narrative Structure

The five basic structural elements of epiphany are: introduction, appearance, message, departure, and conclusion.[300] This framework will be used to examine Paul's encounter with Jesus on the Damascus road in order to construct a comprehensive narrative summary of the event.

Introduction

Two of the most common features of the introduction are title and setting. The introduction to Paul's defense of the gospel in Gal 1 contains a title: "... the gospel preached by me is ... by the revelation of Jesus Christ" (11–12). This statement summarizes Paul's broader argument in defense of the gospel, not just the DRE itself. Nonetheless, it does capture the essence of Paul's experience: the revelation of Jesus Christ. Such identification of the epiphanic figure is a common feature of titles.[301]

The background of Paul's life prior to his encounter with Jesus is well attested.[302] Paul's former life was characterized as being "in Judaism" (ἐν τῷ Ἰουδαϊσμῷ, Gal 1:13). His genealogical and physical credentials were impeccable: an Israelite of the tribe of Benjamin who had been circumcised on the eighth day (Phil 3:5). While his genealogy was important, Paul also actively pursued a life within Judaism. He was a Pharisee (Phil 3:5),[303] which suggests that he studied and observed the Jewish law. In fact, he claimed that he had advanced in Judaism beyond many of his peers (Gal 1:14), zealously pursued the traditions of his fathers (Gal 1:14), and considered himself to be blameless before the law (Phil 3:6). Coupled with this was an active persecution of the "church of God" (Gal 1:13; Phil 3:6; 1 Cor 15:9), to the extent that he sought to destroy it (Gal 1:13). Both of these goals, the pursuit of Judaism and the persecution of the church, were sought with zeal (Phil 3:6; Gal 1:14).

---

300. See pp. 36–41 above.

301. See pp. 36–41 above.

302. For further discussion, see Hurtado, *Lord Jesus Christ*, 87–93; Kim, *Origin*, 32–50; Schnelle, *Apostle Paul*, 57–86.

303. Segal, "Presuppositions," 159. Segal acknowledges that Paul was likely a Pharisee, albeit it "extremist" (170) and "intolerant" (171).

Despite the abundance of background information, Paul provides few specifics regarding the day of the event, such as whether he was alone or with others, or when the event took place. It does seem that he was in or near Damascus, since he claims that he "again returned" to Damascus after departing for Arabia (Gal 1:17). Chronologically, Paul places the event after the resurrection of Jesus (1 Cor 15:3–8; cf. Rom 1:1–5).

Thus, it seems that Paul's primary concern in the period leading up to Jesus's appearance was his identity within Judaism. He took pride in his Jewish heritage, his zeal for Jewish traditions, and his persecution of Jesus's followers. Paul repeatedly presents his pursuit of Judaism as the background for understanding his encounter with Jesus. Particular details of Jesus's appearance, such as the time and place, are omitted. For Paul, the immediate setting was apparently insignificant compared to his past life, and the person he was about to encounter.

Appearance

Paul's narration of Jesus's appearance is remarkably terse. The three salient features of the appearance are: first, the transition from the introduction to the appearance; second, the identity of the epiphanic figure; and third, the imagery of revelation and sight.

The first aspect of the appearance involves the transition from the introduction into the account of the event itself. In Gal 1:15, the transition is marked by three shifts in the narrative.[304] First, the transitional conjunction δέ marks the shift in content. Second, the temporal particle ὅτε marks the shift in time. Third, the third-person verb εὐδόκησεν marks the shift in perspective, from Paul's life to God's revelation of Jesus. These three factors point to the abrupt, unexpected nature of the event. Paul gives no hint that he anticipated or requested Jesus's appearance. Rather, the event was an unexpected interruption in Paul's life, which occurred at the time of God's choosing.

The second aspect of the appearance involves the identification of the epiphanic figure. Paul clearly and consistently identifies that figure as Jesus. Paul uses a noticeably varied range of terms to describe Jesus: Ἰησοῦ Χριστοῦ (Gal 1:12); τὸν υἱόν (Gal 1:16); Ἰησοῦν τὸν κύριον (1 Cor 9:1); Χριστός (1 Cor 15:3); Χριστοῦ [Ἰησοῦ] (Phil 3:12). These

---

304. See pp. 116–20 above.

direct characterizations of Jesus will be discussed in greater detail in the next section.³⁰⁵

The third aspect of the appearance involves Paul's categorization of the event using the imagery of revelation and sight. Paul characterizes the event using the noun ἀποκάλυψις (Gal 1:12), and its verbal cognate ἀποκαλύπτω (Gal 1:16). The language of revelation indicates that his encounter with Jesus was not something Paul sought; rather, God the Father chose to unveil Jesus to Paul. Indeed, Jesus appeared to Paul at the pleasure of God (cf. Gal 1:15).³⁰⁶ In 1 Corinthians, Paul invokes the language of sight with ἑόρακα (9:1) and ὤφθη (15:8), both from the verb ὁράω. The language of sight speaks to the reality of the event. For Paul, Jesus's appearance was not something that he imagined; rather, it was an encounter that involved the perception of reality.³⁰⁷ These concepts of revelation and sight form two sides of the same coin. Jesus's appearance involved the revelation of Jesus to Paul, as well as Paul's perception of that revelation.

Since Paul speaks of having seen Jesus, it is unusual that he does not provide a physical description of the appearance. Jesus's features are not mentioned, nor are any of the attendant circumstances. Instead, the event is presented simply, with emphasis on transition, identity, and revelation: Paul experienced the unexpected revelation of Jesus Christ.

There is uncertainty regarding the kind of appearance Paul experienced. Terms such as "appearance" (Gal 1:16) and "seen" (1 Cor 9:1) could be used of an external encounter or a vision. Perhaps the best evidence is found in 1 Cor 15. Paul lists the DRE as part of a series of encounters. Moreover, he also uses the same verb (ὁράω) to describe his encounter as he does for the earlier encounters. If the previous encounters (including an appearance to over 500 people at one time) were external, then the DRE is likely external as well. Therefore, it is possible that the experience was external,³⁰⁸ although the evidence is not certain. It is also interesting to note that Paul apparently placed little value on whether or not a vision was external (cf. 2 Cor 12:2–3).

305. See pp. 166–73 below.

306. For more information regarding the initiative of the DRE see pp. 154–57 below.

307. Haacker characterizes the event from Paul's perspective as *ein Erkenntnisakt*, an act of cognition. Haacker, "Die Berufung," 11.

308. Cf. Wright, *Resurrection*, 317–18.

Message

Paul emphasizes Jesus's message more than any other aspect of his encounter. He does so repeatedly, and on numerous occasions. For example, the first two chapters of Galatians are a defense of the message Paul received from Jesus: "The gospel preached by me is . . . by revelation from Jesus Christ" (Gal 1:12). Paul gives insight into the content of the message shortly thereafter: "[God] was pleased . . . to reveal his son to me so that I might preach him among the nations" (Gal 1:15–16).[309] This suggests that the message pertained to Jesus ("him"), and involved a specific audience, the Gentiles.

The epistles to the Corinthians reiterate these claims. The opening verse of each epistle reaffirms Paul's apostleship. He also asserts that he was called to preach, not to baptize (1 Cor 1:17), and that his work among the Corinthians was in direct fulfillment of Jesus's commission (1 Cor 9:1).

The Epistle to the Romans also addresses the content of Jesus's message. Paul opens the letter by claiming to be "called as an apostle" (1:1); in other words, he was appointed to his task, and sent as an emissary. His destination, "among all the Gentiles" (1:5), is not mentioned until later in the salutation. Paul repeats his claim to be Jesus's messenger to the Gentiles using the terms ἐθνῶν ἀπόστολος (11:13) and λειτουργὸν Χριστοῦ Ἰησοῦ εἰς τὰ ἔθνη (15:15).

Unlike many other epiphany accounts, Paul does not mention the precise words or actions of Jesus, nor does he give any indication of his own immediate verbal or physical responses to Jesus's message.

In summary, then, Paul presents three aspects of Jesus's message as primary: first, that Jesus called Paul to be his messenger; second, that Jesus gave Paul his message, the gospel;[310] third, that Jesus gave Paul his audience, the Gentile nations. Once again, Paul leaves us wanting more in his recounting of Jesus's message. We find nothing of the words Jesus spoke, nothing of Paul's immediate response. Yet the content of Jesus's

---

309. Kim observes, "From [Gal 1:16] it is clear that for Paul the Christophany on the Damascus road constituted both his gospel (see also Gal 1.12) and his apostolic commission for the Gentile mission." Kim, *Origin*, 57.

310. Kim discusses Paul's gospel in the context of the DRE at length in Kim, *Origin*, 67–99. He also discusses the Christology and soteriology as aspects of the gospel in the following chapters.

message is plain and unmistakable. Jesus appeared to Paul in order to call him to bring the gospel to the Gentiles.[311]

Departure

As we have seen, Paul's description of Jesus's appearance was brief. The description of Jesus's departure is even briefer: Paul makes no mention of how Jesus departed, or of his own reaction to the departure.

Conclusion

Paul conveys little regarding the immediate effects of Jesus's appearance. This is understandable if one considers that Paul's epistles were not written to narrate the DRE; instead, the DRE is presented in support of the arguments within each epistle.

Paul comes closest to giving a conclusion in Galatians, when he states that he went to Damascus and Arabia, and not Jerusalem, after his encounter (1:16–17). Indeed, Paul spends the remainder of the first two chapters of Galatians recounting his actions in the years following Jesus's appearance. Paul's ongoing faithfulness to the message he received is confirmed elsewhere (Rom 15:18–20; 1 Cor 15:10; Phil 3:12). However, these confirmations are from a distance, and do not reflect the immediate effects of Jesus's appearance. Thus, Paul says little regarding the immediate effects of Jesus's appearance. Yet that event became the signal source of a permanent, diametrical change in his life.

Therefore, it is possible to reconstruct the narrative structure of the DRE, from introduction to conclusion, using the various comments Paul makes throughout his letters. Some common, expected features of epiphany narratives are not present. However, Paul clearly describes his background in Judaism, the abrupt nature of the appearance of Jesus, the content of the message he received, and his faithfulness to that message in the years that followed.

Divine Initiative

What brought about Jesus's appearance on the Damascus road? Was it the final step in a long process of searching on the part of the apostle, or

---

311. In discussing Paul's call, Hurtado writes: "It is not clear, however, how soon after the 'revelation' that secured his assent to Christian faith Paul became convinced of his special calling, and how quickly he began his efforts to secure the obedience of Gentiles to the gospel." Hurtado, *Lord Jesus Christ*, 96. However, Paul seems to indicate that the call not only came as part of the DRE, it was indeed the purpose for the DRE.

was it an entirely unexpected event?[312] At first glance, the latter appears to be the obvious answer. Yet the question deserves careful consideration. First, the initiative for Jesus's appearance is critical for several theories related to the nature of the DRE. For example, if Jesus's appearance was a form of *merkabah* vision, then there should be some indication that Paul was seeking an encounter with the divine. Second, some scholars have argued that Paul initiated the DRE.[313] Third, the obvious answer is not always correct. For example, in Gal 1:15 Paul claims that Jesus appeared when God was pleased (εὐδόκησεν) for him to do so. This might appear to be incontrovertible evidence in favor of a divine initiative behind Jesus's appearance. Yet it is also possible that God's pleasure might have been brought about by a human petition. For example, Ps 39:14 (LXX) uses the verb εὐδοκέω in just such a petition. Therefore, it is necessary to undertake a detailed examination of the evidence before reaching a conclusion, no matter how foregone it might appear.

The natural starting point in any consideration of the initiative for Jesus's appearance is Gal 1:14–16. There are at least eight distinct factors that point to divine, rather than human, initiative. First, Paul was persecuting the church of God before Jesus appeared (14). Second, he was actively pursuing his calling within Judaism, apart from Jesus, with no indication of any dissatisfaction in that pursuit (14; cf. Phil 3:4b–6). Third, when Jesus is about to be revealed, Paul changes the subject from himself to God (15). This indicates that God is the principal actor, in contrast to the preceding verses in which Paul was the subject. Fourth, Paul speaks passively about being "set apart" (15). This indicates that Paul did not act, but was acted upon by God. Fifth, Paul's call is described as being "from his mother's womb" (15), indicating that God's plan was in effect even prior to Paul's ability to make any decisions of his own. Sixth, God is said to have acted "by his grace" (15), again indicating God's divine sovereignty despite Paul's actions to the contrary. Seventh, Paul says that Jesus was revealed to him, not that he had found Jesus (16). Eighth,

---

312. Dietzfelbinger addresses the question of "inner preparation" and concludes that it is impossible to know what preparations Paul made, if any, and that it is idle to speculate over it. Dietzfelbinger, *Berufung*, 87.

313. See Gager, *Reinventing*, 53–54. Gager claims that "in some sense Gentiles must have been an underlying factor leading up to the conversion." His first corroborating evidence is rather unpersuasive: "Sanders speculates . . ." He also cites Gaston's claim that "On the basis of Gal 5:11 . . . many have also concluded that Paul had been a missionary to the Gentiles even before his commissioning." Gaston, *Paul*, 28.

Paul was called to act against his prior aims (16). Based on the weight of this evidence, it appears that the DRE exhibits divine initiative rather than human initiative.

Conspicuously absent from this account is any indication that Paul had sought Jesus prior to the DRE. Other epiphanies of the period do not hesitate to describe a desire for heavenly visions (e.g., *Jub.* 12:21; *3 Bar.* 1:1–2; *Apoc. Ab.* 7:12—8:2), yet Paul gives no such indication.

Indeed, other passages confirm the conclusion that Jesus's appearance was solely a result of God's actions, not Paul's. For example, Paul's self-designation of choice, apostle (Rom 1:1; 11:13; 1 Cor 1:1; 9:1; 15:9; 2 Cor 1:1; Gal 1:1), is a passive title, indicating that he had been sent by someone else. Jesus's appearance is described as a revelation (Gal 1:12), which again places the initiative for the DRE outside Paul. In addition, Paul is consistent in speaking passively about his encounter with Jesus: "I have been entrusted with the gospel" (Gal 2:7); "the grace given to me" (Gal 2:9); "set apart for the gospel" (Rom 1:1); "received" (Rom 1:5); "called" (Rom 1:1); "called . . . by the will of God" (1 Cor 1:1); "I was obtained by Christ" (Phil 3:12). Furthermore, Paul's claim to be a slave (Rom 1:1) is a tacit admission that he was obtained by Jesus. The statement "Christ sent me" (1 Cor 1:17) confirms that Jesus commissioned Paul. Finally, Paul frequently associates Jesus's appearance with grace (Rom 1:5, 7; 15:15; 1 Cor 15:10; Gal 1:3, 6, 15), indicating that God had acted toward him in a totally undeserved and unexpected way.

Furthermore, Paul consistently attributes a divine purpose to the DRE. In Galatians, Paul claims that Jesus appeared in order that he might preach him among the Gentiles, ἵνα εὐαγγελίζωμαι αὐτὸν ἐν τοῖς ἔθνεσιν (Gal 1:16).[314] It is possible that ἵνα could indicate result rather than purpose. However, ἵνα is more frequently used to express purpose rather than result.[315] The context also appears to support the view that ἵνα is expressing purpose. The ἵνα clause modifies a subordinate clause that describes his encounter with Jesus (Gal 1:15–16a), and is followed by a recollection of subsequent events (Gal 1:16b—2:20). Therefore, the ἵνα clause indicates purpose for Jesus's appearance.[316]

---

314. See pp. 120–22 above.

315. *GGBTB*, 677.

316. "The purpose of the revelation, that Paul should proclaim the gospel of Christ among the Gentiles, was part of the revelation itself." Bruce, *Galatians*, 93. See also Fung, *Galatians*, 66; Longenecker, *Galatians*, 32.

Paul's Epistles

Other texts confirm that Jesus appeared for the purpose of calling Paul to preach the gospel to the Gentiles. For example, in 1 Corinthians Paul repeats the claim that he was called to be an apostle (1:1), and sent by Jesus to preach the gospel (1:17). In Romans, Paul claims that he was "called as an apostle" and "set apart for the gospel of God" (1:1), given grace and apostleship "for the gospel of God" (1:5), and given grace from God "in order to be a servant of Christ Jesus among the Gentiles" (15:16). In Philippians, Paul was "attained" by Jesus (3:12). Thus, the purpose of the DRE was entirely divine. Jesus appeared in order to call Paul to be his apostle to the Gentiles.[317]

Given the abundant nature of the evidence, we may reasonably conclude that Paul's encounter with Jesus fits the pattern of Divine Initiative.

MERKABAH MYSTICISM

One of the recent trends in scholarship has been to view the DRE as a kind of *merkabah* vision. Since Kim's initial proposal,[318] scholars such as Segal, Newman, and Eskola have also suggested that the DRE should be interpreted as a *merkabah* vision.

Kim

In *The Origin of Paul's Gospel*, Kim proposes that the DRE is a *merkabah* vision.[319] After a discussion of several passages not directly related to the DRE,[320] Kim proceeds to "*the most convincing evidence*" for his proposal, "namely, 2 Cor 3.1—4.6."[321] Kim's discussion focuses squarely on the εἰκὼν τοῦ θεοῦ (4:4), from which he develops the twofold εἰκών-

---

317. "Ziel dieses Offenbarungsaktes ist nicht die persönliche Glaubenserkenntnis des Paulus als Individuum, sondern seine Sendung, sein Apostolat." Haacker, "Die Berufung," 11.

318. See pp. 5–7 above.

319. "As a secondary thesis in my *Origin*, I submitted that on the Damascus road Paul saw the exalted Christ on the *merkabah*-throne." Kim, *Paul*, 194–95.

320. Kim, *Origin*, 224–29. Since Kim states at the beginning of the section, "we submit that *Paul obtained his conception of Christ as the* εἰκὼν τοῦ θεοῦ *at the Damascus Christophany*," it is apparent that 2 Cor 4:4 will be central to his discussion.

321. Ibid., 229.

Christology of the DRE related to Wisdom Christology[322] and Adam Christology.[323]

Kim's argument is based on the association of 2 Cor 4:4–6 with the DRE. We have already argued at length that this passage does not pertain to the DRE.[324] Since the elements within it that Kim relies on (glory, light, and image) do not appear in any Pauline DRE text, Kim's assertion that the DRE is a *merkabah* vision has not been substantiated. Furthermore, the christological corollaries pertaining to the εἰκὼν τοῦ θεοῦ are also not connected to the DRE directly.[325]

Segal

Segal claims that the DRE must be viewed in the tradition of *merkabah* visions.[326] To validate this claim, he discusses numerous Pauline texts. He begins not with Paul's account of the DRE itself, but with the ecstatic vision of 2 Cor 12:1–9,[327] which he admits is likely not a description of the DRE.[328] He then provides a lengthy discussion of *merkabah* visions and other similar mystical encounters.[329] Segal applies his pattern of *merkabah* visions to Paul, focusing on 2 Cor 3:18—4:6[330] and Phil 2:5–11, neither of which pertains to the DRE.[331] His discussion of Gal 1:16 consists of interpreting the dative ἐν ἐμοί as "being united with Christ's heavenly image,"[332] rather than simply identifying the "experiencer of an event."[333]

---

322. Ibid., 260–67.

323. Ibid., 258–60.

324. See pp. 130–35 above.

325. See pp. 187–88 below.

326. See pp. 8–9 above.

327. Segal, *Paul the Convert*, 35–37.

328. "It would be unwise to proclaim that 2 Corinthians 12 was definitely Paul's conversion." Segal, *Paul the Convert*, 37.

329. Ibid., 40–58. Segal again restates the claim that "Ezekiel 1 was one of the central visions that Luke, and Paul, used to understand Paul's conversion." Ibid., 39. Yet the only evidence he presents in favor of this conclusion for the Pauline material seems to be the mention of Glory in Ezek 1 and 2 Cor 4.

330. Ibid., 58–62.

331. Ibid.*t*, 62–63.

332. Ibid., 64.

333. L&N, §90.56. Cf. BDF, §220(1); BDAG, 329. See pp. 118–19 above. Recall also Gaventa's claim that "*en emoi* refers to the revelation to Paul (simple dative) that enabled him to preach to the Gentiles." Gaventa, *Darkness*, 27.

He continues with a discussion of 1 Cor 15:21–58 and 2 Cor 5:15–6:1,[334] neither of which is a DRE text. He then discusses union with the crucified Christ using a variety of non-DRE texts,[335] and concludes with a brief synopsis of disputed Pauline material.[336] Segal concludes that "Paul construes his first Christian experience as (ecstatic) conversion."[337]

Segal argues forcefully in favor of viewing the DRE as a *merkabah*-like event. Yet his argument does not address many DRE-related texts in depth, relying rather on applying conclusions regarding other "mystical" experiences (e.g., 2 Cor 12:1–9) to the DRE.[338] Furthermore, his primary evidence that the DRE was a mystical experience is based on a highly speculative interpretation of a single preposition (ἐν, Gal 1:16).[339]

Segal's other arguments in favor of a *merkabah* interpretation of the DRE are similar to those of Newman. We will consider them below, since Newman develops them in greater detail. However, it should be noted that Hengel and Schwemer also argue against Segal's proposal that the DRE was a *merkabah* vision. They suggest that the vision of 2 Cor 12, not 2 Cor 4, more closely fits the *merkabah* paradigm.[340]

Newman

Newman proposes that "the Damascus Christophany led Paul to weld together various strands of the Glory tradition to arrive at the identification of Christ as δόξα."[341] He also claims that δόξα is a "sign" of the Christophany.[342] Newman bases his argument on the assertion that the DRE was a heavenly ascent in the tradition of *merkabah* visions.[343]

---

334. Segal, *Paul the Convert*, 64–68.

335. Ibid., 68–69.

336. Ibid., 69.

337. Ibid., 69–70.

338. Hays makes a similar observation: "the inferential leaps [on page 47] are characteristic of Segal's discussion. He proposes analogies but rarely makes sustained exegetical arguments." Hays, "New Reading," 185.

339. See pp. 118–19 above.

340. "Segal . . . imagines the vision of Christ before Damascus in the context of Jewish visionary experiences from Ezekiel to Merkaba mysticism. However, that appears more to II Cor. 12.1ff than to the vision at the call, which has the stamp of its own." Hengel and Schwemer, *Unknown Years*, 341 n. 165.

341. Newman, *Glory-Christology*, 211–12.

342. Ibid., 184.

343. "Paul heuristically read his Christophany against the grid of mystical apocalyptic Judaism, specifically the heavenly ascents of Jewish apocalypses, and therefore

Having reviewed the various Pauline DRE texts, we can now analyze Newman's proposal in more detail.

A major difficulty with Newman's argument is that the term δόξα does not appear in his primary DRE texts (1 Cor 9:1-2; 15:1-11; Gal 1:11-17; Phil 3:2-15).[344] Newman seeks to overcome this seemingly insurmountable hurdle in a variety of manners. For 1 Cor 9:1-2 and 15:1-11, Newman notes that several OT passages associate δόξα with ὁράω, which does appear in the 1 Corinthians texts (9:1; 15:8).[345] For Gal 1:11-17, Newman connects the DRE to the vision described in 2 Cor 12 (which also fails to reference δόξα), concluding that the DRE is a *merkabah* vision, and then drawing a connection to appearance of God's glory in Ezek 1-2.[346] Newman's final DRE passage, Phil 3:2-15,[347] also omits δόξα. Newman extends his discussion of this passage to verse 21, which does reference δόξα.[348] Since the connection between δόξα and 1 Cor 9, 15 is superficial,[349] and since Paul does not mention δόξα in Phil 3:2-15, the weight of Newman's argument rests on the Gal 1:11-17 connection between the DRE and *merkabah*.

Newman's claim that the Damascus christophany was a *merkabah*-type vision is based on his interpretation of Gal 1:11-17.[350] To establish

---

interpreted the Christophany as a throne vision in which the special agent of God was equated with the Glory of God." Ibid., 207. For a summary of Newman's study see pp. 16-17 above.

344. These are the texts Newman discusses in chapter 9 in relation to the DRE. Newman, *Glory-Christology*, 184–212. Newman acknowledges that "Paul never made the surface argument that Christ = δόξα," yet concludes that "one can still deduce that such an identification occurred at the convictional level for Paul" that involved a transformation of Paul's "symbolic world" through the DRE. Ibid., 211.

345. Ibid., 190–92.

346. The two passages are "certainly not depicting the *same* event Buttrick, ed., *IDB*. could reflect the same *kind* of ecstatic experience." Ibid., 202.

347. "The autobiographical statements of Galatians 1:11–17 and Philippians 3:2–15 highlight the Christophany as the turning point in Paul's religious life." Ibid., 165.

348. Ibid., 207–10. Newman gives no reason for extending the passage to include verses 16–21, after initially claiming that the DRE-related material extends to verse 15 only.

349. For example, Newman does not appear to connect δόξα to the encounters with Peter, the Twelve, five hundred others, and James (1 Cor 15:5–7), each of which also use ὁράω.

350. "The examination of Galatians 1:11–17 therfore [sic] leads to the following conclusions:... Paul read his [Damascus] Christophany" as a heavenly ascent, a "throne vision." Newman, *Glory-Christology*, 207.

this claim, Newman first states that 2 Cor 12 describes a heavenly ascent.[351] He then seeks to establish a connection between the experiences of Gal 1 and 2 Cor 12 on the basis of three similarities: the word ἀποκάλυψις (Gal 1:12; 2 Cor 12:1, 7); a genitive to identify the one Paul encountered (Ἰησοῦ Χριστοῦ, Gal 1:12; κυρίου, 2 Cor 12:1); and an "affirm[ation] that some sort of mystery was revealed" (εὐαγγέλιον, Gal 1:11; ἄρρητα ῥήματα, 2 Cor 12:4).[352]

The first similarity involves the word ἀποκάλυψις. Newman acknowledges that ἀποκάλυψις is used to describe a wide variety of experiences, including "theophanies, heavenly visions and dreams" as well as "received information or knowledge."[353] This suggests that the term ἀποκάλυψις alone cannot be used to identify a vision as *merkabah*; additional evidence is required to make such a distinction.

The second similarity involves the use of a genitive to describe the one who appears. The construct δι' ἀποκαλύψεως Ἰησοῦ Χριστοῦ, which Newman claims "places the [Damascus] Christophany squarely within the heavenly ascents and throne visions of Jewish apocalypses," is not used exclusively by Paul in this manner. In fact, Paul uses ἀποκάλυψις with an objective genitive on five other occasions (Rom 2:5; 8:19; 16:25; 1 Cor 1:7; 2 Thess 1:7) without reference to a *merkabah* vision.[354]

The third similarity is that a message was received in the vision. Messages are a common feature of all types of visions, particularly Divine Initiative epiphanies.[355] In 2 Cor 12:4, Paul describes what he heard as the mysterious ἄρρητα ῥήματα. Yet the content of the message of Gal 1:11 is the εὐαγγέλιον, which Paul was called to preach publicly to the Gentiles (Gal 1:16). Therefore, the messages received in the two visions appear to be more distinct than similar.

Thus, Newman claims that Gal 1:11–17 describes a *merkabah* vision because Paul received a revelation (first similarity) of Jesus (second

---

351. Newman makes this assertion without providing any supporting evidence. Ibid., 201–2. From the verb ἁρπάζω ("caught up," 2 Cor 12:2, 4) and the phrases ἕως τρίτου οὐρανοῦ (2 Cor 12:2) and εἰς τὸν παράδεισον (2 Cor 12:4), it is likely that Paul is describing a heavenly ascent and/or *merkabah* vision.

352. Ibid., 202.

353. Ibid., 200–201.

354. It should be noted that ἀποκάλυψις takes an objective genitive. BDAG, 112.

355. The centrality of the message element was discussed at length throughout chapter 2. The message element for many epiphanies is noted in Appendix A: Narrative Structure of Selected Epiphanies.

similarity) concerning the gospel (third similarity). But these features could describe nearly any type of epiphany, and are insufficient to warrant the conclusion that Gal 1:11–17 describes a *merkabah* vision.

Furthermore, Gal 1:11–17 contains none of the typical features of *merkabah*. There is no multitiered heavenly realm (2 Cor 12:2), no ascent (2 Cor 12:2, 4) or descent, and no heavenly escort. In fact, it fits the pattern of Divine Initiative. This argues strongly against the notion that the DRE was a *merkabah* vision, since the DRE did not occur as a result of Paul's preparations.

Therefore, Newman's conclusion that Gal 1:11–17 and 2 Cor 12 describe "similar sorts of experiences" (i.e., heavenly ascents and throne visions) is unlikely. His conjecture that the DRE was a *merkabah*-type experience is also unlikely, since he has not demonstrated that Gal 1:11–17 corresponds to 2 Cor 12.[356]

Newman also discusses the DRE in relation to 2 Cor 3:4—4:6.[357] Newman argues at length that 2 Cor 3–4 is connected to both the Sinaitic use of glory[358] and theophanic use of glory in relation to Gen 1–2.[359] However, in his discussion of 2 Cor 3:4—4:6, Newman assumes that the passage refers to the DRE without providing any supporting evidence.[360] As we have seen, it is likely that Paul is not referring to the DRE in this passage.[361] Newman seems to acknowledge his own uncertainty by placing the discussion of the passage not with his primary DRE texts[362] but with 1 Cor 2:8 (clearly not a DRE text) in a section entitled

---

356. Newman also claims in passing that the DRE was an ecstatic event because it "ocurred [sic] ἐν ἐμοί." Newman, *Glory-Christology*, 204–7. L&N, §90.56. Cf. BDF, §220(1); BDAG, 329. Yet we have seen evidence that this ἐν is used to identify the experiencer of the event (see pp. 118–19 above), does not define the type of event. Pate summarizes the two views on the meaning of the preposition ἐν in Pate, *Reverse*, 184–85 n. 31.

357. Newman, *Glory-Christology*, 218–35. Newman devotes a section to 2 Cor 3:4—4:6 (229–35), but also discusses the passage extensively in the preceding section (218–29).

358. Ibid., 218–19.

359. Ibid., 221–22.

360. For example, "Paul's clearest, most extensive use of the Glory tradition occurs in 2 Corinthians 3:4–4:6. Paul employs the Sinaitic Glory construal . . . in the [Damascus] Christophany." Ibid., 229.

361. See pp. 130–35 above.

362. Newman, *Glory-Christology*, 184–212.

"Glory as a 'Word-on-Target': Two Examples."³⁶³ Newman's conclusions regarding Paul's use of glory in 2 Cor 3:4—4:6 may be correct. However, his assumption that these conclusions may also be applied to the DRE is less than certain.

In summary, Newman's conclusions regarding Paul's use of glory in connection to Jesus are substantial. However, Newman's case for closely associating Paul's glory Christology with the DRE is not convincing, since Paul does not use δόξα in the context of the DRE, since the connection between Gal 1 and 2 Cor 12 does not demonstrate that Gal 1 is a *merkabah* vision, and since 2 Cor 3:4—4:6 is not a DRE text.

Eskola

Eskola poses the question, "Could it be that Paul's experience was a merkabah vision?"³⁶⁴ After presenting three arguments in the affirmative, he claims that "only one conclusion can be drawn": that Paul interpreted the DRE as a *merkabah* vision.³⁶⁵

Eskola's first point is that Paul saw a vision of Christ.³⁶⁶ He acknowledges that there is no mention of a throne or chariot in either Gal 1 or Acts 9. Eskola's second point involves the assumption that Paul interpreted his vision according to the throne vision of Ezek 1–2. Yet there is no textual evidence to support this conjecture. However, Paul did interpret his vision using the language of both Isaiah and Jeremiah,³⁶⁷ which makes the lack of reference to Ezekiel troublesome. If Paul did interpret the DRE in the pattern of Ezek 1–2, why would he make no mention of this, but rather allude to both Isaiah and Jeremiah? Therefore, it is unreasonable to conclude that the DRE was a *merkabah* vision based on this argument.³⁶⁸

Eskola's final argument involves the title "Son of God." He claims that "Son of God" is usually a reference to the Davidic messiah, which is a feature of *merkabah* mysticism. Therefore, any mention of "Son of God" in the context of the DRE must be understood as a reference to

---

363. Ibid*y*, 229–40.

364. Eskola, *Messiah and Throne*, 200.

365. Ibid., 201.

366. Ibid., 200.

367. See the discussion of Gal 1:15–16a on pp. 116–20 above.

368. Eskola acknowledges the weakness of this argument in Eskola, *Messiah and Throne*, 200 n. 144.

merkabah mysticism.³⁶⁹ This argument appears to be too ambitious. First of all, Eskola only cites two passages in support of the claim that "Son of God" refers to the Davidic messiah (Rom 1:2–4; 1 Cor 15:25–28); he also suggests a third possibility (cf. 1 Thess 1:10). Eskola does not even claim that the reference to "Son" in Gal 1:16 refers to the Davidic messiah. Yet Paul uses the title "Son" (of God)" on numerous other occasions without reference to the Davidic messiah (Rom 1:9; 5:10; 8:3, 29, 32; 1 Cor 1:9; 15:28; 2 Cor 1:19; 6:18; Gal 1:16; 2:20; 4:4, 6). Eskola himself suggests that two of these passages present Jesus as high priest (Rom 5:9 [cf. 10]; 8:32) rather than the Davidic messiah. This demonstrates that Paul uses the title "Son of God" in a variety of contexts other than as the Davidic messiah;³⁷⁰ therefore, the title is not exclusively a reference to the Davidic messiah. Eskola's claim that the title must then refer to *merkabah* mysticism is also unlikely.

Perhaps the strongest argument against viewing the DRE as a *merkabah* vision is, in fact, Eskola's admonition that "we should pay attention to the general pattern that is present in all merkabah passages."³⁷¹ The Pauline DRE texts lack a heavenly journey, a vision of God's throne in the highest heaven, or any of the other expected features of *merkabah* mysticism. In fact, the evidence suggests quite the opposite: that the DRE was a Divine Initiative experience in which Jesus appeared to Paul unexpectedly, without any preparation leading to an ascent, and without a vision of the heavenly temple.

Summary

It appears that Paul does not present the DRE as a *merkabah*-like experience. The passage most frequently cited in support of the *merkabah* hypothesis, 2 Cor 4:4–6, does not pertain to the DRE. Other evidence presented in favor of the *merkabah* hypothesis, such as the noun ἀποκάλυψις, the preposition ἐν, and the christological title υἱός τοῦ θεοῦ, are all frequently used outside the context of *merkabah* visions; therefore, it is not reasonable to conclude that these alone are evidence that Paul presents the DRE as a *merkabah* vision. Furthermore, Paul's DRE accounts contain none of the typical features of *merkabah* mysti-

---

369. Ibid., 201.

370. Gal 1:16; Rom 1:3, 4. See pp. 171–73 below. The title also appears in Acts 9:20—see pp. 242–43 below.

371. Eskola, *Messiah and Throne*, 156.

cism, including contemplation of the throne, heavenly ascent, a multi-tiered heavenly realm, a climactic vision of God and/or the throne, or a heavenly escort. In fact, the DRE is presented as a Divine Initiative epiphany, which argues against a *merkabah* interpretation of the Pauline DRE texts. Paul presents the DRE as an unanticipated event in which he received an unexpected message rather than an experience precipitated by throne meditation. Therefore, we may reasonably conclude that Paul does not describe DRE as a kind of *merkabah* vision even though he was familiar with the language of *merkabah* mysticism (cf. 2 Cor 12:1–4).

The Significance of the Damascus Road Encounter

Paul describes the DRE as a Divine Initiative epiphany.[372] The pattern of Divine Initiative is inconsistent with earlier psychological interpretations of the DRE, since Jesus's appearance to Paul is unexpected. Paul does not describe any internal conflict leading up to the DRE, but encounters Jesus apparently without prior warning. Divine Initiative also argues against a *merkabah* interpretation of the DRE, since Paul does not describe any preparations prior to the DRE. In fact, Paul's accounts do not contain any of the typical features of *merkabah* visions.[373]

Since the DRE is a Divine Initiative epiphany, it is not surprising that the purpose of the appearance is also divine. Paul indicates on numerous occasions that Jesus appeared in order to call him to be the apostle to the Gentiles (Gal 1:16; cf. Rom 1:5; 15:16; 1 Cor 1:1, 17; Phil 3:12). This is consistent with the pattern we have seen in other Divine Initiative epiphanies, where the purpose for the appearance is revealed in the message section. Heavenly beings rarely appear in Divine Initiative epiphanies without revealing the purpose for their appearance. This argues against Donaldson's assertions that Jesus appeared to Paul without revealing the purpose of the encounter, and that Paul later concluded that he should bring the gospel to the Gentiles.[374]

Perhaps the most significant implication of the DRE's pattern of Divine Initiative involves the identity of the one who appeared to Paul. In describing the events surrounding the DRE, Paul indicates that Jesus's appearance was unexpected. Therefore, the identity of Jesus as revealed in the DRE was neither anticipated by Paul nor constructed by him prior

---

372. See pp. 154–57 above.
373. See pp. 157–65 above.
374. See pp. 19–21 above.

to the event. By presenting the DRE as a Divine Initiative epiphany Paul suggests that the identity of the one who appeared was revealed in the appearance itself. Paul's understanding of Jesus was not the result of a progression leading up to the DRE, but rather the product of a seminal event. While Paul's understanding of Jesus certainly grew in the period following the DRE, the encounter on the Damascus road must be viewed as foundational to Paul's understanding of who Jesus is.

Thus, the Divine Initiative pattern of the DRE is significant for several reasons. First, the unexpected nature of the DRE supports the view that it was not a *merkabah* vision. Second, the purpose of the DRE was revealed in the event itself, rather than being derived later by Paul. Third, the Divine Initiative of the DRE suggests that Paul's Christology is rooted in the DRE. It is to the Christology of the DRE that we now turn our attention.

Characterization of Jesus

In the DRE texts of the undisputed epistles, Paul characterizes Jesus in numerous ways. We will first consider Paul's direct characterization of Jesus through the use of names and titles, and then his indirect characterization through the use of descriptive terms, syntax, and other means.[375]

DIRECT

Keck suggests that the "concentration on titles finally makes the christologies of the NT unintelligible as christologies, and insignificant theologically."[376] Nevertheless, the study of the names and titles of Jesus forms a necessary part of NT Christology, and the Christology of the DRE in particular. Paul directly characterizes Jesus in the DRE texts using the substantives Jesus, Christ, Lord, and Son.[377]

---

375. Direct and indirect characterization are discussed on pp. 30–31 above.

376. Keck, "Renewal," 368. For a general overview of christological names and titles, see Hengel, *Studies*, 359–89; Kim, *Origin*, 104–36; Schnelle, *Apostle Paul*, 437–42.

377. Bruce observes the connection between these terms and the DRE: "Lord, Christ, Son of God—these are near synonyms: to believe that Jesus is one of these is to believe that he is all of these, and all of them are given to him as the risen and exalted one." Bruce, "Jesus," 24. See also Dietzfelbinger, *Berufung*, 63–75. Kim also discusses these titles, not only in the DRE texts but the entire Pauline corpus, in Kim, *Origin*, 104–36. However, his primary interest is in Jesus as the εἰκών τοῦ θεοῦ, which does not appear in the DRE texts (2 Cor 4:4; Col 1:15). Kim, *Origin*, 137–268. Concerning the

Ἰησοῦς

Paul frequently uses the name[378] Jesus to identify the one who appeared to him (Rom 1:1,4, 6; 15:16–17; 1 Cor 1:1; 9:1; 2 Cor 1:1; Gal 1:1, 3, 12; Phil 3:8, 12, 14). Paul is clearly referring to Jesus of Nazareth, who had recently been crucified (1 Cor 15:3–5), whose followers Paul had been actively persecuting (Gal 1:13; Phil 3:6). The immediate implications of Jesus's appearance would have been enormous for Paul. Prior to the DRE, Paul must have assumed that Jesus was dead and buried. When Jesus appeared, he was faced with the inescapable reality that Jesus had been resurrected from the dead (cf. Phil 3:10; 1 Cor 15).

Χριστός

Another of Paul's frequent designations for Jesus is Χριστός (Rom 1:1, 4, 6; 15:16–20; 1 Cor 1:1, 17; 15:3; 2 Cor 1:1; Gal 1:1, 3, 6, 7, 10, 12; Phil 3:7–9, 12, 14). The term Χριστός is frequently used of Jesus in the NT.[379] Χριστός was originally a title referring to the "anointed one."[380] There has been much debate over whether Χριστός is used in the NT as a name or as a messianic title. Many scholars have argued for a messianic use of Χριστός. Wright challenges the notion that "when Paul used the word Χριστός, he did not mean to evoke in his hearers' minds, and did not in fact evoke in his own, the meaning 'Messiah'";[381] furthermore, "there is ample evidence, once we know what we are looking for, to support the claim that Messiahship remained a central concept."[382] With regard to

---

connection of these terms to the DRE, Murphy O'Connor remarks, "Thus, right from the beginning of his life as a Christian, 'Jesus', 'Christ', 'Lord', and 'Son' would have been intimately associated in Paul's mind, because they were rooted in his experience of the power of Jesus." Murphy-O'Connor, *Paul*, 24.

378. BDAG, 471.

379. See Cullmann, *Christology*, 111–36; Hahn, *Titles*, 136–239; Hengel, *Between Jesus and Paul*, 65–77; Moule, *Origin*, 31–35; Taylor, *Names*, 18–23; Witherington, "Christ," 96; Wright, *Climax*, 41–49; Wright, *Paul*, 42–50.

380. BDAG, 1091. De Jonge asserts that the term "anointed" was rarely used, and "clearly not an essential designation for any future redeemer." De Jonge, "Anointed," 147. Dunn outlines the messianic ideas prevalent at the time of Jesus as: Davidic or royal messiah; hoped-for priest figure; prophet; "potentially messianic ideas" such as the suffering servant of Isaiah; and glorified humans and heavenly intermediaries, a category which Dunn dismisses. Dunn, "Messianic," 80–84.

381. Wright, *Climax*, 41.

382. Ibid., 43. Unfortunately, Wright does not examine the DRE texts in the subsequent discussion.

the application of the title to Jesus, Conzelmann suggests that Χριστός "does not represent the relationship between God and Jesus, but rather the connection between promise and fulfillment."[383] Other scholars have claimed that Χριστός functions as a name in the NT, or more precisely, "The personal name ascribed to Jesus."[384] For example, Bousset proposed that "in the Pauline era the title 'Christ' is about to change from a title into a proper name."[385]

There is a variety of opinion on the interpretation of Χριστός in 1 Cor 15 in particular. Hurtado,[386] Wright,[387] and Marshall,[388] for example, argue that Χριστός in 1 Cor 15:3 is titular; Dunn,[389] MacRae[390] and Moule[391] disagree. While it is possible to interpret 1 Cor 15:1–11 in messianic terms, it is equally possible to interpret the passage as an

---

383. Conzelmann, *Theology*, 171 n. 2.

384. BDAG, 1091. Recent studies have pointed to a range of meaning beyond "the anointed." Green notes that "in the past quarter century, the established consensus about the messiah in ancient Judaism has begun to break down, and there now are powerful reasons to ditch it altogether. Careful word-studies, fresh and disciplined readings of well-known texts, and a new appreciation of ancient writings as social products and cultural constructions have revealed religious worlds of ancient Jews (and Christians) considerably more diversified and complex than hitherto imagined." Green, "Messiah," 10.

385. Bousset, *Kyrios*.

386. Hurtado bases his argument on the observation that 1 Cor 15:1–11 contains "both the messianic claim and the messianic interpretation of [Christ's] death and resurrection." Hurtado, *Lord Jesus Christ*, 101.

387. Wright comments with respect to 1 Cor 15:3: "Precisely because this is such an early formulation there is no chance that this word could have been a proper name without connotation, and every reason to suppose that the early Christians intended to have its royal designation." Wright, *Resurrection*, 319–20. Yet Wright notes that the "explicitly 'messianic' argument" is not found until verses 20–28. See also Wright's discussion of Χριστός as a messianic title in Paul's epistles in Wright, *Climax*, 41–55.

388. Marshall, *Origins*, 93.

389. Dunn not only affirms that "the belief in Jesus as the Christ has become so firmly established in his mind and message that he simply takes it for granted," but also that "Christ" functions "as a *proper name* for Jesus" even in 1 Cor 15:3. Dunn, *Unity*, 43.

390. "*Christos* is never or virtually never used by Paul as a title in the sense of Messiah, but only as a proper name. Even in passages thought to be pre-Pauline and merely used by Paul (e.g., Rom. 1:4; 1 Cor. 15:3; Phil. 2:11) there is no evidence that we are dealing with more than a name." MacRae, "Messiah," 171.

391. "It is a familiar fact that Χριστός in the Pauline epistles is, broadly speaking, nearer to a proper name than to a title, however much qualification and subtle nuances might be demanded for a more precise definition." Moule, "Christology," 175.

Paul's Epistles

historical summary of Jesus's death and resurrection; replacing Χριστός with Ἰησοῦς would appear to have little or no effect on the meaning of the text. None of the other instances of Χριστός in the DRE texts appear to be explicitly titular.³⁹² Therefore, it is not possible to conclude with certainty that Χριστός has a specifically titular sense in the DRE texts, although this possibility should not be excluded.

Κύριος

The third term Paul uses to characterize Jesus is κύριος (Rom 1:4; 1 Cor 9:1; Gal 1:3; Phil 3:8).³⁹³ Hurtado lists three different ways that the term is used to characterize Jesus: in hortatory statements, as "master"; in eschatological texts, as acting "in the eschatological role of God"; in worship and liturgy, "as the transcendent, exalted one who had been given the divine 'name.'"³⁹⁴

It is possible to interpret the possessive phrases "my Lord" (Phil 3:8) and "our Lord" (Rom 1:4) as a master-slave relationship. This is borne out by Paul's self-designation as δοῦλος Χριστοῦ Ἰησοῦ (Rom 1:1; 15:15–16; Gal 1:10). Furthermore, Jesus's appearance to Paul is presented in the context of Paul's former life in Judaism (cf. Gal 1:13–14; Phil 3:4–6; 1 Cor 15:9). The designation of Jesus as Lord in this context certainly raises the possibility that Paul associates the divine name with Jesus.

---

392. Dahl wisely observes, "It is only natural that in individual cases one cannot clearly distinguish between statements where the name 'Christ' is used only as a proper name and others where the appellative force is still felt." Dahl, "Messiahship," 17–18.

393. See Cullmann, *Christology*, 195–237; Dunn, "ΚΥΡΙΟΣ"; Hahn, *Titles*, 68–135; Hurtado, *Lord Jesus Christ*, 108–18; Moule, *Origin*, 35–44; Taylor, *Names*, 38–51; Wright, *Paul*, 91–96. Bousset outlines some possible meanings for κύριος: "In addition to God and Christ, other heavenly beings also are addressed, but it is also customary among men, with the servant addressing his lord, the son addressing his father, or a man addressing his superior or any honored person." Bousset, *Kyrios*, 122. More recently, Fitzmyer has outlined the four main views on the background of use of κύριος. First is the secular Palestinian Semitic view, which connects κύριος to the Hebrew אדון or the Aramaic מרא. Second is the religious Palestinian Semitic view, where κύριος is derived from a title already used by Palestinian Jews for Yahweh (so Dalman, Foerster, Cullmann, Schweizer, and Fuller). Third is the Hellenistic Jewish view, which proposes that Greek-speaking Jewish Christians used the LXX translation of יהוה to identify Jesus (so Foerster, Quell, Cullmann, and Schweizer). Fourth is the Hellenistic Pagan view, involving the use of κύριος as a title for gods or human roles in the eastern Mediterranean Hellenistic world (so Bousset, Bultmann, Vielhauer, and Conzelmann). Fitzmyer, "Aramean," 115–16.

394. Hurtado, "Lord," 568.

It is certainly true that elsewhere Paul applies the title κύριος to Jesus when quoting OT Yahweh texts.[395] While none of the DRE texts quote the OT in this manner, there is a connection between Gal 1:3–4 and Yahweh's role as the Lord who rescues.[396] Ἐξαιρέω is a *hapax legomenon* in Paul, yet is quite common in the LXX, occurring 131 times in 117 verses. The vast majority of these occurrences identify the Lord as the one who rescues. For example, rescue is most frequently associated with the Lord,[397] the Lord God,[398] both Lord and God,[399] and God.[400] In many other cases, the Lord (as κύριος or θεός) is closely connected with rescue.[401] Conversely, other verses declare that there is no rescue apart from the Lord.[402] In only one case does κύριος not translate יהוה, yet Yahweh is clearly in view (cf. Isa 38:7).[403] Thus, the LXX closely associates ἐξαιρέω with κύριος as a translation for יהוה. In the few remaining

---

395. E.g., Rom 10:13; 14:11; 1 Cor 1:31; 2:16; 10:26; 2 Cor 10:17. See Capes, "Herodian," 125. Capes concludes that "Paul deliberately and unambiguously applies to Jesus Old Testament texts that contain the divine name" (137). Hengel affirms Capes's conclusion: "[The apotheosis of Jesus] progressed *in a very short time*. Its final result was that the statements in the Old Testament in which the inexpressible divine name, the tetragrammaton YHWH or its Qere in the Greek Bible, Kyrios, 'Lord', was used, were now transferred directly to the *Kyrios Jesus*." Hengel, *Son of God*, 77.

Dunn takes the opposite position. Based on the double use of κύριος in Ps 110:1, he argues that "*Paul can hail Jesus as Lord not in order to identify him with God, but rather, if anything, to distinguish him from the one God*" [emphasis in original]. Dunn, *Unity*, 53. In fact, Dunn even claims that "*Paul in fact calls Jesus 'Lord' as much as a means of distinguishing Jesus from God as of identifying him with God*" [emphasis in original]. Dunn, *Partings*, 190.

396. I have not seen the following argument elsewhere in the literature.

397. Exod 18:8, 9, 10; Judg 10:15; 1 Sam 7:3; 12:10, 11, 21; 17:37; 26:24; 30:8; 2 Sam 22:1, 2, 20; Ps 31:1, 2 (LXX 30:2, 3); 37:40 (LXX 36:40); 71:2 (LXX 70:2); 116:8 (LXX 114:8); 119:153 (LXX 118:153); 140:1, 4 (LXX 139:2, 5); 143:9 (LXX 142:9); 144:7, 11 (LXX 143:7); Isa 31:5; 50:2; 57:13; 60:16; Jer 1:8, 17, 19; 15:21; 20:13; 38:11.

398. Deut 23:15; Josh 2:13; 24:10; Judg 6:9; 1 Sam 10:18; 2 Kgs 17:39; 1 Chr 16:35; Jer 41:13; 49:11; Ezek 34:10, 27.

399. Gen 32:12; Exod 3:8; 1 Sam 4:7 (LXX only); Ps 91:15 (LXX 90:15); Isa 48:10, as well as the larger context of many previously mentioned references.

400. Exod 18:4; 1 Sam 4:8; Job 5:19; Ps 50:15 (LXX 49:15); 59:1 (LXX 58:2); 64:1 (LXX 63:2); 82:4 (LXX 81:4); 144:11 (LXX 143:11); Dan 3:17, 28, 29; 6:16, 17, 21, 28.

401. Deut 32:29; 2 Kgs 18:29, 30, 34, 35; 19:12; 2 Chr 25:15; 32:17; Eccl 7:26; Dan 3:15 (cf. 17); Dan 6:15 (cf. 16); Jer 21:12; 22:3; Hos 2:12; 5:14; Zech 1:18.

402. Dan 8:4; 7; Job 5:4; 10:7; Isa 17:12; 42:22; 43:13; 44:17; 44:20; 47:14; Mic 5:7; Zeph 1:18; Zech 11:6.

403. Isa 38:14; cf. Isa 38:7.

passages that do not directly identify the one who rescues,[404] the Lord is often understood to be responsible for the rescue.[405] The only other occurrence in the LXX appears to be the result of a translation error.[406] Thus, the LXX identifies יהוה as the Lord who rescues.[407]

Therefore, Paul's characterization of Jesus as κύριος, the Lord who rescues,[408] uses language formerly reserved for Yahweh. In other words, Paul characterizes Jesus as Yahweh, the Lord who rescues.[409] While it is true that Jesus is characterized as acting in concert with the Father, Jesus is said to be the one who rescues, not the Father. It is κυρίου Ἰησοῦ Χριστοῦ who assumes the role of rescuer, a role previously reserved for Yahweh.

Υἱὸς [τοῦ Θεοῦ]

Paul's fourth direct characterization of Jesus is υἱός [τοῦ Θεοῦ] (Rom 1:3, 4; Gal 1:16).[410] The centrality of this title to the DRE is highlighted by two observations. First, Jesus is characterized solely as υἱός in the appearance section of the Galatians account (1:15–16a).[411] While Paul is clearly referring to Jesus, he chooses to identify him only as "Son" in the heart of the encounter. Second, Paul uses the title more frequently in the DRE texts than elsewhere. Three of the fifteen references to Son

---

404. Gen 37:21, 22; Lev 14:40, 43; Num 35:25; Deut 25:11; Josh 9:26; 10:6; Judg 9:17; 14:9; 18:28; 1 Sam 14:48; 30:18, 22; 2 Sam 14:6; 19:6; 1 Kgs 1:12; Eccl 7:26; Ezek 33:5, 9, 12; Mic 7:3.

405. E.g., for Josh 9:26; 10:6, see Josh 9:24. For 1 Sam 30:18, 22, see 1 Sam 30:8, 23; for 2 Sam 23:12, see 2 Sam 23:12b.

406. Nah 2:1 (LXX 2:2). The entire phrase appears to be mistranslated. Spronk observes that "the reading of the LXX ἐμφυσῶν, 'blowing', only seems to indicate that the translator did not understand the Hebrew word and simply preserved the consonants." Spronk, *Nahum*, 84.

407. Scullion identifies the "God Who Rescues" as one of the four activities of God in the OT. Scullion, "God," 1044–45.

408. Hays refers to the deliverance of Gal 1:4 as "an event signaling eschatological deliverance." Hays, *Conversion*, 120.

409. This contrasts with Segal's assertion that "Paul uses *Lord* as a term of respect." Segal, *Paul the Convert*, 7.

410. See Burton, *Galatians*, 404–17; Hengel, *Son of God*, 21–56; Hurtado, *Lord Jesus Christ*, 101–8; Moule, *Origin*, 22–31. Hurtado notes that "the most explicit and direct way that Paul links Jesus with God is to refer to Jesus as God's Son." Hurtado, "Christology," 191.

411. Hurtado observes that "something about the vision itself apparently communicated Christ's honorific status as God's Son." Hurtado, *One God*, 118.

of God occur in the DRE texts (Rom 1:3-4; Gal 1:16), which means that Paul uses the title six times more frequently in relation to the DRE than elsewhere.[412] Therefore, the title Son (of God) is significant to the Christology of the DRE.[413]

The meaning of the title Son of God is significant, given its prominent place in the DRE texts.[414] In the Pauline DRE passages, the title relates Jesus to God the Father. Each passage that identifies Jesus as Son also identifies God as Father (Gal 1:1, 3, 4; Rom 1:7). Therefore, the title Son denotes Jesus's relationship with God the Father. Furthermore, the title υἱός emphasizes the uniqueness of this relationship. Just as Jesus is contrasted with humanity (cf. Gal 1:1), only he is joined with God the Father (Gal 1:1) as his Son (Gal 1:16). Hurtado affirms this interpretation, writing that the title is used to "communicate Jesus's unique status and intimate relationship with God."[415]

---

412. We have considered 58 verses related to the DRE (Rom 1:1-6; 11:13; 15:15-20; 1 Cor 1:1, 17; 9:1; 15:1-11; 2 Cor 1:1; 10:8, 13; Gal 1:1-17; Phil 3:4-14), compared to 1,464 verses in the undisputed Paulines (by my count). In the DRE texts, the frequency is 3/58; elsewhere, it is 12/1,406. Therefore, the title occurs 6.06 times more frequently ((3/58)/(12/1,406)) in the DRE passages.

413. Hengel claims that the title was not significant for Paul, noting that he only uses it fifteen times compared to 184 times for "Lord." Hengel, *Son of God*, 3. Wright disagrees: "the crucial revelation was of 'the son of god.'" Wright, *Resurrection*, 380.

414. The origin of Paul's understanding of this term has been debated. Bousset proposed that Paul's use of the term "Son of God" had a Hellenistic Gentile origin. Bousset, *Kyrios*, 91-98, 206-10. See also Bultmann, *Theology*, 1:128-29; Schoeps, *Paul*, 153.

Hengel opposes the Hellenistic Gentile view: "This means that the alleged lapse into the speculative Hellenization of Christology must have already taken place in the early church before the time of Paul!" Hengel, *Son of God*, 7. He argues instead that Paul's concept of the Son of God makes Jesus "identical with a divine being, before all time, mediator between God and his creatures." Ibid., 15. He associates the title Son of God with "the sending of the pre-existent Son into the world" and "the giving up of the Son to death." Ibid., 10-12.

According to Longenecker, Son and Son of God are "titles . . . which among the earliest Jewish believers seem to have been used in a more functional manner to denote Jesus' unique relationship to God and his obedience to the Father's will." Longenecker, "Conviction," 483.

415. Hurtado, "Son of God," 900. Wright links the title Son of God to Jesus's messiahship, claims that the primary meaning of the title is "not 'the second person of the Trinity' but 'Israel's Messiah.'" Wright, *Climax*, 43. See the discussion of Χριστός on pp. 167-69 above. Eskola's suggestion that the title alludes to the Davidic messiah in connection with *merkabah* mysticism is discussed on pp. 163-64 above.

Thus, Paul's characterization of Jesus as υἱός pertains to the unique relationship between Jesus and God the Father.[416] Yet the precise nature of this relationship cannot be ascertained from the Pauline DRE texts alone. Some have speculated that Jesus's Sonship involves pre-existence and a divine nature.[417] While this is certainly possible, it cannot be established from the Pauline DRE texts alone.

Summary

Paul uses four names and titles to directly characterize Jesus in the DRE: Ἰησοῦς, Χριστός, κύριος, and υἱός. The name Ἰησοῦς identifies the epiphanic figure as a familiar human whose followers Paul was persecuting prior to the DRE. The term Χριστός appears to function as another name for Jesus, although it may be titular in 1 Cor 15:3. The title κύριος evokes the OT language of Yahweh, the Lord who rescues, and thereby characterizes Jesus as divine. The title υἱός places Jesus in a unique relationship with God the Father. Thus Paul characterizes Jesus in unique relationship with God the Father, and as divine.

INDIRECT

Paul indirectly characterizes Jesus using at least five different methods. First, he identifies Jesus by placing him within a particular historical context. Second, he compares and contrasts Jesus with other characters, including humans, angels, and God the Father. Third, he relates Jesus to God the Father using grammatical constructions. Fourth, he speaks of Jesus in ways typically reserved for God. Fifth, he refers to Jesus and God the Father interchangeably on different occasions. Each of these methods of indirect characterization will help us to understand more fully how Paul presents Jesus to his readers.

---

416. Wright stresses that the principal meaning of the title Son of God is "Israel's Messiah." Wright, *Resurrection*, 380. Yet Hurtado seems closer to the mark in claiming that title refers to Jesus's "uniquely favored status and relationship to God." Hurtado, *Lord Jesus Christ*, 108.

417. Cranfield argues "the evidence of Romans [including 1:3–4] is surely ... that its author firmly believed in the pre-existence of Jesus, in the sense that as the Son of God he has shared the divine life from all eternity, and in the Incarnation, in the sense that at a particular time the eternal Son of God assumed our human nature for the sake of mankind and of the whole creation." Cranfield, "Comments," 280. See also Gathercole, *Pre-existent*.

Historical Context

We have seen that Paul characterizes Jesus as a specific person through his use of his name, Ἰησοῦς. He provides further evidence for this by placing Jesus within particular historical settings. In Rom 1, Paul places Jesus in an historical setting (2–4) even before identifying him by name (Ἰησοῦ Χριστοῦ, 4). Jesus is the one who was prophesied in the Hebrew Scriptures (2); who was a descendant of David (3); who rose from the dead (4). Each of these settings helps the reader to identify Jesus as a specific person. Similarly, 1 Cor 15 provides a nearly creedal account of Jesus's death and resurrection: Jesus died (3); was buried (4); was raised on the third day (4); appeared to Peter and the other disciples (5); appeared to five hundred others (6); appeared to James and "all the apostles" (7); and finally appeared to Paul (8). These accounts leave little doubt that Paul identifies the one who appeared to him as the person Jesus.[418]

Comparison and Contrast

Paul indirectly characterizes Jesus through the use of contrast. This is most evident in Gal 1. From the outset of the epistle, Paul takes great pains to emphasize that his gospel was not received from (ἀπό) humans or through (διά) a human (1). He then contrasts humanity with both Jesus and God the Father (2). A little later, Paul contrasts himself and angels with Jesus with respect to his message (7–8). Further on, Paul distinguishes humans from God (10a), then humans from Jesus (10b). Several verses later, he places the revelation of Jesus in contrast to any human involvement (κατά, 11; παρά, 12).

Thus, Paul presents Jesus in contrast to three different types of beings: humans, angels, and God the Father. First, Jesus is contrasted with humans (1, 7–8, 10a, 11, 12). We have already demonstrated that Paul viewed Jesus as a person, as shown directly by the name Jesus, and indirectly by historical context. Therefore, it is remarkable that he should contrast Jesus with humans. Second, Jesus is contrasted with angels (7–8). This is an interesting contrast, since it argues against the possibility that Jesus is a semi-divine figure subordinate to God. Third, Jesus is grouped together with God the Father (1, 10). In fact, Jesus is consistently pre-

---

418. Wright concurs: "The language he uses [in 1 Cor 15] is not the language of mystical vision, of spiritual or religious experiences without any definite objective referent." Wright, *Saint Paul*, 35.

sented together with the Father in contrast to both humans and angels. Paul's contrast of Jesus apart from humanity, despite his obvious human identity, makes the comparison together with God the Father even more striking. By characterizing Jesus together with God the Father, yet apart from humans and angels, Paul invites his readers to conclude that Jesus is divine.

Grammar

Paul indirectly characterizes Jesus through certain grammatical features including agency, object of preposition, and chiasm.

Agency

Agency[419] refers to the means by which an action is accomplished. The ultimate agent, also known as principal or sole cause, or the source, refers to the one who is finally responsible for an action. The intermediate agent, also known as the efficient cause, or simply the agent, refers to one who may be used by an ultimate agent to complete an action.[420] We have already seen that Paul ascribes the role of ultimate agent to God the Father (Gal 1:1; Rom 15:15), and the role of intermediate agent to the Son, Jesus (Gal 1:1; Rom 1:5). Thus, Paul viewed his apostleship as a result of God the Father's ultimate agency, through Jesus's intermediate agency.[421]

Object of Preposition

In the salutation of the Epistle to the Galatians, Paul unites Ἰησοῦς Χριστός and θεός πατήρ under the preposition διά (1:1b). Similarly, Jesus and God the Father are also united under the preposition ἀπό as the joint source of grace and peace (1:3). Since Paul had just differentiated Jesus from humanity (1:1a), this close connection between Jesus

---

419. Grammatical agency should not be confused with Hurtado's concept of divine agency, or "heavenly figures described as occupying a position second only to God and acting on God's behalf in some major capacity." Hurtado, *One God*, 17.

420. For more information, see *GGBTB*, 431–33.

421. Wanamaker draws a similar conclusion regarding Gal 1:3–5: "[Verse 5] implies that Jesus Christ died as the agent of God." Wanamaker, "Divine Agent," 523. While it is not a DRE-related text, 1 Cor 8:6 also captures the essence of this relationship between Jesus as the intermediate agent and God the Father as the ultimate agent: "One God, the Father, from whom are all things, and we in him, and One Lord, Jesus Christ, through whom are all things, and we through him."

and God the Father is astonishing. Although it is not possible to conclude that Paul is characterizing Jesus as divine,[422] he is characterizing Jesus in close relationship to God the Father.

Chiasm

A chiasm is a "literary form that has as its most obvious feature a reverse parallelism. Two or more terms, phrases, or ideas are stated and then repeated in reverse order."[423]

The usefulness of chiasms in relation to Paul's epistles has been debated. Bligh, for example, postulated a chiastic outline for the entire Galatian epistle.[424] These claims have, quite sensibly, been rejected by most scholars. In contrast to this, Paul does appear to make occasional and effective use of chiasms within smaller sections of his epistles. As Murphy O'Connor remarks, "The search for concentric structures covering a complete letter has little to recommend it. . . . The situation is completely different with regard to parts within a letter."[425]

Paul makes interesting use of chiasm in the salutation of Galatians. As previously demonstrated,[426] Jesus and God the Father are interchanged in a pair of complementary chiasms.[427] In the first chiasm (1:1), Paul alternates Jesus and God the Father:

A – Jesus Christ and
 B – God the Father
 B' – Who raised
A' – Him from the dead.

---

422. Richardson concludes that while this construction is "theologically very significant," "it is going beyond the evidence to conclude that Thiselton, *1 Corinthians*, prove[s] that Paul regards Jesus as God." Richardson, *Language*, 262.

423. Bailey and Vander Broek, *Literary Forms*, 49.

424. Bligh, *Galatians*. The entire work is cited since a chiastic analysis of Galatians forms the basis of the entire commentary.

425. Murphy-O'Connor, *Letter-Writer*, 90.

426. See pp. 105–7 above.

427. It may be objected that these figures would be better described as examples of *inclusio* rather than chiasm. However, the figures do alternate the ideas of Jesus (A) and God the Father (B), which does appear to meet a minimal definition of chiasm.

Later in the salutation (3–5), he uses a similar chiasm:

> B – God our Father and
>   A – the Lord Jesus Christ
>   A' – who gave himself for our sins
>   A" – that he might rescue us from this present evil age
> B' – according to the will of God our Father

Paul does not hesitate to give the priority of first mention to Jesus, as the first chiasm demonstrates (1). Yet Paul gives first mention to God the Father in the second chiasm (3). In the second chiasm, Jesus and God the Father are given different roles: the former gave himself for our sins (4); the latter raised Jesus from the dead (1). Yet these different roles do not prevent Paul from presenting Jesus and God the Father as a chiastic unity. Paul only distinguishes between Jesus and God the Father by role; otherwise, the two are so intimately intertwined as to be essentially inseparable.

This close connection between Jesus and God the Father is demonstrated by the lengths to which Paul goes to maintain it. The Epistle to the Galatians opens with what appears to be yet another chiasm. It begins with a twofold denial of the origin of the gospel: not from humans, nor through a human. This is followed by the affirmation "but through Jesus Christ and God the Father" (1:1):

> A – not from humans
>   B – nor through a human
>   B' – but through Jesus Christ
> [A'?] – and [from?] God our Father

Paul affirms the one through whom the gospel came, yet strangely fails to name the one from whom it came. This appears to be a case of anacoluthon. The mere mention of Jesus leads directly to God the Father, despite the fact that this destroys the symmetry of the opening statement, and leaves unanswered the obvious question from the opening line: from whom is Paul an apostle? In other words, the close association between Jesus and God the Father is more significant than the structure of Paul's argument. For Paul, Jesus and God the Father are inseparable.

Thus, through the use of chiasm, Paul characterizes Jesus in close association with God the Father.

Divine Roles

Paul indirectly characterizes Jesus in ways normally associated with God. We will now examine five roles that Paul associates with Jesus in the context of the DRE: the name of Jesus, knowing Jesus, seeing Jesus, serving Jesus, and, being sent by Jesus.[428]

Name of Jesus

Paul refers to the name of Jesus twice in the context of the DRE (Rom 1:5; 15:20).[429] Hurtado discusses the "name of Christ" as an aspect of the early Christian "mutation."[430] Early Christians used the name of Jesus as part of the rite of baptism, called on the name of the Lord (Jesus), and invoked the name of Jesus in judgment. Each of these uses relates to the "distinctive devotional pattern" of early Christianity.[431] However, the reference to the name of Jesus in Rom 1:5 appears to be more theological than devotional in nature. The reason Paul performs his ministry is "for the sake of [Jesus's] name."

While the phrase ὑπὲρ τοῦ ὀνόματος does not appear in the LXX, it parallels various translations of the OT phrase לְמַעַן שֵׁם. The LXX uses several different prepositions in conjunction with ὄνομα to translate לְמַעַן שֵׁם, including ἕνεκεν (Ps 23:3; 25:11; 31:3 [4 LXX]; 79:9; 106:8; 109:21; 143:11; Isa 48:9), εἰς (1 Kgs 8:41), διά (2 Chr 6:32; Jer 14:21), and ὅπως (Ezek 20:9, 14, 22, 44).[432] Each of these prepositions conveys the meaning "for the sake of" or "on account of," as does ὑπέρ in Rom 1:5.[433] In each case, לְמַעַן שֵׁם refers to the name Yahweh. Thus, Paul is making an obvious allusion to the divine name Yahweh in speaking of "the sake of his name." In so doing, he gives the name of Jesus divine significance. Paul's reference to the name of Jesus characterizes Jesus in a manner previously reserved for Yahweh.

---

428. A possible sixth such association, Jesus as "the Lord who rescues," has been discussed on pp. 169–71 above.

429. The "name of Christ" is one of Hurtado's six expressions of the early christological mutation. Hurtado, *One God*, 99, 108–11.

430. Ibid., 108–11.

431. Ibid., 111.

432. Jer 14:7 reads ἕνεκεν σοῦ, omitting ὄνομα.

433. For the full range of markers indicating cause and/or reason, see L&N, §89.15–38.

Knowing Jesus

Paul speaks of knowing Jesus using both the noun γνῶσις (Phil 3:8), and the cognate verb γινώσκω (Phil 3:10).[434] Since Paul discusses the knowledge of Jesus in the context of the DRE, this suggests that his knowledge of Jesus arose from the DRE.

In the LXX, the Hebrew verb יָדַע is translated by 22 verbs, 3 nouns, and 8 adjectives. It is primarily translated by γιγνώσκω (490) and its compounds (55),[435] as well as οἶδα (185) and ἐπίσταμαι (42). The substantive דַּעַת is translated by 21 nouns, most commonly γνῶσις (29) and ἐπίγνωσις (5), but also by others including σοφία (2).[436] In the OT, the verb יָדַע has three primary semantic ranges: secular, religious, and revelatory. The first pertains to visual and auditory perception, historical knowledge and skill, emotional and sexual knowledge, and wisdom.[437] The second involves God's knowledge, but also the knowledge of God ("to know Yahweh") and its counterpart, ignorance of God ("not to know Yahweh").[438] The third involves general revelation of God through history and salvation. It also involves divine self-revelation, as God makes himself known.[439]

Lewis also makes a strong connection between knowledge and God. The most common Hebrew verb meaning "to know," יָדַע, encompasses many forms of knowledge. These forms range from God's awareness of humanity and our ways, to human knowledge involving personal acquaintance, learning, and sexual intimacy. The two forms of knowledge most relevant to this discussion are intimate acquaintance and relationship with the divine.[440] Relationship with the divine is a form of intimate acquaintance; of necessity, knowing God requires self-revelation by the

---

434. Koperski discusses the historical origin of this expression in Koperski, *Knowledge*, 20–65.

435. Lightfoot comments that γινώσκω is "not simply 'know', but 'recognise, feel, appropriate.'" He also connects γινώσκω via the LXX to the Hebrew יָדַע. Lightfoot, *Philippians*, 150.

436. Bergman and Botterweck, "יָדַע," 5:453.

437. E.g., Num 24:16; Deut 11:2; 1 Sam 26:12; Neh 4:5; Isa 29:15. Bergman and Botterweck, "יָדַע," 5:461–68.

438. E.g., Gen 18:19; Exod 5:2; 33:12, 17; Ps 91:14. Bergman and Botterweck, "יָדַע," 5:468–70.

439. E.g., Gen 41:39; Exod 6:3; 1 Sam 16:3; Ezek 6:3. Bergman and Botterweck, "יָדַע," 5:470–79.

440. Lewis, "יָדַע," 366.

divine.⁴⁴¹ Both aspects are present in Paul's reference to knowing Jesus, with Jesus in the place of the divine.

The cognate Hebrew noun for knowledge, דַּעַת, is also used in a variety of ways. Perhaps most relevant to this discussion is the "prophetic concept of 'knowledge of God,'" which "is derived from those outstanding historical events in which God has evidenced and has revealed himself to chosen individuals such as Abraham and Moses."⁴⁴² Once again, Paul's knowledge of Jesus fits the paradigm of the OT knowledge of the divine.

Thus, Paul describes knowing Jesus in a manner consistent with the OT pattern of knowing God. In fact, in the DRE texts Paul only refers to knowing Jesus (Phil 3:8, 10) and not God the Father. This supports the notion that by speaking of knowing Jesus, Paul is characterizing Jesus as divine.

Seeing Jesus

Third, Paul speaks of seeing Jesus (1 Cor 9:1; 15:8). The LXX uses εἶδον, ὁράω, and βλέπω to translate the Qal of רָאָה "generally" and "with no discernible distinction."⁴⁴³ The term רָאָה most commonly refers to everyday visual perception.⁴⁴⁴ More specialized uses involve military, legal, royal, and cultic contexts, or wisdom and divination.⁴⁴⁵ Finally, there is a category of theological usage, which refers to the vision of God or his messengers:

> The earlier narrative traditions in particular speak quite naively of seeing God, God's face, or God's messenger. . . . Aside from all mythological encoding, however, it emphasizes the reality of the encounter and the fact of vision as the authentication of an experience.⁴⁴⁶

---

441. For instance, at Sinai Moses speaks of being known by God, and requests that God reveal himself so that he might know him (Exod 33:12–13, 17). A similar paradigm is found in Samuel's initial encounter with God: "And Samuel did not yet know Yahweh; the work of Yahweh had not yet been revealed to him" (1 Sam 3:7). Samuel would know God only after God had revealed himself.

442. Lewis, "יָדַע," 367.

443. Fuhs, "רָאָה," 13:242. Qal forms constitute 1,129 of 1,303 occurrences in the OT. Ibid., 13:212.

444. E.g., Gen 12:15; Exod 2:6; 1 Sam 9:17. Ibid., 13:214–28.

445. E.g., Deut 34:1; 1 Sam 6:19; 14:16; 1 Kgs 18:2. Ibid., 13:214–28.

446. E.g., Exod 24:10. Ibid., 13:229.

Fuhs claims that the theological usage extends to messengers as well as God/Yahweh. Yet his examples (Judg 6:22; 13:23) argue otherwise. In Judg 6, the Angel of Yahweh (22) and Yahweh (14) are identical.[447] Fuhs's other example involving a messenger is found at the conclusion of the appearance of the Angel of Yahweh to Manoah and his wife. Again, the Angel of Yahweh is identical to God in this epiphany.[448] The verse in question even makes direct reference to God[449] and not the Angel of Yahweh. Therefore, the theological usage of seeing is restricted to God alone. Culver reaches a similar conclusion in defining רָאָה as "the act of an authentic prophet in receiving oracles from God" (e.g., Num 12:6; Gen 46:2; 1 Sam 3:15; Ezek 1:1; 8:3; 40:2; 43:3; Dan 10:7–8, 16).[450]

In 1 Cor 9:1 Paul asks the rhetorical question, "Have I not seen Jesus our Lord?" In addition to the obvious external reality (cf. Judg 13:23), this question fits Culver's metaphorical definition since Paul's role as apostle is quite similar to that of the OT prophet.[451] Furthermore, Paul claims to have received an oracle; namely, that he should preach the gospel of Jesus to the Gentiles (Gal 1:16).

Thus, in claiming to have seen Jesus (1 Cor 9:1; 15:8), Paul uses theologically significant language. Paul speaks of seeing Jesus as one would discuss a vision of Yahweh alone. Furthermore, the object of Paul's sight is Jesus "our Lord" (1 Cor 9:1). The "Lord" in Paul's vision is not Yahweh, but Jesus. Therefore, when Paul speaks of seeing Jesus he situates Jesus in the place of Yahweh, as divine.

Slave of Jesus

Fourth, Paul identifies himself as a slave of Jesus using the terms δοῦλος (Rom 1:1; Gal 1:10) and λειτουργός (Rom 15:16). Paul's claim to be a servant of Jesus requires careful attention. In order to understand how Jesus is being characterized in relation to Paul's service, we must understand how both the master and the type of service are described.

---

447. See p. 90 above.

448. See p. 90 above.

449. "We have seen God" (Judg 13:23).

450. Culver, "רָאָה," 823. In addition to the obvious reference to physical vision with the eyes, Culver lists four other metaphorical definitions: to believe a message; to accept, especially on the part of God; to provide; and "to have respect to." These are not relevant to our discussion.

451. Indeed, Paul couches his apostolic call using OT prophetic call language (cf. Gal 1:15–16)

Paul identifies his master as Jesus (Χριστοῦ, Gal 1:10; Χριστοῦ Ἰησοῦ, Rom 15:16). Jesus cannot be identified as a typical human master for two reasons. First, Paul presents Jesus as having died and risen from the dead (Rom 1:4; 1 Cor 15:3–4) prior to the DRE. This suggests that Jesus is not a typical human. Second, Paul has repeatedly contrasted Jesus from humanity in the broader context of Gal 1,[452] and even in 1:10 itself.[453] Therefore, we must conclude that Paul's master is not a typical human, given that Jesus is presented as having died and risen, and no longer residing in the earthly realm, and given the repeated contrast that Paul draws between Jesus and humanity in the immediate context of Gal 1 and indeed in 1:10.

The nature of Paul's service to Jesus is essential to our understanding of how Jesus is being characterized. In Romans, Paul describes his service using the cultic language of priesthood (λειτουργός and ἱερουργέω, Rom 15:16).[454] In Gal 1, Paul presents his service in prophetic terms. Paul describes his service to Jesus, namely his call to bring the gospel of Jesus to the Gentiles (1, 11–16), using prophetic language that alludes to both Isaiah and Jeremiah.[455] Thus, Paul's slavery to Jesus involves both cultic and prophetic service.

Paul's slavery to Jesus reflects the OT pattern of service to God. The terms δοῦλος, λειτουργός, and their cognates are frequently used in the LXX to reflect OT patterns of service to God through the Hebrew verb עָבַד and the noun עֶבֶד.[456] The verb עָבַד may be used without objects, with inanimate objects, or with personal objects.[457] The other use is with respect to serving Yahweh or foreign gods. This category consists of uses

---

452. See pp. 174–77 above.

453. See p. 108 above.

454. See pp. 142–44 above.

455. See pp. 119–20 above.

456. Qal forms of עָבַד (271 times; 18 in other stems) are "usually" translated with δουλεύω (114 times) and λατρεύω (75), although εργάζομαι (37), λειτουργέω (13), and several other verbs "in isolated instances." The noun עֶבֶד (805) is translated primarily with δοῦλος (314), παῖς (336), and θεράπων (42). The noun עֲבֹדָה (145) is primarily translated with λειτουργία or ἔργον, but also δουλεία, ἐργασία, or λατρεία. Rütersworden et al., "עָבַד," 10:381.

457. E.g., Gen 2:5; 29:18; Exod 20:9; Mal 3:17. Rütersworden et al., "עָבַד," 10:3818–4.

where cultic service is implied, as well as the Deuteronomistic use, which "far transcends any specific cultic context."[458]

Similarly, the noun עֶבֶד may refer to a slave, the Israelites in Egypt, vassals, the servant of the king, as a self-designation of obsequiousness, or as a self-designation in the Psalms.[459] It also is used for servants of Yahweh in particular, and for prophets as Yahweh's servants.[460] The latter category is of particular interest. The term "servant of Yahweh" is used of Moses "in a special sense in comparison with the prophets," although prophets are also referred to as Yahweh's servants:

> It is Yahweh himself who calls the prophets. . . . As such, they are Yahweh's spokespersons through whom he warns Israel and makes his will known. . . . He has repeatedly sent these prophets to his people . . . and it is through them that he speaks to Israel. . . . They speak in the name of Yahweh, and through them Yahweh makes his commandments known.[461]

Thus, by speaking of slavery to Jesus in relation to both cultic and prophetic service, Paul characterizes Jesus in a manner formerly reserved for Yahweh. Harris also affirms that "the very existence of the phrase 'slave of Christ' alongside 'slave of God' in New Testament usage testifies to the early Christian belief in Jesus' deity."[462] Harris actually understates the case in relation to the DRE. Paul's service to Jesus is presented as an immediate consequence of the DRE. Furthermore, Paul does not use the phrase "slave of God" with respect to the DRE; his earliest confessions of servitude are to Jesus alone. Paul may have considered himself to be a slave of God the Father as well as Jesus, but the DRE texts only present Paul as a slave of Jesus. Paul characterizes Jesus as divine through his cultic and prophetic devotion to Jesus.

---

458. E.g., Exod 3:12; Deut 6:13; 28:47; Judg 2:19; Ps 100:2. Rüterswörden et al., "עֶבֶד," 10:384–87.

459. E.g., Gen 32:5; Exod 21:7; Lev 25:44; 2 Kgs 16:7; Ps 119:17. Rüterswörden et al., "עֶבֶד," 10:387–94, 396–403.

460. See also Kaiser, "עֶבֶד," 639.

461. Rüterswörden et al., "עֶבֶד," 10:394–95.

462. Harris, *Slave*, 134. This statement is explored more fully in 127–38.

Sent by Jesus

Fifth, Paul claims to be sent by Jesus (1 Cor 1:17).⁴⁶³ The analogous Hebrew verb for sending in the OT is שָׁלַח.⁴⁶⁴ Van der Velden claims that "the subjects doing the sending may be either divine or human," which he further distinguishes as either "natural persons" or "God."⁴⁶⁵

Similarly, Austel claims that Yahweh is usually the one who commissions individuals to divine tasks.⁴⁶⁶ In Exod 3:10, for example, Moses is sent by God to Pharaoh. Den Hertog observes that "if elsewhere in the Hebrew Bible being 'sent' is at issue, it usually concerns a prophet."⁴⁶⁷

Yet in 1 Cor, Paul identifies the one who sent him as Jesus (1:17). The task that Jesus assigns to Paul is not a task to which a mere human could conceivably call someone. Once again, Paul has characterized Jesus in a manner reserved for God.

Jesus and God Used Interchangeably

In discussing his experience on the Damascus road, Paul associates certain terms with God on some occasions and with Jesus on others. The best examples of this phenomenon are seen in relation to εὐαγγέλιον and χάρις.⁴⁶⁸

First, Paul describes the gospel as εὐαγγέλιον θεοῦ in Rom 1:1, and τὸ εὐαγγέλιον τοῦ θεοῦ in Rom 15:16 (cf. 2 Cor 11:7; 1 Thess 2:2, 8, 9). Elsewhere, he defines it as τὸ εὐαγγέλιον τοῦ Χριστοῦ in both Rom 15:19 and Gal 1:7 (cf. 1 Cor 9:12; 2 Cor 2:12; 9:13; Phil 1:27; 1 Thess 3:2).⁴⁶⁹ As previously noted,⁴⁷⁰ there does not appear to be any logic behind this alternation; Paul appears to choose freely between God the Father and

---

463. Cf. ἀπόστολος, Rom 1:1; 11:13; 1 Cor 1:1; 15:9; 2 Cor 1:1; Gal 1:1, 17.

464. "In the case of the LXX it is possible to say: 'ἀποστέλλειν is the Gk. Term for the OT שלח.'" Hossfeld et al., "שָׁלַח," 15:71.

465. Hossfeld et al., "שָׁלַח," 15:59.

466. Austel, "שָׁלַח," 928.

467. Den Hertog, "Prophetic Dimension," 222–23. Den Hertog lists the relevant passages (Jer 14:14, 15; 23:21, 32; 27:15; 28:9, 15; 29:9, 31; 43:2; Ezek 13:6; Neh 6:21), as well as several others related to Moses (Num 16:28–29; Exod 4:13).

468. A third example involves the disputed Pauline epistles. The term ἀπόστολος is qualified as being "of Christ Jesus" (Χριστοῦ Ἰησοῦ) in 1 Cor 1:1 and 2 Cor 1:1, but "of God" (θεοῦ) in Titus 1:1.

469. In the context of his encounter with Jesus, Paul is even careful not to describe the gospel as his own: "the gospel which was preached by me" (Gal 1:11).

470. See p. 139 above.

Jesus with respect to the gospel. This is reminiscent of the free alternation in the multiple characterization of God in numerous OT passages.[471]

As well, Paul describes the grace he received as being from God (τὴν χάριν τὴν δοθεῖσάν μοι ὑπὸ τοῦ θεοῦ, Rom 15:15; ἡ χάρις τοῦ θεοῦ, 1 Cor 15:10) and from Christ (χάριτι Χριστοῦ, Gal 1:6).[472] The phrase ἡ χάρις τοῦ κυρίου Ἰησοῦ is commonly used elsewhere by Paul (1 Cor 16:23; 2 Cor 13:14; Phil 4:23; Phlm 25). A more specific use of χάρις is quite interesting. Paul uses χάρις in conjunction with καλέω only twice. Both instances are found in Gal 1, both in the context of the DRE. The subject of the first instance is Jesus (6), of the second is God the Father (15).[473]

Thus, Paul associates both the gospel and grace with God in some cases and with Jesus in others. This does not necessarily mean that Paul is characterizing Jesus as divine. But Paul does present Jesus and God the Father in extremely close relationship by freely interchanging the two with respect to grace and gospel.

Summary

In the context of the DRE, Paul identifies Jesus in numerous ways, both directly and indirectly. Based on the preceding discussion, it is now possible to draw some conclusions regarding the identity of Jesus in the context of Paul's DRE. In fact, Paul presents Jesus in unique relationship to God the Father and also as divine.[474]

First, Paul uses both direct and indirect means to characterize Jesus in unique relationship with God the Father. He does so directly through the title υἱός. He does so indirectly in numerous ways: by comparing Jesus together with God the Father in contrast to both humans and angels; by identifying God the Father as the ultimate agent and Jesus as

---

471. Cf. Gen 18–19; Exod 3–4; Ezek 1–3. Also see the discussion on the characterization of the Angel of Yahweh, pp. 89–91.

472. There is some textual uncertainty regarding the presence of Χριστοῦ in Gal 1:6. It is absent from some key Western witnesses ($\mathfrak{P}^{46vid}$ G H^{vid} it$^{g, ar}$), but present in many other witnesses ($\mathfrak{P}^{51}$ ℵ A B Ψ 33 81 614 1739 vg syr$^{p, h, pal}$ cop^{bo} goth arm). The alternate reading Ἰησοῦ Χριστοῦ is less frequent (D it^d syrh with*). See *TCGNT*, 520–21.

473. In addition, Jesus and God the Father are united under the preposition ἀπό as the single source of grace (and peace; Gal 1:3).

474. Although his conclusions do differ from mine, Porter uses similar categories to characterize Jesus under three headings: "Jesus the Man"; "Jesus as Lord," which he describes as a "divine filial relation"; and "Jesus Christ as God." Porter, "Images," 97–112.

the intermediate agent responsible for Paul's commissioning; by uniting Jesus and God the Father under one preposition; by freely interchanging Jesus and God the Father in alternating chiasms; by interchanging Jesus and God the Father with respect to both gospel and grace.

Second, Paul characterizes Jesus as divine, both directly and indirectly. He does so directly through the title κύριος as the Lord who rescues. He also characterizes Jesus as divine indirectly by speaking of the name of Jesus, knowing Jesus, seeing Jesus, being a slave of Jesus, and being sent by Jesus.

Thus, Paul characterizes Jesus in the DRE texts both in unique relationship to God the Father, and as divine. It is significant that Paul should present such a detailed and consistent characterization within the context of his first encounter with Jesus. This suggests that Paul associated the essence of his Christology with the DRE.

Patterns of Characterization in Ancient Jewish Epiphanies

Our earlier discussion of ancient Jewish epiphanies found two basic patterns of characterization for heavenly beings.[475] Type-I involves depictions of God in angelic or human form. Type-II involves increased fluidity between humans and heavenly beings with an impermeable boundary between God and other beings. Paul's characterization of Jesus does not appear to correspond to either pattern. The depiction of Jesus in unique relationship to God the Father is consistent with the Type-II pattern involving exalted humans. However, the depiction of Jesus in ways previously reserved for Yahweh is not consistent with the clear distinction that Type-II maintains between God and other beings.

Paul's characterization of Jesus in the DRE also appears to be inconsistent with Type-I. Jesus is described in unique relationship with God the Father in distinction from humanity, which is inconsistent with the Type-I characterization of humans as humans only. Furthermore, Paul characterizes Jesus as divine in numerous ways, which is also inconsistent with the Type-I distinction between God and all other beings.

Two separate conclusions may be drawn from these observations. First, it may be that Paul's characterization of Jesus is new and unique to ancient Jewish epiphanies. This is consistent with Hurtado's assertion

---

475. See pp. 88–97 above.

that early Christian devotion to Jesus was a "significant mutation or innovation in Jewish monotheistic tradition."[476]

The second possibility is that Paul understood Jesus to be not only divine but also pre-existent. In this case, the characterization of Jesus in unique relationship to God the Father and as divine is accommodated by the Type-I pattern. Furthermore, the Type-I pattern would accommodate Jesus's incarnation as the appearance of God as a human. However, the incarnation is a significant variation from the typical Type-I pattern, since God is not described elsewhere as appearing in human form from birth to death. We have not seen evidence in the Pauline DRE texts of Jesus being characterized as pre-existent. However, Paul does appear to do so elsewhere.[477] Hurtado observes that belief in the pre-existence of Jesus "must ... have begun remarkably early."[478]

If Paul's characterization of Jesus is interpreted according to the Type-II pattern, then it represents a significant modification to this pattern. On the other hand, if Paul's characterization of Jesus is interpreted according to the Type-I pattern, we must conclude that as part of the DRE Paul understood Jesus to be pre-existent and that the human existence of Jesus was the ultimate epiphany, from birth to death. The evidence is insufficient to warrant a conclusion either way; however, it is interesting to note that Paul does appear to develop his Christology along the lines of the Type-I pattern by incorporating pre-existence into his later Christology.

Other Christological Approaches

Our conclusions regarding the Christology of the DRE will be compared to those of Seyoon Kim as a typical approach to the names and titles of Jesus, and to Charles Gieschen as representative of angelomorphic approaches.

Kim

The Christology we have seen in the DRE texts is similar to what has been presented by other scholars.[479] For example, Kim develops his

---

476. Hurtado, *One God*, 99.

477. Hurtado discusses the Pauline texts related to the pre-existence of Jesus in Hurtado, "Pre-Existence," 744–46.

478. Ibid., 746.

479. See the discussions in chapter 1 on pp. 1–23 above.

Christology in relation to the titles Christ, Lord, and Son of God.[480] However, Kim's discussion differs from ours in several significant ways. First, Kim includes aspects of Pauline Christology that are not associated with the DRE. Kim relies on 2 Cor 4:4–6 not only for the development of Adam Christology and Wisdom Christology in relation to Jesus as the εἰκὼν τοῦ θεοῦ,[481] but also in his discussion of the titles Christ, Lord, and Son of God.[482] Second, our discussion has considered additional evidence that has been previously neglected. Not only have many aspects of indirect characterization been previously overlooked as relevant to the DRE,[483] but so also has the direct characterization of Jesus as the "Lord who rescues."[484] Finally, our discussion has attempted to locate the characterization of Jesus within the pattern of ancient Jewish epiphanies in general, and not just within the pattern of *merkabah* mysticism.[485]

Gieschen

In addition to *merkabah* mysticism, another recent trend involves the search for christological antecedents among the various heavenly figures in the literature of the Second Temple period.[486] Gieschen's angelomorphic Christology is typical of this approach. While Gieschen does not discuss the DRE directly, he does characterize Jesus as God's angel. In doing so, he relies on a text that has a parallel in the Pauline DRE accounts. Gieschen states that "Galatians 4.14 is the one place in the Pauline corpus where there is an overt reference to Jesus as God's angel."[487] He rightly acknowledges that "most exegetes interpret this positioning in terms of distinct and increasing comparisons."[488] In fact,

---

480. Kim, *Origin*, 100–136.
481. Ibid., 137–268.
482. Ibid., 115–36.
483. See pp. 173–85 above.
484. See pp. 170–71 above.
485. See pp. 157–65 above.
486. For example, Casey asserts that "the figure of Jesus was developed in the same way as other messianic and intermediary figures." Casey, *Christology*, 124. Horbury succinctly summarizes this approach: "Particular attention has been given to the appearance in apocalypses and mystical texts of one exalted angel almost indistinguishable from God himself, like the 'angel of the Lord' in the Old Testament." Horbury, *Messianism*, 119.
487. Gieschen, *Angelomorphic Christology*, 315.
488. Ibid., 324.

in Gal 4:14 Paul appears to use an increasing sequence of exaggeration for effect, as he does elsewhere (cf. 1 Cor 13:1; Gal 1:8). If this is true, then Paul is actually distinguishing Jesus from the ἄγγελος θεοῦ. If, however, Gieschen is correct that the two terms in the comparison are to be equated, then by the same logic Paul must be an "angel from heaven" (Gal 1:8). Since this is clearly absurd, we must conclude that Gieschen's assertion that Jesus is "God's Angel"[489] is also incorrect. Since Gieschen admits that this is the only place in the Pauline epistles where Jesus is characterized as an angel, it does not appear that Paul characterizes Jesus in angelomorphic terms.[490]

CONCLUSION

We have now considered the Damascus road encounter between Paul and Jesus with respect to both the nature of the event and the characterization of Jesus within the event. Paul describes his encounter with Jesus according to the pattern of Divine Initiative epiphanies. This suggests that the DRE should not be interpreted as a *merkabah* vision. It also suggests that Paul's apostolic call was received in the DRE, rather than being a conclusion that Paul reached at a later point. The divine initiative of the event also emphasizes the significance of Paul's characterization of Jesus in the DRE accounts, since it is in the DRE that Paul claims to have become aware of whom Jesus really is.

Paul's DRE Christology is fascinating. Paul characterizes Jesus as divine, and also in unique relationship with God the Father. Jesus is characterized as divine both directly as the Lord who rescues, and indirectly by the name of Jesus, knowing Jesus, seeing Jesus, being a slave of Jesus, and being sent by Jesus. Jesus is characterized in unique relationship with God the Father both directly by the title υἱός, and indirectly: by comparison with God the Father in contrast to both humans and angels; by identification as God the Father's intermediate agent; by being united with God the Father under a single preposition; by being interchanged

---

489. Ibid., 316.

490. Hengel provides a still-timely caveat for the recent trend towards angelomorphic Christology: "A not unimportant difference between the New Testament and the majority of Jewish texts is of course that New Testament christology *a priori* put the exalted Jesus, as Son, *above all angelic beings*. . . . A real *angel christology* could only become significant on the fringe of the Jewish-Christian sphere." Hengel, *Son of God*, 85.

with God the Father in alternating chiasms; by being interchanged with God the Father in relation to both gospel and grace.

Paul's characterization of Jesus as divine and in unique relationship with God the Father is atypical of both Type-I and Type-II patterns of characterization. In order for the Type-II pattern to correlate with Paul's characterization of Jesus, it must be modified to account for Paul's characterization of Jesus as divine. The Type-I pattern must be modified to include incarnation, and Jesus must also be presumed to be pre-existent.

Given the unusual nature of these findings, it is with great anticipation that we now turn our attention to Luke's three-fold presentation of the Damascus road encounter in the book of Acts.

4

Acts 9, 22, and 26

INTRODUCTION

THE BOOK OF ACTS contains three accounts of the Damascus road encounter between Jesus and Paul. The first account (Acts 9:1–9) is in narrative form similar to many other ancient Jewish epiphany accounts. The second and third accounts (Acts 22:3–11; 26:4–20) occur within speeches.[1] In other words, the DRE is diegetic in Acts 9, and metadiegetic in Acts 22 and 26.[2]

Some scholars disparage Acts as a source for understanding the life of the apostle Paul,[3] while others view Acts as invaluable.[4] Our intent is not to determine "what happened," but rather how the event is described in Acts, and how this compares to Paul's account. While Acts is not a

---

1. The form of the speeches is discussed by many writers. For example, Winter outlines the Acts 26 speech as: *exordium* (2–3); *narratio* (4–18); *confirmatio* (19–20); *refutatio* (21); *peroratio* (22–23). Winter, "Speeches," 327–31. Our concern in Acts 22 and 26 is not the form of the speeches, but the underlying narrative of the DRE.

2. Genette designates the universe of the first narrative as the diegesis; the world of the second narrative, or metanarrative, as the metadiegesis. Genette, *Narrative Discourse*, 228.

3. "Relative to incidents in the life of the apostle, Paul's letters possess higher value as evidence than does the book of Acts. This point requires no further explanation." Lohfink, *Conversion*, 21. Bousset also disparages Acts as a source for understanding early Christology. Bousset, *Kyrios*, 32, 120. Yet he follows this with a seemingly contradictory acceptance of the Synoptics, including Luke, as valid sources (33). He even cites a reference in Acts in sole support of a foundational claim: "It is one of the most important established facts that the universal religious community of Antioch, consisting of Jews and Hellenes, developed without Paul (Acts 11:19ff.)." Bousset, *Kyrios*, 120.

4. For example, Jervell states that "in order to get at the historical Paul, we can not do without Acts and Luke." Jervell, "Paul in Acts," 300. So also Carson, Moo, and Morris: "The relegation of Acts to a secondary status in the construction of a life of Paul is simply not legitimate." Carson et al., *Introduction*, 224.

first-hand source for the DRE, it does contain the earliest record of the DRE outside Paul's epistles.[5] Furthermore, our primary interest in Acts is literary rather than historical.[6] Instead of seeking to establish the veracity of Luke's[7] accounts, our goal is to consider Luke's portrait of Jesus within the DRE.

This investigation of Acts will follow the same path used for Paul's epistles. We will begin with an exegetical analysis of each DRE account. This will be followed by a literary analysis of the three accounts, with particular attention to the event itself and to the characterization of Jesus. We will also compare Luke's presentation of the DRE with Paul's.

EXEGESIS

Acts contains three separate accounts of Paul's DRE (9:1-9; 22:3-11; 26:4-20). These accounts, as well as several related texts, will be examined exegetically.[8]

Acts 9:1-9

The first account of the Damascus road encounter is found in Acts 9:1-9:[9]

> **9:1** Saul, still breathing murderous threats upon the disciples of the Lord, went to the high priest **2** and requested letters from him to the synagogues in Damascus, that if he found any who were of the Way,[10] both men and women, he might bring them as prisoners to Jerusalem.

---

5. "To place Luke-Acts as late as the 2d century . . . is excessive." Johnson, "Luke-Acts," 404.

6. Gaventa notes that earlier research focused on the history of Paul's conversion (what "had actually happened"). This gave way to source analysis. Gaventa, "Enemy," 439. It is hoped that this study will help reinforce the importance of the literary approach to the DRE.

7. For the sake of simplicity, the (implied) author of the book of Acts will be referred to as Luke, with no implication as to the identity of the actual author.

8. Fletcher-Louis discusses these accounts, although unfortunately not in detail, in Fletcher-Louis, *Luke Acts*, 50-57.

9. Gaventa discusses this account in Gaventa, *Darkness*, 54-61. For a literary analysis of Acts 8:26—9:31, see Baban, *Encounters*, 207-26.

10. Metzger indicates that there are six variant readings involving this phrase (*TCGNT*, 316-17). The two most viable options involve word order. Other less likely variants involve either the insertion of ταύτης, or the omission of ὄντας. None of the variants affects our interpretation of the text.

3 As he traveled, he drew near to Damascus. Suddenly a light from heaven flashed around him. **4** As he fell to the ground, he heard a voice from heaven saying to him, "Saul, Saul, why do you persecute me?"[11] **5** And he said, "Who are you, Lord?" He replied, "I am Jesus[12] whom you are persecuting.[13] **6** Now stand up and enter into the city, and it will be told to you what you must do." **7** The men who traveled together with him stood speechless, hearing the voice but seeing no one.[14] **8** Saul got up from the ground.[15] Although his eyes were opened he saw nothing; taking him by the hand, they led him into Damascus. **9** And he was three days without seeing, and he neither ate nor drank.

Outline

The Acts 9 DRE narrative conforms to the basic narrative structure of epiphany.[16] It consists of an introduction (1–3a), appearance (3b–5), message (6), and conclusion (8–9), as well as a parenthesis describing the reaction of Paul's companions (7).[17] The narrator is extradiegetic and omniscient.[18]

---

11. A very few manuscripts, including E and 431, insert the clause σκληρόν σοι πρὸς κέντρα λακτίζειν after the initial question; others insert it at the end of the next verse. The phrase appears to be a later addition based on the account in Acts 26:14.

12. Several manuscripts, including A C E and 104, have ὁ Ναζωραῖος after Ἰησοῦς, but this appears to be a later addition based on the text of Acts 22:8.

13. The Textus Receptus contains the clearly spurious addition σκληρόν σοι πρὸς κέντρα λακτίζειν. τρέμων τε καὶ θαμβῶν εἶπε, Κύριε, τί με θέλεις ποιῆσαι; καὶ ὁ κύριος πρὸς αὐτόν: ("'It is hard for you to kick against the goads.' [cf. Acts 26:14] Trembling and astounded, he said 'Lord, what shall I do?' [cf. Acts 22:9] And the Lord [said] to him ...").

14. The reading μηδένα is supported by $\mathfrak{P}^{74}$ ℵ A* B and others. A few manuscripts (A^c C E Ψ 1739 𝔐) read οὐδένα, "no one."

15. Metzger notes that several Western witnesses have modified the statement to be a request by Paul to his companions (it^{h, p} vg^{mss}), and their compliance (it^h Ephraem). *TCGNT*, 318.

16. See pp. 36–41 above. Newman notes the similarity to OT call narratives. Newman, "Acts," 441–42. He outlines the passage as an introductory word (1–3a), divine confrontation (3b–4), objection (5a), commissioning (5b–6, 10–18), sign of reassurance (9, 18–19). Weiser suggests that Acts 9:1–9 is too complex to conform to a preconceived literary *Gattung*. Weiser, *Apostelgeschichte*, 1:219.

17. Funk outlines the narrative as an introduction (1–2), a nucleus (3–8a) consisting of two focalizers (light and voice, 3–4) followed by direct discourse, and a conclusion (8b–9). Funk, *Poetics*, 156–57.

18. Kurz, *Reading Luke-Acts*, 126.

Introduction (Acts 9:1–3a)

Luke prefaces his account of the Damascus road encounter with a summary of Paul's life prior to the DRE (9:1–2), as well as providing the setting for the event itself (9:3a).

Background (Acts 9:1–2)

Luke begins this section by introducing one of the central figures of this pericope, Σαῦλος. Clearly, Saul is synonymous with the apostle Paul (cf. Acts 13:9), whose epistles we have just considered. For the sake of consistency, he will henceforth be referred to as Paul.

The adverb ἔτι (1) is used temporally, as a reminder that Paul had been previously introduced during the account of Stephen's martyrdom (7:57—8:3). Stephen's death was witnessed (7:58) and approved (8:1) by Paul. Luke also makes it clear that Paul was not merely a passive witness to the violence against Christians. Paul sought to "destroy" (ἐλυμαίνετο) the church in a very personal fashion, going into the houses of Christians and "dragging" (σύρων) to prison not only the men, but also the women (8:3). After this brief introduction, Luke turns his attention away from Paul. The intervening pericopes concern Philip (8:4–8), Simon the Sorcerer (8:9–25), and Philip with the Ethiopian eunuch (8:26–40). Now, in Acts 9, Luke returns to the story of Paul.[19]

Luke summarizes Paul's continuing activities against the church with the graphic participial phrase, ἐμπνέων ἀπειλῆς καὶ φόνου εἰς τοὺς μαθητὰς τοῦ κυρίου. The verb ἐμπνέω, meaning "blow or breathe upon,"[20] is a *hapax legomenon* in the NT. The intimate nature of the breathing is seen in Liddell and Scott's examples of playing the flute, of a lover, and of a horse "so close behind as to *breathe upon* one's back."[21] Luke invokes the imagery of ἐμπνέω to capture the intensely personal nature of Paul's hatred.

The content of Paul's breath is expressed in the compound genitive phrase ἀπειλῆς καὶ φόνου, meaning literally "threats and murder." Although Paul had been a witness to the death of Stephen, murder must be seen as a progression from the earlier threat of imprisonment (8:3).

---

19. "As the ετι [sic] (still) indicates in 9:1, we are meant to see the material of Acts 9 as a continuation of what has previously been said about Saul in 8:3." Witherington, *Acts*, 302.

20. LSJ, 546.

21. Ibid.

Since murder is a rather ominous threat, this phrase might be read as a hendiadys, "murderous threats."[22]

The objects of Paul's wrath are identified as "the disciples of the Lord" (τοὺς μαθητὰς τοῦ κυρίου). The term μαθητής is commonly used to describe Jesus's adherents.[23] It is therefore surprising to note that the phrase "disciples of the Lord" is unique not just in Acts, or even Luke-Acts, but in the entire NT.[24] This phrase expresses the intimate connection between the disciples and their Lord. This close relationship stands in poignant contrast to Paul's murderous threats against them. It also foreshadows an even closer association that Jesus himself makes with his followers (4–5).

Finally, the verb ἐμπνέω belongs to a class of verbs that take a genitive for "smelling of."[25] This puts the final point on Luke's imagery. Paul is "breathing the scent of murderous threats upon the Lord's disciples."[26]

The plot now shifts from general threats against followers of Jesus to a specific instance of persecution. The threat is initiated when Paul approaches the high priest.[27] Paul's access to the high priest demonstrates his progress within Judaism, and that he sought approval for his actions from the highest religious authorities.

Paul's project is outlined in verse 2. He asks the high priest for letters to the synagogues at Damascus. At the time, Damascus may have been part of the Nabataean kingdom[28] or, more likely, part of the Roman province of Decapolis.[29] In either case, this would have required the right of extradition on the part of the high priest. Barrett, citing Josephus,[30] takes

---

22. Fitzmyer, *Acts*, 422. Yet this interpretation is not certain. Barrett, *Acts*, 1:445.

23. The term μαθητής occurs 28 times in Acts, 65 times in Luke-Acts, and 261 times in the NT.

24. This appears to have escaped the notice of the commentators.

25. BDF, §174.

26. Gaventa memorably refers to this as "Saul's fearsome breath." Gaventa, *Acts*, 148.

27. It is not certain who was high priest at this time. Bruce suggests that Caiaphas was "probably still in office." Bruce, *Acts of the Apostles*, 233.

28. Ibid., 242.

29. Ibid., 233.

30. Josephus reports that "Herod's formidable influence extended, moreover, beyond his realm to his friends abroad; for no other sovereign had been empowered by Caesar, as he had, to reclaim a fugitive subject even from a state outside his jurisdiction." *J.W.* 1:474. Even this citation recognizes that Herod held this extraordinary power, and

the view that the high priest would have had no such authority. Paul's mission would have depended on the "good will" of the Damascus synagogues to hand over any Christians who would, in effect, "disappear."[31]

Regardless of the political situation and the legality of the mission, Paul intended to target Jesus's followers in Damascus. This is made plain in the protasis of the following third-class conditional statement, ὅπως ἐάν τινας εὕρῃ τῆς ὁδοῦ ὄντας. Here ὄντας, from εἰμί, connotes belonging through association.[32] Thus, Luke describes those Paul sought as "belonging to the Way," or "being of the Way." This is Luke's first use of the term ὁδός as a designation for Christians.[33] Paul's mission to Damascus involved seeking both men and women, ἄνδρας τε καὶ γυναῖκας, echoing Acts 8:3. This illustrates the depths to which Paul was willing to descend in order to destroy Jesus's disciples.

Luke finally reveals the goal of Paul's expedition, δεδεμένους ἀγάγῃ εἰς Ἰερουσαλήμ. The priority of Jerusalem is seen in Paul's desire to "bring them bound to Jerusalem," rather than simply dealing with them in Damascus. Not only did Paul seek approval for his persecution of Christians from the high priest in Jerusalem, it appears he also intended for his prisoners to be dealt with by the proper religious authorities. The main verb ἀγάγῃ, from ἄγω, means "bring" in the sense of "take into custody."[34] The adverbial participle δεδεμένους, from δέω, indicates the manner in which the prisoners would be brought to Jerusalem; specifically, bound in chains, as captive prisoners.[35]

Paul's application to the high priest was successful (cf. Acts 9:3), indicating that Paul's actions met with the approval of the highest religious officials.

Thus, Luke reveals two related aspects of Paul's character prior to the DRE. First, Paul was seriously committed to the destruction of the Way. He was willing to go to any length, including murder, sparing neither women nor men. He was willing to cross dangerous political

---

says nothing of whether the Jewish religious community might also have had special authority.

31. Barrett, *Acts*, 1:446.
32. BDAG, 285.
33. For more instances of ὁδός see Acts 16:17; 18:25, 26; 19:9, 23; 22:4; 24:14, 22.
34. BDAG, 16.
35. Danker suggests the translation "bring someone as a prisoner" for δεδεμένον ἄγειν τινά. BDAG, 221.

borders. He had access to the highest Jewish religious authorities. He sought, and received, their approval for his actions. In other words, Paul knew no limits in his attempt to destroy the Way. Second, Luke portrays Paul as being committed to Judaism. His persecution of the Way appears to have been firmly rooted in religious fervor. He sought the approval of the high priest. His mission started and ended in Jerusalem, although it involved Jesus's disciples in Damascus. In other words, Paul's hatred of Jesus and his followers was rooted in an equally zealous commitment to Judaism.

Setting (Acts 9:3a)

Luke describes both temporal and spatial settings for Paul's Damascus road encounter. The temporal setting is found in the phrase ἐν δὲ τῷ πορεύεσθαι, "while he was traveling." Here, ἐν τῷ is followed by the infinitive πορεύεσθαι. In the NT, a preposition with the dative of the articular infinitive is only found with ἐν τῷ, and then mainly in Luke.[36] The meaning is temporal; "while." Evidently Paul had been successful in obtaining authorization from the high priest, and had set out on his journey to Damascus. Unfortunately, the temporal setting is typological rather than chronological,[37] making it impossible to date the event.

The spatial setting is found in the phrase ἐγένετο αὐτὸν ἐγγίζειν τῇ Δαμασκῷ. Bruce notes that ἐγένετο with the accusative and infinitive is "Luke's favorite septuagintalism."[38] Here, ἐγένετο functions as the Hebrew וַיְהִי,[39] by introducing a disjunctive clause containing parenthetic information about the setting:[40] Paul is drawing near to Damascus.

Thus, Luke provides both temporal and spatial settings for the DRE. The event happened while Paul was traveling, as he drew near to Damascus.

---

36. BDF, §404.

37. Typological setting refers to the kind of time (e.g., "by night"), while chronological refers to the particular point in time (e.g., "on September 23, 1967") or length of time ("for forty years"). See Powell, *Narrative Criticism*, 72–74.

38. Bruce, *Acts of the Apostles*, 149.

39. MHT, 1:16.

40. Putnam observes that "disjunctive clauses also present parenthetic information, which tends to be either flashback, information about setting, or other proleptic information that the reader will need in order to understand upcoming events in the narrative." Putnam, *Biblical Hebrew*.

Appearance (Acts 9:3b–5)

The shift from introduction to appearance is marked by the adverb ἐξαίφνης, "suddenly."[41] Louw and Nida group ἐξαίφνης together with several other terms that pertain to "an extremely short period of time between a previous state or event and a subsequent state or event."[42] There may also be an implication of unexpectedness, which seems to be "a derivative of the context as a whole and not a part of the meaning of the lexical items."[43] Since Luke gives no indication that Paul expected anything to happen, the context suggests that the event was not only sudden, but also unexpected.[44]

Luke continues his narration of the appearance with the words αὐτὸν περιήστραψεν φῶς ἐκ τοῦ οὐρανοῦ. As anticipated by ἐξαίφνης, the subject changes from Paul to "a light."[45] Luke describes the light in several ways: it was "from heaven," and it "shone brightly around" Paul.[46] Jervell identifies the light as the glory of the risen Lord,[47] although this seems to go beyond what the text admits.

Two events are described in verse 4. First, Paul reacts to the light by falling to the ground, πεσὼν[48] ἐπὶ τὴν γῆν. Falling is a typical human response to epiphany (cf. Ezek 1:28). Second, Paul hears a voice speaking to him. The voice, apparently also from heaven, has been compared to the *bat qol*.[49] This rabbinic term, meaning "daughter of the voice," describes heavenly voices heard after the dormancy of the spirit following the destruction of the first Jerusalem temple.[50] Dalman indicates that

---

41. BDAG, 344.

42. L&N, §67.113. The other terms include αἰφνίδιος, ἐξάπινα, ἐξαυτῆς, ἄφνω, ἄρτι, and παραχρῆμα.

43. Ibid., §67.113.

44. Barrett goes even further, claiming that "the suddenness emphasises the supernatural character of the event; see D. Daube . . ." Yet Daube does not appear to support Barrett's observation. Barrett, *Acts*, 1:449; Daube, *The Sudden*, 28–34.

45. Barrett notes that light is "a common feature of theophanies." Barrett, *Acts*, 1:449. Michel discusses the close connection of light and epiphany: "Feuerzeichen und Stimme, Herrlichkeit und Anrede, Licht und Wort sind von alters her Begleiterscheinungen der göttlichen Berufung." Michel, "Das Licht."

46. L&N, §14.45.

47. "Sie ist die Doxa des erhöhten Herrn." Jervell, *Apostelgeschichte*, 280.

48. BDF discusses the use of the supplementary participle with verbs of perception and cognition (§416[1]).

49. Bruce, *Book of Acts*, 182.

50. Horn, "Holy Spirit," 264.

the voice occurs specifically in instances where there is no appearance.[51] Therefore, given both the light and the presence of Jesus, it seems that Paul experienced something more than a *bat qol*.[52]

Luke provides a sensory description of the appearance involving both sight and hearing. Paul certainly heard the voice; he was also seemingly aware of the light, since it precipitated his fall. Yet did he actually see the one who appeared? Luke does not give a physical description of Jesus here, nor chapters 22 or 26. Lohfink views this as a disagreement between Paul and Acts.[53] Yet Luke does not state that Paul did not see the one who appeared. Therefore, it is not certain from this verse alone whether Paul actually saw Jesus.[54]

Paul's interlocutor initiates the conversation with the question, Σαοὺλ Σαούλ, τί με διώκεις; The epanadiplosis[55] "Saul, Saul" involves a double vocative. This construction is common to OT epiphanies (cf. Gen 22:11; 46:2; Exod 3:4; 1 Sam 3:4, 10). Yet double vocatives are not unique to epiphanies: Jesus even uses a double vocative from the cross (Matt 27:46; Mark 15:34).[56]

The voice's question must have been surprising to Paul: "Why are you persecuting me?" Apparently, the interlocutor is intimately connected with those Paul was persecuting.[57] Paul does not address this question, but responds with a query of his own: τίς εἶ, κύριε; He is clearly struggling to identify the one who has appeared.[58]

The figure identifies himself in response to Paul's query with the words ἐγώ εἰμι Ἰησοῦς ὃν σὺ διώκεις. It is possible that ἐγώ εἰμι is an

---

51. "When the term is applied to a divine manifestation, it implies that it was audible to the human hearing without a personal theophany." Dalman, "Bath Qol."

52. Beaujour discusses the issue of voice and presence. "Indeed, until recently, voice implied presence, a spatial and temporal coincidence between a speaker and at least one hearer.... Voice manifested presence. A voice-event was an epiphany." Beaujour, "Phonograms," 3:273.

53. "Paul's 'I have seen the Lord' [1 Cor 9:1] points to another discrepancy. As unequivocal as this Pauline statement sounds, according to Acts it would seem that Paul never saw the Lord at all." Lohfink, *Conversion*, 25.

54. But see the discussion of Acts 9:27 below on pp. 203–4.

55. The "repetition of an important word for emphasis." BDF, §492.

56. Although this is likely a quotation from Ps 22:1.

57. The implications of this connection are discussed on pp. 243–44.

58. For a discussion of Paul's use of κύριε see pp. 240–42 below.

echo of the divine name, Yahweh; yet this is far from certain.[59] The interlocutor identifies himself by name, "Jesus." He then repeats the initial complaint (4) with the appositional phrase ὃν σὺ διώκεις, "whom you are persecuting."

Message (Acts 9:6)

Following the brief opening interchange, Jesus moves directly to his message.[60] Jesus's message is shockingly succinct: ἀλλὰ ἀνάστηθι καὶ εἴσελθε εἰς τὴν πόλιν καὶ λαληθήσεταί σοι ὅ τί σε δεῖ ποιεῖν. It is possible that ἀνάστηθι καὶ εἴσελθε could be viewed as a Hebraism; however, Paul had fallen, so the command to stand is appropriate in its own right.[61]

Jesus commands Paul to enter into the city. Given that Paul had previously planned to enter the city (3), the only new information is found in the rather oblique clause, "and it will be told you what you must do." The words ὅ τί introduce the answer to an indirect question[62] that is here left unspoken.[63] Conzelmann claims that Paul did not receive his commissioning from Jesus in the DRE.[64] Yet this is a hasty judgment, since chapters 22 and 26 have yet to be considered.

Parenthesis: Paul's Travel Companions (Acts 9:7)

The description of Paul's travel companions (7) is a parenthetical internal analeptic anachrony. It is analeptic, in that it appears in the discourse following its occurrence in story time. It is also parenthetical, in that it is of secondary importance compared to Paul's interaction with Jesus.

The first indication that Paul was not alone occurs in the phrase οἱ δὲ ἄνδρες οἱ συνοδεύοντες αὐτῷ. The substantive participle συνοδεύοντες, meaning "travel together with," is a *hapax legomenon* in the NT, from

---

59. See p. 247 below.

60. The variations between Acts 9, 22, and 26, and the purpose for this repetitive narration are discussed on pp. 225–29 below.

61. Bruce notes that the parallel phrase ἀναστὰς πορεύου in Acts 22:10 is "more than a Semitic redundant." Bruce, *Acts of the Apostles*, 456. Blass suggests the reading "go on your way." BDF, §336.

62. BDF, §300(1).

63. I.e., "What must I do?" Cf. Acts 22:10.

64. "In contrast to Gal 1:12–13 Paul does not learn of the gospel in the vision itself. He is directed to the church, which is the mediator of this teaching." Conzelmann, *Acts*, 71.

συνοδεύω. The pronoun αὐτῷ is dative of association.⁶⁵ In other words, others were traveling with Paul when Jesus appeared. Their response is described in the next two words. The verb εἱστήκεισαν, "stood," is pluperfect from ἵστημι. The manner of standing, ἐνεοί, is plural of ἐνεός meaning "speechless." This is also a *hapax legomenon* in the NT. In other words, Paul's companions reacted to the appearance by standing speechless.

Luke further describes the companions' awareness of the event with the phrase ἀκούοντες μὲν τῆς φωνῆς μηδένα δὲ θεωροῦντες. They heard the voice, but saw no one. Clearly they were aware that something unusual had happened, but were not aware of the content. This vision was meant for Paul alone. Yet the fact that the companions could apparently perceive the sound, if not the light, invalidates the theory that Luke is describing an epileptic fit or some other form of inner experience.

Conclusion (Acts 9:8-9)

In what may be the first indication of his obedience to the message, Paul arose from the ground (cf. Acts 26:19). The physical ramifications of the vision are immediate. Although Paul's eyes are opened, he can see nothing (ἀνεῳγμένων δὲ τῶν ὀφθαλμῶν αὐτοῦ οὐδὲν ἔβλεπεν).⁶⁶ Paul was led by the hand, χειραγωγοῦντες, into Damascus, where he remained three days without sight, food, and water.

Related Passages

While the account of Jesus's appearance to Paul concludes in verse 9, it is followed by three closely related pericopes that contain valuable information pertaining to the DRE.

Ananias (Acts 9:10-19a)

Jesus's appearance to Ananias is not part of the DRE, yet it is closely connected.⁶⁷ Ananias's story is a fascinating contrast to Paul's. Ananias is described as a disciple (10), in contrast to Paul, who is described as persecuting the Lord's disciples (1). The Lord calls Ananias by name (10), as he did with Paul (4). Ananias responds with an affirmative statement,

---

65. *GGBTB*, 159.

66. Pritchard claims that the blindness was psychosomatic, yet there is no indication of this in the text. Pritchard, *Literary Approach*, 151.

67. Tannehill notes Ananias's central role in Acts 9: "This episode is more than the story of Saul; it is the story of Saul and Ananias, a story of how the Lord encountered both and brought them together." Tannehill, *Narrative Unity*, 2:115.

ἰδοὺ ἐγώ, κύριε (10), in contrast with Paul's question, τίς εἶ, κύριε (5). Yet in both responses, the one who appeared is identified as κύριε. Both Ananias (11) and Paul (6) are commanded to get up and go. Finally, in Acts 9 Jesus reveals Paul's call to Ananias (15–16), yet not to Paul himself.

The one who appeared to Ananias is characterized as κύριος by both the narrator (10, 11, 15) and Ananias (10, 13). Ananias also describes Jesus in verse 17: τὸ ὁ κύριος ἀπέσταλκέν με, Ἰησοῦς ὁ ὀφθείς σοι ἐν τῇ ὁδῷ ᾗ ἤρχου, ("the Lord has sent me, Jesus who appeared to you on the road on which you were coming").

The Lord describes Paul as σκεῦος ἐκλογῆς ἐστίν μοι οὗτος τοῦ βαστάσαι τὸ ὄνομά μου ἐνώπιον ἐθνῶν τε καὶ βασιλέων υἱῶν τε Ἰσραήλ (15).[68] This identifies Paul as "my chosen instrument," "bearing my name." The "name of the Lord" is repeated in the next verse, ὑπὲρ τοῦ ὀνόματός μου (16).[69] These descriptions, while spoken of Paul, provide a means for characterization of the Lord. It is interesting to observe that while Jesus does inform Ananias of Paul's call, Ananias does not inform Paul.[70]

Paul's New Message (Acts 9:19b–22)

Tannehill observes that "the episode is not over with Saul's healing and baptism."[71] As a result of his encounter with Jesus, Paul's message was entirely changed. He "immediately" begins to preach that Jesus is the Son of God (20) and the Christ (22).

Verse 20 reads, καὶ εὐθέως ἐν ταῖς συναγωγαῖς ἐκήρυσσεν τὸν Ἰησοῦν[72] ὅτι οὗτός ἐστιν ὁ υἱὸς τοῦ θεοῦ. Εὐθέως indicates that the change was immediate, and by implication, a direct outcome of Jesus's appearance. Paul's new message is seen in his proclamation that Jesus is the Son of God. The term "son" in respect of Jesus is rare in Acts. Jesus is described elsewhere as the "son of man" (7:56) and as the "son" (13:33, quoting Ps 2:7). Yet the title Son of God in verse 20 is unique in Acts.

---

68. Lohfink argues that τοῦ βαστάσαι τὸ ὄνομά μου κτλ. suggests public confession rather than a worldwide missionary call. Lohfink, "Meinen Namen," 109.

69. Some Western variants also insert the phrase ἐν τῷ ὀνόματι Ἰησοῦ Χριστοῦ after χεῖρας in verse 17. See Head, "Texts," 431.

70. As Weiser observes, "aber Hananias teilt dies nicht dem Saulus mit, sondern heilt und tauft ihn nur." Weiser, *Apostelgeschichte*, 1:217.

71. Tannehill, *Narrative Unity*, 2:122.

72. The majority of early witnesses, including 𝔓$^{45, 74}$ ℵ A B C D E 61, read Ἰησοῦν. Others, including H L P, read Χριστόν instead of Ἰησοῦν. *TCGNT*, 320.

Bruce draws attention to this fact: "It is more significant than might be supposed at first glance that the once occurrence of the title 'Son of God' in Acts should be in this report of Saul's early preaching,"[73] and not only in his early preaching, but in his earliest preaching as an immediate consequence of the DRE.

Another aspect of Paul's new message is revealed in verse 22: οὗτός ἐστιν ὁ χριστός, "this is the Christ." The antecedent for οὗτος is apparently Jesus (cf. Acts 9:20).

Thus, Paul's new message consisted of the confessions that Jesus is the Son of God, and Jesus is the Christ. These confessions will be explored in greater detail in the section on Luke's characterization of Jesus.[74]

Paul in Jerusalem (Acts 9:26–28)

In this passage Luke narrates Barnabas's defense of Paul before the disciples in Jerusalem. Barnabas convinces the disciples that Paul had seen the Lord (27) and spoken to him (27) on the Damascus road.[75] Since Barnabas affirms Paul's calling, there is no reason to conclude that his evaluative point of view is not reliable.[76] Therefore, Lohfink's assertion that Paul never saw Jesus according to Acts is incorrect. His conclu-

---

73. Bruce, *Book of Acts*, 190.

74. See pp. 240, 242–43 below.

75. Gill notes the parallel structure of the events in Damascus (13–25) and Jerusalem (26–30), comparing the Lord's reassurance to Barnabas's. Gill, "Structure," 547–48.

76. The "evaluative point of view" relates to the veracity of a particular characterization. Powell, speaking of the Gospels, states that "there are only two basic points of view, the 'true' and the 'untrue,' and the evaluative points of view of all characters may be defined accordingly.... Since the narrators of our Gospels are reliable, their evaluative points of view are always true." Powell, *Narrative Criticism*, 54. The same logic also applies to writers of other, similar texts. Identification by the narrator is the most obvious and trustworthy source. A character may provide self-identification. If we know that a character is trustworthy, we may conclude that the data is also accurate. Powell observes that "the evaluative point of view of God is by definition true." Powell, *Narrative Criticism*, 54. A character may also be identified by other characters. In discussing other characters in a narrative, Powell states, "The reader will judge whether their evaluative points of view are true by comparing them with the points of view of the narrator, God, and Satan." Powell, *Narrative Criticism*, 54. In the case of epiphany, the evaluative point of view of the human recipient(s) is frequently true as well, since God has chosen them to receive a divine message. For a further discussion on reliability, see Rimmon-Kenan, *Narrative Fiction*, 101–4.

sion that Acts therefore disagrees with Paul's account (1 Cor 9:1) is also incorrect.[77]

Barnabas concludes by describing how Paul had spoken "in the name of Jesus" (27). Paul then goes out and speaks "in the name of the Lord" (28).

Thus, Acts 9 presents the DRE not only in a narrative text (1–9), but also in the later accounts of Ananias (10–19a), Paul (19b–22), and Barnabas (26–28).

Acts 22:3–11

Luke's second account of the DRE is found in Acts 22.[78] At the end of Acts 21, Jews from Asia Minor have created a disturbance against Paul for supposedly bringing a Gentile into the temple, thereby defiling it (27–30). As the Roman soldiers take Paul into custody (33), he is given permission by their commander to defend himself before the crowd (39–40). In his speech, Paul recounts the details of his Damascus road experience. Thus, the DRE account in 22:3–21 consists of a narrative within a speech within a narrative.[79] Therefore, Paul is an intradiegetic,[80] obtrusive narrator.[81]

Once again, we will begin with a translation of the text, followed by an exegetical examination of Paul's speech. The related accounts of Ananias (12–16) and Paul's temple vision (17–21) will also be explored.

All pertinent text critical questions have been footnoted in the following translation. Most are inconsequential, with the possible exception of the companions' fearful response to the light (9).

> **22:3** I am a Jew, born in Tarsus of Cilicia but brought up in this city, strictly educated[82] by Gamaliel in the ancestral law, being

---

77. "Paul's 'I have seen the Lord' [1 Cor 9:1] points to another discrepancy. As unequivocal as this Pauline statement sounds, according to Acts it would seem that Paul never saw the Lord at all." Lohfink, *Conversion*, 25.

78. Gaventa discusses this appearance in Gaventa, *Darkness*, 67–73.

79. With dialog within the narrative within the speech within the narrative. For more on diegetic levels see p. 40 n. 32 above.

80. "An intradiegetic narrator appears in the first narrative and narrates a story within the first narrative." Funk, *Poetics*, 304.

81. Since his "influence on the narration is made explicit." Kurz, *Reading Luke-Acts*, 128.

82. D has the present participle, παιδευμένος.

zealous for God[83] just as you all are today. **4** I persecuted this Way until death, binding and handing over to prison both men and women, **5** as also the high priest[84] testifies for me, and all the council of elders. Having received letters to the brothers I traveled to Damascus in order to bring those in that place bound to Jerusalem to be punished. **6** As I was traveling and drawing near to Damascus about noon, suddenly from heaven a very bright light flashed around me. **7** I fell[85] to the ground and heard a voice speaking to me, "Saul, Saul, why are you persecuting me?"[86] **8** And I answered, "Who are you, Lord?" He said to me, "I am Jesus of Nazareth, whom you are persecuting. **9** Those with me saw the light[87] but did not hear the voice that spoke to me. **10** I said, "What shall I do, Lord?" And the Lord said to me, "Arise and go into Damascus, and there you will be told about all that I have appointed for you to do." **11** But[88] since I could not see[89] because of the brightness of that light, I came into Damascus being led by the hand by those with me.

Outline

The outline of the DRE story in Acts 22 is similar to that of Acts 9. The main difference is the position of the parenthesis describing Paul's travel companions (22:9), which is presented prior to the message.

Introduction (Acts 22:3–6a)

Once again, Luke provides both background and setting for the second account of Paul's Damascus road encounter.

---

83. The genitive τοῦ θεοῦ is disputed. Ψ 614, 1505, and other witnesses, including various Vulgate manuscripts, omit it. 88 and the Vulgate replace it with "of the law" (τοῦ νόμου).

84. The high priest is named Ἀνανίας in 614 and a few others.

85. A corrector of D includes minor revisions to verse 6 and the preceding portion of verse 7.

86. The sentence σκληρόν σοι πρὸς κέντρα λακτίζειν from Acts 26:14 is included in E gig and various Vulgate and Syriac manuscripts.

87. The response of Paul's companions to the light, καὶ ἔμφοβοι ἐγένετο, is included in D E Ψ 1739 𝔐 gig sy[h] sa, but is not present in 𝔓[74] ℵ A B H 049 33 326 1175 1241 2464 and various other manuscripts and versions. Metzger regards this as "a natural expansion in Western and other witnesses." *TCGNT*, 430.

88. A few manuscripts, d gig, and several versions read ἀναστάς instead of ὡς.

89. Two sparsely attested variants differ from the reading in the text, οὐκ ἐνέβλεπον. B reads οὐδὲν ἔβλεπεν. E 2464 and a few other manuscripts read οὐκ ἔβλεπον.

Background (Acts 22:3–5)

Paul initially identifies himself as ἀνὴρ Ἰουδαῖος, "a Jewish man."[90] He then gives a brief autobiographical sketch. He was born in Tarsus but brought up ἐν τῇ πόλει ταύτῃ, "in this city" (3). It is likely that "this city" refers to Jerusalem rather than Tarsus, since that is where the speech is being delivered.[91]

The remainder of verse 3 emphasizes the strong religious influence during Paul's formative years. The phrase ἀνατρέφω παρὰ τοὺς πόδας is an idiom meaning "taught (by)."[92] Paul was not only taught by Gamaliel,[93] but taught "strictly,"[94] κατὰ ἀκρίβειαν. The object of Paul's study was the law of his fathers or ancestors, τοῦ πατρῴου νόμου (cf. πατρικῶν, Gal 1:14). The phrase ζηλωτὴς ὑπάρχων is also used by Paul with respect to his background in Judaism (Gal 1:14). In Galatians, the zeal pertains to the ancestral traditions; here, it is directed toward God.[95]

Paul next describes his persecution of Jesus's followers. The verb διώκω is also used by Paul (Gal 1:12; Phil 3:6). The description of Jesus's disciples as the "way," ὁδός, echoes Acts 9:2.[96] The language used to describe Paul's actions, δεσμεύων καὶ παραδιδοὺς εἰς φυλακάς, and his targets, ἄνδρας τε καὶ γυναῖκας, also echoes Acts 9:2. In this earlier account, the language is used of Paul's intent for Christians in Damascus; here, it apparently refers to his actions against Christians in Jerusalem.

Luke builds on the account in Acts 9 by having Paul seek approval for his expedition not only from the high priest (9:1), but also from the

---

90. Ἰουδαῖος is a noun, but here is used adjectivally to designate a person (cf. Acts 2:14; 10:28). BDF, §242.

91. Bruce agrees, referring to those who see "Tarsian influences" as having "given free rein to imagination." Bruce, *Book of Acts*, 415. Van Unnik reaches the same conclusion after a lengthy investigation. Van Unnik, "City," 301. He later reaffirmed this conclusion in van Unnik, "City," 327. However, as Fitzmyer notes, a "case could be made for either interpretation, which the Greek would tolerate." Fitzmyer, *Acts*, 704. Indeed, after an exhaustive and detailed study Du Toit concludes, "Exactly when he went to Jerusalem is unclear." Du Toit, "Two Cities," 401. The salient point here is not the physical setting of Paul's upbringing, but its Jewish nature.

92. L&N, §33.232.

93. Jeremias concludes that Paul does appear to have been a student of the Hillelite rabbinic school. Jeremias, "Paulus," 94.

94. L&N, §72.20.

95. Although see p. 205 n. 83 above.

96. Lyonnet seems to identify the "way" as a "way of life" in Lyonnet, "La Parole."

full council of elders (πρεσβυτέριον, 22:5). He even claims that the high priest and the council of elders can verify the accuracy of his claims (μαρτυρεῖ μοι).

The purpose of Paul's Damascus expedition is described using the participle δεδεμένους, which is repeated from 9:2. The ultimate destination, Ἰερουσαλήμ, is also repeated. The final purpose, ἵνα τιμωρηθῶσιν, "that they might be punished," is made explicit here, but is surely implied in 9:2. The verb τιμωρέω is used uniquely in the NT by Luke in reference to Paul's pre-DRE persecutions (cf. 26:11).

Thus, the presentation of Paul's background in Acts 22 is quite similar to those of both Acts 9 and the Pauline epistles.

Setting (Acts 22:6a)

The setting is introduced with the Hebraism ἐγένετο δέ ... περιαστράψαι (cf. 9:3). The temporal and spatial details are similar to 9:3, with the addition of an extra temporal detail. The time of day, περὶ μεσημβρίαν, draws attention to the brightness of the impending light.

Appearance (Acts 22:6b–8)

The description of the appearance in 22:6b–8 is quite similar to 9:3b–5, with several additions. The heavenly light is further qualified with ἱκανὸν περὶ ἐμέ. Ἱκανός indicates its considerable brightness[97] or intensity.[98]

Paul's reaction and the initial dialog are also quite similar to Acts 9. Once again Paul falls to the ground[99] and hears a voice calling his name[100] and asking the familiar question: τί με διώκεις; Paul's question in response, τίς εἶ, κύριε, also appears verbatim from 9:5; Jesus's response, ἐγώ εἰμι Ἰησοῦς ὁ Ναζωραῖος, ὃν σὺ διώκεις, is also identical to Acts 9, save for the additional identifier ὁ Ναζωραῖος. This identifies Jesus as being from Nazareth.[101]

---

97. BDAG, 472.

98. L&N, §78.14.

99. The word for ground in Acts 9:4, γῆ, has been replaced by the synonym ἔδαφος (cf. L&N, §1.39–45), which is a *hapax legomenon* in the NT.

100. Rosenblatt notes that Paul, rather than Saul, has been used since 13:9; the vocative Σαούλ is an anachrony. Rosenblatt, "Recurring Narration," 98.

101. L&N, §93.538.

Parenthesis: Paul's Travel Companions (Acts 22:9)

In Acts 9, the parenthesis describing Paul's companions was analeptic, following the message. In Acts 22 it is proleptic, preceding the message. Since Jesus's appearance only affects Paul's companions indirectly, the placement of this parenthetical information appears to be inconsequential. In Acts 22, Paul's companions "saw the light but did not hear the voice." This contrasts to the Acts 9 account, where they "heard the voice but saw no one." The apparent conflict between these accounts will be discussed in greater detail in the summary section.[102]

Message (Acts 22:10)

The message in 22:10 essentially repeats the message from 9:6. Here, however, Paul initiates the message with the question τί ποιήσω, κύριε, "What shall I do, Lord?" This direct question complements the indirect question (ὅ τί . . .) of 9:6. Paul's task is also refined. It is no longer just "what you must do," but "all that I have appointed for you to do."

Conclusion (Acts 22:11)

Now blind, Paul is led by the hand into Damascus (cf. 9:8). Paul's blindness is attributed to the brightness of the light, ἀπὸ τῆς δόξης τοῦ φωτὸς ἐκείνου.

Related Passages

The larger narrative of Acts continues with two events that pertain directly to Paul's encounter with Jesus. The first involves Ananias (22:12–16). The second describes a later appearance of Jesus to Paul (22:17–21).

Ananias (Acts 22:12–16)

Acts 9:10–18 recounts the story of the Lord's appearance to Ananias. Acts 22 presents Ananias from Paul's perspective.[103] Two interesting details are found in Ananias's message to Paul. First, Ananias refers to Jesus as τὸν δίκαιον, the "righteous one" (14).[104] Second, Ananias makes a vague reference to Paul's call, ὅτι ἔσῃ μάρτυς αὐτῷ πρὸς πάντας ἀνθρώπους ὧν ἑώρακας καὶ ἤκουσας (15). The audience, "all people," is suggestive of Paul's call to the Gentiles.[105]

---

102. See p. 224 below.

103. According to Luke.

104. See p. 243 below.

105. This is not certain, since "all" could be interpreted within a strictly Jewish context (cf. Acts 22:3–5).

Paul's Jerusalem Temple Vision (Acts 22:17–21)

Paul's Jerusalem temple vision[106] is relevant to the DRE, for in 22:21 the implied reader learns for the first time that Paul received his commission to the Gentiles directly from Jesus.

The epiphanic figure is first identified as αὐτός (18), which appears to have no antecedent.[107] It is therefore necessary to look forward. Not only does Paul refer to the interlocutor as κύριος (19), he also speaks of persecuting "those who believe in you" (τοὺς πιστεύοντας ἐπὶ σέ). Based on this later context, we may conclude that αὐτός refers to Jesus.

Jesus's message concludes with the words, ἐγὼ εἰς ἔθνη μακρὰν ἐξαποστελῶ σε (21). In other words, Jesus is sending Paul to the distant nations. Given the clarity of the message, two related questions arise. First, how does the message function in the context of Paul's speech before the angry crowd (cf. 21:27–22:2)? Second, is this the point at which Paul learns of his call?

The first question is typically answered by noting that the mere mention of Gentiles causes the crowd to interrupt Paul.[108] Others see the mention of Jesus as the source of offence.[109] Marguerat is more nuanced in seeing a "double provocation": first, that the κύριος who appears in the temple is not God, but Jesus; and second, the "adjunction of vv. 17–21 transfers from Ananias (9.10–16) to Saul the literary form of the prophetic call account."[110] While these are all accurate, none seems to capture the full extent of Paul's provocative claim. Their claim against Paul was that he had brought a Gentile into the temple. Paul's response infuriates the crowd, for he completely inverts this complaint. First, Paul claims that Jesus appeared to him in the temple, thereby placing Jesus at the very seat of Yahweh, in the temple. Second, Paul claims that Jesus sent him from the temple, reversing the direction of the crowd's accusation. Finally, Paul replaces the offense of a single Gentile with a call to all the Gentiles, by Jesus, from the temple. It is scarcely possible to imagine a more provocative response to their

---

106. Roloff claims that Acts 22:17–21 is a Lukan fabrication: "Lukas hat ihn kaum ganz frei erfunden." Roloff, *Apostelgeschichte*, 320.

107. See Marguerat, "Saul's Conversion," 150 n. 57.

108. See Marshall, *Acts*, 358.

109. Harrisville claims "that Jesus sent Paul forth moves the crowd to wild tumult." Harrisville, "Acts 22," 185.

110. Marguerat, "Saul's Conversion," 149–50.

complaint against Paul. Therefore, the revelation of Paul's call as part of the Jerusalem temple vision appears to serve an essential function in answering the crowd's accusation (21:29).

The second question involves the placement of Paul's call in the Jerusalem temple vision rather than in the DRE. Some scholars assume that Paul received his commission for the first time during the temple vision. For example, Fitzmyer states that the "commission to bear witness 'to the Gentiles' is thus conferred on Paul in the very heart of Judaism's religious cult, in the precincts of the Jerusalem Temple."[111] In contrast, Bruce opines that for Paul the temple vision "reaffirmed what he had already learned on the Damascus road—that his call was to be Christ's witness among the Gentiles."[112] Based on an analysis of Acts 22 alone, or even together with Acts 9, it is impossible to decide the issue definitively, due to Luke's silence on the issue. Clearly, Paul does not mention his call in this recounting of the DRE. Yet, he does not rule out the possibility, either. It seems plausible that Luke included Paul's call within the temple vision in order to serve the specific function of addressing the complaint of the crowd. Therefore, it is not necessary to conclude that Paul received his commission for the first time in the temple vision. Indeed, it would seem prudent to reserve judgment on this matter until Acts 26 has been considered.

Acts 26:4–20

The third DRE account is found in Acts 26.[113] After the events of Acts 22, Paul is transferred to the custody of Felix, the Roman governor of the province of Judaea. Two years later, Felix is replaced by Festus (24:27). At some point, Herod Agrippa II and his sister Bernice visit Festus, who shares with them his difficulty in deciding how to deal with Paul. Agrippa requests to hear from Paul himself (25:22). Festus consents and summons Paul (25:23). During his defense, Paul tells Agrippa of his Damascus road encounter with Jesus. Derrida comments,

> In the second autobiographical narrative, the destination of this testimony of conversion is seen to be even more clearly assigned.

---

111. Fitzmyer, *Acts*, 708.

112. Bruce, *Book of Acts*, 419.

113. See Gaventa, *Darkness*, 77–88. For a summary of the speech, see Squires, *Plan of God*, 32–35.

It is a question, this time, of converting others and turning their eyes—open at last—toward the light, a question of turning them away from darkness and from Satan (the angel of light but also of blindness) in order to recall them to God, in order for God to call them back to Him.[114]

Acts 26:4–20 is now presented in translation. Text-critical notes are included in the footnotes.

> **26:4** Therefore all[115] Jews have known my life from my youth, which was from the beginning among my people in Jerusalem; **5** they know me from that time, if they wish to testify, that according to the strictest sect of our religion I lived as a Pharisee. **6** And I am on trial now for the hope of the promise made by God to our[116] fathers, **7** to which our twelve tribes earnestly, night and day, hope to attain. It is concerning this hope I am accused by the Jews, O King.[117] **8** Why is it considered unbelievable by you if God raises the dead? **9** So I thought it was necessary for me to do many hostile acts to the name of[118] Jesus of Nazareth, **10** which I also did in Jerusalem. I locked up many holy ones in prisons, receiving authority from the high priests. I cast my vote against them when they were being condemned to death. **11** Frequently punishing them in all the synagogues, I tried to compel them to blaspheme; being furiously enraged at them, I was pursuing them even to foreign cities. **12** In this situation, as I was traveling to Damascus with the authority and authorization of[119] the high priests, **13** at midday along the way, O King, I saw a light from

---

114. Derrida, *Memoirs of the Blind*, 116. Lohfink remarks, "Now finally Paul is actually sent forth, and this immediately by Christ and directly outside Damascus." Lohfink, *Conversion*, 95.

115. The article οἱ is included before Ἰουδαῖοι in ℵ A C² P, most miniscules, and the Textus Receptus. It is absent from $\mathfrak{P}^{74}$ B C* E Ψ 33 81 323 614 945 1175 1505 1739 1875 1884 1891 2495. Metzger argues for the shorter reading; the meaning of the text is little changed by either reading. *TCGNT*, 438.

116. Most witnesses include ἡμῶν, although H L P 049 1241 𝔐 do not.

117. Paul's address to Agrippa is βασιλεῦ Ἀγρίππα in 104 945 1739 1891, Syriac, and a few others; Ἀγρίππα βασιλεῦ in M; βασιλεῦ in ℵ B C E 096 33 81 1175 2464, Vulgate and Coptic versions; and not present in A Ψ 36 453 and a few others. Thus it appears that the weight of evidence favors βασιλεῦ.

118. A few manuscripts, including $\mathfrak{P}^{74}$ ℵ*, include the article τοῦ before Ἰησοῦ.

119. Instead of the simple genitive ἐπιτροπῆς, some witnesses (C Ψ 33 1739 𝔐) include the preposition παρά. The weight of evidence ($\mathfrak{P}^{74}$ ℵ A B E 048^{vid} 096 81 614 1175 1505) supports ἐπιτροπῆς.

heaven,[120] brighter than the sun, shining around me and those traveling with me. **14** After we all fell to the ground,[121] I heard a voice speaking to me[122] in the Aramaic language, "Saul, Saul, why are you persecuting me? It is hard for you to kick against the goads." **15** And I said, "Who are you, Lord?" And the Lord[123] said, "I am Jesus[124] whom you are persecuting. **16** But get up and stand on your feet; I appeared to you for this reason: to appoint you servant and witness both of what you have seen[125] and of what I will show to you **17** rescuing you from the people and from the Gentiles to whom I am sending[126] you, **18** to open their[127] eyes, so that they may turn from darkness to light, and from the authority of Satan to God, so that they may receive forgiveness of sins and a place with those who have been sanctified by faith in me." **19** For this reason, King Agrippa, I was not disobedient to the heavenly vision, **20** but to all in Damascus first, and also in Jerusalem, and[128] the region of Judea and among the Gentiles I commanded them to repent and to turn to God, performing works worthy of repentance.

Outline

Luke's third account of the DRE is quite similar to the previous two in many respects. Yet the speech in Acts 26 is stylistically different from the

120. Οὐρανόθεν is omitted by 𝔓[74vid].

121. The text does appear to be correct. However, several Western witnesses (614 2147 gig sy[hmg] sa bo[mss]) include διὰ τὸν φόβον ἐγὼ μόνος. This variant alters the text in two ways. First, it provides a motivation for the falling (although the reason is strongly suggested by the text). Second, it emphasizes that Paul alone heard the heavenly voice.

122. There are several variations to λέγουσαν πρός με, none of which affect the meaning of the text.

123. H P 049 323 1241 𝔐 omit κύριος.

124. Many witnesses (048 6 104 614 1175 gig vg[mss] sy[p, h**]) include ὁ Ναζωραῖος.

125. NA[27] includes με (B C[vid] 614 945 1175 1505 1739 1891 2464) in square brackets, in order "to represent the balance between external evidence and transcriptional probability." *TCGNT*, 438. While this is certainly the more difficult reading, I prefer to omit on the strength of the evidence (𝔓[74] ℵ A C[2] E Ψ 096 𝔐).

126. The text reads ἀποστέλλω, supported by ℵ A B E 048[vid] 𝔐 . The three variants, ἀποστελῶ, ἐξαποστέλλω, ἐξαποστελῶ, have less support, and little affect the meaning of the text.

127. E 096, and some Vulgate manuscripts, replace αὐτῶν with τυφλῶν, "of the blind."

128. Some witnesses, including E Ψ 33 1739 𝔐, insert the preposition εἰς. The text has the support of 𝔓[74] ℵ A B vg[mss] in omitting.

preceding accounts. Bruce observes that "the construction of the speech is more careful than usual, the grammar more classical, and the style more literary."[129] For example, ἴσασι (26:4) is an unusual form of οἶδα which "stems from literary language."[130] The superlative ἀκριβεστάτην (5) is the only one of three NT superlatives in -τατος that has a strictly superlative meaning.[131] The term used to describe the heavenly origin of the light, οὐρανόθεν (13), is a literary term[132] occurring only once elsewhere in the NT (Acts 14:17). Yet despite its classical style, the speech also exhibits some of the diachronic developments of first-century Greek. For example, the time of Jesus's appearance, ἡμέρας μέσης or "at midday," is expressed using a genitive of time, which is not a classical usage.[133]

In addition to the stylistic and grammatical embellishments, the vocabulary is also quite unusual. Some of the words that are *hapax legomena* in the NT include: βιωσίν, "way of life" (4); the superlative ἀκριβεστάτην, "strictest" (5); θρησκεία, "religion" or "worship" (5); ἐμμαίνομαι, "to be enraged" (11); ἐπιτροπή, "authority" (12); and λαμπρότης, "brightness" (13).[134] The story also contains the first known occurrence of δωδεκάφυλον,[135] which Blass describes as an "attributive compound showing mutation."[136] Words that are *dis legomena* in the NT include: κατακλείω, "lock up" (10; Luke 3:20); ψῆφος, the pebble used by Paul to vote against Christians (10; Rev 2:17); τιμωρέω, "punish" (11; 22:5); οὐρανόθεν (13); and περιλάμπω, "shining around" (13; Luke 2:9). Finally, some words are *tris legomena* in the NT, including: καταφέρω, "to cast" (10; 20:9; 25:7); and προχειρίζομαι, "to choose in advance, appoint" (16; 3:20; 22:14).

Bearing these differences in mind, let us now examine the text in detail.

---

129. Bruce, *Book of Acts*, 461.
130. BDF, §99(2).
131. This is discussed in "The decline of the superlative." BDF, §60(1).
132. Bruce, *Acts of the Apostles*, 500.
133. BDF, §186(2).
134. L&N, §14.49.
135. Bruce, *Acts of the Apostles*, 498.
136. BDF, §120(3).

Introduction (Acts 26:4–13a)

As in Acts 9 and 22, the introduction provides both background (26:4–11) and setting (26:12–13a).

Background (Acts 26:4–11)

Paul's pre-DRE autobiography in Acts 26 is similar to that of Acts 22. It describes Paul's upbringing in Jerusalem (4), and his persecution of Christians (10–11).

Several additional details are worth noting. Paul claims to have lived as a Pharisee, ἔζησα Φαρισαῖος (5).[137] Paul's attitude toward Jesus is explicitly stated in verse 9: Ἐγὼ μὲν οὖν ἔδοξα ἐμαυτῷ πρὸς τὸ ὄνομα Ἰησοῦ τοῦ Ναζωραίου δεῖν πολλὰ ἐναντία πρᾶξαι. This statement identifies the close connection that Paul makes between the "name of Jesus of Nazareth" and those he then sought to persecute (10–11), and this prior to Jesus's appearance.

Paul describes two additional features of his persecuting activities. He cast his vote against Christians when they were being condemned to death (10).[138] He also sought to make Christians blaspheme (βλασφημεῖν, 11) against the "name of Jesus of Nazareth" (9). The finite verb in verse 11, ἠνάγκαζον, is imperfect,[139] indicating that Paul's attempts to make the Christians blaspheme were to no avail.[140]

Thus, in the introduction of the third DRE account, Paul presents a fuller picture of his activities against Christians prior to his encounter with Jesus on the Damascus road.

Setting (Acts 26:12–13a)

Paul places the setting within the context of the preceding background information using the phrase ἐν οἷς, which means "in these circumstances."[141] Paul again gives the temporal setting as "while I was

---

137. In making the case that Paul was actually a "Zealot," not just a Pharisee, Fairchild notably omits any reference to this verse. Fairchild, "Pre-Christian."

138. The political significance and legality of capital punishment is discussed in Witherington, *Acts*, 742.

139. This is generally taken as a conative imperfect (BDF, §326; BDAG, 60; *GGBTB*, 551).

140. Luke gives no indication that Paul's attempts were successful (cf. Acts 4:18–21; 5:27–41; 7:51—8:4). However, it is possible that the imperfect may be iterative or customary rather than conative (Steve Walton, private e-mail; cf. *GGBTB*, 547–48).

141. Bruce, *Acts of the Apostles*, 500.

traveling to Damascus" (Ἐν οἷς πορευόμενος εἰς τὴν Δαμασκὸν, 12) and "at midday" (ἡμέρας μέσης, 13). The spatial setting is less specific than before, "along the way" (κατὰ τὴν ὁδὸν, 13).

Appearance (Acts 26:13b–15)

Once again, a bright light suddenly appears from heaven. Two progressions are apparent with respect to the light. First, the light increases in intensity from "a light" (9:3) and "a very bright light" (22:6) to "a light brighter than the sun" at midday (26:13). Second, the light also increases in scope, from "shining around" (9:3), and "shining around me" (22:6), to "shining around me and those traveling with me" (26:13)

Two further progressions are evident in the human response to the light. First, in 9:4 and 22:7 only Paul falls, yet in 26:14 "all of us" (πάντων... ἡμῶν) fall. Second, the common verb for falling, πίπτω,[142] is found in 9:4 and 22:7, but the much less frequent καταπίπτω[143] is found in 26:14.[144]

In 26:14 we learn for the first time that the voice spoke in Aramaic.[145] The unusual spelling of "Saul" (Σαούλ), also present in the previous accounts (9:4; 22:7), may be another indication that Jesus spoke in Aramaic. Jesus's initial remarks are also expanded from the accounts in Acts 9 and 22. The phrase σκληρόν σοι πρὸς κέντρα λακτίζειν is common in classical literature.[146] Bultmann also notes that the phrase "is a widespread proverbial expression that means that man cannot withstand the divine," and therefore "does not refer to an inner struggle."[147] Jervell interprets the phrase as a theological passive: "Paulus kann nicht gegen Gott selbst kämpfen."[148]

---

142. 90 occurrences in the NT.

143. Only three occurrences in the NT.

144. Although καταπίπτω is not necessarily an intensification from πίπτω, Moulton notes that it "is used metaphorically of the accidents of fortune" in *Vettii Valentis Anthologiarum Libri*. Moulton and Milligan, *Vocabulary*, 331.

145. The term Ἑβραΐδι is "generally taken to mean the Aramaic language." Marshall, *Acts*, 395.

146. Bruce, *Acts of the Apostles*, 501. Bruce claims that the goads "were not the prickings of an uneasy conscience over his persecuting activity but the new forces which were now impelling him in the opposite direction."

147. Bultmann, *Existence*, 114.

148. Jervell, *Apostelgeschichte*, 593.

The epiphanic figure is identified in several different ways at several different levels of the narrative. Paul identifies the figure as κύριος, both in the dialog with the divine interlocutor (τίς εἶ, κύριε, 15), and in his narration of the event to Agrippa (ὁ δὲ κύριος εἶπεν, 15).[149] The figure identifies himself as Ἰησοῦς,[150] "whom you are persecuting" (15).

Message (Acts 26:16-18)

Finally in verse 16, after issuing the command to stand, Jesus reveals the purpose for his appearance. The purpose is marked by the phrase εἰς τοῦτο γάρ. Jesus identifies Paul's role, message, and audience. Jesus himself appoints Paul. The verb for appoint, προχειρίζω, is rare in the NT, occurring elsewhere only in Acts 3:20 and 22:14. Here, Jesus is the one who appoints; in 22:14, it is the "God of our fathers" who appoints. Paul is to be a servant (ὑπηρέτης, 16) and a witness (μάρτυρα, 16). Paul's message involves the rather cryptic "things you have seen and things which will appear to you" (ὧν τε εἶδές [με] ὧν τε ὀφθήσομαί σοι, 16). Paul's audience is the Gentiles, τῶν ἐθνῶν, to whom Jesus now sends him (εἰς οὓς ἐγὼ ἀποστέλλω σε, 17).

The message is further refined in verses 17 and 18. Jesus promises to rescue (ἐξαιρούμενος, 17) Paul from "the people and the Gentiles to whom I am sending you." This reference to the Lord who rescues echoes Gal 1:3. In the NT, ἐξαιρέω occurs eight times. The occurrences in Matthew are idiomatic and hence not relevant here.[151] Of the remaining instances, three refer to God or the Lord,[152] and another involves rescue by a human.[153] The final two instances are found in the context of Paul's DRE: once in Acts (26:17), and once in Paul (Gal 1:4). It is noteworthy that such an unusual NT word should be used in the context of the DRE by both Luke and Paul.

---

149. Although see p. 212 n. 123 above for a textual variant.

150. Many Western witnesses (see p. 212 n. 124) also include ὁ Ναζωραῖος, "of Nazareth." This reading is not likely original; it is also not necessary for our argument, since ὁ Ναζωραῖος does appear in Acts 22:8.

151. Matt 5:29; 18:9. These repeat a saying of Jesus, "If your [right] eye causes you to stumble, cast it out."

152. The subject of Acts 7:10 is God; of 7:34, the Lord, in a clear reference to יהוה. In 2:11 the subject is the Lord, which is likely a reference to God; so Dunn, *Christology*, 249.

153. Acts 23:27.

Scholarly discussion of ἐξαιρούμενός in 26:17 has focused on its meaning, and its connection to prophetic commissioning. Page had proposed that it should be translated with its classical sense of "choosing,"[154] but recent interpreters favor "delivering" or "rescuing."[155] The connection with OT prophetic commissioning, particularly that of Jeremiah (Jer. 1:7-8; cf. 1 Chr 16:35; Ezek 2:3; Isa 42:7, 16), is also well noted.[156] The theological implications of Jesus identifying himself as the one who rescues have been largely ignored. As we have seen,[157] the verb ἐξαιρέω is almost exclusively used in the LXX with reference to the Lord, κύριος, as Yahweh. This connection between κύριος and ἐξαιρέω is critical to Luke's characterization of Jesus.[158]

Paul's message involves opening people's eyes and turning them from darkness to light, from Satan to God, in order that they would be forgiven and have a future place with the saints (18). Jesus concludes his message by claiming that sanctification comes "by faith in me."[159]

Conclusion (Acts 26:19-20)

Paul concludes his account by mentioning his obedience to the heavenly vision (19). He then gives a brief overview of his post-DRE activities (20). Squires notes that 26:19-23 is "virtually a new segment" not present in either Acts 9 or 22.[160]

Summary

The Damascus road encounter between Paul and Jesus is presented on three separate occasions in Acts. Luke first describes the event at its proper chronological place in the discourse, and recounts it twice more in speeches by Paul. Each account provides a slightly different perspective on what is perhaps the central event in the book of Acts.

---

154. Page, *Acts*, 248-49.

155. Barrett, *Acts*, 2:1160; Bruce, *Acts of the Apostles*, 502; Conzelmann, *Acts*, 211; Gaventa, *Acts*, 344; Haenchen, *Acts*, 686.

156. Barrett, *Acts*, 2:1160; Bruce, *Book of Acts*, 466-67; Bruce, *Acts of the Apostles*, 502; Fitzmyer, *Acts*, 759.

157. See pp. 170-71 above.

158. See pp. 240-42 below.

159. The message is discussed in greater detail on pp. 225-29 below.

160. Squires, *Plan of God*, 35.

LITERARY ASPECTS OF THE DAMASCUS ROAD ENCOUNTER

We will next consider the DRE from a literary perspective. The first literary issue to be addressed is the relationship between the accounts of Acts 9, 22, and 26. In many ways, the three accounts are quite similar. Yet there are also areas where they appear to diverge. For example, 9:7 states that Paul's companions remained standing, while 26:14 says that they all fell to the ground. In 9:7, Paul's companions heard the voice but saw no one, while in 22:9, they saw the light but did not hear the voice. In addition, in Acts 9 and 22 Paul confers with Ananias regarding his calling, while in 26:16–18 Jesus calls Paul personally.[161]

Luke's use of repetition has perplexed scholars for years, and remains "even today a *crux interpretum* in Acts research."[162] Some of the previous explanations for the variations include source criticism, redaction criticism, form criticism, ancient historiography, stylistic variation, adaptation to context, and narrative criticism, as well as simply mistakes or carelessness on the part of Luke.[163] Of course, there are variations within each of the basic approaches, and various combinations of different approaches have also been proposed. Each of these theories will now be considered in turn.

The source critical approach attributes the difference to Luke's use of multiple sources. It also typically presupposes that the three accounts are incompatible. For example, Hirsch views the message elements of Acts 9 and 26 as contradictory, and therefore proposes that Acts 22 was introduced by Luke as a compromise.[164] Other scholars who argue that

---

161. Meyer, "Light and Voice," 28–29. For a discussion of the first two issues, see pp. 229–31 below; for the third, see p. 225–29 below.

162. Marguerat, "Saul's Conversion," 128. Tannehill raises the issue of how the variations would be understood by Luke's readers: "The free way in which Paul reformulates the account of his commission carries a certain risk that some hearers or readers will doubt the accuracy of his account." Tannehill, *Narrative Unity*, 2:322.

163. For an excellent summary of recent approaches see Clark, *Parallel Lives*, 150–65.

164. Dibelius summarizes Hirsch's position as follows: "Chapter 22 is intended to furnish a compromise between the accounts in Chapters 9 and 26. As Hirsch plainly asserts, this judgement presupposes that the two accounts, in 9 and 26, 'are incompatible'. That is just the question. Hirsch, quite rightly, sees the chief discrepancy in the fact that the call to become a missionary to the Gentiles is given to Paul in Chapter 26 only by the voice from heaven; in Chapter 9 there is only the Lord's command to Ananias and, in Chapter 22, though hinted at in the words of Ananias, the charge is openly given for

the variations in the DRE accounts are due to multiple sources include Pritchard,[165] Jervell,[166] and Budesheim.[167] Barrett notes that the multiple source theory is "now very generally abandoned."[168]

Redaction criticism is also proposed as an explanation for the variations.[169] Dibelius is a prominent proponent of this approach. He argues against Hirsch's source critical approach,[170] speculating instead that Acts 9 is the original DRE account, with Acts 22 and 26 being redactional variants.[171] Haenchen, building on Dibelius's work, emphasizes Luke's "dramatic technique of scene-writing" in which "edifying material" is completely reworked to express Luke's theological concerns.[172]

The DRE narratives are also approached from a form-critical perspective.[173] Hedrick suggests that "Acts 9:1–19 is basically a miracle story of the healing of Paul's blindness. Acts 22:4–16 appears to be a healing narrative that has been redacted into a commissioning narrative; Acts

---

the first time in the vision in the temple." Dibelius, *Acts*, 158–59 n. 47.

165. "Luke's three reports of [Paul's mystical experience near Damascus] in Acts quite probably represent three slightly varying traditions." Pritchard, *Literary Approach*, 150.

166. Jervell claims that Acts 22:17–21 "can only be explained by Luke's having before him various traditions regarding the story of Paul's conversion that he does not want to 'suppress.'" Jervell, *People of God*, 166.

167. Budesheim notes the "sparse attention given of late to source-criticism of the speeches of Acts," complaining that the situation was "not entirely felicitous." In an effort to rectify this perceived deficiency, he proposes that the speeches in Jerusalem (Acts 22:1–21) and Miletus (20:18–35) "one speech which Luke reworked, divided into two parts, and situated in reverse order into the progression of his 'history' of the early Church." Budesheim, "Paul," 9–10.

168. Barrett, *Acts*, 1:444. As early as 1961, Dibelius's argument against multiple sources was accepted as "proven." Klein, *Zwölf Apostel*, 144.

169. For example, see Burchard, *Zeuge*, 119–22; Löning, *Die Saulustradition*, 18–19.

170. "The question is whether these variations may all be attributed to Luke. Once we have seen that we are concerned primarily with what the account is intended to signify, rather than with its historical reliability, then we can conclude that they are to be attributed to him." Dibelius, *Acts*, 158–59 n. 47.

171. Dibelius, *Acts*, 160.

172. Haenchen, *Acts*, 107–10.

173. See Barrett, *Acts*, 1:439–45; Witherington, *Acts*, 303–15.

26:12–18 is a commissioning narrative."[174] Hubbard,[175] Mullins,[176] and Lohfink[177] have also considered the three accounts from a form-critical perspective.

Another explanation involves ancient historiography. Lohfink concludes that "the speeches contained in ancient historical documents are *a medium of free and creative literary compositional expression*."[178] Dunn takes the same position.[179]

Some suggest that the differences are due to unintentional mistakes or careless redaction. For example, Haenchen views the variations as evidence of "careless Lukan redaction."[180] In other words, Haenchen presumes that Luke was using multiple divergent sources, and did not remove the discrepancies due to carelessness.

Stylistic concerns have also been suggested as a possible explanation for the differences. For example, Jervell suggests that Luke uses repetition for emphasis.[181] Others have proposed that the variations are due to context, Stanley being one of the first to suggest this.[182] Similarly, Schille attributes the differences to Lukan literary devices.[183] Others taking this position include Gaventa,[184] Bruce,[185] and Wright.[186] Still others view the three accounts as intentionally divergent; that is, Luke introduced the

---

174. Hedrick, "Paul's Conversion," 417. Hedrick's interpretation of the appearance of the resurrected Jesus as healing narrative seems utterly inadequate.

175. Hubbard, "Commissioning Stories," 103–26.

176. Mullins, "Commission Forms," 603–14.

177. Lohfink, *Conversion*, 61–80.

178. Lohfink, *Conversion*, 53. He makes this generalization after citing one example from Josephus. (Emphasis in original.)

179. Dunn, *Acts*, 117.

180. So Marguerat, "Saul's Conversion," 129.

181. "Lukas benutzt die Wiederholung, um das besonders Wichtige zu betonen." Jervell, *Apostelgeschichte*, 278.

182. "The triple narrative of that supremely critical hour in a life fraught with crises deserves to be studied from another aspect: the function assigned it in the exposition of his theme by the author of the book of Acts." Stanley, "Paul's Conversion," 315.

183. Schille, *Apostelgeschichte*, 218.

184. "Luke tells the story in a different manner each time, depending on the demands of the context." Gaventa, *Darkness*, 90.

185. "The different accounts are subtly adapted to their varying circumstances." Bruce, *Acts of the Apostles*, 232.

186. "The main differences between the accounts are easily explained in terms of the audience Luke envisages for each occasion." Wright, *Resurrection*, 390.

discrepancies in modifying the narrative to fit the context. Kilgallen is typical of this view, suggesting that "in Acts 26, Paul does away with the intermediacy of Ananias in order to underline the directness and divinity of the authority which stand behind all that Paul subsequently did in his life."[187] Segal suggests the discrepancies reflect a general unawareness of the event: "These differences show that the details of Paul's conversion were not well known and not part of a carefully guarded literary tradition."[188]

Recently, scholars have proposed a number of literary approaches. For example, Marguerat explains the variations using a combination of five rules.[189] Witherup proposes that the variations are an example of functional redundancy.[190] Witherington suggests that Luke employs repetition and variation for "cumulative effect."[191]

Various combinations of these views have also been espoused. For example, Barrett advocates either stylistic variation or source criticism.[192] O'Toole appears to suggest that Acts 26 was redacted from Acts 22 for context and stylistic concerns.[193] Townsend suggests that Acts 9 was derived from a combination of multiple sources[194] and stereotypical

---

187. Kilgallen, "Paul before Agrippa," 185, 191.

188. Segal, *Paul the Convert*, 7.

189. His five rules are focus, inculturation, variation, actualization, and narrative situation setting. Marguerat, "Saul's Conversion," 127–55.

190. "The so-called redundancy found in Acts 9, 22 and 26 is not a happenstance of repetition but a functional, rhetorical and literary tool which exalts the portrait of Paul as apostle to the Gentiles and elaborates the story of the growth of the Christian faith." Witherup, "Functional Redundancy," 85.

191. Witherington, *Acts*, 665–66. See Hedrick, "Paul's Conversion," 415–32.

192. "Either Luke is deliberately introducing variation, so as to achieve the emphasis that comes from repetition and at the same time avoid the risk of losing the reader, or he is using different traditions. The former alternative is more probable." Barrett, *Acts*, 2:1159.

193. Of Acts 26, O'Toole writes: "Less significant details are dropped, but the central and more important ones are emphasized through expansion. Luke thus highlights and enlivens his last apology of Paul; he is more definite, clearer, more explicit. Moreover, Luke better organizes and unifies the last apology of Paul. The apology of 22:1–21 is somewhat scattered; we have two reports about Paul as a persecutor (22:4–5, 19–20), two visions (22:7–11, 17–21), and the addition of another main character who gives Paul his mission. So the report of 26:12–18 is more compressed than 22:6–16." O'Toole, *Climax*, 45.

194. Acts 9 "can be understood as a tradition which arose from a simple elaboration of certain bits of accurate information." Townsend, "Tradition," 97.

features of epiphany.[195] Lüdemann cites a combination of literary[196] and redactional factors.[197] Weiser attributes the variations to a combination of inattentiveness (perhaps), intensification, or accommodation to the particular situation.[198] Wenham suggests either a "lack of interest in historical precision" or "different sources."[199]

Thus, the variation among the three DRE accounts remains an open issue. None of the current approaches appears to explain the data adequately.

I will propose a new reading that does account for the repetition and variation among the three narratives. This new approach is presented below in the discussion of the message.

Let us then consider the literary aspects of Luke's DRE narratives. We will begin with the event itself, including the structure, initiative, and purpose of the appearance. We will then examine the characterization of Jesus in the DRE.

Event

Luke's three-fold narration of the DRE is elegant in its simplicity. Yet the three accounts contain variations that merit close attention.

NARRATIVE STRUCTURE

The three Acts DRE narratives, and the message in particular, have been the subject of much debate.[200] A new approach to reconciling the three accounts will be presented in our discussion of the message.

---

195. He explains the heavenly light as an "expected" feature of epiphanies, and Paul's blindness as "a testimony to the intensity of the light." Townsend, "Acts 9," 129–30.

196. Lüdemann, *Christianity*, 116.

197. Lüdemann views Acts 26 as "a redactional composition by Luke," citing Wellhausen's claim that it is "mere excrescence." Lüdemann, *Christianity*, 256.

198. Weiser, *Apostelgeschichte*, 2:610.

199. Wenham, "Parallels," 219.

200. See pp. 218–22 above. Lohfink proposed an alternate structure based on several OT accounts: Redeeinführung (Discourse introduction), Verdoppelter Anruf (Double call), Frage Christi (Christ's question), Redeeinführung (Discourse introduction), Frage des Paulus (Paul's question), Redeeinführung (Discourse introduction), Selbstpräsentation Christi (Christ's Self-presentation), Auftrag (Commission). "Ein in dieser Art geformtes Gespräch innerhalb einer Erscheinung begegnet nicht erst in der Apg. Beispiele dafür finden sich schon im AT, und zwar an drei Stellen." Lohfink, "Darstellungsform."

Introduction

Luke provides an introduction to each account. Furthermore, each introduction consists of both background (9:1–2; 22:3–5; 26:4–11) and setting (9:3a; 22:6a; 26:12–13a).

Background

Luke provides background information about Paul prior to the DRE. In particular, three facets of Paul's life are described: his upbringing, his persecution of the church, and his expedition to Damascus. These are presented chronologically, from a more distant time until immediately prior to Jesus's appearance. They also progress from the general to the specific, from a discussion of Paul's religious upbringing and his persecution of the church, to the details of the expedition to Damascus.

Paul's upbringing is discussed in 22:3 and 26:4–5. He is described as a Jew (22:3), born in Tarsus (22:3), but likely raised in Jerusalem (22:3; 26:4). He was taught by Gamaliel (22:3). He is also described as a Pharisee (26:5), and being "zealous for God" (22:3). Paul's persecution of the church is described with increasing detail in each successive account, from simply "breathing murderous threats" (9:1), through persecuting "unto death" and imprisonment (22:4), to committing "many hostile acts" against the name of Jesus, including imprisoning Christians, forcing them to blaspheme Jesus, and voting to condemn them to death (26:9–11). Each account concludes with a description of the mission to Damascus. Paul received authorization from the high priest for the expedition in order to deport Christians back to Jerusalem (9:1–2; 22:5; 26:12a) to be punished (22:5).

Thus, Luke presents Paul as a devout Jew, a Pharisee, who was zealous for God and sought to live according to the precepts of Judaism. This is demonstrated in his request for approval from the high priest (9:1–2) and the council of elders (22:5) for his actions, as well as his intention to return his prisoners to Jerusalem to face punishment (9:2; 22:5). Even his votes condemning Christians to death (26:10) show that Paul was attempting to meet the requirements of Judaism as he understood them.

Luke also presents Paul in opposition to Jesus and his followers. Luke describes the range of Paul's persecuting activities, including making threats (9:1), forcing Christians to blaspheme (26:11), arresting both men and women (9:2; 22:4), and even voting for capital punishment

(26:10). Paul's activities were not limited geographically. He even pursued Christians to foreign cities (26:11).

Thus, prior to the DRE Paul is characterized as a devout Jew who was violently opposed to Jesus and his followers.

Setting

Jesus's appearance is given both temporal and spatial setting. Temporally, the DRE is set during Paul's journey to Damascus (9:3; 22:6; 26:12), at noon (22:6; 26:13). Spatially, the DRE occurs "near Damascus" (9:3; 22:6). While neither the temporal nor spatial setting is too specific, each gives a general sense of when and where the DRE is about to occur.

Appearance

Luke describes the appearance in each account (9:3b–5; 22:6b–8; 26:13b–15). Most of the key features are repeated in each instance: the suddenness; the light from heaven; Paul's fall; the voice; the double vocative, "Saul, Saul"; the initial question, "Why are you persecuting me"; Paul's query in reply, "Who are you, Lord?"; and the answer, "I am Jesus, whom you are persecuting." There is some variation among the accounts. For example, the voice is said to speak in Aramaic (τῇ Ἑβραΐδι) in 26:14. In the same verse, the initial question is followed by the proverbial statement about kicking against the goads.

However, the greatest variation involves the light, both in its brightness and scope, and in the response to it. The light is described with increasing intensity, from "a light" (9:3), and "a very bright light" (22:6), to "a light brighter than the sun" at midday (26:13). The light is also described with increasing scope, from "shining around" (9:3), and "shining around me" (22:6), to "shining around me and those traveling with me." The human reaction to the light also increases, from Paul alone falling (9:4; 22:7) to "all of us," πάντων ... ἡμῶν (26:14).

Thus, it appears that Luke's repetitive narration in the appearance section, particularly with respect to the description of the light and the subsequent human response, is presented as an increasing sequence.[201]

---

201. The sequence has a definite order (Acts 9, 22, 26). Each account uses increasingly precise and heightened language.

Message

The message element is prominent in each of the three Lukan DRE accounts (9:6; 22:10; 26:16–18). As we have seen, scholarly attention has focused on the variations among them. I will now propose a new reading of Luke's DRE narrative that accounts for both the frequency and repetition of the message, as well as the variations among the three accounts.

In discussing Forster's *A Passage to India*, Kermode remarks, "I spend much of my time among learned men who were devoted colleagues and friends of Forster and who know *Passage* well, but they never seem to talk about its secrets, only about its message and what, in their view, is wrong with it."[202] The same appears to be true of Luke's DRE narrative in Acts. Too much has been made of what seems to be wrong, and too little attention has been paid to the secret behind Luke's purposeful repetition.

Luke's DRE narrative cannot be properly interpreted apart from the literary concepts of repetition[203] and frequency.[204] The DRE is a repeating narrative that occurs once but is narrated more than once. The pattern of repetition is perhaps less obvious, since Luke does not merely repeat the message verbatim each time. Yet we have already seen evi-

---

202. Kermode, "Secrets," 88.

203. Miller observes, "in a novel, what is said two or more times may not be true, but the reader is fairly safe in assuming that it is significant." Miller, *Repetition*, 2. Ricoeur claims that repetition implies the "existential deepening" of time. Ricoeur, "Narrative Time," 184. Alter proposes a "scale of repetitive structuring and focusing devices": *leitwort*, where cognates and synonyms of a word are repeated; *motif*, where an action, image, or object recur; *theme*, where a particular value, be it "moral, moral-psychological, legal, political, historical, [or] theological," is repeated; *sequence of actions*, involving the threefold, or threefold plus one, repetition of an event, "with some intensification or increment from one occurrence to the next, usually concluding either in a climax or a reversal"; *type-scene*, involving "an episode occurring at a portentous moment in the career of the hero which is composed of a fixed sequence of motifs," such as the "the annunciation of the birth of the hero, the betrothal by the well, the trial in the wilderness." Alter, *Biblical Narrative*, 96. For a discussion on repetition in the context of narrative time, see Ricoeur, "Narrative Time," 180–90. Cadbury discusses Luke's use of repetition and variation, particularly in the context of the three DRE accounts of Acts 9, 22, and 26. Cadbury, "Four Features," 88–97.

204. Frequency involves "relations between the repetitive capacities of the story and those of the narrative." Genette, *Narrative Discourse*, 35. An event that occurs once and is narrated once is singulative, or a singular narrative. An event that occurs more than once but is narrated only once is called iterative narrative. An event that occurs once but is narrated more than once is called repeating narrative. Genette, *Narrative Discourse*, 114–16.

dence that the three accounts form an increasing sequence. For example, the description of Paul's persecutions increase from "breathing murderous threats" (9:1) and "I persecuted this Way unto death, binding and handing over to prison both men and women" (22:4), to "many hostile acts," "locked up many holy ones in prisons," "I cast my vote against them when they were being condemned to death," "frequently punishing them in the synagogues," "I tried to compel them to blaspheme," and "I was pursuing them even to foreign cities" (26:9–11). Similarly, the brightness of the light is described in increasing terms, from "a light from heaven" (9:3) and "a very bright light" (22:6) to "a light from heaven, brighter than the sun" (26:13). The scope of the light also increases, from "around him" (9:3) and "around me" (22:6) to "around me and those traveling with me" (26:13). The response to the light increases from "he fell to the ground" (9:7) and "I fell to the ground" 22:7) to "we all fell to the ground" (26:14). Lohfink also identifies the continual increase ("fortwährende Steigerung") with respect to Paul's call to mission, from call (Christ to Ananias), call to mission (Ananias to Saul), and announcement of the mission (Christ to Saul in Jerusalem), to immediate mission (Christ to Saul from Damascus).[205]

Thus, it appears that the Lukan DRE accounts are an increasing sequence, which is a typical literary pattern of repetition.[206] In Acts 26, the implied reader learns for the first time that Paul received his call to the Gentiles from Jesus on the Damascus road. If Luke intended to reveal this at the end of the sequence, we should find evidence of an increasing sequence with respect to this purpose in Acts 9 and 22. In fact, we have already seen that the evidence does exist but, like Forster's secret in *A Passage to India*, appears to have gone unnoticed.

In the first account, Jesus's message consists of the cryptic statement, ἀλλὰ ἀνάστηθι καὶ εἴσελθε εἰς τὴν πόλιν καὶ λαληθήσεταί σοι ὅ

---

205. Lohfink attributes the sequence to the "bewußte Redaktions- und Kompositionstechnik des Lukas," which has "ein theologisches Ziel"; namely, the mission-work of Paul and the development of the church among the Gentiles. Lohfink, "Meinen Namen," 114.

206. Alter remarks that folktales often consist of "three consecutive repetitions ... with some intensification or increment ... concluding in either a climax or a reversal." Alter, *Biblical Narrative*, 95–6. Resseguie suggests that "a series of three may indicate that an action is complete, finished. There may be an intensification of an action from one occurrence to the next, with the third in the series representing a climax." Resseguie, *Narrative Criticism*, 49.

τί σε δεῖ ποιεῖν (Acts 9:6). As we have seen, ὅ τί indicates an implied question. Given Jesus's response, Paul's implied question must have been, "What must I do?" Jesus does not answer the question at this point. The second account contains the very question that was implied in the first account: εἶπον δέ· τί ποιήσω, κύριε (22:10). Yet surprisingly, Jesus avoids the question; his response (22:10) is utterly insufficient. The third account is even more surprising. Jesus answers Paul's question (26:16–18), even though Paul does not pose it!

The sequence, then, consists of an implied question with no answer (Acts 9), an explicit question with no answer (Acts 22), and Jesus's answer to the unasked question (Acts 26). In other words, Luke has intentionally constructed the entire sequence to culminate with the revelation of the purpose of the DRE in Jesus's answer in the third account (26:16–18). Thus, Luke's purpose in the three DRE accounts is to reveal that Paul received his call to the Gentiles from Jesus himself on the Damascus road.

A close reading of Acts 9, 22, and 26 supports this hypothesis. Since Paul begins to fulfill his calling prior to Acts 26, it is necessary for the implied reader to be aware of Paul's call after the initial DRE account in Acts 9. Indeed, Luke informs the implied reader of Paul's call in Jesus's appearance to Ananias (9:15). Yet the implied reader remains ignorant of Paul's knowledge of his call, since Ananias does not reveal it to Paul. In Acts 22, the implied reader learns that Paul received his call to the Gentiles from Jesus (22:21), yet is still not informed whether Paul received his call on the Damascus road. In Acts 26, Luke finally reveals to the implied reader that Paul received his call to the Gentiles from Jesus on the Damascus road.

Luke accomplishes this without introducing contradictions into the narrative. Acts 9 does not indicate that Jesus did not call Paul on the Damascus road. In fact, the implied reader is informed of Paul's call through Ananias, but Ananias does not inform Paul. This leaves the implied reader in suspense as to how Paul was informed of his call. In Acts

22, Luke does not exclude the possibility that Jesus called Paul on the Damascus road. The implied reader does not know if Paul was made aware of his call prior to the Jerusalem temple vision, but this only serves to heighten the suspense. Finally in Acts 26, the implied reader learns for the first time that Jesus called Paul on the Damascus road. Thus, it appears that Luke has introduced instabilities into the narrative in order to create tension[207] for the implied reader, which is resolved at the end of the sequence.

This reading conforms to Lodge's three basic effects of narrative.[208] The sequence involves suspense, since the reader is unaware of the true nature of Paul's call until the final account. It also involves curiosity, since the question is hinted at in Acts 9 and asked in Acts 22, but is not answered until Acts 26. Furthermore, the sequence also involves peripeteia. The implied reader may have reasonably assumed that Paul was first informed of his call to the Gentiles in Acts 9 by Ananias or in Acts 22 in the Jerusalem temple vision. Yet in Acts 26 it is finally revealed to the implied reader that Jesus appeared to Paul on the Damascus road in order to send him to the Gentiles.

If it is true that Luke's purpose was finally to reveal that Paul received his call to the Gentiles from Jesus himself on the Damascus road, then we are also able to resolve some other questions that have perplexed scholars.[209] For example, the function of Ananias in the DRE narratives has been the subject of speculation. Lundgren suggests that Ananias serves a twofold purpose: to heal and baptize Paul, and to affirm that Paul was divinely called by Jesus.[210] If our reading is correct, Ananias actually serves a literary purpose: to inform the implied reader of the real purpose for Jesus's appearance, while leaving unanswered until Acts 26 the question of whether Jesus called Paul on the Damascus road. This

---

207. Phelan defines tension as the second form of instabilities: "In general, the story-discourse model of narrative helps to differentiate between two main kinds of instabilities: the first are those occurring within the story, instabilities between characters, created by situations, and complicated and resolved through actions. The second are those created by the discourse, instabilities—of value, belief, opinion, knowledge, expectation—between authors and/or narrators, on the one hand, and the authorial audience on the other." Phelan, *Reading People*, 15.

208. Namely, suspense, curiosity, and peripeteia. Lodge, "Realist Text," 8.

209. "It is most improbable that Ananias is a fictitious character, though Luke may not have known precisely who he was or what he did." Barrett, *Acts*, 1:444.

210. Lundgren, "Ananias," 122.

also explains why Ananias is present in Acts 9 and 22, where the purpose of the DRE has not been fully revealed, but absent from Acts 26, where Ananias is no longer needed.

A failure to appreciate the significance of Luke's purpose in narrating the DRE has led not only to misinterpretations of the Lukan DRE narrative,[211] but also to false comparisons between Luke and Paul. For example, Roloff's initial comment on Acts 9 involves the perceived differences between the DRE accounts of Luke and Paul. Rather than taking the entire sequence into account, Roloff misconstrues Luke's presentation in Acts 9 as a conversion. He then concludes that this differs from Paul's emphasis on the appearance of Jesus and the call to the Gentiles.[212] Similarly, Jervell views the relationship between Acts 22 and 26 as one of inconsistency rather than increasing sequence, which leads to the conclusion that "the Gentile mission is not what is of primary importance for Luke."[213]

Thus, Luke's purpose in the DRE narrative is to reveal that Paul was called as apostle to the Gentiles by Jesus himself on the Damascus road. The three DRE accounts are a crescendo that culminates in the fortissimo of Acts 26:16–18. In other words, Acts 26 is the pinnacle toward which Luke has been climbing since Acts 9.[214]

The message itself is quite startling as well. On the Damascus road, Jesus himself appoints Paul (26:16; cf. 22:14) to be his servant and witness (26:16), with a message (26:17–18) about Jesus ("of what I will show you," 16; sanctified by "faith in me," 18), to the Gentiles (17).

Parenthesis: Paul's Companions

Paul's companions are mentioned in each DRE account. The companions do not speak; their responses are non-verbal.[215] In the first account, the companions stand speechless, hear the voice, and see no one (9:7); in the second, they see the light but do not hear the voice (22:9); in the third,

---

211. In other words, the entire sequence of Acts 9, 22, and 26.
212. Roloff, *Apostelgeschichte*, 144.
213. Jervell, *People of God*, 166.
214. Given the significance of the revelation in Acts 26, it would be interesting to consider the possibility that Acts 26 is the climax not only of the DRE sequence, but also of the entire book of Acts.
215. For an introduction to the narrative use of non-verbal communication, see Korte, *Body Language*, 3–22.

they fall to the ground (26:14). There are apparent discrepancies among the three accounts, yet none seems beyond reconciliation.[216]

The first apparent contradiction concerns whether the companions stood (9:7) or fell (26:14). Bruce rightly notes that this discrepancy is "immaterial: presumably the others were able to get up while Saul remained lying on the ground."[217] In fact, Revelations contains an instance where the angels in heaven stand (εἱστήκεισαν) and fall (ἔπεσαν) around the throne in the same verse (Rev 7:11)!

The second apparent contradiction concerns whether the companions heard (9:7) or did not hear (22:9) the voice. Both accounts contain the verb ἀκούω. The former has an accusative object; the latter, genitive. Blass[218] and Wallace[219] have demonstrated that the case of the object cannot explain the difference between the two verses. Haenchen sees little significance in the details. Both the standing and the hearing/seeing are "contradictions," but "it is only the means of expression which are changed, not the sense of the statement."[220] It is possible to hear the sound of a voice, but not to hear what is said. A similar situation is found in John 12:29, where a voice from heaven is heard (ἀκούω) by the crowd but not understood. Furthermore, the parenthetical observations appear at different points chronologically within discourse time.[221] In Acts 9, the observation regarding Paul's travel companions is presented after the message; in Acts 22, it is presented prior to the message.[222] Thus, it is possible that the companions did not hear the voice at first (Acts 22:9), but became aware of the voice as the encounter continued.[223]

The third apparent contradiction concerns what the companions saw (22:9) or did not see (9:7). This can be understood by the difference in the direct object. In Acts 22, the companions saw the light. In Acts 9,

---

216. For a good summary of the debate, see Barrett, *Acts*, 2:1038–39.

217. Bruce, *Book of Acts*, 184–85.

218. "The NT wavers between genitive and accusative in phrases meaning 'to hear a sound.' . . . The construction for 'to hear a speech' is also doubtful in classical Greek." BDF, §173.

219. *GGBTB*, 133.

220. Haenchen, *Acts*, 322–23.

221. Conzelmann notes the shift, but attributes it to "the intensification of the light imagery." Conzelmann, *Acts*, 187.

222. Gaventa notes that "22:9 appears at a different point in the account than does 9:7." Gaventa, *Darkness*, 71.

223. I am not aware of any others that have made this observation.

the companions did not see the one who appeared. Therefore, it is not necessary to conclude that Acts 9 and 22 are contradictory with respect to what the companions saw.

Thus, the three accounts in Acts 9, 22, and 26 are not irreconcilable. It is not necessary to conclude that the three accounts are contradictory, or that Luke varied the accounts with no regard for accuracy.[224]

Regardless of the variations among the accounts, the more significant literary question remains: why does Luke mention Paul's companions in the DRE story? Perhaps the best answer to this question lies in the comparison and contrast with Paul. The companions are aware of Jesus's appearance, which confirms the reality of Paul's experience.[225] Furthermore, the contrast between Paul and the companions serves to elevate the importance of Paul. Paul is the one to whom Jesus fully appears; the others are only vaguely aware of Jesus's presence, and therefore are much less significant.[226]

Departure

None of the three accounts records Jesus's departure.

Conclusion

Each account contains a conclusion (Acts 9:8–9; 22:11; 26:19–20). Those of Acts 9 and 22 emphasize the traumatic effect of the encounter. Paul is blinded by Jesus's appearance, and is led by the hand into Damascus. The conclusion in Acts 26 emphasizes Paul's obedience to the call he received from Jesus on the Damascus road.

Summary

Luke's narration of the Damascus road encounter between Jesus and Paul is a literary masterpiece. With great precision Luke weaves his story through the repeated narration of three separate accounts in an increas-

---

224. This seems to be what Barrett is suggesting: "Luke was writing up a freshly familiar story, and in each case included what seemed to him to be impressive details in the most impressive way he could think of." Barrett, *Acts*, 2:1038–39.

225. It also confirms that the appearance was an external event, rather than an internal experience such as a vision or epileptic seizure.

226. Similarly, Gaventa comments with respect to Acts 22:9 as it contrasts with 9:7: "However, if we give adequate attention to the function of this verse in the story, the differences cease to have much weight." Gaventa, *Darkness*, 71.

ing sequence that culminates in a startling revelation: Paul received his call to the Gentiles directly from Jesus himself on the Damascus road.

Luke's account of the DRE may be compared to Paul's own testimony. While some scholars have chosen to emphasize the differences between the two accounts,[227] it appears that they are in fact quite similar.

In the introduction, both Luke and Paul provide background information. Both describe Paul's upbringing in Judaism (Acts 22:3; Gal 1:13) as a Pharisee (Acts 26:5; Phil 3:5) with zeal (Acts 22:3; Gal 1:14). Both describe his persecution of Jesus's followers (Acts 9:1; 22:4; 26:9-11; Gal 1:13; Phil 3:6; 1 Cor 15:9).[228] Only Luke describes the preparation for the mission to Damascus (Acts 9:1-2; 22:5; 26:12), and the setting for the encounter at noon (Acts 22:6; 26:13) on the way to Damascus (Acts 9:3; 22:6; 26:12; cf. Gal 1:17).

Regarding the appearance, both Luke and Paul speak of Paul seeing Jesus (Acts 9:27; 1 Cor 9:1; 15:8). Only Luke describes the light and voice, Paul's response, and the initial dialog between Jesus and Paul (Acts 9:3b-5; 22:6b-8; 26:13b-15).

In the message section, both Luke and Paul describe Jesus as the source of Paul's call (Acts 26:16; Gal 1:12, 15-16). Both describe Paul as a messenger, with Luke using the term witness (Acts 26:16), and Paul using the term apostle (Rom 1:1; 11:13; 1 Cor 1:1; 1 Cor 9:1; 15:9; 2 Cor 1:1; Gal 1:1). Both also identify Paul as a servant (ὑπηρέτης, Acts 26:16; δοῦλος, Rom 1:1; Gal 1:10; λειτουργός, Rom 15:16). Both indicate that Paul was given a message; Luke provides a brief description (Acts 26:16-18), while Paul frequently refers to the message as the gospel (εὐαγγέλιον, Rom 1:1,

---

227. For example, Harrisville claims that "Luke's portrait of Paul in Acts is disturbingly different from the portrait drawn from Paul's own letters." Harrisville, "Acts 22," 181. Roloff suggests that the DRE account in Acts 9 portrays conversion, while Paul's own description emphasizes the appearance of Jesus. Roloff, *Apostelgeschichte*, 144. Gabel also posits that Acts differs from Paul's epistles. "What then is Luke trying to do in his portrait of Paul? He is trying to domesticate him, to pull him firmly within the orbit of the Church, to tone down his radical theology, to contain his freedom." Gabel et al., *Bible as Literature*, 236. Wilckens writes that Luke and Paul do not agree: "We must simply not expect theological agreement between Luke and Paul.... Luke takes very seriously the historicity of the church in the world, and his doing so causes his concepts to be different from those of Paul." Wilckens, "Interpreting Luke-Acts," 68.

228. Despite the remarkable similarities between the two versions, Hultgren concludes that Paul's account is "different" and "undoubtably more accurate." Hultgren, "Pre-Christian," 110-11.

3; 15:16; 1 Cor 1:17; Gal 1:6–9, 11). Both also identify Paul's audience as the Gentiles (Acts 26:17; Rom 1:5; 15:16; 1 Cor 9:1).

Both Luke and Paul omit the departure.

In the conclusion, both Luke and Paul describe how Paul was faithful to his call (Acts 26:19–20; Rom 15:18–20; 1 Cor 15:10; Phil 3:12; cf. Gal 1:16c-2:20). Only Luke describes Paul being led blind into Damascus (Acts 9:8–9; 22:11).

Thus, most of the details of Paul's DRE narrative are repeated in Acts. Where the two overlap, Luke does not appear to contradict Paul, but seems to affirm what Paul says. On the other hand, Luke does provide additional information, consisting primarily of description and dialog. In the introduction, Luke describes the preparation for Paul's mission to Damascus, and the setting for Jesus's appearance at noon on the Damascus road. In the appearance, Luke describes the light, the voice, Paul's fall, and the initials dialog between Jesus and Paul.[229] In the message, Luke's content is similar to Paul's (including the elements of call, role, message, and audience), yet Luke presents the message in the words of Jesus, rather than indirectly as does Paul. Finally, in the conclusion, Luke describes the circumstances immediately following Jesus's departure, as the blinded Paul is led into Damascus.

It is natural that Acts should contain more descriptive details and dialog than Paul, since Acts is in narrative form while Paul's accounts are found in epistles where the DRE is a secondary concern. While the additional information in Acts is obviously not corroborated by Paul, it does not contradict Paul's testimony. Therefore, we may conclude that Acts affirms the details of Paul's DRE account, and provides additional information that is not inconsistent with Paul's account.

Divine Initiative

Acts presents the DRE as a Divine Initiative epiphany. Prior to the DRE, Luke gives no indication that Paul was seeking an encounter with the divine. Rather, Paul appears to be completely satisfied in his pursuit of

---

229. Fletcher-Louis compares the DRE to an angelophany by noting that "many of the essential features of Paul's experience such as the bright light and the falling to the ground are precisely those to be expected when a mortal encounters an angel." Fletcher-Louis, *Luke Acts*, 55. Yet we have seen that these features are shared by appearances of God and other beings. Therefore, Fletcher-Louis has not established his claim that the DRE presents Jesus in angelomorphic form.

Judaism and persecution of the church.²³⁰ The adverb ἐξαίφνης ("suddenly," 9:3b; 22:6) also implies that the appearance was unexpected.²³¹ Furthermore, Paul's reaction ("Who are you?," 9:5; 22:8; 26:15) also indicates that he was not expecting to see the one who appeared. Therefore, it appears that the initiative for the appearance came not from Paul, but rather from the one who appeared.²³² Thus, the DRE is portrayed in each of the Acts accounts as a Divine Initiative epiphany.

Acts also presents a divine purpose for the DRE. The purpose is revealed at the culmination of the third account in Acts 26:16: "I appeared to you for this reason: to appoint you servant and witness . . ." This purpose is confirmed powerfully through Luke's use of repetition. The three accounts of Acts 9, 22, and 26 form an increasing sequence that climaxes with the revelation that Jesus appeared to Paul on the Damascus road in order to call him as his witness to the Gentiles (26:16). The implied reader is made aware of the purpose in Acts 9:15–16 through Jesus's appearance to Ananias, and in Acts 22:21 through Jesus's appearance to Paul in the temple. However, the revelation that Paul's call came directly from Jesus on the Damascus road is not disclosed until Acts 26. Even though the purpose is not fully revealed until the third account, it is certainly implied by Paul's implicit and explicit questions in the first two accounts. Therefore, the purpose of the DRE is divine: Jesus appeared in order to call Paul as his witness to the Gentiles.

By depicting the DRE as a Divine Initiative epiphany with a divine purpose, Acts shares the same basic pattern as Paul.²³³

Merkabah Mysticism

It has been suggested that the DRE was a *merkabah*-like vision. In fact, the connection between the DRE and *merkabah* mysticism was first proposed in relation to Acts rather than Paul. We will consider Bowker's original hypothesis in detail, as well as briefly examining Segal's similar proposal.

---

230. See pp. 223–24 above.

231. Munck assumes that the initiative for the appearance lies with Jesus: "Un trait remarquable de la conversion de Paul et de sa vocation est précisément le fait que le Christ arrêta son persécuteur d'une manière aussi soudaine." Munck, "La vocation," 133.

232. "Paul's conversion results from divine initiative." Gaventa, *Darkness*, 92.

233. See pp. 154–57 above.

Bowker

Bowker proposes that the Acts DRE accounts are presented in the form of a *merkabah* vision. He cites seven "points of contact" to establish this thesis.[234] We will first consider the points of contact between the Acts DRE accounts and *merkabah* visions cited by Bowker, and then consider the Acts DRE accounts with respect to the unique features of *merkabah* visions.

Bowker's first and second points of contact involve setting. The first point of contact is the location, "on the road" (Acts 9:3; 22:6; 26:12f.).[235] It is not unusual for epiphanies, or any narrative, to include the location as part of the setting. In fact, Baban has demonstrated that "on the road" is used as part of a larger pattern of post-resurrection divine encounters including not only the DRE (Acts 9), but also the Emmaus road encounter (Luke 24:13–35) and Philip's encounter with the Ethiopian (Acts 8:26–40).[236] Therefore, "on the road" in Acts 9 appears to be a Lukan rhetorical device rather than an indication of *merkabah*. The second point of contact involves the time of the event (Acts 22:6; 26:13).[237] Time is a common type of setting in many narratives, not just visions. In fact, Bowker admits that the type of time setting for the DRE differs from that of the Johanan *merkabah* visions.[238] Thus, it is unlikely that the specification of a time and place for the setting of the DRE indicates a point of contact with *merkabah* visions.

Bowker's third and fifth points of contact involve the appearance of the divine being. The third point, a heavenly light (Acts 9:3; 22:6; 26:13),[239] has long been associated with God's presence and is certainly not a unique feature of *merkabah* visions (cf. Gen 1:3; Ps 4:6; 18:28; 36:9; 76:4; 89:15; 104:2). The fifth point, a voice (Acts 9:4f.; 22:7; 26:14),[240] is also common to many types of visions other than *merkabah* visions (cf.

---

234. Bowker, "Merkabah Visions," 167–70.

235. Ibid., 167.

236. "In essence, the post-Easter *hodos* paradigm communicates a model of divine encounter that can be perceived both as good literature and as challenging theology." Baban, *Encounters*, 279.

237. Bowker, "Merkabah Visions," 167–68.

238. "The notes are different in content (time and season), but evidently the same in intention." Ibid., 167.

239. Ibid., 168.

240. Ibid.

Artap. 3.27:21; *T. Job* 3:1; *Lad. Jac.* 3:1–2; *4 Ezra* 14:1b). Therefore, there is nothing unique about Jesus's appearance that suggests a *merkabah* vision.

The fourth point involves Paul's response to Jesus's appearance: he falls to the ground (Acts 9:4; 22:6; 26:14).[241] Once again, this response is a common feature of many kinds of epiphanies, not just *merkabah* visions (cf. Gen 17:3; Num 22:31; Josh 5:14; Ezek 1:28; Tob 12:16b).

Bowker's sixth point of contact is the apparent uncertainty among Paul's traveling companions over what had occurred (Acts 9:7; 22:9).[242] Bowker draws an analogy between this and variations among the accounts of Johanan's visions. Yet the discrepancies between accounts of Johanan's visions pertain to the adept himself rather than his companions. Furthermore, *merkabah* visions are surely not the only type of vision that exhibit variations among multiple accounts.[243] Therefore, it is unreasonable to suggest that apparent discrepancies between Acts 9, 22, and 26 indicate that the DRE is being presented as a *merkabah* vision.

The seventh and final point of contact pertains to consequences of the vision (Acts 9:9).[244] This point of contact is based on the notion that "those who practised visionary contemplation were frequently in a trance-condition."[245] Yet Acts does not describe Paul as being in a trance at any point during or following the DRE. Bowker suggests that Paul's blindness may be an indication of a trance.[246] He also notes that a trance is mentioned in Acts 22:17, yet this pertains to a separate vision. Therefore, while it may be conjectured that Paul experienced a trance as part of the DRE, there is no evidence from Acts to support this claim.

In summary, then, Bowker's points of contact between the DRE and *merkabah* visions involve: the setting, the appearance of a heavenly being, and a human response to the appearance, each of which is quite common among many different kinds of epiphanies; apparent discrepancies between multiple accounts of an event, which is common to all

---

241. Ibid.

242. Ibid., 168–70.

243. For example, see the discussion of rewritten OT epiphanies in *Jubilees* (pp. 62–65) and Josephus (pp. 80–82).

244. Bowker, "Merkabah Visions," 170.

245. Ibid.

246. "[Paul's] condition is one of blindness, though perhaps also one of trance." Ibid.

types of narratives, including other kinds of epiphanies; and trances, even though there is no evidence of a trance in the Acts DRE narratives. Thus, Bowker's points of contact do not appear to identify the DRE as a *merkabah* vision.[247]

Furthermore, the Acts DRE accounts lack the unique features of *merkabah* visions. There is no ascent to the heavenly realm, no multitiered heavenly realm, and no heavenly being to guide Paul on his heavenly journey. Perhaps the most damaging evidence against Bowker's *merkabah* hypothesis is that the DRE is presented as a Divine Initiative event, while *merkabah* visions require preparation on the part of the adept.[248] Since there is no indication that Paul made any preparation prior to his encounter with Jesus on the Damascus road, it is reasonable to conclude that the DRE is not presented as a *merkabah* vision in Acts.[249]

Segal

Segal claims that the DRE accounts in Acts should be interpreted in the *merkabah* tradition through five parallels with Ezek 1.[250] However, none of these parallel features is by any means unique to *merkabah*-like visions. A heavenly voice,[251] falling,[252] a command to go,[253] a human figure,[254] and the appearance of the "Glory [of God]"[255] are not exclusive features of *merkabah*.

Therefore, neither Bowker nor Segal provide evidence to support the conclusion that the Acts DRE accounts take the form of a *merkabah* vision in contrast to other types of epiphanies.

---

247. Bowker acknowledges that "some of the features are likely to occur in the account of *any* vision." Ibid.

248. Bowker acknowledges the necessity of preparation for *merkabah* visions in the following statement: "the contemplation necessary for the vision was regarded as a kind of 'higher education.'" Ibid.

249. Gaventa makes a similar observation: "it is probably unwise to try to connect Paul too closely with the Merkabah tradition." Gaventa, "Conversion," 185.

250. Segal, *Paul the Convert*, 9. "Ezekiel 1 was one of the central visions that Luke, and Paul, used to understand Paul's conversion" (39).

251. Artap. 3.27:21; *T. Job* 3:1; *Lad. Jac.* 3:1–2; *4 Ezra* 14:1b.

252. Gen 17:3; Num 22:31; Josh 5:14; Ezek 1:28; Tob 12:16b.

253. Ezekiel to Jews, and Paul to Gentiles. Gen 12:1; Exod 3:10; *Jub.* 12:22.

254. Gen 18–19.

255. Exod 33:18, 22; 40:34, 35; Lev 9:6, 23; Num 14:10.

Summary

Acts is remarkably similar to Paul in its depiction of the Damascus road encounter. Both Acts and Paul present the DRE as a Divine Initiative epiphany with a divine purpose. Acts emphasizes the importance of the DRE's purpose, namely, Paul's call as Jesus's witness, through the threefold repeated sequence of Acts 9, 22, and 26. Neither Acts nor Paul presents the DRE as a *merkabah*-type vision. Thus, the basic details of the DRE are presented in similar terms by Acts and Paul. The significance of our findings in Acts therefore mirrors that of the Pauline DRE accounts.[256]

Characterization of Jesus

In the previous chapter we considered Paul's DRE Christology.[257] We shall now consider the DRE Christology of Acts. One aspect of the Acts DRE narratives that differs significantly from Paul's accounts is the presence of multiple characters. Multiple characters are not a factor in the Pauline epistles, since the reader learns of the DRE from Paul alone. In Acts, other characters such as Ananias and Barnabas are present, Paul is no longer the main narrator,[258] and Jesus speaks directly to Paul. Therefore, it is necessary to consider the evaluative point of view[259] of those who are characterizing Jesus. Since the implied author of Acts presents himself as reliable (Acts 1:1; cf. Luke 1:1–4), we may consider his evaluative point of view to be true. Similarly, Jesus, Paul, Ananias, and Barnabas are presented as reliable characters in the narrative; therefore their evaluative points of view are also true.[260]

Bearing this in mind, let us turn our attention to the characterization of Jesus in the three DRE accounts of Acts. We will first consider Luke's direct characterization of Jesus through the use of names and titles. We will then examine Luke's indirect characterization of Jesus through the use of descriptive terms, syntax, and other means.

---

256. See pp. 165–66 above.
257. See pp. 166–73 above.
258. Although he is the intradiegetic narrator in Acts 22 and 26.
259. See p. 203 n. 76 above.
260. Nevertheless, it may be significant in certain cases to note who is characterizing Jesus. As Berlin notes, "It is especially interesting to note the way the narrator refers to different characters, in contrast to the way they refer to each other." Berlin, *Poetics*, 87.

Direct

In the three Acts DRE accounts Jesus is directly characterized by five different names and titles: Ἰησοῦς [ὁ Ναζωραῖος], χριστός, κύριος, υἱός τοῦ θεοῦ, and δίκαιος.

It can be exceedingly difficult to determine the precise meaning of a particular title in a specific context.[261] We have already seen this in the Pauline epistles.[262] For example, the title υἱός may entail more than a unique relationship to God, yet in the context of Gal 1 it is difficult to reach a more precise conclusion. Similarly, the term χριστός in 1 Cor 15 may have messianic overtones, but the context does not permit a more precise judgment. The meaning of the title κύριος would be equally uncertain were it not for its qualification as the Lord who rescues.

There are two primary reasons why the same difficulty arises in the study of christological DRE titles in Acts. First, Luke does not always provide sufficient context for a precise determination to be made. For example, the proclamation that Jesus is "the Christ" (Acts 9:22) is made without qualification. The reference to "the Righteous One" (Acts 22:14) is in a similarly isolated context. Second, most of the titles have a widely attested range of meanings, not only within Luke-Acts and the NT, but also in the literature of the Second Temple period, as well as the OT and LXX. Therefore, even if Luke is using a title in a specific way, it may be impossible to ascertain his intended meaning with certainty given both the range of semantic possibilities and the limited context of the DRE narratives. Nevertheless, the situation is not beyond hope. In many cases the context does permit a more precise interpretation.

With these reservations in mind, let us consider how Jesus is directly characterized in the three Acts DRE narratives.

Ἰησοῦς [ὁ Ναζωραῖος]

The name Ἰησοῦς is used by Paul (9:20; 26:9), Ananias (9:17), Barnabas (9:27), and Jesus himself (9:5; 22:8; 26:15) to identify Jesus. This characterizes Jesus as a human being. Ananias and Barnabas were followers of Jesus prior to the DRE (9:10; cf. 9:27a). Furthermore, Jesus identifies

---

261. Recall Dahl's observation with respect to the term χριστός: "In individual cases one cannot clearly distinguish between statements where the name 'Christ' is used only as a proper name and others where the appellative force is still felt." Dahl, "Messiahship," 17–18.

262. See pp. 167–69 above.

himself as Ἰησοῦς ὁ Ναζωραῖος (22:8; 26:15). Thus, Luke characterizes Jesus as the historical person, Jesus of Nazareth.

Χριστός

Paul uses the term χριστός to characterize Jesus after the DRE (9:22). In the Pauline DRE accounts, it is uncertain whether χριστός is used as a title;[263] in Acts 9:22, there can be little doubt, since the term appears as a predicate nominative describing Jesus.[264] As such, it appears to be a confession of Paul's newfound faith, signifying Paul's radical new Christology following the DRE. Yet the precise meaning of "Christ" in the context of the DRE alone cannot be established with any certainty, for Paul simply states that "this is the Christ."[265]

Κύριος

Luke characterizes Jesus as Lord in numerous places throughout the three DRE narratives.[266] At the pinnacle of the Acts DRE sequence, Jesus identifies himself as the Lord (κύριος, 26:15) who rescues (ἐξαιρούμενος, 26:17). For such an unusual word[267] to be used by both Luke and Paul to characterize Jesus as Lord in the DRE is quite remarkable. As we have seen, the designation "Lord who rescues" is reserved for Yahweh. Therefore, Jesus is being characterized in a manner previously reserved for Yahweh.[268]

Acts and Paul differ in the types of rescue they describe. In Galatians, Jesus is said rescue Paul and the Galatians from "the present evil age" (1:4); in Acts, Jesus promises to rescue Paul from "the [Jewish] people and from the Gentiles to whom I am sending you" (26:17). This

---

263. See pp. 167–69 above.

264. Conzelmann claims that Christ "is used throughout Acts as a title." Conzelmann, *Acts*, 74.

265. Moule cites four texts (Acts 17:3; 18:5, 28; 26:23) where "the whole point is that Jesus is identified as the Christ," which he defines as "the long-expected Anointed One." Moule, "Christology," 175.

266. Acts 9:1, 5; 22:8, 10, 19; 26:15; cf. 9:10, 11, 13, 15, 17, 27, 28.

267. Ἐξαιρέω is rare in the NT, occurring only five times in Acts (7:10, 34; 12:11; 23:27; 26:17), once in Paul (Gal 1:4), and twice elsewhere (Matt 5:29; 18:9).

268. See pp. 169–71 above. This reference to the "Lord who rescues" suggests a more complete Christology than Dunn is willing to recognize. Dunn claims that the application of the title Lord to Jesus is probably "indicative of an unreflective stage in early Christology." Dunn, "ΚΥΡΙΟΣ," 253.

difference may be attributed to the fact that the rescue of Acts 26:17 is directly toward Paul specifically, while the rescue of Gal 1:4 is addressed more broadly to both Paul and his readers ("for our sins," "rescue us").

A related question involves Paul's use of κύριος immediately after Jesus's appearance (9:5; 22:8; 26:15). Why would Paul identify Jesus as "Lord" when it is unlikely he already recognized the one who had just appeared? This question is typically approached in opposite ways. The first approach admits that Paul did not yet identify the figure as Jesus, but did recognize that the figure was divine. For example, Bruce suggests that Paul uses "Lord" to acknowledge the apparent divinity of the epiphanic figure.[269] Conversely, the second approach denies that Paul could have known that the one who appeared was divine. For example, Gaventa favors the translation "sir," since the identity of the figure is still uncertain.[270] Both positions have considerable merit. Yet each approach seems to ignore the function of κύριος in its literary context.

In Acts 9,[271] and indeed throughout Luke-Acts,[272] the term κύριος is applied to Jesus. For example, we have already established that κύριος identifies Jesus with Yahweh as the Lord who rescues. Therefore, the implied reader is already aware that κύριος applies to Jesus, and that it has theological implications. However, Paul cannot know the identity of the epiphanic figure at this point in the narrative. Hence, Paul's use of κύριε is an example of verbal irony,[273] since the implied reader is aware that

---

269. Bruce, *Acts of the Apostles*, 235. Similarly, Barrett writes: "Saul is aware that he is confronted by a superhuman being; the context . . . shows that though Saul has not yet identified his interlocutor κύριε is not simply a polite address to a fellow man." Barrett, *Acts*, 1:450.

270. Gaventa, *Darkness*, 58; Gaventa, *Acts*, 149. So also Fitzmyer: "*He asked, 'Who are you, sir?'* Saul uses *Kyrie* . . . but at this stage of his career, it could not yet have had for him the connotation of 'Lord,' with which he would so often later use it." Fitzmyer, *Acts*, 425.

271. Cf. Acts 9:1, 9, 10, 11, 13, 15, 17, 27, 28.

272. For a summary of κύριος in Acts, see Dunn, "ΚΥΡΙΟΣ."

273. Irony is defined as "a mode of discourse for conveying meanings different from—and usually opposite to—the professed or ostensible ones." Childs and Fowler, eds., *Literary Terms*, 123. The two main categories of irony are situational and verbal. According to Muecke, every instance of irony utilizes three essential elements. First, irony is a "double-layered" or "two-story" phenomenon. The lower level is the situation "either as it appears to the victim of irony (where there is a victim) or as it is deceptively presented by the ironist (where there is an ironist)." Muecke, *Irony*, 19. Second, there is an opposition between the two levels, possibly involving "contradiction, incongruity, or incompatibility." Muecke, *Irony*, 19. Third is the element of innocence. "Either a victim

Paul is correct in identifying the epiphanic figure as κύριος even though Paul himself is not aware of the epiphanic figure's identity at this point in the narrative.[274]

Thus, κύριος is used to characterize Jesus as Yahweh, the Lord who rescues. It is also used ironically by Paul, since he correctly identifies Jesus as κύριος without being fully aware of the implications at the time.

Υἱὸς τοῦ Θεο

Paul characterizes Jesus as the Son of God in his post-DRE confession: οὗτός ἐστιν ὁ υἱὸς τοῦ θεοῦ (Acts 9:20).[275] The meaning of this title has been debated. For instance, Marshall and Weiser interpret it messianically,[276] while Fitzmyer claims that it expresses the unique relationship between Jesus and God.[277]

It is impossible to understand the meaning of Paul's confession that Jesus is the Son of God without considering the larger context of Luke-Acts.[278] At this point in the narrative of Luke-Acts, the implied author expects the implied reader to recognize the implications of this confession without further elaboration.[279] Indeed, there is a narrative thread relating to the Son of God that runs throughout Luke-Acts. It begins when the angel foretells that Jesus would be the Son of God (Luke 1:35). The devil (Luke 4:3, 9) and demons (Luke 4:41; 8:28) confess that Jesus is the Son of God. The high priest condemns Jesus to death because he will not deny that he is the Son of God (Luke 22:70). Finally, Paul's first words after the DRE are in recognition that Jesus is the Son of God. Therefore, the statement οὗτός ἐστιν ὁ υἱὸς τοῦ θεοῦ is a primal confession ex-

---

is confidently unaware of the very possibility of there being an upper level or point of view that invalidates his own, or an ironist pretends not to be aware of it." Ibid., 20. See also Resseguie, *Narrative Criticism*, 67–75.

274. I have not seen this argument in the literature.

275. Schweizer speculates that the characterization of Jesus as the Son of God developed in a "two-stage Christology." Schweizer, "Son of God," 186–87.

276. "It expressed the position of Jesus as the Messiah (2 Sa. 7:14) who had been exalted by God to sit at his right hand (Ps. 2:7)." Marshall, *Acts*, 174. "Jesus als der Sohn Gottes ist für Lukas der von Gott Erwählte." Weiser, *Apostelgeschichte*, 1:233.

277. "The title expressed a unique relationship of Jesus to Yahweh, the God of the OT." Fitzmyer, *Acts*, 435.

278. Polhill notes the obvious connection to Gal 1:16 and Rom 1:1–4. Polhill, *Acts*, 239.

279. This despite Barrett's assertion to the contrary: "It can hardly be claimed that [this occurrence] is one that was of special significance to Luke." Barrett, *Acts*, 1:463.

pressing Paul's newfound perspective. The implied reader may reasonably conclude that Paul would not have made this confession prior to the DRE. In fact, it appears that Paul persecuted Jesus's followers precisely because of their confession that Jesus is the Son of God.

Thus, the title Son of God is likely indicative of the unique relationship between Jesus and God, a relationship so unique that it warranted Jesus's execution and Paul's persecution of Jesus's followers. By affirming Jesus's divine sonship, Paul reveals his newfound perspective resulting from the DRE.

Ὁ Δίκαιος

Ananias characterizes Jesus as the "Righteous One" (Acts 22:14). Since Ananias does not elaborate on this title,[280] its precise meaning in this context is elusive. Scholars have noted its OT usage as a title for the descendants of David (Jer 23:5–6; 33:15),[281] its presence in *1 En.* 37–71,[282] and two earlier instances in Acts (by Peter, 3:14; by Stephen, 7:52). Marshall suggests that the title has messianic overtones.[283] Perhaps the best that can be said is that it speaks to Jesus's unique character.

INDIRECT

In the DRE narratives of Acts, Jesus is characterized not only directly through various names and titles, but also indirectly. This indirect characterization is done primarily through the use of metonymy and the assignment of divine roles.

Metonymy

In the introduction to the first DRE narrative, Luke uses the unique phrase "disciples of the Lord" (9:1).[284] This statement reveals a close relationship between Jesus and his disciples, and foreshadows two later metonymical comments. The first of these is found in the question, "Why are you persecuting me" (9:4; 22:6; 26:14); the second, in the self-identification,

---

280. See Ibid., 2:1041.
281. Gaventa, *Acts*, 308.
282. Hays, "Righteous One," 194.
283. Marshall, *Acts*, 356.
284. This is the only NT occurrence of the phrase "disciple(s) of the Lord" in any form.

"Jesus, whom you are persecuting" (9:5; 22:8; 26:15). In each case, Jesus closely associates himself with his followers.

This metonymy is significant to the characterization of Jesus in at least two ways. First, by claiming Jesus's followers as his own, the epiphanic figure identifies himself as Jesus. Second, it reveals the closeness of the relationship between Jesus and his followers. The disciples belong to Jesus (9:1). Therefore, any attack on them is equivalent to an attack on Jesus himself.

Therefore, through the use of metonymy Jesus is characterized as a human being in close relationship with his followers.

Divine Roles

Luke characterizes Jesus indirectly through the roles that Jesus claims for himself. We have already seen that Jesus is the Lord who rescues.[285] We will now examine six other roles associated with Jesus.

Name of Jesus

The "name of Jesus" appears frequently in the Acts DRE narratives.[286] It is interesting to note that one of Paul's attacks against Jesus's followers involved compelling them to blaspheme not against the name of God, but against the name of Jesus of Nazareth (26:9–11).

As previously discussed,[287] the reference to the "name of Jesus" characterizes Jesus in the manner that Yahweh is characterized in the OT. This conclusion is corroborated by Moule[288] and Davis.[289]

---

285. See pp. 240–42 above.

286. Acts 9:14, 15, 16, 21, 27, 28; 22:16; 26:9. Davis cites Acts 9:14, 21; 22:16. Davis, *Name*, 128–29.

287. See p. 178 above.

288. The third of Moule's three "striking phenomena" in Luke's use of κύριος is "the use of the phrase ἐπικαλεῖσθαι τὸ ὄνομα which, undoubtedly used in certain instances with reference to the name of Jesus, is irresistibly reminiscent of the Old Testament idea of invoking the name of Yahweh (cf. Acts 2:21 with 7:59; 9:14, 21; 22:16) and implies the invocation of the divine." Moule, "Christology," 161.

289. "The Old Testament and intertestamental background of Joel 2.32[3.5] is one which suggests 'calling on the name of the LORD' was a cultic activity directed to Israel's God. In pre-Christian Judaism I found little evidence that this phrase applied to a non-divine figure." He offers two possibilities: either Jesus is "God's final, fully authorized agent," or Luke was "hinting at something far more." Davis, *Name*, 139.

Appointed by Jesus

In Acts 22:14–15, Ananias states that "the God of our fathers" has appointed (προεχειρίσατο) Paul to be his witness. At this point in the narrative, the implied reader has not yet seen the third DRE account. Luke has yet to reveal fully his purpose in the sequence: that Paul was called by Jesus on the Damascus road.

The verb προχειρίζω is exceedingly rare, occurring only three times in the NT, each in Acts (3:2; 22:14; 26:16). Therefore, it would certainly be memorable for the implied reader to encounter the same unusual term again in the third DRE account, having just encountered it in connection to the second DRE account. At the pinnacle of the third account Luke reveals that Jesus is the one who appoints (προχειρίσασθαι) Paul. Luke is clearly describing the same appointment: to be a witness of what he has experienced to the people. In other words, Luke reveals Jesus in the place of "the God of our fathers" at the climax of the DRE sequence as the one who appoints to divine tasks.

The verb προχειρίζω is also rare in the LXX, making it difficult to draw a direct comparison to the OT. It appears only three times outside the Apocrypha, notably in God's appearance to Moses at the burning bush. In Exod 4:13, Moses pleads with Yahweh to appoint someone else (Δέομαι, κύριε, προχείρισαι δυνάμενον ἄλλον, ὃν ἀποστελεῖς). It is God who appoints in this verse. In other places, however it is used of human appointment (e.g., Josh 3:12; Dan 3:22; 2 Macc 3:7; 8:9).

Therefore, the verb προχειρίζω does not necessarily characterize Jesus as divine. However, it does affirm that Jesus is the one who appointed Paul on the Damascus road (Acts 26:16).

Sent by Jesus

Jesus commissions Paul by sending him to the Gentiles (ἀποστέλλω, Acts 26:17; cf. ἐξαποστέλλω, 22:21). As we have seen, God is the one who sends humans on divine tasks.[290] The task of being a witness of the resurrected Jesus to the Gentile nations must surely be considered a divine task. Therefore, Jesus takes the place of God in the act of sending Paul. Luke emphasizes this characterization in two ways. First, he places Paul's sending in the words of Jesus himself, and not of Paul or the narrator. Second, he emphasizes that Jesus is the one who sends Paul not

---

290. See p. 184 above.

only with a first-person verb, but also with the first-person pronoun: ἐγὼ ἀποστέλλω σε (26:17). Thus, Luke leaves no doubt that Paul was sent by Jesus himself on the Damascus road. In other words, Luke characterizes Jesus as divine, and emphatically so, through the act of sending of Paul on a divine mission.

Servant of Jesus

In Acts 26:16, Jesus appoints Paul to be his servant, ὑπηρέτης. This term is relatively rare in the NT, occurring only 20 times.[291] It is even more rare in the LXX, occurring only twice (Prov 14:35; Isa 32:5). Given its rarity, it is difficult to establish a direct connection to either the LXX or the OT. Therefore, it is not possible to conclude that the term ὑπηρέτης characterizes Jesus as divine, as was possible with the term δοῦλος in the Pauline epistles.[292]

However, there is a semantic connection between ὑπηρέτης and δοῦλος. Louw and Nida list ὑπηρέτης under the domain "Serve,"[293] along with most of the cognates that are used to translate עֶבֶד and עֲבֹדָה.[294] In fact, ὑπηρέτης translates עֶבֶד in Proverbs 14:35. Therefore, we may conclude that Luke's use of the term ὑπηρέτης complements Paul's own self-characterization as Jesus's slave.[295]

Witness of Jesus

In Acts 26:16, Jesus appoints Paul as his witness. In Acts, μάρτυς is used almost exclusively with respect to Jesus and his resurrection.[296] This use of the term is not reflected in the LXX or the OT. The term μάρτυς is used 55 times in the LXX; 45 of those translate עֵדוּת.[297] Yet neither term is used for those who are sent by God; rather, it is used of Yahweh himself as a witness.[298] Therefore, even though being a witness of Jesus is closely

---

291. Six of these are in Luke-Acts (Luke 1:2; 4:20; Acts 5:22, 26; 13:5; 26:16).

292. See pp. 181–83 above.

293. L&N, §35.19–30.

294. Rüterswörden et al., "עֶבֶד," 10:381. Louw and Nida do not include δοῦλος in the "Serve" domain, although its cognate δουλεύω is included.

295. See pp. 181–83 above.

296. Cf. Acts 1:8, 22; 2:32; 3:15; 5:32; 10:39, 41; 13:31; 22:15, 20; 26:16. The only exceptions involve false witnesses (6:13), and witnesses at the death of Stephen (7:58).

297. Simian-Zofre and Ringgren, "אָמַן," 10:500.

298. E.g., 1 Sam 12:5; Jer 42:5; Mal 3:5. Simian-Zofre and Ringgren, "אָמַן," 10:505–6.

connected with being sent by Jesus and being a servant of Jesus, it is not possible to draw any further christological conclusions from the term μάρτυς alone.[299]

Faith in Jesus

In Acts 26:18, Jesus claims that sanctification comes by "faith [that is placed] in me." It is difficult to establish a linguistic connection between the NT and OT concepts of faith. For example, πίστις is found 32 times in the LXX; none are used with God as the object. Perhaps the closest Hebrew nominal form is אֱמוּנָה and its verbal cognate, אָמַן. Again, the connection to the NT is uncertain. As Schreiner remarks, "It is not very easy to correctly evaluate the immediate significance of the OT idea for the development of 'faith' in the NT."[300] Therefore, it is not possible to draw any definite conclusions regarding the identity of Jesus based on his claim that those who believe in him will be sanctified.

Ἐγώ εἰμι

In each of the three DRE narratives in Acts, Jesus's self-identification begins with the words ἐγώ εἰμι (9:5; 22:8; 26:18). On the surface, it may appear that this is an allusion to the Divine Name יהוה (cf. Exod 3:13–15). However, the usage of this phrase throughout Luke-Acts does not support this conclusion. Jesus uses the phrase in several other places, without a certain reference to the Divine Name (Luke 22:70; 24:39; Acts 18:10). In fact, others also use the phrase. For example, the angel Gabriel introduces himself to Zechariah with the same words (Luke 1:19). Both Peter (Acts 10:21) and Paul (Acts 26:29) also use the phrase. Even Paul begins his speech in the second DRE account with ἐγώ εἰμι (Acts 22:3).

Therefore, it is less than certain that these words mean anything other than a simple "I am," with no allusion to deity.

Summary

The DRE Christology of Acts appears to complement that of Paul. First, both characterize Jesus as a human being through the name Ἰησοῦς and through specific historical details: for Paul, through historical setting; for Luke, through Jesus's followers.

---

299. For a discussion of witness in Acts see Bolt, "Mission."

300. Schreiner, "אָמַן," 1:309. It may be possible to connect πίστις with בָּטַה, although this seems even more dubious.

Second, both characterize Jesus in unique relationship to God through the title υἱός. The confession that Jesus is the Son (of God) is fundamental to both Acts and Paul. In Acts, the characterization of Jesus as the Son of God is Paul's initial response to the DRE (9:20); in the appearance element of the DRE, Paul characterizes Jesus solely as υἱός (Gal 1:16). Given the relative rarity of υἱός as a christological title in both Acts and Paul,[301] it is noteworthy that both Luke and Paul characterize Jesus as υἱός at such critical points in their DRE narratives.

Third, both Luke and Paul also characterize Jesus as divine. Both characterize Jesus as the Lord who rescues, even though the verb "rescue," ἐξαιρέω, only occurs eight times in the NT. Both also characterize Jesus as divine by reference to the name of Jesus and being sent by Jesus. The correspondence between Luke's and Paul's references to the name of Jesus is reinforced by their use of the phrase ὑπὲρ ὀνόματος. This phrase is quite rare in the NT, occurring only six times (Acts 5:41; 9:16; 15:26; 21:13; Rom 1:5; 3 John 7). It is striking, then, that it should be used both by Luke (Acts 9:16) and Paul (Rom 1:5) in the context of the DRE.[302]

The Christologies of Acts and Paul differ in several areas. Paul alone characterizes Jesus in close relationship to God through the use of comparison and contrast, by using Jesus and God interchangeably, and through grammar (including agency, object of preposition, and chiasm). Paul alone characterizes Jesus as divine by reference to knowing Jesus, seeing Jesus, and being a slave of Jesus (although this is complemented in Acts by the language of servanthood). In each case, the evidence strengthens existing conclusions and does not contradict Luke's characterization of Jesus.

Conversely, Luke alone characterizes Jesus as ὁ δίκαιος, although the precise meaning of this term in the context of Acts 22:14 is uncertain. Luke alone uses metonymy to identify Jesus with his followers. While Paul does not identify Jesus with his followers through metonymy, he does make a similarly close connection in the phrase τοῦ δόντος ἑαυτὸν ὑπὲρ τῶν ἁμαρτιῶν ἡμῶν (Gal 1:4). In other words, Jesus died "in the place of our sins," which is similar to the metonymy of Acts. Finally, a difference was noted between Luke's use of χριστός as a title, and Paul's

---

301. See p. 172 n. 412 above.

302. It is also interesting that each instance refers to Jesus rather than God the Father (3 John 7 may be the sole exception, although this is debatable).

use as a name. However, this is not necessarily contradictory, since Paul may be using χριστός as a title.[303]

Therefore, Luke and Paul present remarkably similar portraits of Jesus in the DRE. Luke does provide additional information in certain cases, and less in others. Nevertheless, the areas of overlap are large, and the differences appear to complement the points of commonality.

CONCLUSION

Our study of Luke's DRE narratives has yielded some surprising results. Luke's portrayal of the event is remarkably consistent with Paul's account. Both present the DRE as a Divine Initiative epiphany with a divine purpose, and not a *merkabah* vision. The repeated narration of Acts 9, 22, and 26 forms an increasing sequence that reveals Luke's purpose in telling the DRE story: Paul received his call to the Gentiles on the Damascus road from Jesus himself. This call did not come at a later point, or from anyone other than Jesus himself. Similarly, the Christology of the DRE in Acts complements Paul's depiction of Jesus as being in unique relationship to God, and as divine.

---

303. The context of 1 Cor 15:3 does not permit a precise determination. See pp. 167–69 above.

5

The Significance of the Damascus Road Encounter

THIS STUDY HAS EXAMINED the Christology of the Damascus road encounter within the context of the genre of ancient Jewish epiphany up to the first century CE. The findings are summarized below.

ANCIENT JEWISH EPIPHANIES

We first considered the genre of ancient Jewish epiphany. Previous attempts at classifying epiphanies have tended to focus on specific subgenres such as angelophanies, heavenly ascents, and *merkabah* visions. Therefore, they are prone to mistake features that are common to all types of epiphanies as distinguishing features of a specific subgenre.[1] To avoid this potential difficulty, our survey considered the genre of ancient Jewish epiphany as a whole.

This survey produced significant results related to the narrative structure of epiphanies, the distinction between Divine Initiative and Divine Response epiphanies, and the identification of two patterns of characterization for God, other heavenly beings, and humans. The narrative structure for the genre of ancient Jewish epiphany consists of five elements: introduction, consisting of background and setting for the epiphany; appearance, which depicts the initial contact between the human and heavenly beings; message, in which the human and heavenly beings interact; departure, which depicts the separation of the parties; and conclusion, which describes the immediate effects of the encounter.[2]

---

1. For example, see Bowker's points of contact between the DRE and *merkabah* visions on pp. 234–37 above, and Segal's on p. 237 above.

2. The basic narrative structure of epiphanies is discussed on pp. 36–41 above.

The survey also produced a substantial finding related to how epiphanies are initiated.[3] A Divine Initiative epiphany is initiated by God without any preparation or prior awareness on the part of the human recipient. A Divine Initiative epiphany therefore has a divine purpose, typically involving a divinely initiated message or action. The purpose of a Divine Initiative epiphany is normally accomplished, since God has initiated the encounter. On the other hand, a Divine Response epiphany results from a human request or other human preparation. The purpose of a Divine Response epiphany is typically human rather than divine, since it usually relates to the human request that initiated the encounter. However, it is possible for a Divine Response epiphany to have a divine purpose, since God is not bound to perform the human request. As a result, the human purpose in initiating a Divine Response epiphany may not be accomplished. For example, many heavenly ascents never culminate in a vision of God or his throne.

The final discovery relates to the characterization of human and heavenly beings.[4] Two patterns of characterization emerged. In Type-I characterization, God may be characterized in angelic or human form, and angels may be depicted in human form, but humans are not described in anything other than human form. This pattern of characterization is most frequent in early OT epiphanies such as the appearance of God and two angels in human form to Abraham and Lot (Gen 18–19), as well as numerous Angel of Yahweh epiphanies. In Type-II characterization, God remains transcendent and does not appear in the form of any other kind of being. Angels may still be characterized as human (e.g., *2 En.* 1:4), while humans may also be depicted in exalted form (e.g., the Son of Man, *1 En.* 37–71; Adam, *L.A.E.* 13:1—16:3).

There is no definite correlation between the patterns of initiative and character. It appears that Type-I characterization tends to be found in Divine Initiative epiphanies, while Divine Response epiphanies tend to exhibit Type-II characterization. However, it is also possible for Type-II characterization to appear in Divine Initiative epiphanies.

---

3. The concepts of Divine Initiative and Divine Response are discussed on p. 41 and pp. 85–88 above.

4. See pp. 88–97 above.

THE DAMASCUS ROAD ENCOUNTER ACCORDING TO PAUL

It is possible to reconstruct Paul's account of the DRE based on the somewhat fragmentary evidence of the undisputed Pauline epistles.[5] Galatians 1:1–17 contains Paul's most substantial account of the DRE.[6] Other passages that pertain to the DRE include 1 Cor 1:1,17; 9:1; 15:1–11; 2 Cor 1:1; 10:8, 13; Rom 1:1–6; 11:13; 15:15–20; Phil 3:4–14.[7] Another passage that has received attention as a DRE text is 2 Cor 4:4–6. Entire theories are related to the nature and Christology of the DRE on the assumption of a connection between 2 Cor 4:4–6 and the DRE. However, we have argued in detail that this passage does not pertain to the DRE, but rather involves pre-Pauline creation-incarnation imagery.[8] The language of glory, light, and image is used in relation to this creation-incarnation metaphor in John 1:14 and Col 1:15, but not in any of the Pauline DRE texts. Therefore, 2 Cor 4:4–6 should not be considered a DRE text.

Using references to the DRE in the passages cited above, it is possible to reconstruct the basic Pauline DRE narrative. Paul's account of the DRE begins with his background as a strict adherent to Judaism and persecutor of the early Christian church.[9] Jesus appeared to Paul unexpectedly, presumably in the vicinity of Damascus. Unfortunately, Paul provides little narrative detail of the encounter itself or of the one who appeared to him.[10] However, he is emphatic on one point: that Jesus appeared in order to call Paul as his apostle to the Gentiles.[11]

Paul presents the DRE as a Divine Initiative epiphany.[12] This is significant for at least three reasons. First, it provides further evidence that Paul did not view the DRE as a *merkabah*-like vision.[13] Second, the pattern of Divine Initiative is consistent with Paul's emphatic claim of purpose, that Jesus appeared in order to call Paul as his apostle to the

---

5. The disputed Pauline epistles tend to corroborate these findings. See pp. 148–49 above.

6. See pp. 100–22 above.

7. These passages are discussed on pp. 123–49 above.

8. See pp. 130–35 above.

9. The introduction section is discussed on pp. 150–51 above.

10. The appearance section is discussed on pp. 151–52 above.

11. The message section is discussed on pp. 153–54 above.

12. See pp. 154–57 above.

13. See pp. 157–65 above.

The Significance of the Damascus Road Encounter

Gentiles.[14] Third, the Divine Initiative of the DRE has christological significance. Since the DRE was Paul's initial encounter with the resurrected Jesus, Paul's understanding of who Jesus is began at the DRE. Not only did Paul learn of his apostolic call in the DRE, he also came to know the one who commissioned him.

With respect to Christology, Paul characterizes Jesus as divine, and in unique relationship with God the Father.[15] Paul characterizes Jesus as divine by describing Jesus as the Lord who rescues, and also by referring to the name of Jesus, knowing Jesus, seeing Jesus, being a slave of Jesus, and being sent by Jesus. Paul characterizes Jesus in unique relationship with God the Father by the title υἱός, and also by comparing Jesus together with God the Father in contrast to both humans and angels, by identifying God the Father as the ultimate agent and Jesus as the intermediate agent responsible for Paul's commissioning, by uniting Jesus and God the Father under one preposition, by freely interchanging Jesus and God the Father in alternating chiasms, and by interchanging Jesus and God the Father with respect to both gospel and grace.

The Christology of the DRE appears to be a new innovation among ancient Jewish epiphanies since it does not correspond to either of the patterns of characterization of heavenly beings. The characterization of Jesus in unique relationship with God the Father is consistent with the Type-II pattern for exalted humans. However, the characterization of Jesus as divine is not consistent with Type-II, since it breaks the impermeable boundary between God and other heavenly creatures. Similarly, Paul's characterization of Jesus requires modification of the Type-I pattern. Type-I cannot account for the characterization of Jesus either in unique relationship to God the Father or as divine, unless Paul also assumed that Jesus was pre-existent as divine.[16] Even if we grant this assumption, the characterization of Jesus as human goes beyond the typical epiphany since Jesus did not merely appear in human form from birth to death in the incarnation, but also appears as Jesus in the DRE. Thus, Paul's characterization of Jesus in the DRE must be viewed as an innovation among ancient Jewish epiphanies.

---

14. See pp. 154–57 above.

15. Paul's characterization of Jesus is discussed on pp. 166–87 above.

16. While Paul does not characterize Jesus as pre-existent in the DRE texts, it is interesting to note that he does so elsewhere (e.g., Phil 2:6–11).

THE DAMASCUS ROAD ENCOUNTER ACCORDING TO ACTS

Acts contains three accounts of the DRE.[17] Each of the accounts in Acts presents it as a Divine Initiative epiphany.[18] The three narratives form an increasing sequence that culminates with the revelation that Paul received his vocational call from Jesus in the DRE.[19] Thus, the Acts DRE narratives echo the Divine Initiative and divine purpose of Paul. Similarly, the Acts narratives also do not depict the DRE as a *merkabah* vision.[20]

The Christology of the DRE in Acts is also similar to that of Paul.[21] Jesus is depicted as divine by reference to the Lord who rescues. Jesus is characterized in unique relationship to God through the title υἱός.[22] Therefore, the conclusions regarding Paul's characterization of Jesus in relation to the two patterns of characterization for heavenly beings in ancient Jewish epiphanies also pertain to Acts.

Thus, Acts repeats the main themes of Paul's account of the DRE. Acts presents the DRE as a Divine Initiative epiphany with a divine purpose. The DRE Christology of Acts involves the characterization of Jesus as divine and in unique relationship with God, as well as in close relationship with his followers.

CONCLUSION

The Damascus road encounter between Jesus and Paul, as described by both Paul and Acts, is a prime example of a Divine Initiative epiphany. Jesus unexpectedly appeared in order to call Paul as his apostle to the Gentiles. The Christology of the DRE is perhaps even more significant than the call. From his earliest encounter, Paul characterizes Jesus as divine and in unique relationship with God the Father. This represents a significant innovation from other ancient Jewish epiphanies, since the characterization of a human in divine form either breaches the boundary between God and other beings, or implies a presumption of Jesus's pre-existence.

---

17. See pp. 191–92 above.
18. See pp. 233–34 above.
19. See pp. 225–29 above.
20. See pp. 234–37 above.
21. See pp. 238–49 above.
22. Acts also characterizes Jesus in close relationship to his followers. See p. 248 above.

Appendix A

Narrative Structure of Selected Epiphanies

The following table summarizes the basic narrative structure of many epiphany texts. The introduction, appearance, message, departure, and conclusion elements of each epiphany are listed where they occur. The message is rarely omitted, while the departure is rarely described.

Table 2: Narrative Structure of Selected Epiphanies

Epiphany Text	Introduction	Appearance	Message	Departure	Conclusion
Gen 3:8–24	(1–7)	8	9–19		21–24
Gen 16:7–14	7	(7a)	8–12		13–14
Gen 17:1–22	1a	1b	1c-21	22	
Gen 18:1–33	1	2–9	10–32	33	
Gen 19:1–29	1a	2–11	12–22		23–29
Gen 21:17–21		17a	17b-18		19
Gen 22:11–19		11	12–18		19
Gen 28:10–22	10–11	12–13a	13b-15		16–22
Gen 31:10–13	10	11	12–13		
Gen 32:1–2	1a	1b-2a			2b
Gen 32:22–30	22–24a	24b-26	27–29		30
Gen 35:1			1		
Gen 35:9–15	9a	9b	10–12	13	14–15
Exod 3:1–4:17	3:1	3:2–6	3:7–4:17		
Exod 19:1–13	1–2	3a	3b–13		
Exod 19:16–33:3	19:16a	19:16b-20	19:21—33:3		33:4–6
Num 7:89	7:89a	7:89b			
Num 11:24–25	24	25a	25b		
Num 12:1–15	1–2	4–5	9		10–15
Num 14:1–35	1–10a	10b	11–35		
Num 16:1–40	1–19a	19b	20–38		39–40
Num 16:41–50	41–42a	42b	43–50		

Epiphany Text	Introduction	Appearance	Message	Departure	Conclusion
Num 22:9-12		9a	9b-12		
Num 22:20		20a	20b		
Num 22:21-35	21-22a	22a-31	32-35a		35b
Deut 31:14-22	14	15	16-21		22
Josh 1:1-9	1a	1b	2-9		
Josh 3:7-8			7-8		
Josh 5:13—6:5	5:13a	5:13a-15	2-5		
Josh 7:6-15	6-9	10	11-15		
Judg 2:1-5		1a	1b-3		4-5
Judg 6:11-24	11b	11a	12-21a	21b	22-24
Judg 6:25-27	25a		25b-26		27
Judg 13:1-8	1-2	3a	3b-5		6-8
Judg 13:9-23	9a	9b-11a	11b-19a	19b-20	21-23
1 Sam 3:1-21	1-3	4a-10	11-14		15
1 Sam 28:1-25	1-11	12-14	16-20		21-25
1 Kgs 3:5-15	5a	5b	5c-14	15a	15b
1 Kgs 19:1-18	1-5a 8b-9a	5b 7a 9b-13a	5c 7b 13b-18		6 8a
2 Kgs 1:3-4			3-4		
2 Kgs 1:15			15		
2 Kgs 2:11-12	11a	11b		11c	12
2 Kgs 19:35	35a		35b		35c
1 Chr. 21:14-30	15-17	18		19-30	
2 Chr. 1:7-12	7a	7b	7c-12		
2 Chr. 32:21					
Job 38:1—42:9		38:1	38:2—41:34 42:7-8		42:1-6 42:9
Isa 6:1-13	1a	1b-7	8-13		
Isa 37:36					
Jer 1:4-10		4	5-10		
Ezek 1:1—3:15	1:1-2	1:3-28	2:1-3:11	3:12-14	3:15
Ezek 3:16-—5:17	3:16a	3:16b-24a	3:24—5:17		
Ezek 8:1—11:25	8:1a	8:1b-4	8:5—11:23	11:24	11:25
Ezek 37:1-14		1	2-14		
Ezek 40-48	40:1a	40:1b-3	40:3—48:35		

Narrative Structure of Selected Epiphanies

Epiphany Text	Introduction	Appearance	Message	Departure	Conclusion
Dan 3:25–30					
Dan 4	1–10a 29–31a	10b–13 31b	14–17 31c–32		18 33
Dan 5:1–6	1–4	5–6	[25–28]		
Dan 7:1–28	1		2–14; 15–27		28
Dan 8:1–27	1		2–14; 15–26		27
Dan 9:20–27	20	21	22–27		
Dan 10:1—12:13	10:1–4	10:5–10	10:11—12:4; 12:5–13		
Tob 5:4—12:22	5:4a	5:4b	5:5—12:19	12:20–21	12:22
Jub. 12:16–24	16–22	22a	22b–24		
Jub. 15:1–24	1–2	3a	3b–21	22	23–24
Jub. 16:1–4	1a	1b	1c–4		
T. Levi 2:1—5:7	2:1–4	2:5–12	3:1–5:6		5:7
T. Job 2:1—5:3	2:1–4	3:1–2a	3:2b–5:1	5:2a	5:2b–3
Jos. Asen. 14–17	14:1a	14:1b–15	15:1—17:6	17:7–8	17:9
2 En. 1–42	1:1–3	1:4—2:4	3:1—42:14		
Lad. Jac. 1–7	1:3a 3:1a	1:3b–8 3:1b–5	1:9—2:1 4:1—7:3		2:2–22
3 Bar. 1–17	1:1–2	1:3a	1:3b—17:1		
4 Ezra 3:1—5:20	3:1–36	4:1	4:2—5:13		5:14–20
4 Ezra 5:21—6:35	5:21–30	5:31	5:32—6:34		6:35
4 Ezra 6:36—9:26	6:36–59	7:1	7:2—9:25		9:26
4 Ezra 9:27—10:59	9:27–37	9:38–40	9:41—10:59a		10:59b
4 Ezra 11:1—12:39	11:1a 12:3b–9	11:1b	11:1c—12:3a 12:10–39		
4 Ezra 13:1–58	13:1a 13:14b–20	13:1b	13:1c–13 13:21–56		13:14a 13:57–58
4 Ezra 14:1–26	14:1a	14:1b–2	14:3–26		
Apoc. Ab. 1–32	1:1—8:1a	8:1b–2 9:1 10:3—11:6	8:3–4 9:2—10:2 12:1—32:6		8:5–6
T. Ab. A1:1—20:15	A1:1–7	A2:1–12	A3:1—20:15		
T. Ab. B1:1—12:16	B1:1–3	B2:1–13	B3:1—12:13	B12:14	B12:15–16
T. Ab. B13–14	B13:1–2	B13:3–5	B13:6—14:9		
T. Isaac 2:1—3:19	2:1a	2:1b–4	2:5—3:19		

Appendix B

Epiphany in Non-Jewish Literature

While our focus is primarily on Jewish literature, it is interesting to compare epiphanies in Jewish literature with those in non-Jewish narratives.[1]

Squires has a brief discussion on epiphanies in Hellenistic historiography.[2] He presents evidence that Stoics reasoned from divination to the existence of the gods, as well as vice versa.[3] Squires also discusses several dreams. He considers a dream seen by both Publius and Marcus Tarquinius;[4] Aeneas' founding of Alba Longa in obedience to a divine message; another vision of Aeneas leading to a treaty between Trojans and Greeks and the introduction of democratic reforms in Rome in response to visions, portents, and oracles.[5] Squires finds two primary functions of epiphanies in Luke-Acts: they "confirm divine providence," and "they predict the course of future events."[6] While this may be true of some epiphanies in Luke-Acts, it does not appear to be an accurate assessment of the DRE in Acts. Jesus appeared to Paul on the Damascus road in order to call him as his messenger to the Gentiles.[7]

1. Segal provides a brief summary of non-Jewish heavenly ascent narratives in Segal, "Heavenly Ascent," 2.32.2:1341-51. Tabor also reviews ancient Sumerian, Mesopotamian, and Greek ascents in Tabor, *Things Unutterable*, 61-6.

2. Squires, *Plan of God*, 103-8.

3. Squires, *Plan of God*, 103-4. As the title suggests, Cicero's interest in *De Divinatione* is not epiphanies, but divination. For example, he mentions "two kinds [of forewarning] which are classed as natural means of divination—the forewarnings of dreams, or of frenzy" (1.6.12).

4. Dionysius does not record an epiphany within the dream: "For frightful visions haunted them in their dreams whenever they slept, threatening them with dire punishments if they did not desist and abandon their attempt; and at last they thought that they were pursued and beaten by some demons, that their eyes were gouged out, and that they suffered many other cruel torments." Dionysius of Halicarnassus, *Roman Antiquities* 5.54.1-2 (Earnest Cary, LCL). See Squires, *Plan of God*, 106.

5. Squires, *Plan of God*, 106-8.

6. Squires, *Plan of God*, 120.

7. See pp. 233-34 above.

Seaford compares the "earthquake scene" of Euripides' *Bacchae* (576–603) to Acts 9:3–7 and 16:25–30. He argues that thunder, lightning, and earthquake are a common method of "mystic initiation."[8] Yet there is no mention of thunder, lightning, or earthquake in any of the DRE texts.

Strelan also discusses some non-Jewish parallels to the DRE, including Ovid's *Metamorphosis*.[9]

Perhaps the most striking example of epiphany in non-Jewish literature is found in the Greek Magical Papyri. The "Mithras Liturgy" (*PGM* IV.475–829)[10] contains a spell "which the great god Helios Mithras ordered to be revealed to me by his archangel, so that I alone may ascend into heaven as an inquirer and behold the universe" (475–85). After a sequence of events (486–620), the ascender will see "a youthful god, beautiful in appearance, with fiery hair, and in a white tunic and a scarlet cloak, and wearing a fiery crown" (635–39). The theme of seven is prominent. There are seven immortal gods (620, 674–93), seven virgins (662), seven days (735). The process is termed ἀπαθανατισμός, "immortalization" (749). The similarities to the 2TP pattern are striking. Since the text contains a spell to invoke the great god, the initiative is clearly human. The purpose is also human: to behold the universe. The spell is consistent with the 2TP pattern, since it involves immortalization, or transformation of being. In each of these ways, however, it differs from the OT pattern of epiphany.

These non-Jewish sources provide a fascinating background for epiphany in Jewish literature. Yet they also reveal that the DRE corresponds much more closely with the OT pattern of epiphany than either 2TP Jewish or non-Jewish epiphanies.

---

8. Seaford, "Thunder," 139.

9. Strelan, *Acts*, 165–79. "Then did the shrine and the laurel-tree and the quiver which the god himself bears quake together, and the tripod from the inmost shrine gave forth these words and stirred their hearts trembling with fear: 'What you seek from this place you should have sought, O Roman, from a nearer place. And even now seek from that nearer place. Nor have you any need of Apollo to abate your troubles, but of Apollo's son. Go with kindly auspices and call on my son.'" Ovid *Metamorphoses* 15.633–40 (Frank J. Miller, LCL). See also Segal, *Paul the Convert*, 24.

10. For the liturgy in translation, see Betz, *Papyri*, 48–52.

Bibliography

PRIMARY SOURCES

Abegg, Martin G., Jr. *Qumran Sectarian Manuscripts*. Bellingham, WA: Logos Research Systems, 1999-2003.

Alexander, P. "3 (Hebrew Apocalypse of) Enoch: A New Translation and Introduction." In *OTP* 1:223-315. New York: Doubleday, 1983.

Andersen, F. I. "2 (Slavonic Apocalypse of) Enoch: A New Translation and Introduction." In *OTP* 1:91-221. New York: Doubleday, 1983.

The Babylonian Talmud: Seder Mo'ed Hagigah. Translated by Israel Abrahams. New York: Saphrograph, 1959.

Betz, Hans Dieter. *Galatians: A Commentary on Paul's Letter to the Churches in Galatia*. Hermeneia. Philadelphia: Fortress, 1979.

Black, Matthew. *The Book of Enoch, or 1 Enoch: A New English Edition with Commentary and Textual Notes*. Leiden: Brill, 1985.

Borgen, Peder, Kåre Fuglseth, and Roald Skarsten. *The Works of Philo: Greek Text with Morphology*. Bellingham, WA: Logos Research Systems, 2005.

Burchard, Christoph. "Joseph and Asenath: A New Translation and Introduction." In *OTP* 2:177-247. New York: Doubleday, 1983.

———. *Joseph und Asenath: Kritisch Herausgegeben*. Leiden: Brill, 2003.

Charlesworth, James H. "The History of the Rechabites: A New Translation and Introduction." In *OTP* 2:443-61. New York: Doubleday, 1983.

Cicero. Translated by Harry Caplan, H. M. Hubbell, E. W. Sutton, H. Rackham, G. L. Hendrickson, J. H. Freese, L. H. G. Greenwood, H. Grose Hodge, C. MacDonald, N. H. Watts, R. Gardner, Walter C. A. Ker, Clinton W. Keyes, J. E. King, Walter Miller, W. A. Falconer, and D. R. Shackelton Bailey. 39 vols. LCL. Cambridge: Harvard University Press, 1954-2001.

Collins, John J. "Artapanus: A New Translation and Introduction." In *OTP* 2:889-903. New York: Doubleday, 1983.

Crane, Gregory R. *Perseus Digital Library Project*. Online: http://www.perseus.tufts.edu.

Diodorus Siculus. Translated by C. H. Oldfather, C. L. Sherman, C. Bradford Welles, Russel M. Geer and Francis R. Walton. 12 vols. LCL. Cambridge: Harvard University Press, 1933-67.

Dionysius of Halicarnassus. Translated by Earnest Cary and Stephen Usher. 9 vols. LCL. Cambridge: Harvard University Press, 1937-85.

Euripides. Translated by David Kovacs. 6 vols. LCL. Cambridge: Harvard University Press, 1994-2003.

Gaylord, H. E., Jr. "3 (Greek Apocalypse of) Baruch: A New Translation and Introduction." In *OTP* 1:653-79. New York: Doubleday, 1983.

Harlow, Daniel C. *The Greek Apocalypse of Baruch (3 Baruch)*. Leiden: Brill, 1996.

Ibn Ezra. *Exodus (Shemot)*. Translated by H. Norman Strickman and Arthur M. Silver. New York: Menorah, 1996.

Isaac, E. "1 (Ethiopic Apocalypse of) Enoch: A New Translation and Introduction." In *OTP* 1:5–89. New York: Doubleday, 1983.

Josephus. Translated by H. St. J. Thackeray, Ralph Marcus, Allen Wickgren, and Louis H. Feldman. 13 vols. LCL. Cambridge: Harvard University Press, 1926–65.

Kee, H. C. "Testaments of the Twelve Patriarchs: A New Translation and Introduction." In *OTP* 1:775–828. New York: Doubleday, 1983.

Lehrmah, S. M. *Exodus*. Midrash Rabbah. Edited by H. Freedman. London: Soncino, 1939.

Martínez, Florentino García, and Eibert J. C. Tigchelaar. *The Dead Sea Scrolls Study Edition*. 2 vols. Leiden: Brill, 1997.

Metzger, B. M. "The Fourth Book of Ezra: A New Translation and Introduction." In *OTP* 1:516–59. New York: Doubleday, 1983.

Milik, J. T. *The Books of Enoch: Aramaic Fragments of Qumran Cave 4*. Oxford: Clarendon, 1976.

Moore, Carey A. *Tobit: A New Translation with Introduction and Commentary*. AB 40A. New York: Doubleday, 1996.

Neusner, Jacob. *Genesis Rabbah: The Judaic Commentary to the Book of Genesis*. 3 vols. Atlanta: Scholars, 1986.

———. *The Mishnah: A New Translation*. New Haven: Yale University Press, 1988.

Nickelsburg, George W. E., and James C. VanderKam. *1 Enoch: A New Translation Based on the Hermeneia Commentary*. Minneapolis: Fortress, 2004.

Ovid. Translated by Grant Showerman, J. H. Mozley, Frank J. Miller, J. G. Frazer, A. L. Wheeler and G. P. Goold. 6 vols. LCL. Cambridge: Harvard Universty Press, 1914–89.

Parry, Donald W., and Emanuel Tov, editors. *The Dead Sea Scrolls Reader*. 6 vols. Brill: Leiden, 2005.

Philo. Translated by F. H. Colson, G. H. Whitaker, and Ralph Marcus. 12 vols. LCL. Cambridge: Harvard University Press, 1929–53.

Philonenko, Marc. *Joseph et Asénath*. Leiden: Brill, 1968.

Preisendanz, Karl, editor. *Papyri graecae magicae: Die griechischen Zauberpapyri*. 2 vols. Stuttgart: Teubner, 1928, 1931.

Rahlfs, Alfred, editor. *Septuaginta: With Morphology*. Stuttgart: Deutsche Bibelgesellschaft, 1935, 1979, 1996.

Rubinkiewicz, R. "Apocalypse of Abraham: A New Translation and Introduction." In *OTP* 1:681–705. New York: Doubleday, 1983.

Sanders, E. P. "Testament of Abraham: A New Translation and Introduction." In *OTP* 1:871–902. New York: Doubleday, 1983.

Spittler, Russell P. "Testament of Job: A New Translation and Introduction." In *OTP* 1:829–68. New York: Doubleday, 1983.

Stinespring, W. F. "Testament of Isaac: A New Translation and Introduction." In *OTP* 1:903–11. New York: Doubleday, 1983.

———. "Testament of Jacob: A New Translation and Introduction." In *OTP* 1:913–18. New York: Doubleday, 1983.

Wintermute, O. S. "Jubilees: A New Translation and Introduction." In *OTP* 2:35–142. New York: Doubleday, 1983.

Yonge, Charles Duke. *The Works of Philo: Complete and Unabridged*. Peabody, MA: Hendrickson, 1993–96.

SECONDARY SOURCES

Abbott, H. Porter. *The Cambridge Introduction to Narrative*. Cambridge: Cambridge University Press, 2002.

Addinall, Peter. "Exodus III 19B and the Interpretation of Biblical Narrative." *VT* 49 (1999) 289–300.

Alexander, Philip S. "Retelling the Old Testament." In *It Is Written: Scripture Citing Scripture*, edited by D. A. Carson and H. G. M. Williamson, 99–121. Cambridge: Cambridge University Press, 1988.

Allen, Leslie C. *Ezekiel 1–19*. WBC 28. Dallas: Word, 1994.

———. "The Structure and Intention of Ezekiel 1:1." *VT* 43 (1993) 145–61.

Allison, Dale C. *Testament of Abraham*. CEJL. Berlin: de Gruyter, 2003.

Alston, Wallace M., Jr. "Genesis 18:1–11." *Int* 42 (1998) 397–402.

Alter, Robert. *The Art of Biblical Narrative*. London: Allen & Unwin, 1981.

———. *The David Story*. New York: Norton, 1999.

———. *Genesis: Translation and Commentary*. New York: Norton, 1996.

Attridge, Harold W. "Historiography." In *Jewish Writings of the Second Temple Period: Apocrypha, Pseudepigrapha, Qumran Sectarian Writings, Philo, Josephus*, edited by Michael Edward Stone, 157–184. Philadelphia: Fortress, 1984.

Austel, Hermann J. "שָׁלַח." In *TWOT* 927–28.

Baban, Octavian D. *On the Road Encounters in Luke-Acts: Hellenistic Mimesis and Luke's Theology of the Way*. Milton Keynes: Paternoster, 2006.

Bailey, James L., and Lyle D. Vander Broek. *Literary Forms in the New Testament: A Handbook*. Louisville: Westminster John Knox, 1992.

Bar-Efrat, Shimon. *Narrative Art in the Bible*. JSOTSup 70. Sheffield: Sheffield Academic, 2000.

Barclay, John M. G. "Manipulating Moses: Exodus 2.10–15 in Egyptian Judaism and the New Testament." In *Text as Pretext: Essays in Honour of Robert Davidson*, edited by Robert P. Carroll, 28–46. Sheffield: Sheffield Academic, 1992.

———. "Paul's Story: Theology as Testimony." In *Narrative Dynamics in Paul: A Critical Assessment*, edited by Bruce W. Longenecker, 133–56. Louisville: Westminster John Knox, 2002.

Barnett, Paul. "Revolutionary Movements." In *DPL*, 813–19. Downers Grove, IL: InterVarsity, 1993.

———. *The Second Epistle to the Corinthians*. NICNT. Grand Rapids: Eerdmans, 1997.

Barrett, C. K. *A Critical and Exegetical Commentary on the Acts of the Apostles*. 2 vols. ICC. Edinburgh: T. & T. Clark, 1994, 1998.

———. *The First Epistle to the Corinthians*. BNTC. London: Black, 1968.

Barth, Karl. *A Shorter Commentary on Romans*. Translated by D. H. van Daalen. London: SCM, 1959.

Barthes, Roland. *Image, Music, Text*. Translated by Stephen Heath. Glasgow: Fontana, 1977.

———. *S/Z*. Translated by Richard Miller. Oxford: Blackwell, 1974.

Bauckham, Richard. *God Crucified: Monotheism and Christology in the New Testament*. Carlisle: Paternoster, 1998.

Beaujour, Michel. "Phonograms and Delivery: The Poetics of Voice." In *Notebooks in Cultural Analysis*, edited by Norman F. Cantor, 3:266–79. Durham, NC: Duke University Press, 1986.

Behm, Johannes. "ἀνάθεμα, ἀνάθημα, κατάθεμα." In *TDNT* 1:354–55.

Beker, J. Christiaan. *Paul the Apostle: The Triumph of God in Life and Thought.* Philadelphia: Fortress, 1980.

Ben Zvi, Ehud. "The Dialogue between Abraham and YHWH in Gen. 18.23–32: A Historical-Critical Analysis." *JSOT* 53 (1992) 27–46.

Bergman, J., and G. Johannes Botterweck. "יָדַע." In *TDOT* 5:448–81.

Berlin, Adele. *Poetics and Interpretation of Biblical Narrative.* Sheffield: Almond, 1983.

Berry, George Ricker. "The Title of Ezekiel (1:1–3)." *JBL* 51 (1932) 54–57.

Betz, Hans Dieter. *The Greek Magical Papyri in Translation, Including the Demotic Spells.* 2nd ed. Chicago: University of Chicago Press, 1992.

———. "Paul (Person)." In *ABD* 5:186–201. New York: Doubleday, 1992.

Blenkinsopp, Joseph. *Ezekiel.* Interpretation. Louisville: John Knox, 1990.

———. "The Judge of All the Earth: Theodicy in the Midrash on Genesis 18:22–33." *JJS* 41 (1990) 1–12.

Bligh, John. *Galatians.* Householder Commentaries. London: St. Paul, 1970.

Block, Daniel I. *Ezekiel 1–24.* NICOT. Grand Rapids: Eerdmans, 1997.

Bockmuehl, Markus. *A Commentary on the Epistle to the Philippians.* BNTC. London: Black, 1997.

Bohak, Gideon. *Joseph and Asenath: And the Jewish Temple in Heliopolis.* SBLEJL 10. Atlanta: Scholars, 1996.

Bolt, Peter. "Mission and Witness." In *Witness to the Gospel: The Theology of Acts*, edited by I. Howard Marshall and David Peterson, 191–214. Grand Rapids: Eerdmans, 1998.

Booth, Wayne C. *The Rhetoric of Fiction.* Chicago: University of Chicago Press, 1961.

Borgen, Peder. "Philo of Alexandria." In *ABD* 5:333–42. New York: Doubleday, 1992.

Bousset, Wilhelm. *Kyrios Christos.* Translated by John E. Steely. Nashville: Abingdon, 1913, 1970.

———. *Kyrios Christos: Geschichte des Christusglaubens von den Anfängen des Christentums bis Irenaeus.* Göttingen: Vandenhoeck & Ruprecht, 1921.

Bowker, John Westerdale. "'Merkabah' Visions and the Visions of Paul." *JSS* 16 (1971) 157–73.

Brooke, George J. "Men and Women as Angels in *Joseph and Asenath*." *JSP* 14 (2005) 159–77.

Brooks, Roger. "Mishnah." In *ABD* 4:871–73. New York: Doubleday, 1992.

Bruce, F. F. *The Acts of the Apostles: The Greek Text with Introduction and Commentary.* 3rd rev. ed. Grand Rapids: Eerdmans, 1990.

———. *The Book of the Acts.* Rev. ed. NICNT. Grand Rapids: Eerdmans, 1988.

———. *The Epistle to the Galatians.* NIGTC. Exeter: Paternoster, 1982.

———. "'Jesus is Lord.'" In *Soli Deo Gloria: New Testament Studies in Honor of William Childs Robinson*, edited by J. McDowell Richards, 23–36. Richmond, VA: John Knox, 1968.

Brueggemann, Walter. *Genesis.* Interpretation. Louisville: John Knox, 1982.

———. *Theology of the Old Testament: Testimony, Dispute, Advocacy.* Minneapolis: Fortress, 1997.

Budesheim, T. L. "Paul's Abschiedsrede in the Acts of the Apostles." *HTR* 69 (1976) 9–30.

Bultmann, Rudolph. *Existence and Faith: Shorter Writings of Rudolph Bultmann.* Translated by Schubert M. Ogden. London: Hodder and Stoughton, 1961.

———. *Theology of the New Testament*. Translated by Kendrick Grobel. 2 vols. London: SCM, 1952.
Burchard, Christoph. *Der dreizehnte Zeuge: Traditions- und kompositionsgeschichtliche Untersuchungen zu Lukas' Darstellung der Frühzeit des Paulus*. FRLANT 103. Göttingen: Vandenhoeck & Ruprecht, 1970.
———. "The Text of *Joseph and Asenath* Reconsidered." *JSP* 14 (2005) 83–96.
Burton, Ernest de Witt. *The Epistle to the Galatians*. ICC. Edinburgh: T. & T. Clark, 1980.
Cadbury, Henry J. "Four Features of Lucan Style." In *Studies in Luke-Acts*, edited by Leander E. Keck and J. Louis Martyn, 87–102. Philadelphia: Fortress, 1966, 1980.
Calvin, John. *Genesis*. Wheaton: Crossway, 2001.
Campbell, Antony F. *1 Samuel*. The FOTL 7. Grand Rapids: Eerdmans, 2003.
Capes, David B. "YHWH Texts and Monotheism in Paul's Christology." In *Early Jewish and Christian Monotheism*, edited by Loren T. Stuckenbruck and Wendy E. S. North, 120–37. JSNTSup 263. London: T. & T. Clark, 2004.
Carroll, Robert P. "Strange Fire: Abstract of Presence Absent in the Text: Meditations on Exodus 3." *JSOT* 61 (1994) 39–58.
Carson, D. A., Douglas J. Moo, and Leon Morris. *An Introduction to the New Testament*. Grand Rapids: Zondervan, 1992.
Casey, P. M. *From Jewish Prophet to Gentile God: The Origins and Development of New Testament Christology*. Cambridge: James Clark, 1991.
Charlesworth, James H. "The Jewish Roots of Christology: The Discovery of the Hypostatic Voice." *SJT* 39 (1986) 19–41.
———. "Pseudepigrapha, OT." In *ABD* 5:537–40. New York: Doubleday, 1992.
Chatman, Seymour. *Story and Discourse: Narrative Structure in Fiction and Film*. Ithaca, NY: Cornell University Press, 1978.
Chesnutt, Randall D. *From Death to Life: Conversion in Joseph and Asenath*. JSPSup 16. Sheffield: Sheffield Academic, 1995.
Childs, Brevard. *Exodus*. OTL. London: SCM, 1974.
Childs, Peter, and Roger Fowler, editors. *The Routledge Dictionary of Literary Terms*. New York: Routledge, 2006.
Clark, Andrew C. *Parallel Lives: The Relation of Paul to the Apostles in the Lucan Perspective*. Carlisle: Paternoster, 2001.
Coats, George W. *Genesis: With an Introduction to Narrative Literature*. FOTL. Grand Rapids: Eerdmans, 1983.
Coggins, R. J., and Michael A. Knibb. *The First and Second Books of Esdras*. Cambridge: Cambridge University Press, 1979.
Collins, John J. "*Joseph and Asenath*: Jewish or Christian?" *JSP* 14 (2005) 97–112.
———. "Powers in Heaven: God, Gods and Angels in the Dead Sea Scrolls." In *Religion in the Dead Sea Scrolls*, edited by John J. Collins and Robert A. Kugler, 9–28. Grand Rapids: Eerdmans, 2000.
———. *The Scepter and the Star: The Messiahs of the Dead Sea Scrolls and Other Ancient Literature*. ABRL. New York: Doubleday, 1995.
———. "Testaments." In *Jewish Writings of the Second Temple Period: Apocrypha, Pseudepigrapha, Qumran Sectarian Writings, Philo, Josephus*, edited by Michael Edward Stone, 325–55. Philadelphia: Fortress, 1984.
Conzelmann, Hans. *Acts of the Apostles*. Translated by James A. Limburg, Thomas Kraabel, and Donald H. Juel. Philadelphia: Fortress, 1987.

———. *1 Corinthians*. Translated by James W. Leitch. Hermeneia. Philadelphia: Fortress, 1975.

———. *The Theology of St. Luke*. Translated by Geoffrey Buswell. London: Faber, 1960.

Cranfield, C. E. B. *Romans*. 2 vols. ICC. Edinburgh: T. & T. Clark, 1975–79.

———. "Some Comments on Professor J. D. G. Dunn's *Christology in the Making* with Special Reference to the Evidence of the Epistle to the Romans." In *The Glory of Christ in the New Testament: Studies in Christology in Memory of George Bradford Caird*, edited by L. D. Hurst and N. T. Wright, 267–80. Oxford: Clarendon, 1987.

Crawford, Sidnie White. "The Rewritten Bible at Qumran." In *The Hebrew Bible and Qumran*, edited by James H. Charlesworth, 173–95. The Bible and the Dead Sea Scrolls 1. Richland Hills, TX: BIBAL, 2000.

Culler, Jonathan. *Structuralist Poetics: Structuralism, Linguistics and the Study of Literature*. Ithaca, NY: Cornell University Press, 1975.

———. *Literary Theory: A Very Short Introduction*. Oxford: Oxford University Press, 1997.

Cullmann, Oscar. *The Christology of the New Testament*. Rev. ed. Philadelphia: Westminster, 1959.

Culver, Robert D. "רָאָה." In *TWOT* 823–25.

Dahl, Nils Alstrup. "The Messiahship of Jesus in Paul." In *Jesus the Christ: The Historical Origins of Christological Doctrine*, edited by Donald H. Juel, 15–25. Minneapolis: Fortress, 1991.

Dalman, G. "Bath Qol." In *NSHE* 2:4. London: Educational Book Company, 1908.

Dancy, J. C. *The Shorter Books of the Apocrypha*. CBC. Cambridge: Cambridge University Press, 1972.

Dancy, John. *The Divine Drama: The Old Testament as Literature*. Cambridge: Lutterworth, 2001.

Darr, John A. *On Character Building: The Reader and the Rhetoric of Characterization in Luke-Acts*. Louisville: Westminster John Knox, 1992.

Daube, David. *The Sudden in the Scriptures*. Leiden: Brill, 1964.

Davidson, Maxwell J. *Angels at Qumran: A Comparative Study of 1 Enoch 1–36; 72–108 and Sectarian Writings from Qumran*. JSPSup 11. Sheffield: Sheffield Academic, 1992.

Davis, Carl Judson. *The Name and Way of the Lord: Old Testament Themes, New Testament Christology*. JSNTSup 129. Sheffield: Sheffield Academic, 1996.

De Jonge, Marinus. "The Use of the Word 'Anointed' in the Time of Jesus." *NovT* 8 (1966) 132–48.

Den Hertog, Cornelis. "The Prophetic Dimension of the Divine Name: On Exodus 3:14a and Its Context." *CBQ* 64 (2002) 213–28.

Derrida, Jacques. "The Law of Genre." *CI* 7 (1980) 55–81.

———. *Memoirs of the Blind: The Self-Portrait and Other Ruins*. Translated by Pascale-Anne Brault and Michael Naas. Chicago: University of Chicago Press, 1993.

DeSilva, David A. *Introducing the Apocrypha: Message, Context, and Significance*. Grand Rapids: Baker, 2002.

Dibelius, Martin. *Studies in the Acts of the Apostles*. Translated by Mary Ling. London: SCM, 1956.

Dietzfelbinger, Christian. *Die Berufung des Paulus als Ursprung seiner Theologie*. WMANT 58. Neukirchen-Vluyn: Neukirchener, 1985.

Bibliography

Docherty, Susan. "*Joseph and Asenath*: Rewritten Bible or Narrative Expansion?" *JSJ* 35 (2004) 27–48.

Docherty, Thomas. *Reading (Absent) Character: Towards A Theory of Characterization in Fiction*. Oxford: Clarendon, 1983.

Donaldson, Terence L. *Paul and the Gentiles: Remapping the Apostle's Convictional World*. Minneapolis: Fortress, 1997.

Driver, G. R. "Ezekiel's Inaugural Vision." *VT* 1 (1951) 60–62.

Driver, Samuel Rolles. *The Book of Genesis*. 15th ed. WC. London: Methuen, 1948.

Dunn, James D. G. *The Acts of the Apostles*. Peterborough: Epworth, 1996.

———. *The Christ and the Spirit: Christology*. Grand Rapids: Eerdmans, 1998.

———. *The Epistle to the Galatians*. BNTC. London: Black, 1993.

———. *The Epistles to the Colossians and to Philemon: a Commentary on the Greek Text*. NIGTC. Grand Rapids: Eerdmans, 1996.

———. "Jesus—Flesh and Spirit: An Exposition of Romans 1:3-4." In *The Christ and the Spirit: Christology*, 126–53. Grand Rapids: Eerdmans, 1998.

———. "Jesus—Flesh and Spirit: An Exposition of Romans I. 3–4." *JTS*, n.s., 24 (1973) 40–68.

———. "ΚΥΡΙΟΣ in Acts." In *The Christ and the Spirit: Christology*, 241–53. Grand Rapids: Eerdmans, 1998.

———. "'A Light to the Gentiles': the Significance of the Damascus Road Christophany for Paul." In *The Glory of Christ in the New Testament: Studies in Christology in Memory of George Bradford Caird*, edited by L. D. Hurst and N. T. Wright, 251–66. Oxford: Clarendon, 1987.

———. "Messianic Ideas and Their Influence on the Jesus of History." In *The Christ and the Spirit: Christology*, 78–95. Grand Rapids: Eerdmans, 1998.

———. "The Narrative Approach to Paul: Whose Story?" In *Narrative Dynamics in Paul: A Critical Assessment*, edited by Bruce W. Longenecker, 217–30. Louisville: Westminster John Knox, 2002.

———. *The Partings of the Ways: Between Christianity and Judaism and their Significance of the Character of Christianity*. London: SCM, 1991.

———. "Paul: Apostate or Apostle of Israel." *ZNQ* 89 (1998) 256–71.

———. *Romans*. 2 vols. WBC 38A, B. Dallas: Word, 1988.

———. "'Son of God' as 'Son of Man' in the Dead Sea Scrolls? A Response to John Collins on 4Q246." In *The Scrolls and the Scriptures: Qumran Fifty Years After*, 198–210. Sheffield: Sheffield Academic, 1997.

———. *The Theology of Paul the Apostle*. Grand Rapids: Eerdmans, 1998.

———. *Unity and Diversity in the New Testament: An Inquiry into the Character of Earliest Christianity*. London: SCM, 1977.

———. "Was Christianity a Monotheistic Faith from the Beginning?" In *The Christ and the Spirit: Christology*, 315–44. Grand Rapids: Eerdmans, 1998.

Durham, John I. *Exodus*. WBC 3. Waco, TX: Word, 1987.

Eichrodt, Walther. *Ezekiel*. Translated by Cosslett Quin. OTL. London: SCM, 1970.

Eskola, Timo. *Messiah and the Throne: Jewish Merkabah Mysticism and Early Christian Exaltation Discourse*. WUNT 2.142. Tübingen: Mohr, 2001.

Evans, Craig A. "Scripture-Based Stories in the Pseudepigrapha." In *Justification and Variegated Nomism: The Complexities of Second Temple Judaism*, edited by D. A. Carson, Peter T. O'Brien, and Mark A. Seifrid, 57–72. WUNT 140. Grand Rapids: Baker, 2001.

Fairchild, Mark R. "Paul's Pre-Christian Zealot Associations: A Re-Examination of Gal 1:14 and Acts 22:3." *NTS* 45 (1999) 514–32.

Fee, Gordon D. *The First Epistle to the Corinthians*. NICNT. Grand Rapids: Eerdmans, 1987.

———. *Paul's Letter to the Philippians*. NICNT. Grand Rapids: Eerdmans, 1995.

Feldman, Louis H. "Josephus." In *ABD* 3:981–98. New York: Doubleday, 1992.

———. *Judean Antiquities 1–4*. Flavius Josephus: Translation and Commentary. Edited by Steve Mason. Leiden: Brill, 2000.

———. "Rearrangement of Biblical Material in Josephus' *Antiquities*, Book 1." *SBLSP* (1999) 246–62.

Firmat, Gustavo Pérez. "The Novel as Genres." *Genre* 12 (1979) 269–92.

Fitzgerald, John T. "Philippians, Epistle to the." In *ABD* 5:318–26. New York: Doubleday, 1992.

Fitzmyer, Joseph A. *The Acts of the Apostles: A New Translation with Introduction and Commentary*. AB 31. New York: Doubleday, 1998.

———. *The Dead Sea Scrolls and Christian Origins*. Grand Rapids: Eerdmans, 2000.

———. *Romans*. AB 33. New York: Doubleday, 1993.

———. "The Semitic Background of the New Testament *Kyrios*-Title." In *A Wandering Aramean: Collected Aramaic Essays*, edited by Joseph A. Fitzmyer, 115–42. SBLMS 25. Missoula, MT: Scholars, 1979.

———. *Tobit*. CEJL. Berlin: de Gruyter, 2003.

Fletcher-Louis, Crispin H. T. "Alexander the Great's Worship of the High Priest." In *Early Jewish and Christian Monotheism*, edited by Loren T. Stuckenbruck and Wendy E. S. North, 71–102. JSNTSup 263. London: T. & T. Clark, 2004.

———. "Heavenly Ascent or Incarnational Presence? A Revisionist Reading of the Songs of the Sabbath Sacrifice." *SBLSP* 37 (1998) 367–99.

———. *Luke-Acts: Angels, Christology, and Soteriology*. Philadelphia: Coronet, 1997.

———. "Some Reflections on Angelomorphic Humanity Texts among the Dead Sea Scrolls." *DSD* 7 (2000) 292–312.

Forster, Edward Morgan. *Aspects of the Novel*. London: Edward Arnold, 1974.

Fredriksen, Paula. "Paul and Augustine: Conversion Narratives, Orthodox Traditions, and the Retrospective Self." *JTS*, n.s., 37 (1986) 3–34.

Frennesson, Björn. *"In a Common Rejoicing": Liturgical Communion with Angels in Qumran*. SSU 14. Uppsala: Uppsala University Library, 1999.

Frye, Northrop. *Anatomy of Criticism: Four Essays*. Princeton: Princeton University Press, 1957.

Fuhs, H. F. "רָאָה." In *TDOT* 13:208–42.

Fung, Ronald Y. K. *The Epistle to the Galatians*. NICNT. Grand Rapids: Eerdmans, 1988.

Funk, Robert W. *The Poetics of Biblical Narrative*. Sonoma: Polebridge, 1988.

Furnish, Victor Paul. *II Corinthians*. AB 32A. Garden City, NY: Doubleday, 1984.

Gabel, John B., Charles B. Wheeler, and Anthony D. York. *The Bible as Literature: An Introduction*. 3rd ed. Oxford: Oxford University Press, 1996.

Gager, John G. *Reinventing Paul*. Oxford: Oxford University Press, 2000.

Garvey, James. "Characterization in Narrative." *Poetics* 7 (1978) 63–78.

Gaster, T. H. "Angel." In *IDB* 1:128–34. Nashville: Abingdon, 1962.

Gaston, Lloyd. *Paul and the Torah*. Vancouver: University of British Columbia Press, 1987.

Gathercole, Simon J. *The Pre-existent Son: Recovering the Christologies of Matthew, Mark, and Luke.* Grand Rapids: Eerdmans, 2006.

Gaventa, Beverly Roberts. *The Acts of the Apostles.* ANTC. Nashville: Abingdon, 2003.

———. *From Darkness to Light: Aspects of Conversion in the New Testament.* OBT 20. Philadelphia: Fortress, 1986.

———. "The Overthrown Enemy: Luke's Portrait of Paul." *SBLSP* 24 (1985) 439–49.

———. "Paul's Conversion: A Critical Sifting of the Epistolary Evidence." PhD diss., Duke University, 1978.

Genette, Gérard. *Narrative Discourse: An Essay in Method.* Ithaca, NY: Cornell University Press, 1980.

Gianotti, Charles R. "The Meaning of the Divine Name YHWH." *BSac* 142 (1985) 38–51.

Gieschen, Charles A. *Angelomorphic Christology: Antecedents and Early Evidence.* AGJU 42. Leiden: Brill, 1998.

Gill, David. "The Structure of Acts 9." *Bib* 55 (1974) 546–8.

Gnuse, Robert Karl. *The Dream Theophany of Samuel: Its Structure in Relation to Ancient Near Eastern Dreams and Its Theological Significance.* Lanham, MD: University of America Press, 1984.

———. "Dreams in the Night—Scholarly Mirage or Theophanic Formula?: The Dream Report as a Motif of the So-Called Elohist Tradition." *BZ* 39 (1995) 28–53.

Goulder, Michael. "The Pauline Epistles." In *The Literary Guide to the Bible*, edited by Robert Alter and Frank Kermode, 479–502. Cambridge: Belknap/Harvard University Press, 1987.

Green, William Scott. "Messiah in Judaism: Rethinking the Question." In *Judaisms and Their Messiahs at the Turn of the Christian Era*, edited by Jacob Neusner, William Scott Green, and Ernest S. Frerichs, 1–13. Cambridge: Cambridge University Press, 1987.

Greenberg, Moshe. *Ezekiel 1–20.* AB 22. New York: Doubleday, 1983.

Gunkel, Hermann. *Genesis: Translated and Interpreted.* Translated by Mark E. Biddle. Macon, GA: Mercer University Press, 1997.

Gunn, David M. "Narrative Criticism." In *To Each Its Own Meaning: An Introduction to Biblical Criticisms and Their Application*, edited by Steven L. McKenzie and Stephen R. Haynes, 171–95. London: G. Chapman, 1993.

Haacker, Klaus. "Die Berufung des Verfolgers und die Rechtfertigung des Gottlosen." *TBei* 6 (1975) 1–19.

Habel, N. "The Form and Significance of the Call Narratives." *ZAW* 77 (1965) 297–323.

Haenchen, Ernst. *The Acts of the Apostles: A Commentary.* Translated by R. McL. Wilson. Oxford: Blackwell, 1971.

Hahn, Ferdinand. *The Titles of Jesus in Christology: Their History in Early Christianity.* Translated by Harold Knight and George Ogg. London: Lutterworth, 1969.

Hals, Ronald M. *Ezekiel.* FOTL. Grand Rapids: Eerdmans, 1989.

Hamilton, Victor P. *Genesis 18–50.* NICOT. Grand Rapids: Eerdmans, 1995.

Harlow, Daniel C. "The Christianization of Early Jewish Pseudepigrapha: The Case of *3 Baruch*." *JSJ* 32 (2001) 416–44.

Harris, Murray J. "Prepositions and Theology in the Greek New Testament." In *NIDNTT* 3:1171–215.

———. *The Second Epistle to the Corinthians: A Commentary on the Greek Text.* NIGTC. Grand Rapids: Eerdmans, 2005.

———. *Slave of Christ: A New Testament Metaphor for Total Devotion to Christ*. NSBT 8. Leicester: Apollos, 1999.
Harrisville, Roy A. "Acts 22:6–21." *Int* 42 (1988) 181–85.
Hawthorne, Gerald F., and Ralph P. Martin. *Philippians (Revised)*. WBC 43. Dallas: Word, 2004.
Hayman, A. Peter. "The 'Man from the Sea' in 4 Ezra 13." *JJS* 49 (1998) 1–16.
Hays, Richard B. "Christology and Ethics in Galatians: The Law of Christ." *CBQ* 49 (1987) 268–90.
———. *The Conversion of the Imagination: Paul as Interpreter of Israel's Scripture*. Grand Rapids: Eerdmans, 2005.
———. *The Faith of Jesus Christ: An Investigation of the Narrative Substructure of Galatians 3:1—4:11*. SBLDS 56. Chico, CA: Scholars, 1983.
———. "A New Jewish Reading of Paul." *Int* 46 (1992) 184–87.
———. "'The Righteous One' as Eschatological Deliverer: A Case Study in Paul's Apocalyptic Hermeneutics." In *Apocalyptic and the New Testament*, edited by Joel Marcus and Marion L. Soards, 191–215. JSNTSup. Sheffield: Sheffield Academic, 1989.
Head, Peter. "Acts and the Problem of its Texts." In *The Book of Acts in Its Ancient Literary Setting*, edited by Bruce W. Winter and Andrew D. Clarke, 415–44. Grand Rapids: Eerdmans, 1993.
Hedrick, Charles W. "Paul's Conversion/Call: A Comparative Analysis of the Three Reports in Acts." *JBL* 100 (1981) 415–32.
Hengel, Martin. *Between Jesus and Paul: Studies in the Earliest History of Christianity*. Translated by John Bowden. London: SCM, 1983.
———. *The Son of God: The Origin of Christology and the History of Jewish-Hellenistic Religions*. Philadelphia: Fortress, 1976.
———. *Studies in Early Christology*. Edinburgh: T. & T. Clark, 1995.
Hengel, Martin, and Anna Maria Schwemer. *Paul Between Damascus and Antioch: The Unknown Years*. Translated by John Bowden. London: SCM, 1997.
Hernadi, Paul. *Beyond Genre: New Directions in Literary Classification*. London: Cornell University Press, 1972.
Hertzberg, Hans Wilhelm. *I & II Samuel*. OTL. London: SCM, 1964.
Hiebert, Theodore. "Theophany in the OT." In *ABD* 6:505–11. New York: Doubleday, 1992.
Hochman, Baruch. *Character in Literature*. London: Cornell University Press, 1985.
Horbury, William. *Jewish Messianism and the Cult of Christ*. London: SCM, 1998.
———. "Jewish and Christian Monotheism in the Herodian Age." In *Early Jewish and Christian Monotheism*, edited by Loren T. Stuckenbruck and Wendy E. S. North, 16–44. JSNTSup 263. London: T. & T. Clark, 2004.
Horn, F. W. "Holy Spirit." In *ABD* 3:260–80. New York: Doubleday, 1992.
Hossfeld, F.-L., F. van der Velden, and U. Dahmen. "שָׁלַח." In *TDOT* 15:49–73.
Hubbard, Benjamin J. "Commissioning Stories in Luke-Acts: A Study of Their Antecedents, Form and Content." *Semeia* 8 (1977) 103–26.
———. "The Role of Commissioning Accounts in Acts." In *Perspectives on Luke-Acts*, edited by Charles H. Talbert, 187–98. Edinburgh: T. & T. Clark, 1978.
Hübner, Hans. *Biblische Theologie des Neuen Testaments: Des Theologie des Paulus und ihre neutestamentliche Wirkungsgeschichte*. 3 vols. Göttingen: Vandenhoeck & Ruprecht, 1993.

Hultgren, Arlan J. "Paul's Pre-Christian Persecutions of the Church: Their Purpose, Locale, and Nature." *JBL* 95 (1976) 97–111.

Hurtado, Larry W. "Convert, Apostate or Apostle to the Nations: The 'Conversion' of Paul in Recent Scholarship." *SR* 22 (1993) 273–84.

———. "First-Century Jewish Monotheism." *JSNT* 71 (1998) 3–26.

———. "Jesus' Divine Sonship in Paul's Epistle to the Romans." In *Romans and the People of God: Essays in Honor of Gordon D. Fee on the Occasion of his 65th Birthday*, edited by Sven K. Soderlund and N. T. Wright, 217–33. Grand Rapids: Eerdmans, 1999.

———. "Lord." In *DPL*, 560–69. Downers Grove, IL: InterVarsity, 1993.

———. *Lord Jesus Christ: Devotion to Jesus in Earliest Christianity*. Grand Rapids: Eerdmans, 2003.

———. *One God, One Lord: Early Christian Devotion and Ancient Jewish Monotheism*. 2nd ed. London: T. & T. Clark, 1998.

———. "Paul's Christology." In *The Cambridge Companion to St. Paul*, edited by James D. G. Dunn, 185–98. Cambridge: Cambridge University Press, 2003.

———. "Pre-Existence." In *DPL*, 743–46. Downers Grove, IL: InterVarsity, 1993.

———. "Son of God." In *DPL*, 900–906. Downers Grove, IL: InterVarsity, 1993.

Inglis, G. J. "The Problem of St. Paul's Conversion." *ExpTim* 40 (1928–29) 227–31.

Jacobsen, Thorkild. "The Graven Image." In *Ancient Israelite Religion*, edited by Patrick D. Miller Jr., Paul D. Hanson, and S. Dean McBride, 15–32. Philadelphia: Fortress, 1987.

Janzen, J. Gerald. "And the Bush Was Not Consumed." *JBQ* 31 (2003) 219–25.

Jasper, David, and Stephen Prickett, editors. *The Bible and Literature: A Reader*. Oxford: Blackwell, 1999.

Jeremias, Joachim. "Paulus als Hillelit." In *Neotestamentica et Semitica*, edited by E. Earle Ellis and Max Wilcox, 88–94. Edinburgh: T. & T. Clark, 1969.

Jervell, Jacob. *Die Apostelgeschichte*. KEK 17. Göttingen: Vandenhoeck & Ruprecht, 1998.

———. *Luke and the People of God*. Minneapolis: Augsburg, 1972.

———. "Paul in the Acts of the Apostles: Tradition, History, Theology." In *Les Acts des Apôtres: Traditions, rédaction, théologie*, edited by J. Kremer, 297–306. Leuven: Leuven University Press, 1979.

Johnson, Luke Timothy. "Luke-Acts, Book of." In *ABD* 4:403–20. New York: Doubleday, 1992.

Jones, Peter R. "1 Corinthians 15:8: Paul the Last Apostle." *TynBul* 36 (1984) 3–34.

Kaiser, Walter C. "עָבַד." In *TWOT* 639–40.

Kahn, Pinchas. "The Mission of Abraham: Genesis 18:17–22:19." *JBQ* 30 (2002) 155–63.

Keck, Leander E. "Toward the Renewal of New Testament Christology." *NTS* 32 (1986) 362–77.

Keen, Suzanne. *Narrative Form*. New York: Palgrave MacMillan, 2003.

Keesey, Donald. *Contexts for Criticism*. Mountain View, CA: Mayfield, 1998.

Kermode, Frank. "Secrets and Narrative Sequence." *CI* 7 (1980) 83–101.

Kilgallen, John. "Paul before Agrippa (Acts 26:2–23) Some Considerations." *Bib* 69 (1988) 170–95.

Kim, Seyoon. *The Origin of Paul's Gospel*. WUNT 2.4. Tübingen: Mohr, 1984.

———. *Paul and the New Perspective: Second Thoughts on the Origin of Paul's Gospel*. Grand Rapids: Eerdmans, 2002.

Klein, Günter. *Die Zwölf Apostel: Ursprung und Gehalt einer Idee.* FRLANT 77. Göttingen: Vandenhoeck & Ruprecht, 1961.

Klein, Ralph W. *1 Samuel.* WBC 10. Waco, TX: Word, 1983.

Kloppenborg, John. "An Analysis of the Pre-Pauline Formula 1 Cor 15:3b-5 in Light of Some Recent Literature." *CBQ* 40 (1978) 351–67.

Knapp, John V. "Introduction: Self-Preservation and Self-Transformation: Interdisciplinary Approaches to Literary Character." In *Literary Character,* edited by John V. Knapp, 1–16. Lanham, MD: University Press of America, 1990.

Knibb, Michael A. "Temple and Cult in Apocryphal and Pseudepigraphical Writings From Before the Common Era." In *Temple and Worship in Biblical Israel,* edited by John Day, 401–16. LHBOTS 422. London: T. & T. Clark, 2005.

———. "The Translation of *1 Enoch* 70.1: Some Methodological Issues." In *Biblical Hebrews, Biblical Texts,* edited by Ada Rapoport-Albert and Gillian Greenberg, 340–54. JSOTSup. Sheffield: Sheffield Academic, 2001.

Knights, Chris H. "Towards a Critical Introduction to 'The History of the Rechabites.'" *JSJ* 26 (1995) 324–42.

Koet, Bart J. "Trustworthy Dreams? About Dreams and References to Scripture in 2 Maccabees 14–15, Josephus' *Antiquities Judaicae* 11.302–347, and in the New Testament." In *Persuasion and Dissuasion in Early Christianity, Ancient Judaism, and Hellenism,* edited by Pieter W. van der Horst, Maarten J. J. Menken, Joop F. M. Smit, and Geert Van Oyen, 87–107. Leuven: Peeters, 2003.

Koperski, Veronica. *The Knowledge of Christ Jesus My Lord: The High Christology of Philippians 3:7–11.* CBET. Kampen: Kok Pharos, 1996.

Korte, Barbara. *Body Language in Literature.* Toronto: University of Toronto Press, 1997.

Kraemer, Ross Shepard. *When Asenath Met Joseph: A Late Antique Tale of the Biblical Patriarch and His Egyptian Wife, Reconsidered.* Oxford: Oxford University Press, 1998.

Kraft, Robert A., Harold W. Attridge, Russell P. Spittler, and Janet Timbie, editors. *The Testament of Job: According to the SV Text.* SBLTT 5. Missoula, MT: University of Montana Press, 1974.

Kreitzer, L. Joseph. *Jesus and God in Paul's Eschatology.* JSNTSup 19. Sheffield: Sheffield Academic, 1987.

Kugel, James. "The Ladder of Jacob." *HTR* 88 (1995) 209–27.

Kurz, William S. *Reading Luke-Acts: Dynamics of Biblical Narrative.* Louisville: Westminster John Knox, 1993.

Kutsko, John F. *Between Heaven and Earth: Divine Presence and Absence in the Book of Ezekiel.* Edited by William Henry Propp. Biblical and Judaic Studies. Winona Lake, IN: Eisenbrauns, 2000.

LaPorte, Jean. "The High Priest in Philo of Alexandria." *SPhilo* 3 (1991) 71–82.

Levison, John R. "The Debut of the Divine Spirit in Josephus's *Antiquities.*" *HTR* 87 (1994) 123–38.

Lewis, Jack P. "יָדַע." In *TWOT* 366–67.

Liddon, H. P. *The Divinity of Our Lord and Saviour Jesus Christ: Eight Lectures Preached before the University of Oxford in the Year 1866.* London: Longmans, Green, 1867, 1908.

Lightfoot, J. B. *Saint Paul's Epistle to the Philippians.* London: Macmillan, 1913.

Lilly, Joseph L. "The Conversion of Saint Paul." *CBQ* 6 (1944) 180–204.

Lind, Werner Allan. "A Text-Critical Note to Ezekiel 1: Are Shorter Readings Really Preferable to Longer?" *JETS* 27 (1983) 135–39.

Lindemann, Andreas. *Der Erste Korintherbrief.* HNT 9. Tübingen: Mohr, 2000.

Lodge, David. "Analysis and Interpretation of the Realist Text: A Pluralistic Approach to Ernest Hemingway's 'Cat in the Rain.'" *PT* 1 (1980) 5–22.

Lohfink, Gerhard. "Eine alttestamentliche Darstellungsform für Gotteserscheinungen in den Damaskusberichten (Apg 9; 22; 26)." *BZ* 9 (1965) 246–57.

———. *The Conversion of St. Paul: Narrative and History in Acts.* Translated by Bruce J. Manila. Chicago: Franciscan Herald, 1976.

———. "Meinen Namen zu tragen ... (Apg 9, 15)." *BZ* 10 (1966) 108–15.

Long, Burke O. "Reports of Visions among the Prophets." *JBL* 95 (1976) 353–65.

Longenecker, Bruce W., editor. *Narrative Dynamics in Paul: A Critical Assessment.* Louisville: Westminster John Knox, 2002.

———. *2 Esdras.* Sheffield: Sheffield Academic, 1995.

Longenecker, Richard N. *The Christology of Early Jewish Christianity.* London: SCM, 1970.

———. "The Foundational Conviction of New Testament Christology: The Obedience / Faithfulness / Sonship of Christ." In *Jesus of Nazareth: Lord and Christ: Essays on the Historical Jesus and New Testament Christology,* edited by Joel B. Green and Max Turner, 473–88. Grand Rapids: Eerdmans, 1994.

———. *Galatians.* WBC 41. Dallas: Word, 1990.

———. "Some Distinctive Early Christian Motifs." *NTS* 14 (1968) 526–45.

Longman, Tremper, III. "The Bible as Literature: A Brief History." In *A Complete Literary Guide to the Bible,* edited by Leland Ryken and Tremper Longman III, 49–68. Grand Rapids: Zondervan, 1993.

Löning, Karl. *Die Saulustradition in der Apostelgeschichte.* Neutestamentliche Abhandlungen 9. Münster: Aschendorff, 1973.

Lüdemann, Gerd. *Early Christianity according to the Traditions in Acts: A Commentary.* Translated by John Bowden. London: SCM, 1989.

Lührmann, Dieter. "Christologie und Rechtfertigung." In *Rechtfertigung,* edited by Johannes Friedrich, Wolfgang Pöhlmann, and Peter Stuhlmacher, 351–63. Tübingen: Mohr, 1976.

Lund, Nils W. *Chiasmus in the New Testament: A Study in the Form and Function of Chiastic Structures.* Chapel Hill: University of North Carolina Press, 1942.

Lundgren, Sten. "Ananias and the Calling of Paul in Acts." *ST* 25 (1971) 117–22.

Lunt, H. G. "Ladder of Jacob: A New Translation and Introduction." In *OTP* 2:401–411. New York: Doubleday, 1983.

Lyonnet, Stanislas. "'La Voie' dans les Actes des Apôtres." In *La Parole de grâce: Études lucaiennes à la mémoire d'Augustin George,* edited by J. Delorme and J. Duplacy, 149–64. RSR 69. Paris: Recherches de science religieuse, 1981.

MacDonald, Nathan. "Listening to Abraham—Listening to Yhwh: Divine Justice and Mercy in Genesis 18:16–33." *CBQ* 66 (2004) 25–43.

MacRae, George. "Messiah and Gospel." In *Judaisms and Their Messiahs at the Turn of the Christian Era,* edited by Jacob Neusner, William Scott Green, and Ernest S. Frerichs, 169–85. Cambridge: Cambridge University Press, 1987.

Malina, Debra. *Breaking the Frame: Metalepsis and the Construction of the Subject.* Columbus: Ohio State University Press, 2002.

Marguerat, Daniel. "Saul's Conversion (Acts 9, 22, 26) and the Multiplication of Narrative in Acts." In *Luke's Literary Achievement*, edited by Christopher M. Tuckett, 127–55. JSNTSup. Sheffield: Sheffield Academic, 1995.
Marshall, I. Howard. *The Acts of the Apostles: An Introduction and Commentary*. TNTC. Leicester: InterVarsity, 1980.
———. *The Origins of New Testament Christology*. ICT. Downers Grove, IL: InterVarsity, 1976.
Martin, Ralph P. *2 Corinthians*. WBC 40. Dallas: Word, 2002.
Martínez, Florentino García. "Apocalypticism in the Dead Sea Scrolls." In *The Encyclopedia of Apocalypticism*, edited by John J. Collins, 162–92. London: Continuum, 2000.
———. *Qumran and Apocalyptic: Studies on the Aramaic Texts from Qumran*. STDJ 9. Brill, 1992.
Martyn, J. Louis. *Galatians*. AB 33A. New York: Doubleday, 1997.
Merenlahti, Petri, and Raimo Hakola. "Reconceiving Narrative Criticism." In *Characterization in the Gospels: Reconceiving Narrative Criticism*, edited by David Rhoads and Kari Syreeni, 13–48. Sheffield: Sheffield Academic, 1999.
Metzger, B. M. *A Textual Commentary on the Greek New Testament*. 2nd ed. London: United Bible Societies, 1994.
Meyer, Marvin W. "The Light and Voice on the Damascus Road." *FF* 1986 (1986) 27–35.
Michel, O. "Das Licht des Messiah." In *Donum Gentilicium: New Testament Studies in Honour of David Daube*, edited by E. Bammel, C. K. Barrett, and W. D. Davies, 40–50. Oxford: Clarendon, 1978.
Miller, J. Hillis. *Fiction and Repetition: Seven English Novels*. Cambridge: Harvard University Press, 1982.
Miller, James E. "The Thirtieth Year of Ezekiel 1:1." *RB* 99 (1992) 499–503.
Moberly, R. Walter L. *Genesis 12–50*. Sheffield: Sheffield Academic, 1992.
———. "To Hear the Master's Voice: Revelation and Spiritual Discernment in the Call of Samuel." *SJT* 48 (1995) 443–68.
———. *The Old Testament of the Old Testament: Patriarchal Narratives and Mosaic Yahwism*. Minneapolis: Fortress, 1992.
Moo, Douglas J. *The Epistle to the Romans*. NICNT. Grand Rapids: Eerdmans, 1996.
Moule, C. F. D. "The Christology of Acts." In *Studies in Luke-Acts*, edited by Leander E. Keck and J. Louis Martyn, 159–85. Philadelphia: Fortress, 1966, 1980.
———. *The Origin of Christology*. Cambridge: Cambridge University Press, 1977.
Moulton, James Hope, and George Milligan. *The Vocabulary of the Greek New Testament: Illustrated from the Papyri and other Non-Literary Sources*. Grand Rapids: Eerdmans, 1930.
Muecke, Douglas Colin. *The Compass of Irony*. London: Methuen, 1969.
Mullins, T. Y. "New Testament Commission Forms, Especially in Luke-Acts." *JBL* 95 (1976) 603–14.
Munck, Johannes. "La vocation de l'Apôtre Paul." *ST* 1 (1947) 131–45.
Munoa, Phillip B. *Four Powers in Heaven: The Interpretation of Daniel 7 in the Testament of Abraham*. JSPSup 28. Sheffield: Sheffield Academic, 1998.
Murphy-O'Connor, Jerome. *Paul: A Critical Life*. Oxford: Clarendon, 1996.
———. *Paul: His Story*. Oxford: Oxford University Press, 2004.
———. *Paul the Letter-Writer: His World, His Options, His Skills*. GNW 41. Collegeville, MN: Liturgical, 1995.
———. "Tradition and Redaction in 1 Cor 15:3–7." *CBQ* 43 (1981) 582–89.

Myers, Jacob M. *I and II Esdras*. AB 42. Garden City, NY: Doubleday, 1974.
Newman, Carey C. "Acts." In *A Complete Literary Guide to the Bible*, edited by Leland Ryken and Tremper Longman III, 436–44. Grand Rapids: Zondervan, 1993.
———. *Paul's Glory-Christology: Tradition and Rhetoric*. NovTSup. Leiden: Brill, 1992.
Newsom, Carol A. "Angels." In *ABD* 1:248–53. New York: Doubleday, 1992.
Nickelsburg, George W. E. *Ancient Judaism and Christian Origins: Diversity, Continuity, and Transformation*. Minneapolis: Fortress, 2003.
———. "The Nature and Function of Revelation in *1 Enoch*, *Jubilees*, and Some Qumranic Documents." In *Pseudepigraphic Perspectives*, edited by Esther G. Chazon and Michael Stone, 91–119. Leiden: Brill, 1999.
———. "Response to Wiard Popkes." In *George W. E. Nickelsburg in Perspective: An Ongoing Dialogue of Learning*, edited by Jacob Neusner and Alan J. Avery-Peck, 1:101–3. JSJSup 80. Leiden: Brill, 2003.
Niehoff, Maren R. *Philo on Jewish Identity and Culture*. TS 86. Tübingen: Mohr, 2001.
Noth, Martin. *Exodus*. Translated by John Bowden. OTL. London: SCM, 1962.
O'Brien, Peter T. *The Epistle to the Philippians*. NIGTC. Grand Rapids: Eerdmans, 1991.
O'Toole, Robert F. *The Christological Climax of Paul's Defense*. AnBib 78. Rome: Biblical Institute, 1978.
Odell, Margaret S. "Ezekiel Saw What He Said He Saw: Genres, Forms, and the Vision of Ezekiel 1." In *The Changing Face of Form Criticism for the Twenty-First Century*, edited by Marvin A. Sweeney and Ehud Ben Zvi, 162–76. Grand Rapids: Eerdmans, 2003.
Orlov, Andrei A. "The Face as the Heavenly Counterpart of the Visionary in the Slavonic *Ladder of Jacob*." In *Of Scribes and Sages: Early Jewish Interpretation and Transmission of Scripture*, edited by Craig A. Evans, 1:59–76. LSTS 51. London: T. & T. Clark, 2004.
———. "The Flooded Arboretums: The Garden Traditions in the Slavonic Version of *3 Baruch* and the *Book of Giants*." *CBQ* 65 (2003) 184–201.
Osborn, Noel D. "This Is My Name Forever: 'I Am' or 'Yahweh.'" *BT* 39 (1988) 410–15.
Otzen, Benedikt. *Tobit and Judith*. Sheffield: Sheffield Academic, 2002.
Page, Thomas Ethelbert. *The Acts of the Apostles*. New York: MacMillan, 1895.
Pate, C. Marvin. *The Reverse of the Curse: Paul, Wisdom, and the Law*. WUNT 2.114. Tübingen: Mohr, 2000.
Petersen, Norman R. *Literary Criticism for New Testament Critics*. Philadelphia: Fortress, 1978.
Phelan, James. *Reading People, Reading Plots: Character, Progression, and the Interpretation of Narrative*. Chicago: University of Chicago Press, 1989.
Pickover, Clifford. "The Vision of the Chariot: Transcendent Experience and Temporal Lobe Epilepsy." *S&S* 10 (1999). Online: http://www.science-spirit.org/article_detail.php?article_id=130.
Poirier, John C. "The Ouranology of the Apocalypse of Abraham." *JSJ* 35 (2004) 391–408.
Polhill, John B. *Acts*. NAC 26. Nashville: Broadman, 1992.
Porter, Stanley E. "Images of Christ in Paul's Letters." In *Images of Christ: Ancient and Modern*, 95–112. Sheffield: Sheffield Academic, 1997.
Porton, Gary G. "Talmud." In *ABD* 6:310–15. New York: Doubleday, 1992.
Powell, Mark Allan. *What is Narrative Criticism?* Edited by Dan O. Via Jr. GBS. Minneapolis: Fortress, 1990.

Prickett, Stephen. "Biblical Hermeneutics." In *Encyclopedia of Literature and Criticism*, edited by Martin Coyle, Peter Garside, Malcolm Kelsall, and John Peck, 653–65. London: Routledge, 1991.

———. "Biblical and Literary Criticism: A History of Interaction." In *The Bible as Literature: A Reader*, edited by David Jasper and Stephen Prickett, 12–43. Oxford: Blackwell, 1999.

Pritchard, John Paul. *A Literary Approach to the New Testament*. Norman: University of Oklahoma Press, 1972.

Prokulski, Walenty. "The Conversion of St. Paul." *CBQ* 19 (1957) 453–73.

Propp, Vladimir. *Morphology of the Folktale*. Translated by Laurence Scott. 2nd ed. AFSBSS 9. Austin: University of Texas Press, 1968.

Propp, William Henry. *Exodus 1–18*. AB 2. New York: Doubleday, 1998.

Putnam, Frederic Clarke. *Toward Understanding and Reading Biblical Hebrew: Part 6*. Online: http://www.fredputnam.org/files/Grammar Part 6.pdf.

Rad, Gerhard von. *Old Testament Theology*. Translated by D. M. G. Stalker. 2 vols. London: SCM, 1975.

Renaud, B. "La Figure Prophétique de Moïse in Exode 3,1–4,17." *RB* 93 (1986) 510–34.

Resseguie, James L. *Narrative Criticism of the New Testament: An Introduction*. Grand Rapids: Baker, 2005.

Richards, I. A. *Principles of Literary Criticism*. 2nd ed. London: Routledge & Kegan Paul, 1926.

Richardson, Neil. *Paul's Language about God*. JSNTSup 99. Sheffield: Sheffield Academic, 1994.

Ricoeur, Paul. "Narrative Time." *CI* 7 (1980) 169–90.

Rimmon-Kenan, Shlomith. *Narrative Fiction: Contemporary Poetics*. 2nd ed. London: Routledge, 2002.

Robinson, Bernard P. "Moses at the Burning Bush." *JSOT* 75 (1997) 107–22.

Rodway, Allan. "Generic Criticism: The Approach through Type, Mode and Kind." In *Contemporary Criticism*, edited by Malcolm Bradbury and David Palmer, 83–105. Stratford-Upon-Avon Studies 12. London: Edward Arnold, 1970.

Roloff, Jürgen. *Die Apostelgeschichte*. NTD 5. Göttingen: Vandenhoeck & Ruprecht, 1988.

Romberg, Bertil. *Studies in the Narrative Technique of the First-Person Novel*. Stockholm: Almqvist & Wiksell, 1974.

Rosenblatt, Marie-Eloise. "Recurring Narration as a Lukan Literary Convention in Acts: Paul's Jerusalem Speech in Acts 22:1–22." In *New Views on Luke and Acts*, edited by Earl Richard, 94–105. Collegeville, MN: Liturgical, 1990.

Rosmarin, Adena. *The Power of Genre*. Minneapolis: University of Minnesota Press, 1985.

Rowland, Christopher. "Apocalyptic Literature." In *It Is Written: Scripture Citing Scripture*, edited by D. A. Carson and H. G. M. Williamson, 170–89. Cambridge: Cambridge University Press, 1988.

———. *The Open Heaven: A Study of Apocalyptic in Judaism and Early Christianity*. New York: Crossroad, 1982.

Runia, D. T. "God and Man in Philo of Alexandria." *JTS*, n.s., 39 (1998) 48–75.

Rüterswörden, U., H. Simian-Zofre, and Helmer Ringgren. "עָבַד." In *TDOT* 10:376–405.

Sanders, E. P. *Judaism: Practice and Belief 63 BCE–66 CE*. London: SCM, 1992.

Sandnes, Karl Olav. *Paul—One of the Prophets? A Contribution to the Apostle's Self-Understanding*. WUNT 43. Tübingen: Mohr, 1991.

Sarna, Nahum M. *Genesis* בראשית: *The Traditional Hebrew Text with the New JPS Translation*. Jewish Publication Society – The JPS Torah Commentary. Philadelphia: Jewish Publication Society, 1989.

———. *Exodus* שמות: *The Traditional Hebrew Text with the New JPS Translation*. JPSTC. Philadelphia: Jewish Publication Society, 1991.

Sasson, Jack M. "The Eyes of Eli: An Essay in Motif Accretion." In *Inspired Speech: Prophecy in the Ancient Near East: Essays in Honor of Herbert B. Huffmon*, edited by John Kaltner and Louis Stulman, 171–90. JSOTSup 378. London: T. & T. Clark, 2004.

Schaller, Berndt. "Zur Komposition und Konzeption des Testaments Hiobs." In *Studies on the Testament of Job*, edited by Michael A. Knibb and Pieter W. van der Horst, 46–92. SNTSMS 66. Cambridge: Cambridge University Press, 1989.

Schenk, Wolfgang. *Die Philipperbriefe des Paulus: Kommentar*. Stuttgart: Kohlhammer, 1984.

Schille, Gottfried. *Die Apostelgeschichte des Lukas*. THKNT 5. Berlin: Evangelische Verlagsanstalt, 1983.

Schmitt, Hans-Christoph. "Das sogenannte vorprophetische Berufungsschema. Zur 'geistigen Heimat' des Berufungsformulars von Ex 3,9-12; Jdc 6,1-24 und 1 Sam 9,1-10,16." *ZAW* 104 (1991) 202-16.

Schnabel, Eckhard J. *Der erste Brief des Paulus an die Korinther*. HTA. Wuppertal: Brockhaus, 2006.

Schnelle, Udo. *Apostle Paul: His Life and Theology*. Translated by M. Eugene Boring. Grand Rapids: Baker Academic, 2003, 2005.

Schoeps, H. J. *Paul: The Theology of the Apostle in the Light of Jewish Religious History*. London: Lutterworth, 1959, 1961.

Scholer, David M., and Klyne R. Snodgrass. "Preface to the 1992 Reprint of Nils W. Lund, Chiasmus in the New Testament." In *Chiasmus in the New Testament: A Study in the Form and Function of Chiastic Structures*, vii–xxi. Peabody, MA: Hendrickson, 1992.

Schrage, Wolfgang. *Der erste Brief an die Korinther*. 4 vols. EKKNT 7. Zürich: Benziger, 1991–2001.

Schreiner, Josef, "אָמֵן." In *TDOT* 1:292–327.

Schreiner, Thomas R. *Romans*. BECNT. Grand Rapids: Baker, 1998.

Schüngel-Straumann, Helen. *Tobit*. HTKAT. Freiburg: Herder, 2000.

Schuller, Eileen. "Worship, Temple, and Prayer in the Dead Sea Scrolls." In *The Judaism of Qumran: A Systematic Reading of the Dead Sea Scrolls: Theory of Israel*, 1:125–43. HO 56. Leiden: Brill, 2001.

Schweizer, Eduard. "The Concept of the Davidic 'Son of God' in Acts and Its Old Testament Background." In *Studies in Luke-Acts*, edited by Leander E. Keck and J. Louis Martyn, 186–93. Philadelphia: Fortress, 1966, 1980.

Scott, Ian W. "Is Philo's Moses a Divine Man?" *SPhilo* 14 (2002) 87–111.

Scullion, John J. "God in the OT." In *ABD* 2:1041–8. New York: Doubleday, 1992.

Seaford, Richard. "Thunder, Lightning and Earthquake in the *Bacchae* and in the Acts of the Apostles." In *What Is a God? Studies in the Nature of Greek Divinity*, edited by Alan B. Lloyd, 139–51. London: Duckworth, 1997.

Segal, Alan F. "Heavenly Ascent in Hellenistic Judaism, Early Christianity and their Environment." In *ANRW* 2.32.2:1333–94. New York: de Gruyter, 1980.

———. *Paul the Convert: The Apostolate and Apostasy of Saul the Pharisee.* New Haven: Yale University Press, 1990.

———. "Paul's Jewish Presuppositions." In *The Cambridge Companion to St. Paul*, edited by James D. G. Dunn, 159–72. Cambridge: Cambridge University Press, 2003.

———. "The Risen Christ and the Angelic Mediator Figures in Light of Qumran." In *Jesus and the Dead Sea Scrolls*, edited by James H. Charlesworth. 302–28. New York: Doubleday, 1992.

———. *Two Powers in Heaven: Early Rabbinic Reports about Christianity and Gnosticism.* Leiden: Brill, 1977.

Seitz, Christopher. "The Call of Moses and the 'Revelation' of the Divine Name: Source-Critical Logic and Its Legacy." In *Theological Exegesis: Essays in Honor of Brevard S. Childs*, edited by Christopher Seitz and Kathryn Greene-McCreight, 145–61. Grand Rapids: Eerdmans, 1999.

Shereen, Faiza W. "Form, Rhetoric, and Intellectual History." In *Literary Theory and Criticism*, edited by Patricia Waugh, 233–44. Oxford: Oxford University Press, 2006.

Silva, Moisés. *Philippians.* 2nd ed. Baker Exegetical Commentary on the New Testament. Grand Rapids: Baker, 2005.

Simian-Zofre, H., and Helmer Ringgren. "אָמַן." In *TDOT* 10:495–516.

Ska, Jean Louis. "L'arbre et la tente: la fonction du décor en Gn 18,1–15." *Bib* 68 (1987) 383–89.

Skemp, Vincent. "Avenues of Intertextuality between Tobit and the New Testament." In *Intertextual Studies in Ben Sira and Tobit*, edited by Jeremy Corley and Vincent Skemp, 43–70. CBQMS 38. Washington, DC: Catholic Biblical Association of America, 2005.

Skinner, John. *A Critical and Exegetical Commentary on Genesis.* 2nd ed. ICC. Edinburgh: T. & T. Clark, 1930.

Speiser, E. A. *Genesis.* Edited by William F. Albright and David Noel Freedman. New York: Doubleday, 1964.

Spronk, Klaas. *Nahum.* HCOT. Kampen: Kok Pharos, 1997.

Squires, John T. *The Plan of God in Luke-Acts.* SNTSMS 76. Cambridge: Cambridge University Press, 1993.

Stanley, David M. "Paul's Conversion in Acts: Why the Three Accounts?" *CBQ* 15 (1953) 315–38.

Stendahl, Krister. *Paul among Jews and Gentiles.* Philadelphia: Fortress, 1976.

Stone, Michael Edward. "The Book of Enoch and Judaism in the Third Century B.C.E." In *Selected Studies in Pseudepigrapha and Apocrypha*, edited by Michael Edward Stone, 184–97. Leiden: Brill, 1991.

———. "The Enochic Pentateuch and the Date of the Similitudes." In *Selected Studies in Pseudepigrapha and Apocrypha*, edited by Michael Edward Stone, 198–212. Leiden: Brill, 1991.

———. *Fourth Ezra.* Hermeneia. Minneapolis: Fortress, 1990.

Strelan, Rick. *Strange Acts: Studies in the Cultural World of the Acts of the Apostles.* BZAW 126. Berlin: de Gruyter, 2004.

Stuckenbruck, Loren T. *Angel Veneration and Christology: A Study in Early Judaism and in the Christology of the Apocalypse of John.* WUNT 70. Tübingen: Mohr, 1995.

———. "'Angels' and 'God': Exploring the Limits of Early Jewish Monotheism." In *Early Jewish and Christian Monotheism*, edited by Loren T. Stuckenbruck and Wendy E. S. North, 45–70. JSNTSup 263. London: T. & T. Clark, 2004.

Tabor, James D. *Things Unutterable: Paul's Ascent to Paradise in Its Greco-Roman, Judaic, and Early Christian Contexts*. Lanham, MD: University of America Press, 1986.

Takahashi, Masashi. "An Oriental's Approach to the Problems of Angelology." *ZAW* 78 (1966) 343–50.

Tannehill, Robert C. *The Narrative Unity of Luke-Acts: A Literary Interpretation*. 2 vols. Minneapolis: Fortress, 1986.

Taylor, S. G. "A Reconsideration of the 'Thirtieth Year' in Ezekiel 1:1." *TynBul* 17 (1966) 119–20.

Taylor, Vincent. *The Names of Jesus*. London: Macmillan, 1953, 1962.

Thiselton, Anthony C. *The First Epistle to the Corinthians*. NIGTC. Grand Rapids: Eerdmans, 2000.

Thompson, Thomas L. "How Yahweh Became God: Exodus 3 and 6 and the Heart of the Pentateuch." *JSOT* 68 (1995) 57–74.

Thrall, Margaret E. *The Second Epistle to the Corinthians*. 2 vols. ICC. Edinburgh: T. & T. Clark, 2000.

Todorov, Tzvetan. *The Fantastic: A Structural Approach to a Literary Genre*. Translated by Richard Howard. Cleveland: Case Western Reserve University Press, 1973.

Toit, Andrie B. du. "Persuasion in Romans 1:1–17." *BZ* 33 (1989) 192–209.

———. "A Tale of Two Cities: 'Tarsus or Jerusalem' Revisited." *NTS* 46 (2000) 375–402.

Townsend, John T. "Acts 9:1–29 and Early Church Tradition." *SBLSS* 27 (1988) 119–31.

———. "Acts 9:1–29 and Early Church Tradition." In *Literary Studies in Luke-Acts*, edited by Richard P. Thompson and Thomas E. Phillips, 87–98. Macon, GA: Mercer University Press, 1998.

Unnik, W. C. van. "Once Again: Tarsus or Jerusalem." In *Sparsa Collecta: The Collected Essays of W. C. van Unnik: Part One*, edited by W. C. van Unnik, 321–27. Leiden: Brill, 1973.

———. "Tarsus or Jerusalem: The City of Paul's Youth." In *Sparsa Collecta: The Collected Essays of W. C. van Unnik: Part One*, edited by W. C. van Unnik, 259–320. Leiden: Brill, 1973.

VanderKam, James C. "Biblical Interpretation in *1 Enoch* and *Jubilees*." In *The Pseudepigrapha and Early Biblical Interpretation*, edited by James H. Charlesworth and Craig A. Evans, 96–125. JSPSup 14. Sheffield: Sheffield Academic, 1993.

———. *The Book of Jubilees*. CSCO 511. Louvain, Belgium: Orientalista, 1989.

———. *The Book of Jubilees: Guides to Apocrypha and Pseudepigrapha*. Sheffield: Sheffield Academic, 2001.

Vermes, Geza. *An Introduction to the Complete Dead Sea Scrolls*. London: SCM, 1999.

Wacholder, Ben Zion. "Creation in Ezekiel's Merkabah: Ezekiel 1 and Genesis 1." In *Of Scribes and Sages: Early Jewish Interpretation and Transmission of Scripture*, edited by Craig A. Evans, 1:14–32. LSTS 51. London: T. & T. Clark, 2004.

Wadenpfuhl, Laura. "Glossary." In *Narrative/Theory*, edited by David H. Richter, 325–30. White Plains, NY: Longman, 1996.

Waldman, Nahum M. "A Note on Ezekiel 1:18." *JBL* 103 (1984) 614–18.

Waltke, Bruce K. *Genesis: A Commentary*. Grand Rapids: Zondervan, 2001.

Wanamaker, C. A. "Christ as Divine Agent in Paul." *SJT* 39 (1986) 517–28.

Watson, Francis. "Is There a Story in These Texts?" In *Narrative Dynamics in Paul: A Critical Assessment*, edited by Bruce W. Longenecker, 230–39. Louisville: Westminster John Knox, 2002.

Watson, Wilfred G. E. "The Structure of 1 Sam 3." *BZ* 29 (1985) 90–93.

Waugh, Patricia, ed. *Literary Theory and Criticism*. Oxford: Oxford University Press, 2006.

Webber, Randall C. "A Note on 1 Corinthians 15:3–5." *JETS* 26 (1983) 265–69.

Weiser, Alfons. *Die Apostelgeschichte*. 2 vols. OTK 5. Gütersloh: Mohn, 1981.

Welch, John W. "Introduction." In *Chiasmus in Antiquity*, edited by John W. Welch, 9–16. Hildesheim: Gerstenberg, 1981.

———. "Criteria for Identifying and Evaluating the Presence of Chiasmus." In *Chiasmus Bibliography*, edited by John W. Welch and Daniel B. McKinlay, 157–74. Provo, UT: Research, 1999.

Wenham, David. "Acts and the Pauline Corpus: II. The Evidence of Parallels." In *The Book of Acts in Its Ancient Literary Setting*, edited by Bruce W. Winter and Andrew D. Clarke, 215–58. The Book of Acts in Its First Century Setting 1. Grand Rapids: Eerdmans, 1993.

Wenham, Gordon J. *Genesis*. 2 vols. WBC 1, 2. Waco, TX: Word, 1994.

Westermann, Claus. *Basic Forms of Prophetic Speech*. Translated by Hugh Clayton White. Louisville: Westminster John Knox, 1991.

———. *Genesis 12–36*. BKAT. Neukirchen-Vluyn: Neukirchener, 1981.

———. *Genesis 12–36: A Commentary*. Translated by John J. Scullion. Minneapolis: Augsburg, 1985.

White, Hayden. "From 'The Value of Narrativity in the Representation of Reality.'" In *Modern Literary Theory*, edited by Philip Rice and Patricia Waugh, 265–72. London: Arnold, 2001.

White, Stephen L. "Angel of the Lord: Messenger or Euphemism?" *TynBul* 50 (1999) 299–305.

Whitley, C. F. "The 'Thirtieth' Year in Ezekiel 1:1." *VT* 9 (1959) 326–30.

Wicke, Donald W. "The Structure of 1 Sam 3: Another View." *BZ* 30 (1986) 256–58.

Wikenhauser, Alfred. *Pauline Mysticism*. Herder: Freiburg, 1960.

Wilckens, Ulrich. *Der Brief an die Römer*. 3 vols. EKKNT 6. Benziger: Neukirchen, 1978–82.

———. "Interpreting Luke-Acts in a Period of Existential Theology." In *Studies in Luke-Acts*, edited by Leander E. Keck and J. Louis Martyn, 60–83. Philadelphia: Fortress, 1966, 1980.

Willett, Tom W. *Eschatology in the Theodicies of 2 Baruch and 4 Ezra*. Journal for the Study of the Pseudepigrapha: Supplement Series 4. Sheffield: Sheffield Academic, 1989.

Winter, Bruce W. "Official Proceedings and the Forensic Speeches in Acts 24–26." In *The Book of Acts in Its Ancient Literary Setting*, edited by Bruce W. Winter and Andrew D. Clarke, 305–36. The Book of Acts in Its First Century Setting 1. Grand Rapids: Eerdmans, 1993.

Witherington, Ben, III. *The Acts of the Apostles: a Socio-Rhetorical Commentary*. Grand Rapids: Eerdmans, 1998.

———. "Christ." In *DPL*, 95–100. Downers Grove, IL: InterVarsity, 1993.

———. "Christology." In *DPL*, 100–115. Downers Grove, IL: InterVarsity, 1993.

Witherup, Ronald D. "Functional Redundancy in the Acts of the Apostles: A Case Study." *JSNT* 48 (1992) 67–86.
Wright, N. T. *The Climax of the Covenant: Christ and the Law in Pauline Theology.* Minneapolis: Fortress, 1991.
———. *Paul: In Fresh Perspective.* Minneapolis: Fortress, 2005.
———. *The Resurrection of the Son of God.* Christian Origins and the Question of God. Minneapolis: Fortress, 2003.
———. *What Saint Paul Really Said: Was Paul of Tarsus the Real Founder of Christianity?* Grand Rapids: Eerdmans, 1997.
Wyatt, N. "The Development of the Tradition in Exodus 3." *ZAW* 91 (1979) 437–42.
———. "The Significance of the Burning Bush." *VT* 36 (1986) 361–65.
Zimmerli, Walther. *Ezekiel: A Commentary on the Book of the Prophet Ezekiel.* 2 vols. Hermeneia. Philadelphia: Fortress, 1979.

Author Index

Abbott, H. Porter, 26–27
Addinall, Peter, 51
Alexander, P., 59, 61, 82, 86, 94
Allen, Leslie C., 55, 56, 58
Allison, Dale C., 71
Alston, Wallace M., Jr., 48
Alter, Robert, 31, 49, 54, 148, 225, 226
Andersen, F. I., 67
Attridge, Harold W., 61, 66

Baban, Octavian D., 3, 192, 235
Bailey, James L., 33, 176
Barclay, John M. G., 61, 98
Bar-Efrat, Shimon, 30
Barnett, Paul, 115, 135, 136
Barrett, C. K., 126, 195–96, 198, 217, 219, 221, 228, 230, 231, 241–42
Barth, Karl, 144
Barthes, Roland, 26, 36
Bauckham, Richard, 17, 23, 28, 29, 30, 72, 93, 94
Beaujour, Michel, 199
Beker, J. Christiaan, 1
Ben Zvi, Ehud, 43
Berlin, Adele, 31, 238
Berry, George Ricker, 55
Betz, Hans Dieter, 99, 104, 105–6, 110, 112, 116, 119, 121, 259
Black, Matthew, 71–73
Blenkinsopp, Joseph, 43, 57
Bligh, John, 104, 176
Block, Daniel I., 55, 56
Bockmuehl, Markus, 145, 147–48
Bohak, Gideon, 67

Bolt, Peter, 247
Booth, Wayne C., 31
Borgen, Peder, 77, 79, 80
Bousset, Wilhelm, 1, 2, 168–69, 172, 191
Bowker, John Westerdale, 4, 5, 23, 136, 234–37, 250
Brooke, George J., 67
Brooks, Roger, 82
Bruce, F. F., 104–6, 112, 114, 117, 119–21, 130, 156, 166, 195, 197–98, 200, 203, 206, 210, 213–15, 217, 220, 230, 241
Brueggemann, Walter, 48–49
Budesheim, T. L., 219
Bultmann, Rudolph, 169, 172, 215
Burchard, Christoph, 67, 219
Burton, Ernest de Witt, 100, 103, 105–6, 112, 115, 121–22, 171
Buttrick, George Arthur, 160

Cadbury, Henry J., 225
Calvin, John, 47–48
Campbell, Antony F., 53
Capes, David B., 170
Carroll, Robert P., 52
Carson, D. A., 191
Casey, P. M., 188
Charlesworth, James H., 58–59, 70, 73, 86, 93
Chatman, Seymour, 23, 39
Chesnutt, Randall D., 67
Childs, Brevard, 33, 50, 241
Childs, Peter, 241
Clark, Andrew C., 218
Coats, George W., 35

Coggins, R. J., 69
Collins, John J., 61, 66–67, 73, 77
Conzelmann, Hans, 124–26, 168–69, 200, 217, 230, 240
Crane, Gregory R., 81
Crawford, Sidnie White, 62
Culler, Jonathan, 23, 26, 37, 39
Cullmann, Oscar, 167, 169

Dahl, Nils Alstrup, 169, 239
Dalman, G., 169, 198–99
Dancy, J. C., 48, 60
Darr, John A., 31
Daube, David, 198
Davidson, Maxwell J., 72, 77
Davis, Carl Judson, 244
De Jonge, Marinus, 167
Den Hertog, Cornelis, 49–50, 184
Derrida, Jacques, 26, 210–11
deSilva, David A., 69
Dibelius, Martin, 218–19
Dietzfelbinger, Christian, 9–13, 99, 115, 130–31, 133, 155, 166
Docherty, Susan, 67
Docherty, Thomas, 30
Donaldson, Terence L., 19–21, 115, 117, 130, 144, 165
Driver, G. R., 56
Driver, Samuel Rolles, 42
Dunn, James D. G., 3, 7–9, 77, 89, 98, 100, 106, 110, 112, 114, 118–20, 134, 138–42, 144, 167–70, 216, 220, 240–41
Durham, John I., 52–53, 89

Eichrodt, Walther, 57
Eskola, Timo, 22–23, 25, 29, 157, 163–64, 172
Evans, Craig A., 67

Fairchild, Mark R., 214
Fee, Gordon D., 123–24, 127, 129, 145, 147
Feldman, Louis H., 80–81

Firmat, Gustavo Pérez, 27
Fitzgerald, John T., 99
Fitzmyer, Joseph A., 60–61, 77, 133, 140–41, 169, 195, 206, 210, 217, 241–42
Fletcher-Louis, Crispin H. T., 18, 76, 82, 92, 94, 192, 233
Forster, Edward Morgan, 28, 225–26
Fowler, Roger, 241
Fredriksen, Paula, 3
Frennesson, Björn, 75
Frye, Northrop, 26
Fung, Ronald Y. K., 100, 104–07, 110, 112, 116, 156
Funk, Robert W., 37, 193, 204
Furnish, Victor Paul, 130, 135

Gabel, John B., 232
Gager, John G., 3, 155
Garvey, James, 30, 31
Gaster, T. H., 48
Gaston, Lloyd, 155
Gathercole, Simon J., 173
Gaventa, Beverly Roberts, 3, 31, 119, 125, 130, 158, 192, 195, 204, 210, 217, 220, 230–31, 234, 237, 241, 243
Gaylord, H. E., Jr., 68
Genette, Gérard, 23, 39–40, 191, 225
Gianotti, Charles R., 50
Gieschen, Charles A., 18–19, 29–30, 89, 187–89
Gill, David, 203
Gnuse, Robert Karl, 33–34
Goulder, Michael, 100
Green, William Scott, 168
Greenberg, Moshe, 57–58
Gunkel, Hermann, 48
Gunn, David M., 43

Haacker, Klaus, 152, 157
Habel, N., 49–50, 55–56
Haenchen, Ernst, 217, 219–20, 230
Hahn, Ferdinand, 167, 169

Author Index

Hakola, Raimo, 23
Hals, Ronald M., 55
Hamilton, Victor P., 43, 46, 49
Harlow, Daniel C., 68
Harris, Murray J., 110, 134, 136, 183
Harrisville, Roy A., 209, 232
Hawthorne, Gerald F., 130, 145
Hayman, A. Peter, 69
Hays, Richard B., 72, 98, 118, 159, 171, 243
Head, Peter, 202
Hedrick, Charles W., 219-21
Hengel, Martin, 159, 166-67, 170-72, 189
Hernadi, Paul, 26
Hertzberg, Hans Wilhelm, 35
Hiebert, Theodore, 33-34
Hochman, Baruch, 26
Horbury, William, 32, 188
Horn, F. W., 198
Hubbard, Benjamin J., 33-34, 220
Hübner, Hans, 100, 120
Hultgren, Arlan J., 232
Hurtado, Larry W., 2, 15, 23, 28-30, 41, 93, 137, 140, 150, 154, 168, 169, 171-73, 175, 178, 186-87

Inglis, G. J., 3
Isaac, E., 65-66, 71, 73, 95, 257

Jacobsen, Thorkild, 52
Janzen, J. Gerald, 50
Jasper, David, 3
Jeremias, Joachim, 206
Jervell, Jacob, 1, 191, 198, 215, 219-20, 229
Johnson, Luke Timothy, 192
Jones, Peter R., 128

Kahn, Pinchas, 45
Keck, Leander E., 166
Kee, H. C., 66
Keen, Suzanne, 26
Keesey, Donald, 27

Kermode, Frank, 225
Kilgallen, John, 221
Kim, Seyoon, 1, 4-9, 15, 23, 99, 100, 125, 130-35, 137, 142, 145-46, 150, 153, 157-58, 166, 187-88
Klein, Günter, 219
Klein, Ralph W., 35
Kloppenborg, John, 128
Knapp, John V., 26
Knibb, Michael A., 60, 62, 69, 72
Knights, Chris H., 73
Koet, Bart J., 82
Koperski, Veronica, 179
Korte, Barbara, 229
Kraemer, Ross Shepard, 67
Kraft, Robert A., 66
Kreitzer, L. Joseph, 93
Kugel, James, 68
Kurz, William S., 193, 204
Kutsko, John F., 58

LaPorte, Jean, 79
Lehrmah, S. M., 83
Levison, John R., 81, 95
Liddon, H. P., 89
Lightfoot, J. B., 179
Lilly, Joseph L., 3
Lind, Werner Allan, 56
Lindemann, Andreas, 126, 128
Lodge, David, 228
Long, Burke O., 23, 55
Longenecker, Bruce W., 25, 69, 98, 110
Longenecker, Richard N., 99, 102, 104-8, 110, 111-12, 117-18, 120, 122, 156, 172
Löning, Karl, 219
Lüdemann, Gerd, 222
Lührmann, Dieter, 3
Lund, Nils W., 104, 106
Lundgren, Sten, 228
Lunt, H. G., 68
Lyonnet, Stanislas, 206

MacDonald, Nathan, 43
MacRae, George, 135, 168
Malina, Debra, 41
Marguerat, Daniel, 209, 218, 220–21
Marshall, I. Howard, 145, 168, 209, 215, 242–43
Martin, Ralph P., 130, 133, 145
Martínez, Florentino García, 74, 76–77
Martyn, J. Louis, 107, 108, 116
Merenlahti, Petri, 23
Metzger, B. M., 69, 101–2, 192, 193, 205, 211
Meyer, Marvin W., 218
Michel, O., 198
Milik, J. T., 71
Miller, J. Hillis, 56, 225, 259
Miller, James E., 56, 225, 259
Milligan, George, 215
Moberly, R. Walter L., 34–35, 50, 89
Moo, Douglas J., 139–41, 143, 191
Moore, Carey A., 60
Morris, Leon, 191
Moule, C. F. D., 167–69, 171, 240, 244
Moulton, James Hope, 215
Muecke, Douglas Colin, 241
Mullins, T. Y., 33, 220
Munck, Johannes, 3, 119, 234
Munoa, Phillip B., 71
Myers, Jacob M., 69

Neusner, Jacob, 82, 83
Newman, Carey C., 1, 2, 16, –17, 34, 99, 157, 159–63, 193
Newsom, Carol A., 33, 89
Nickelsburg, George W. E., 32, 72–73, 77
Noth, Martin, 49, 52

Odell, Margaret S., 55
Orlov, Andrei A., 68
Osborn, Noel D., 50

Otzen, Benedikt, 60

Page, Thomas Ethelbert, 217
Parry, Donald W., 74–76
Pate, C. Marvin, 5, 162
Petersen, Norman R., 23
Phelan, James, 228
Philonenko, Marc, 66–67
Pickover, Clifford, 3
Poirier, John C., 84
Polhill, John B., 242
Porter, Stanley E., 185
Porton, Gary G., 82
Powell, Mark Allan, 23, 25, 40, 44, 197, 203
Prickett, Stephen, 3, 23
Pritchard, John Paul, 201, 219
Prokulski, Walenty, 3
Propp, Vladimir, 27, 35–36
Propp, William Henry, 52
Putnam, Frederic Clarke, 197

Rad, Gerhard von, 34
Renaud, B., 49
Resseguie, James L., 23, 25, 37, 44, 104, 226, 242
Richards, I. A., 23
Richardson, Neil, 176
Ricoeur, Paul, 225
Rimmon-Kenan, Shlomith, 26, 28, 30, 41, 203
Robinson, Bernard P., 52
Rodway, Allan, 27
Romberg, Bertil, 98
Rosenblatt, Marie-Eloise, 207
Rosmarin, Adena, 26–27
Rowland, Christopher, 85–87, 93, 96
Rubinkiewicz, R., 70
Runia, D. T., 79

Sanders, E. P., 19, 32, 65–66, 71, 155
Sandnes, Karl Olav, 119
Sarna, Nahum M., 43–44, 47–48, 50, 52, 89

Sasson, Jack M., 53
Schaller, Berndt, 66
Schenk, Wolfgang, 147
Schille, Gottfried, 220
Schmitt, Hans-Christoph, 33
Schnabel, Eckhard J., 125
Schnelle, Udo, 99, 130, 145, 150, 166
Schoeps, H. J., 172
Scholer, David M., 104
Schrage, Wolfgang, 123, 125, 128, 129
Schreiner, Thomas R., 143, 247
Schüngel-Straumann, Helen, 61
Schuller, Eileen, 76
Schweizer, Eduard, 169, 242
Scott, Ian W., 79, 194
Scullion, John J., 171
Seaford, Richard, 259
Segal, Alan F., 8–9, 13, 15, 23, 33, 78, 82, 88, 130, 131, 134, 136–37, 150, 157–59, 171, 221, 234, 237, 250, 258, 259
Seitz, Christopher, 50
Shereen, Faiza W., 26
Silva, Moisés, 146, 147
Ska, Jean Louis, 44
Skemp, Vincent, 61
Skinner, John, 48
Snodgrass, Klyne R., 104
Speiser, E. A., 47
Spittler, Russell P., 66
Spronk, Klaas, 171
Squires, John T., 210, 217, 258
Stanley, David M., 220
Stendahl, Krister, 3
Stinespring, W. F., 66, 71
Stone, Michael Edward, 69–71
Strelan, Rick, 259
Stuckenbruck, Loren T., 17–18, 30, 74–75, 94

Tabor, James D., 13–14, 136, 258
Takahashi, Masashi, 49
Tannehill, Robert C., 201–2, 218

Taylor, S. G., 56, 167, 169
Taylor, Vincent, 56, 167, 169
Thiselton, Anthony C., 128, 129, 176
Thompson, Thomas L., 53
Thrall, Margaret E., 134–35
Timbie, Janet, 66
Todorov, Tzvetan, 27, 36
Tov, Emanuel, 74, 75, 76
Townsend, John T., 221–22

van Unnik, W. C., 206

Vander Broek, Lyle D., 33, 176
VanderKam, James C., 62, 65, 72
Vermes, Geza, 74–75

Wacholder, Ben Zion, 56
Wadenpfuhl, Laura, 37
Waldman, Nahum M., 56
Waltke, Bruce K., 43, 49
Wanamaker, C. A., 175
Watson, Francis, 98
Watson, Wilfred G. E., 53
Waugh, Patricia, 23
Webber, Randall C., 128
Weiser, Alfons, 193, 202, 222, 242
Welch, John W., 104
Wenham, David, 222
Wenham, Gordon J., 44–45
Westermann, Claus, 34–35, 43, 47–48, 89
Wheeler, Charles B., 232
White, Hayden, 24
White, Stephen L., 89
Whitley, C. F., 56
Wicke, Donald W., 53
Wikenhauser, Alfred, 119
Wilckens, Ulrich, 143, 232
Willett, Tom W., 69
Winter, Bruce W., 191
Wintermute, O. S., 62
Witherington, Ben, III, 28, 167, 194, 214, 219, 221
Witherup, Ronald D., 221

Wright, N. T., 2–3, 99, 119, 125, 127, 129–30, 137, 152, 167–69, 172–74, 220
Wyatt, N., 49–50

York, Anthony D., 232

Zimmerli, Walther, 55

Subject Index

Abraham, 39, 42–50, 62–66, 69–71, 81, 85–87, 89, 95, 180, 251
Aeneas, 258
affinity, 28–29, 78
agency, 103–4, 110–12, 124, 140, 143–44, 175, 253
Agrippa, 210–12, 216
Alexander Polyhistor, 61
Alexander, 82
Alexandria, 77
Ananias, 201–2, 204, 208–9, 218, 221, 226–29, 234, 238–39, 243, 245
Angel of Darkness, 75
angel of God, 61, 108
Angel of the Lord. *See* Angel of Yahweh
Angel of the Presence, 76, 130
Angel of Truth, 75
Angel of Yahweh: in ancient Jewish literature, 33, 48, 50, 52–53, 61–63, 65, 70, 83–85, 87, 95–96; characterization of, 88–91; and Christology, 9, 18; and Paul, 130, 181, 188, 251
angelomorphic Christology, 18–19, 187–89, 233
angelomorphism: and characterization, 88, 91–96; as criterion of divinity, 29; in Dead Sea Scrolls, 76
Anointed One, 72, 240
apostleship of Paul: in 1 Corinthians, 123–26, 129; in 2 Corinthians, 135; agency,

175; Divine Initiative, 156–57, 165; and the DRE message, 153, 229, 232, 252; in Galatians, 100, 102–3, 105–6, 121, 130; like Old Testament prophet, 181; in Romans, 138, 140–43
appearance (element): in Acts, 198–200, 207–8, 215–16, 224; definition, 37–38; in Paul, 116–20, 151–52
appointed by Jesus, 245
Arabia, 102, 122, 151, 154
Aramaic, 76, 169, 215, 224
ascent: as category of epiphanies, 13–14, 250; as characteristic of Divine Response, 41, 251; DRE as, 8–9, 14, 17, 22, 159–65, 237; in New Testament, 136–37; in non-Jewish literature, 258; in Pseudepigrapha, 68, 71, 85–86
Asenath, 67
auditory message dream, 33–34, 53
Azaz'el, 72

Balaam, 40, 81
Balak, 40
Barnabas, 117, 203–4, 238–39
Baruch, 68–69, 85–87
basic narrative structure of epiphany, 36–41, 50, 53, 109, 150–54, 222–33. *See also* appearance (element); conclusion (element); departure (element); introduction (element); message (element)

bat qol, 198–99
Bearer of Divine Light, 11
blasphemy, 149, 214, 223, 244
blindness, 132, 201, 208, 233, 236

call narrative, 33–34, 49, 53, 55
Caravaggio, Michelangelo Merisi da, 29
characterization: of epiphanic beings in ancient Jewish literature, 47–49, 52–54, 57–58, 61, 63–65, 70, 77, 81; of God and other heavenly beings, 29–31; of Jesus in Acts, 238–49, 254; of Jesus by Paul, 166–90, 253; patterns of, 88–97, 250–51; theory, 28; Type-I characterization, 88–92, 94–97, 186–87, 190, 251, 253; Type-II characterization, 91–97, 186–87, 190, 251, 253. See also direct characterization; indirect characterization
characterization of Jesus. See Christology
chariot, 75, 78, 83, 85, 163. See also *merkabah* vision(s)
cherubim, 28, 71, 88
chiasm, 104, 106–7, 176–77
chief of the house of the Most High, 66, 88
Chosen One, 72–73
Christ, 6, 11, 167–69, 239–40
Christology: appointed by Jesus, 245; Christ, 6, 11, 167–69, 239–40; faith in Jesus, 217, 247; "I am", 141, 199–200, 207, 247; Jesus as name, 167, 239; knowing Jesus, 146–47, 179–80, 248; Kyrios, 11, 170; Lord, 6, 169–71, 216, 240–42; Lord who rescues, 170–71, 216–17, 240–42, 248; name of Jesus, 15, 178, 202, 204, 214, 244; seeing Jesus, 126–27, 130–35, 152, 180–81, 248; sent by Jesus, 184, 245–46; slave of Jesus, 126, 138, 142–44, 156, 169, 181–83, 216, 232, 246–48; Son of God, 140, 163–64, 166, 171–73, 188; Wisdom Christology, 6–8, 15, 28, 157–58, 188; witness of Jesus, 216, 232, 234, 245–47.
church, Paul's persecution of: in Acts, 194, 223, 233–34; autobiographical accounts, 10, 114–16, 129, 145, 150, 155, 252
commander of Yahweh's army, 91
companions, Paul's travel, 200–201, 208, 218, 229–31, 236
conclusion (element): in Acts, 200–201, 208, 217, 231; definition, 38; in Paul, 122, 154–55
conversion: and call controversy, 3, 7; and the DRE, 6, 130–36, 159, 232
creation, 62, 131–35, 252
Creator, 29, 79
Cynics, 126

Damascus, 102, 122, 151, 154, 192–93, 195–97, 201, 203, 205–8, 211–12, 215, 223–24, 226–28, 231–33, 252
Daniel, 6, 86
Davidic messiah, 22, 163–64, 167, 172
Decapolis, 196
defocalizer, 37
Delacroix, Eugène, 29
dell' Abate, Nicolò, 29
departure (element): in Acts, 231; definition, 38; in Paul, 154

Subject Index

diegesis, 40–41, 191
direct characterization: of Jesus in Acts, 238–43, 247–49; of Jesus by Paul, 166–73, 185–86, 188; theory, 30–31
disputed Pauline epistles, 5, 7, 23–24, 99, 105, 134, 148–49, 159, 184
divine hand, 88
Divine Initiative: in Acts, 233–34, 237–38, 249, 254; in ancient Jewish epiphanies, 47, 51, 54, 57, 61, 65, 68, 71, 73, 85–88, 96; definition, 41, 250–51; in Paul, 137, 154–57, 161–66, 189, 252–53
Divine Response: in ancient Jewish epiphanies, 63, 66–71, 73–74, 85–88, 96; definition, 41, 250–51; in Paul, 137
double vocative, 50, 70, 199, 209, 224
dreams: as category of epiphanies, 9, 33–35, 42, 161; in non-Jewish literature, 258; in Old Testament, 38, 53; in Pseudepigrapha, 66, 68–69, 71, 82, 93
Dujardin, Karel, xxiv, 28

Easter event, DRE as, 10–11, 13
Egypt, 51–52, 61, 66, 69, 183
Elect One, 72–73, 83
Eli, 53–54
Elohim, 53, 70, 95
Enoch, 15, 19, 67–68, 71–73, 85, 92–94
epanadiplosis, 199
epiphany: as genre, 32–36
eternal holy ones, 76
evaluative point of view, 25, 203, 238
exalted humans, 8, 77–80
Ezekiel, 54–57, 83, 92, 158–59, 163

Ezra, 69–70, 95

face: "before face", 68; of God, 93, 180; of Jesus, 132–33
faith in Jesus, 217, 247
falling to the ground: as response to epiphany, 5, 38, 56, 60, 63–64, 84; Paul in DRE, 198–200, 207, 215, 224, 230, 236–37
fluidity of characterization, 49, 52–53, 70, 76, 186
focalization, 25, 37, 39
focalizer, 37, 193
folktales, 27, 35–36, 226
freedom, 125–27

Gabriel, 83, 91, 247
Gamaliel, 204, 206, 223
genre: in ancient Jewish literature, 55, 58–59, 84–88, 250; theory, 23–27, 250
Gentiles, Paul's call to: in Acts, 208–10, 216, 226–29, 232–34, 245, 258; in Paul, 19–21, 141, 149, 153–57, 161, 165, 181–82, 252–53
glory: Christology, 16, 159–63; of God, 58, 61, 74–76, 83, 86, 130, 237; light as, 132–35, 158, 198, 252
God of gods, 79
God the Father: active in the DRE, 118–19, 122, 124, 139, 216, 245; Paul's commission from, 100; in Philo, 78–79; relationship to Jesus, 104–8, 171–90, 253
grace: and apostleship, 126, 140–41; and call, 118, 122, 129, 142–43, 148–49; and Divine Initiative, 155–57; and gospel, 185; as means, 117; source of, 106, 118, 175, 185

Habakkuk, 86
Hagar, 80
hapax legomenon, 143, 170, 194, 200–201, 207, 213
Haran, 62
heaven(s): fifth, 69, 84, 87; gates of, 66; seventh, 67, 83–85; tenth, 84; third, 4, 84–85, 134, 136–37
Hebraism, 110, 200, 207
Hecataeus, 92
high priest: in Acts, 195–97, 205–7, 223, 242; in ancient Jewish literature, 79, 92–93; Jesus as, 164
Holy Most High, 66
humanity: God's awareness of, 179; and intermediary beings, 78–80; of Jesus, 105–7; Jesus in contrast with, 108, 172, 174–75, 182, 186; source of DRE, 109–11

"I am," 141, 199–200, 207, 247
Iaoel, 70, 85, 91
Ibn Ezra, 50, 52
Image of God: Adam as, 93; Jesus as, 11, 157–58, 188; Logos as, 78
implied question, 208, 227
increasing sequence, 189, 224–29, 231–32, 234, 240, 245, 254
indirect characterization: of Jesus in Acts, 243–49; of Jesus by Paul, 173–86, 188; theory, 30–31
intermediate agency, 103–4, 110–12, 124, 140, 175, 253
introduction (element): in Acts, 194–97, 205–7, 214–15, 223–24, 232–33; definition, 37; in Paul, 109–16, 150–51
irony, 25, 241–42

Isaiah, 24, 85, 163, 182. *See also* Servant of Isaiah
Ishmael, 64

Jacob, xiii, 9, 68, 89, 91, 95
Jeremiah, 24, 120, 122, 163, 182, 217
Jerusalem, 68, 70, 102, 122, 154, 192, 196–98, 203, 205–6, 209–12, 214, 219, 223, 226, 228
Jesus (name), 167, 239
Job, 66, 86, 96
Johanan b. Zakkai, 4
Josephus, 24, 27, 42, 80–82, 95, 195, 220, 236
Joshua, 91

knowing Jesus, 146–47, 179–80, 248
Kyrios, 11, 170. *See also* Lord (Christological title)

La Conversion de Saint Paul (dell' Abate), 29
Levi, 65–66, 85, 115
light: in Acts, 198–99, 201, 204–5, 207–8, 213, 215, 217–19, 222, 224, 226, 229–30, 232–33, 235; in ancient Jewish literature, 66–67, 84; and *merkabah* visions, 5, 252; in Paul, 11, 16, 130, 132–35, 158
lightning, 75, 259
literary-critical methodology, 2, 22–26
Logos, 15, 77–80
Lord (Christological title), 6, 169–71, 216, 240–42
Lord of the Spirits, 72
Lord of the Universe, 85
Lord who rescues, 170–71, 216–17, 240–42, 248
Lot, 42–43, 46–47, 49, 81, 251

Subject Index

Mamre, 44, 69, 89
man from the sea, 69, 88
Manoah, 87, 181
Marcus Tarquinius, 258
Master God, 71, 95
mediator: church as, 200; between God and humans, 8–9, 65; Jesus as, 48, 172
merkabah vision(s): and Acts, 234–38, 249, 254; DRE as, 4–7, 9, 15–17, 19, 22–23, 25; in extra-Biblical Jewish literature, 56, 59, 67, 75–77, 83, 85–86, 250; and Paul, 135–37, 155, 157–66, 172, 188–89, 252
message (element): in Acts, 200–201, 208, 216–17, 225–29; definition, 38; in Paul, 120–22, 153–54
metadiegesis, 40–41, 191
metalepsis, 25, 40–41
Metatron, 86, 94
metonymy, 243–44, 248
Michael, 15, 71, 83–84, 91, 93, 95
Mishnah, 82–83
monolatry, 29–30
monotheism, 18, 29–30, 32
Moses, 15, 49–52, 61–62, 69, 78–79, 83, 86, 92–93, 115, 132–34, 180, 183–84, 245

Nabataean kingdom, 195
name of Jesus, 15, 178, 202, 204, 214, 244
narrative criticism, 2, 22–26
Nebuchadnezzar, 68
new *religionsgeschichtliche Schule*, 2, 24

"on the road", 3, 5, 235

perspective: human and divine, 39–40; shift between Paul and God, 122. *See also* focalization
Phanuel, 68, 85
Pharisee, Paul as, 145, 150, 214, 223, 232
Philo, 6, 22, 42, 77–80
Phinehas, 115, 145
plot, 24, 87
pre-existence, 69
priest(s): in Dead Sea Scrolls, 76; Levi as, 66; Paul as, 143–44, 182
Publius, 258

Rabbi Hiyya, 83
Rabbi Judah (rabbi), 83
Raphael, 60, 61
repetition: in Acts DRE accounts, 218–22, 225–29, 234; in epiphany texts, 45, 54, 75; by Paul, 138–39, 199; theory, 25, 225
rescue, 170–71, 216–17, 240–42, 248
resurrection, 15, 28, 129, 134, 139–40, 147, 167, 174
Righteous One, 72, 208, 239, 243
righteous ones, 73
Rome, 77, 258

Saint Paul Renversé sur le Chemin de Damas (Delacroix), 29
Saint Paul sur le Chemin de Damas (anonymous), 29
Saint Paul sur le Chemin de Damas (Delacroix), 29
Saint Paul sur le Chemin de Damas (Zimmermann), 29
Samuel, 34–35, 53–54, 180
Sarah (wife of Abraham), 42–44, 47, 49, 64–65
Sarah (wife of Tobit), 60–61
Sariel, 68, 95
second God, 78, 92

seeing Jesus, 126–27, 130–35, 152, 180–81, 248
sent by Jesus, 184, 245–46
sequence: increasing, 189, 224–29, 231–32, 234, 240, 245, 254; narrative, 39, 70; temporal, 6
seraphim, 88
Servant of Isaiah, 122, 138, 167
servant of Jesus. *See* slave of Jesus
servants of the Presence, 76
setting: in ancient Jewish literature, 44, 46, 50, 53, 56, 62–64; of DRE in Acts, 197, 205–7, 214–15, 223–24, 232–33, 247; of DRE and *merkabah*, 235–36; in epiphanies, 39–40, 84, 250; theory, 37
shining, 130, 213, 215, 224
Simeon, 115
Sinai, 16, 62, 133–35, 162, 180
slave of Jesus, 126, 138, 142–44, 156, 169, 181–83, 216, 232, 246–48
Sodom, 43, 45–47, 81
Son of God: in Acts, 202–03, 242–43, 248; in ancient Jewish literature, 77; as Christological title, 6, 11; in Paul, 140, 163–64, 166, 171–73, 188
Son of Man, 72–73, 77, 88, 92, 94, 202, 251
Son of the Most High, 69, 88
Stephen, 9, 194, 243, 246
Stoics, 258
suspense, 227–28

Tarsus, 204, 206, 223
temple: defiling of, 204; destruction of, 59, 198; God's glory on, 74; heavenly, 22, 71, 164; Paul's vision in, 204, 209–10, 218–19, 228, 234
tension, 45, 89, 228

The Conversion of Saint Paul (Dujardin), xxiv, 28
The Conversion on the Way to Damascus (Caravaggio), 29
theophany: DRE as, 4, 8; in Josephus, 82; in the Old Testament, 16, 33–34, 47–48, 50, 53–55, 58, 133, 135, 199; in the Pseudepigrapha, 70
throne, 29, 55, 66, 71–72, 92–93, 230, 251. See also *merkabah* vision(s)
thunder, 75, 259
Tobit, 60–61
Torah, 10, 12–13, 20, 115
two gods, 77–78
Type-I characterization, 88–92, 94–97, 186–87, 190, 251, 253
Type-II characterization, 91–97, 186–87, 190, 251, 253

ultimate agency, 103–4, 110–11, 124, 143–44, 175, 253
Ur, 62, 63, 86
Uriel, 69, 91

visions, 9
voice, heavenly: in Acts, 198–201, 205, 207–8, 212, 215, 218, 224, 229–37; in ancient Jewish literature, 56, 61–62, 66, 68–70, 73, 84, 91, 95; and *merkabah* visions, 5

Wisdom Christology, 6–8, 15, 28, 157–58, 188
witness of Jesus, 216, 232, 234, 245–47
worship: of angels, 17; as criterion of divinity, 29–30, 94; of God, 72, 75, 79, 213; in heaven, 22; of humans, 82, 92–93; of Jesus, 15

Yahoel, 126

zeal, 10, 115, 150–51, 206, 223, 232
Zealots, 115
Zechariah (father of John the
    Baptist), 247
Zimmermann, Christoph, 29
Zoar, 46
Zosimus, 73, 91

Ancient Document Index

OLD TESTAMENT

Genesis
1–2	162
1:3	131, 235
2:5	182
3:8–24	255
3:24	88
12:1–3	62
12:1	70, 237
12:15	180
15:9	70
16:1—21:1	35
16:7–14	90–91, 255
16:7–11	61
16:9	80
16:12–13	39
17:1–22	255
17:1–16	63–64
17:1	37
17:3	38, 236–37
18:1—19:29	6, 34, 39, 42–49, 61, 64–65, 81, 85, 87–88, 91, 95–96, 185, 237, 251
18:1	34, 50, 58, 69, 83
18:1–6	81
18:1–15	35
18:1–33	89, 255
18:2	34, 38
18:10b–11	41
18:17–19	39
18:19	179
19:1	34, 38, 49, 58
19:1–29	255
19:13	91
21:17	61, 80
21:17–18	49
21:17–21	90–91, 255
22:2	70
22:11	50, 89, 199
22:11–19	90–91, 255
28:10–22	9, 255
28:11–13	68
29:18	182
31:10	88
31:10–13	90–91, 255
31:13	78
32:1	88
32:1–2	38, 255
32:5	183
32:12	170
32:22–32	89, 91
34	115
35:1	255
35:9–15	255
35:13	38
37:21	171
41:39	179
46:2	50, 181, 199

Exodus
2:6	180
3:1—4:17	42, 49–53, 84–85, 87–91, 95, 134, 185, 255
3	53
3:2	61, 83
3:2–4	69
3:2a	58
3:4	199
3:5	38
3:6	70
3:7—4:17	38

Exodus (cont.)		12:6	181
3:8	170	14:1–35	255
3:10	184, 237	14:10	237
3:12	183	16:1–40	255
3:13–15	247	16:41–50	255
3:15	70	22–24	81
4:13	184, 245	22:2–35	90–91
5:2	179	22:9–12	40, 256
6	53	22:20	40, 256
6:3	179	22:21–35	256
14:19	61, 89	22:22	61
16:28–29	184	22:22–23	38
18:4	170	22:31	38, 236–37
18:8–10	170	24:16	179
19:1–13	255	25:1–18	145
19:16—33:3	255	25:5–8	115
20:2	61	25:11	115
20:9	182	35:25	171
21:7	183		
23:20–33	90–91	*Deuteronomy*	
24:10–11	95	5:6	61
24:19	180	6:13	183
32–33	90–91	11:2	179
33:7—34:28	86	23:15	170
33:12	179	25:11	171
33:12–13	180	28:47	183
33:17	179–80	31:14–22	256
33:18	237	32:29	170
33:22	237	34:1	180
34:6	50		
34:29–35	134	*Joshua*	
40:34–35	237	1:1–9	256
		2:13	170
Leviticus		3:8–9	256
9:6	237	3:12	245
9:23	237	5:13—6:5	91, 256
14:40	171	5:14	38, 236–37
14:43	171	7:6–15	256
25:44	183	9:24	171
		9:26	171
Numbers		10:6	161, 171
7:89	255	14:7	138
11:24–25	255	24:10	170
12:1–15	255	24:29	138

Judges

2:1–5	90–91, 256
2:8	138
2:19	183
6:7–24	49
6:9	170
6:11	34, 38, 40
6:11–24	90–91, 256
6:14	181
6:20	61
6:22	181
6:25–27	256
9:17	171
10:15	170
13	49
13:1–23	90–91, 256
13:23	181
13:2–20	87
13:6	88
13:9	37
13:11b	38
13:20	38
14:9	171
16:17	117
18:28	171

1 Samuel

3:1–21	34, 42, 53–54, 85, 87, 256
3:4	199
3:7	180
3:10	50, 199
3:15	181
4:7–8	170
6:19	180
7:3	170
9:17	180
10:18	170
12:5	246
12:10–11	170
12:21	170
14:16	180
14:48	171
16:3	179
17:37	170
26:12	179
26:24	170
28:1–25	256
30:8	170–71
30:18	171
30:22–23	171

2 Samuel

7:14	242
13:18	143
14:6	171
19:6	171
22:1–2	170
22:20	170
23:12	171
24:15–25	90–91

1 Kings

1:12	171
3:5	34, 38
3:5–15	256
8:41	178
10:5	143
18–19	115
18:2	180
19:1–18	256
19:5–7	89

2 Kings

1:3–4	89, 256
1:15	89, 256
2:11–12	256
2:12	38
4:8–17	35
4:43	143
6:15	143
16:7	183
17:23	138
17:39	170
18:29–30	170
18:34–35	170
19:12	170
19:35	89, 256

1 Chronicles

16:35	170, 217
21:14–30	90–91, 256

2 Chronicles

1:7	88
1:7–12	256
6:32	178
7:12	37, 38
9:4	143
25:15	170
32:17	170
32:21	90–91, 256

Ezra

7:24	143

Nehemiah

4:5	179
6:21	184
10:39	143

Job

1:6–12	39
1:21	117
5:4	170
5:19	170
10:7	170
19:26–27	95
31:35	86
33:26	95
38–42	86, 256

Psalms

2:7	202, 242
4:6	235
11:7	95
17:15	95
18:28	235
22:1	199
22:10	117
23:3	178
25:11	178
31:1–2	170
31:3	178
36:9	235
37:40	170
40:13 (39:14 LXX)	155
50:15	170
59:1	170
63:2	95
64:1	170
71:2	170
71:6	117
76:4	235
79:9	178
82:4	170
89:3	138
89:15	235
91:14	179
91:15	170
100:2	183
103:21	143
104:2	235
104:4	143
106:8	178
109:21	178
110:1	170
116:8	170
119:17	183
119:153	170
140:1	170
140:4	170
143:9	170
143:11	178
144:7	170
144:11	170

Proverbs

14:35	246

Ecclesiastes

7:26	170–71

Isaiah

6:1–13	256
6:2	88
6:6	88

Isaiah (cont.)

17:12	170
29:15	179
31:5	170
32:5	246
37:36	89, 256
38:7	170
38:11	95
38:14	170
42:7	217
42:16	217
42:22	170
43:13	170
44:17	170
44:20	170
47:14	170
48:9	178
48:10	170
49:1	117
49:1–6	119–20, 138
50:2	170
53	120
57:13	170
60:16	170
61:6	143

Jeremiah

1:4–5	119–20
1:4–10	256
1:7–8	217
1:8	170
1:17	170
1:19	170
14:14–15	184
14:21	178
15:21	170
20:13	170
21:12	170
22:3	170
23:5–6	243
23:21	184
23:32	184
27:15	184
28:9	184
28:15	184
29:9	184
29:31	184
33:15	243
38:11	170
41:13	170
42:5	246
43:2	184
49:11	170

Ezekiel

1:1—3:15	22, 42, 54–58, 88, 91–92, 96, 185, 256
1	16, 158, 237
1–2	4, 16, 160, 163
1:1	181
1:26b	58
1:28	38, 198, 236–37
1:28a	58
2:3	217
3:16—5:17	256
3:16	37
6:3	179
8:1—11:25	256
8:1	37
8:3	181
10:1–22	88
13:6	184
20:9	178
20:14	178
20:22	178
20:44	178
33:5	171
33:9	171
33:12	171
34:10	170
34:27	170
37:1–14	256
40–48	77, 256
40:2	181
43:3	181

Daniel

3:15	170
3:17	170
3:22	245
3:25–30	257
3:28–29	170
4	257
5:1–6	257
5:24	88
6:15	170
6:16–17	170
6:21	170
6:28	170
7	16, 77, 257
8	257
8:4	170
8:7	170
8:15–16	91
8:17	38
9:20–27	257
9:21–27	86
9:21	91
10:1—12:13	257
10:4	37
10:7–8	38, 181
10:16	181

Hosea

2:12	170
5:14	170

Joel

2:32	244

Micah

5:7	170
7:3	171

Nahum

2:1	171

Habakkuk

2:1	86
2:2–20	86

Zephaniah

1:18	170

Zechariah

1–3	90–91
1:18	170
11:6	170

Malachi

3:5	246
3:17	182

APOCRYPHA

2 Maccabees

3:7	245
8:9	245

Tobit

3:16–17	61
5–12	85
5:4—12:22	60–61, 257
11:14–15	17
12:15	61
12:16	38, 236–37

PSEUDEPIGRAPHA

Apocalypse of Abraham

	22, 84, 86, 137
1–32	257
7:11	71
7:12—8:2	86, 156
7:12	70, 71
8:2	70
8:4	70
9:1	70
9:5	70
9:8	70
10:1	91
10:3	70
10:4	85
12:1—15:1	70
15:4	70

Ancient Document Index

Apocalypse of Abraham (cont.)
16:3	71, 87, 93
19:1	71, 87
27	70

Apocalypse of Zephaniah
A:(1)	85
B:8	85
2:1	85

Artapanus
3.27:21	61, 236–37
3.27:61	61

3 Baruch
	84, 86–87
1–17	257
1:1–2	86, 156
1:1	85
1:2	37, 69
1:3	68
3:1	91
11:1–2	69, 84, 87, 93, 137

1 Enoch
	17, 22, 92
14	71, 87
14:11	88
15–16	71
17–36	71
37–71	71–73, 94, 243, 251
46	6
46:3	88
61:10	88

2 Enoch
	22, 84–85, 137
1–42	257
1:1–7	67–68
1:4–5	85
1:4	251
3–21	38
21:1–6	68
22	87
22:1	68, 84
22:8–10	19
24:2	68

3 Enoch
1:1–3	85
4:1–16:5	94
48BCD	59

Ezekiel the Tragedian
	92
68–86	92–93

4 Ezra
	22, 69–70, 86
1–2	69
3–14	69
3:1—5:20	257
3:1–36	69, 70
4:1–2	91
4:1	69
5:14–20	85
5:21—6:35	257
5:21–30	70
6:36—9:26	257
6:36–59	70
9:27—10:59	257
9:27–37	70
11:1—12:39	257
12:3b–9	70
13	6, 257
13:14b–20	70
13:37	69, 88
14:1–26	69–70, 257
14:1b	95, 236–37
15–16	69

History of the Rechabites
	86
1:2–3	73
1:3	68, 91
18:1	74

Joseph and Asenath

	86
14–17	66–67, 88, 257
14:1–12	17
15:11–12x 9	17
15:12x	88

Jubilees

1:1b	65
1:5	62
1:7	62
1:26	62
1:27	62, 65, 88
1:29	62
2:1	62
2:2	61
2:18	61
12	87
12:16–27	62–63, 88
12:16–24	65, 257
12:21	86, 156
12:22	65, 237
12:24	95
12:27	38
15:1–24	63–64, 257
15:1	37
15:3	65
16	87
16:1–4	64–65, 85, 95, 257
23:32	62
30:12	62
30:21	62
33:18	62
50:6	62
50:13	62

Liber antiquitatum biblicarum

13:6	17

Life of Adam and Eve

	92
13:1—16:3	93–94, 251

Ladder of Jacob

	22, 85
1–7	257
1:1–12	68
3:1–2	68, 237
4:1–3	95

Martyrdom and Ascension of Isaiah

	84, 137
7:2	85

Testaments of the Twelve Patriarchs

	17, 91

Testament of Levi

	22, 86
2–5	65–66, 85, 87, 257
2:2	37
2:7	84, 91
2:7–9	137
3:4–8	61

Testament of Abraham

	85
A1:1—20:15	257
B1:1—12:16	257
B13–14	257
1:4	71, 95
2:1	71, 95
5:1	71, 95

Testament of Isaac

2:1—3:19	257
2:1	71, 95
5:4	71, 95

Testament of Jacob

1:6	71, 95
2:5	71, 95

Testament of Job

	22, 86
2–5	88, 257
2:1–4	66
3:1–2	236
3:1	66, 237
4:1	66
5:2	66

NEW TESTAMENT

Matthew

5:29	216, 240
18:9	216, 240
27:46	199

Mark

15:34	199

Luke

1:1–4	238
1:2	246
1:19	61, 247
1:35	242
2:9	213
3:20	213
4:3	242
4:9	242
4:20	246
4:41	242
8:28	242
12:37	142
22:70	242, 247
24:13–35	235
24:39	247

John

1:1–18	133
1:1–14	133, 252

Acts

1:1	238
1:8	246
1:22	246
2:11	216
2:21	244
2:32	246
3:2	245
3:14	243
3:15	246
3:20	213, 216
4:18–21	214
5:22	246
5:26	246
5:27–41	214
5:32	246
5:41	248
6:13	246
7:10	216, 240
7:34	216, 240
7:51—8:4	214
7:52	243
7:55–56	9
7:56	202
7:57—8:3	194
7:58	246
7:59	244
8:4–8	194
8:9–25	194
8:26—9:31	192
8:26–40	194, 235
9:1–9	1, 3, 6, 11–12, 131, 163, 191–201, 204–5, 218–22, 238
9:1–3a	194–97
9:1–2	194–97, 223, 232
9:1	1, 201, 206, 226, 232, 240–41, 243–44
9:2	206–7
9:3–9	1
9:3–7	259
9:3	5, 132, 196, 200, 207, 215, 226, 232, 235
9:3a	197, 223–24
9:3b–5	198–200, 207, 224, 232
9:3b	234
9:4–5	195

Acts (cont.)

9:4	5, 19, 201, 207, 215, 235–36, 243
9:5	201, 234, 239–41, 244, 247
9:6	200–201, 208, 225–29
9:7	200–201, 218, 226, 229–31, 236
9:8–9	201–2, 231, 233
9:8	132, 208
9:9	5, 236, 241
9:10–19a	201–2, 204
9:10–18	208
9:10	239–41
9:11	240–41
9:13–25	203
9:13	240–41
9:14	244
9:15	227, 240–41, 244
9:16	244, 248
9:17	239–41
9:19b–22	202–04
9:20	164, 239, 242, 248
9:21	244
9:22	239–40
9:26–30	203
9:26–28	203–4
9:27	199, 232, 239–41, 244
9:28	241, 244
9:29	240
10:21	247
10:39	246
10:41	246
12:11	240
13:2	117
13:5	246
13:9	207
13:31	246
13:33	202
14:17	213
15:26	248
16:17	196
16:25–30	259
17:3	240
18:5	240
18:10	247
18:25–26	196
18:28	240
19:9	196
19:23	196
20:9	213
20:18–35	219
21:23	248
21:27—22:2	209
21:27–40	204
21:29	210
22:3–11	3, 6, 11, 40–41, 191–92, 204–10, 218–22, 238
22:3–6a	205–07
22:3–5	24, 206–8, 223
22:3	232, 247
22:4	196, 226, 232
22:5	213, 232
22:6	5, 132, 215, 226, 232, 234–36, 243
22:6a	207, 223–24
22:6b–8	207, 224, 232
22:7	5, 215, 226, 235
22:8	193, 216, 234, 239–41, 244, 247
22:9	5, 193, 208, 218, 229–31, 236
22:10	200, 208, 225–29, 240
22:11	132, 208, 231, 233
22:12–16	204, 208
22:14–15	245
22:14	213, 216, 239, 243, 245, 248
22:15	246
22:16	244
22:17–21	204, 208–10
22:17	236
22:19	240
22:20	246
22:21	227, 234, 245
23:27	240
24:14	196
24:22	196
24:27	210

Acts (cont.)

25:7	213
25:22–23	210
26:4–20	3, 6, 11, 191–92, 210–22, 238
26:4–13a	214–15
26:4–11	24, 214, 223–24
26:5	232
26:9–11	226, 232, 244
26:9	239, 244
26:11	207
26:12–13a	214–15, 223–24
26:12	5, 232, 235
26:13	5, 132, 226, 232, 235
26:13b–15	215–16, 224, 232
26:14	5, 193, 205, 218, 226, 230–31, 235–36, 243
26:15–16	234
26:15	239–41, 243
26:16–18	216–18, 225–29, 232
26:16	245–46
26:17	240–41, 245–46
26:18	247
26:19–23	217
26:19–20	217, 231, 233
26:19	201
26:23	240
26:29	247

Romans

1:1	5, 10, 21, 99, 105, 117, 126, 139, 141–43, 149, 153, 156–57, 167, 169, 181, 184, 232
1:1–4	242
1:1–5	151, 165
1:1–6	137–41, 172, 252
1:1–17	137
1:2–4	164, 174
1:3–4	139, 164, 171–73
1:3	232
1:4	167–69, 182
1:5	21, 99, 126–27, 129, 142, 149, 153, 156–57, 175, 178, 248
1:6	167
1:7	106, 156, 172
1:9	164
1:15	121
2:5	161
2:15	133
2:16	110
3:5	110
5:3	10, 99
5:5	133
5:9–10	164
5:10	164
5:15	105
7:22	110
8:3	164
8:19	161
8:29	164
8:32	164
10:2–4	5, 99
10:6	133
10:8–9	133
10:15	121
10:13	170
11:3	10, 99
11:13	126–27, 137, 141–43, 149, 153, 156, 172, 184, 232, 252
12:3	10, 99
14:11	170
15:14	137
15:15–20	137, 142–44, 172, 252
15:15–16	169
15:15	10, 21, 99, 129, 149, 153, 156, 175, 185
15:16–20	167
15:16	10, 99, 126–27, 139, 149, 157, 165, 181–82, 184, 232–33
15:18–20	154, 233
15:18	10, 21, 99, 149
15:19	139, 184

Romans (cont.)
15:20	121, 143, 178
16:25	110, 161

1 Corinthians
1:1	5, 10, 21, 99, 123–24, 130, 138, 141, 156–57, 165, 167, 172, 184, 199, 204, 232, 252
1:3	106
1:7	161
1:9	164
1:17	21, 121, 123–25, 153, 156–57, 165, 167, 172, 184, 232–33, 252
1:31	170
2:8	162
2:16	170
3:3	110
3:10	99
7:22	126
7:37	133
8:6	175
8:9	125
9:1	5, 8, 10, 14, 99, 123, 125–27, 129–31, 143, 151–53, 156, 167, 169, 172, 180–81, 232, 252
9:1–2	10, 160
9:3	125
9:8	110
9:12	139, 184
9:16	121
9:16–17	5, 99
9:18	121
10:26	170
12:3	127
13:1	189
15:1–11	123, 127–29, 160, 168, 172, 239, 252
15:1–2	121
15:1	127
15:3–11	99
15:3–8	99, 151, 172
15:3–5	167
15:3–4	182
15:3	151, 167–68, 173, 249
15:5–7	160
15:8–11	99
15:8–10	5, 130
15:8	10, 14, 99, 131, 152, 180–81, 232
15:9	145, 150, 156, 169, 184, 232
15:10	99, 149, 154, 156, 185, 233
15:21–58	159
15:25–28	164
15:28	164
15:32	110
15:45	139
16:23	185

2 Corinthians
1:1	5, 21, 99, 130, 141, 156, 167, 172, 184, 232, 252
1:2	106
1:19	164
1:22	133
2:12	139, 184
3:1—4:6	157
3–4	6
3:2–3	133
3:4—4:6	5, 7, 99, 131–35, 162–63
3:7–11	10, 99
3:16—4:6	6, 7
3:18—4:6	158–59
4:4	166
4:6	2, 10, 11, 99
4:4–6	7, 8, 15, 130–35, 158, 164, 188, 252
5:12	133
5:15—6:1	159
5:16	5, 99
5:17	131
6:17	139
6:18	164

Ancient Document Index

2 Corinthians (cont.)

7:3	133
8:16	133
9:13	139, 184
10:8	135, 172, 252
10:13	131, 135–36, 172, 252
10:16	121
10:17	170
11:7	121, 139, 184
12	4, 14, 19
12:1–9	158–59
12:1–4	99, 134–37, 160–63, 165
12:1	161
12:2–3	152
12:2	4, 161–62
12:4	161–62
12:6–10	9
12:7	161
13:14	185

Galatians

1–2	98
1	131, 137, 141, 163, 239
1:1—2:9	99
1:1	5, 102–6, 110, 112, 115, 124, 140–41, 156, 167, 172, 174–77, 182, 184, 232
1:1–2	138
1:1–4	119
1:1–5	102–7
1:1–17	100–122, 145–46, 172, 252
1:2	114, 174
1:3	129, 140, 142, 156, 167, 169, 172, 175, 185, 216
1:3–4	170
1:3–5	106–7, 175–76
1:4	120, 171–72, 216, 240–41, 248
1:6	118, 121, 129, 139–40, 142–43, 156, 167, 185
1:6–9	232
1:6–10	107–8
1:7	121, 139, 167, 184
1:7–10	109, 174
1:8	107–8, 121, 128, 189
1:8–9	115
1:9	99, 121, 128
1:10	108, 115, 138, 149, 167, 169, 181–82, 232
1:11	10, 99, 113, 121, 127–28, 139, 161, 184, 233
1:11–12	109–13, 115, 118, 150, 172
1:11–14	109–16
1:11–16	182
1:11–17	99, 109–22, 160–63
1:12	99, 149, 151–53, 156, 161, 167, 206, 232
1:12–13	200
1:12–16	99
1:13	10, 117, 129, 145, 150, 167, 232
1:13–14	24, 113–16, 117, 121, 145, 149, 169
1:13–16a	146
1:13–17	5
1:14	145, 150, 206, 232
1:14–16	155
1:15	99, 123, 138, 140, 142, 144, 149, 151–52, 155–56, 185
1:15–16	10, 21, 24, 122, 130, 132, 139, 153, 181, 232
1:15–16a	116–20, 156, 171
1:16	8, 10, 99, 121, 123, 127, 132, 140–41, 149, 151–53, 156, 158–59, 161, 164–65, 171–72, 181, 242, 248
1:16b—2:20	156, 233
1:16b	120–22
1:16c–17	122, 154
1:17	151, 184, 232
1:18—2:20	122–23
1:22–24	10
1:23	121
2:2	10, 99, 139
2:7	139, 156

Galatians (cont.)

2:7–9	10, 99
2:9	129, 140, 142, 156
2:12	139
2:20	164
3:15	110
4:4	164
4:6	164
4:13	121
4:14	108, 188–89
5:11	155

Ephesians

1:1	5
3:1–13	5, 99, 148–49
3:1–12	24
3:13	99
3:17	133

Philippians

1:2	106
1:7	133
1:22	127
1:27	139, 184
2:5–11	158
2:6–11	253
2:11	168
3:1–3	145
3:2–15	99, 160
3:4–6	155, 169
3:4–11	5, 10, 21, 24, 99
3:4–14	144–48, 172, 252
3:5	150, 232
3:5–6	10
3:6	149, 150, 167, 206, 232
3:7–10	167
3:8	169, 179–80
3:10	179–80
3:12	151, 154, 156–57, 165, 167, 233
3:14	167
4:23	185

Colossians

1:1	5
1:15	6, 166, 252
1:15–20	134
1:23c–29	5, 99
1:25	99
1:25–27	149
1:25–29	24
2:18	74
3:15–16	133

1 Thessalonians

1:1	106
1:10	164
2:2	139, 184
2:8–9	139, 184
2:16	10, 99
3:2	139, 184
3:6	121

2 Thessalonians

1:2	106
1:7	161

1 Timothy

1:12–17	24
2:5	105
2:7	24

2 Timothy

1:9	118

Titus

1:1	184

Philemon

3	106
25	185

1 Peter

5:10	118

3 John

7	248

Ancient Document Index

Revelation
1	6
2:17	213
5:3	111
4:4	29
4:5	61
7:11	230
8:2	61
9:20	111

DEAD SEA SCROLLS

1Q28b
III	2–4, 74
IV	24–26, 76
IV	25–26, 61

1QH^a
IX	10–12, 75
XIV	13, 61

1QM
X	10–11, 74

1QS
III	13
IV	1, 75

2Q4
	77

4Q246
	76–77

4Q266
	3, iii, 25, 74

4Q400
	1, i, 1, 76
	1, i, 4, 76
	1, i, 7, 76
	1, ii, 17, 76
	2, 7, 76

4Q403
	I, 1–27, 75
	II, 1–17, 75
	II, 18, 75

4Q404
	2, 4–9, 75
	11, 1–2, 75
	16, 3–4, 75

4Q405
	20–23, 75

4Q491
	11 I, 75

4Q554
	77

4Q555
	77

5Q15
	77

11Q18
	77

11Q19
XXIX	8–9, 74

CD-A
VIII	2–3, 74

PHILO

De fuga et inventione
101	78
106	79
108	79

De migratione Abrahami
102	79

De vita Mosis I
158 — 79

Quod omnis probus liber sit
43 — 79

Quaestiones et solutiones in Genesin
2.62 — 78

De Somniis I
1.228–36 — 78

JOSEPHUS

Jewish Antiquities
1:189 — 80
1:194–95 — 81
1:196–202 — 81
1:196–96 — 95
1:219 — 80
1:325 — 80
1:331–33 — 80
5:213 — 81
5:277 — 81
11:327 — 82

RABBINIC WRITINGS

MISHNAH

m. Ḥagigah
2:1 A–B — 83

m. Megillah
4:10 F, G — 83

TALMUD

b. Ḥagigah
12b — 83

MIDRASH

Genesis Rabbah
48:10 1B — 83, 95

Exodus Rabbah
2:5 — 83, 95

GRECO-ROMAN LITERATURE

CICERO

De Divinatione
1.6.12 — 258

DIODORUS SICULUS
— 92

DIONYSIUS OF HALICARNASSUS

Roman Antiquities
5.54.1–2 — 258

EURIPIDES

Bacchae
576–603 — 259

OVID

Metamorphoses
15.633–40 — 259

Greek Magical Papyri
IV.475–829 — 259